I0764376

The Doubts and Loves of Yehuda Amichai

The Doubts and Loves of Yehuda Amichai

Israeli, European, and International Poet

Ido Bassok

Translated from the Hebrew by Mark Joseph

HAMILTON BOOKS

Lanham • Boulder • New York • London

Published by Hamilton Books
An imprint of The Rowman & Littlefield Publishing Group, Inc.
4501 Forbes Boulevard, Suite 200, Lanham, Maryland 20706
www.rowman.com

86-90 Paul Street, London EC2A 4NE

Copyright © 2024 The Rowman & Littlefield Publishing Group, Inc.

All rights reserved. No part of this book may be reproduced in any form or by any electronic or mechanical means, including information storage and retrieval systems, without written permission from the publisher, except by a reviewer who may quote passages in a review.

British Library Cataloguing in Publication Information Available

Library of Congress Cataloging-in-Publication Data

Names: Bassok, Ido, author. | Joseph, Mark (Translator), translator.
Title: The doubts and loves of Yehuda Amichai : Israeli, European, and international poet / Ido Bassok ; translated from Hebrew by Mark Joseph.
Other titles: Sefeḳot ṿe-ahavot. English
Description: Lanham : Hamilton Books, 2024. | Includes bibliographical references and index. | Summary: "This book presents the life and works of Yehuda Amichai, born Ludwig Pfeuffer in Würzburg, Germany. Amichai, an engaged political poet, was an enlightened, humanitarian European while remaining an authentic Israeli who loved his country and was deeply involved finding solutions to its problems"—Provided by publisher.
Identifiers: LCCN 2024032138 | ISBN 9780761874607 (cloth ; alk. paper) | ISBN 9780761874614 (ebook)
Subjects: LCSH: Amichai, Yehuda. | Poets, Israeli—Biography. | LCGFT: Biographies.
Classification: LCC PJ5054.A65 Z5513 2024 | DDC 892.41/6 [B]—dc23/eng/20240827
LC record available at https://lccn.loc.gov/2024032138

♾™ The paper used in this publication meets the minimum requirements of American National Standard for Information Sciences—Permanence of Paper for Printed Library Materials, ANSI/NISO Z39.48-1992.

Contents

Introduction

Amichai from Inside and Out

YEHUDA AMICHAI AND THE BIOGRAPHER'S DILEMMA

While I was writing this biography of the Israeli Hebrew poet Yehuda Amichai (1924-2000), I often wondered whether knowing more about his life story would enhance or diminish his reputation. Amichai is revered by many Israelis and their Arab neighbors, and others throughout the world. His poetry has penetrated their hearts and led to identification and a rare feeling of mutuality. Beyond his poetry, he was loved for the humility, warmth and convivial love of humanity that he radiated in his lectures and personal exchanges.

In interviews throughout his life, Amichai himself expressed many misgivings about biography as a genre and the biographical impulse. Sometimes he was categorical: "I don't need to know if a great poet was a drunkard or beat his wife," he told an interviewer from the Yale Jewish student newspaper;[1] in his view it was better to ignore the character or opinions of artists and the famous. The American poet Robert Frost, whom Amichai rated highly, was a terrible father and husband, and he was not alone. Amichai acknowledged that great people can have bad character traits. "I am interested in the work of art in and of itself and not how it came to be." Elsewhere he argued that complete self-exposure can inhibit the making of great art.

It is generally thought that Amichai's reservations about biography meant that for much of his life he either did not save material or rebuffed the idea of archiving, which is the prime resource for biographical work. He even told one of his interviewers that he took particular pleasure in consigning drafts to the wastepaper basket.[2] One supposition is that his close friend the poet Ted Hughes urged Amichai to preserve his writings, mainly for economic reasons. Hughes was convinced that drafts of works by Amichai such as his diaries, letters and articles about him would translate into capital. However, the inventory of the archive, which was donated to the Beinecke Library at Yale University and which served as the basis for this biography, casts some doubt on this explanation. The archive preserves nearly all of Amichai's work journals from the 1950s. In addition to many drafts of poems and ideas for subsequent works, there is significant personal material, even though Amichai consistently denied that he kept notebooks or notes.

Surprisingly, given his criticism of biography as a genre in a number of interviews, Amichai talked more than once about the biographical aspects of his work and in particular his poems. When Doron Weber, in a detailed unpublished interview, asked him whether *Poems of Achsiv* "always commemorate a specific person," he answered affirmatively. "And you can follow your own life history through [the poems]?" "Yes, exactly. Poetry to me is also a kind of documentation, a kind of private documentation. But not in the way of a journalist. More like in a museum where you put things on a shelf, which commemorate for you a whole period." In other words, the poem is a kind of essence, abstracted from the biography, not a reflection but rather a metonymic representation. He goes on to vehemently explain – using German for emphasis in this English interview – that "*Dinge! Dinge*! [Things! Things!] [...] provide unwitting testimony to events, they are the authentic proof that the events referred in the poems indeed happened. He compares the objects in his poems to a convincing legal argument where the details of seemingly incidental things contain more truth than a systematic account. The objects in his poems were coincidental, he said; they were something "I just bump my head on."[3]

WRITING AMICHAI'S BIOGRAPHY: THE PERSONAL ANGLE

Why did I choose to write about Amichai? Along with his contemporaries such as Natan Zach, David Avidan, Dahlia Ravikovitch, Dan Pagis and others, Amichai was one of the heroes of my youth. When I began reading modern poetry as a teen, Amichai was the prime representative of the new "young" Hebrew poetry. He would later joke about this when he was still being classified as a young poet in his 40s. *Two Hopes Away* (1958), which was published by *Hakibbutz Hameuchad*, where my father was one of the editors-in-chief, was a kind of a sacred book for me. In the late 1970s, when I began teaching high school, I would begin my first lesson with a poem by Amichai, and I would also read from the book to soldiers while serving as an instructor on my annual stint in the reserves. I would always be amazed how an Amichai poem managed to win over even those who were not drawn to literature, and even less so to poetry.

There is no need to know poets or artists personally to love and value their work to the point of wanting to devote years of one's life to writing their biography. I met Amichai once, when I was in my last year of high school in Jerusalem (at the University High School). He came to talk to our humanities class, invited by our lively homeroom and literature teacher. Amichai generally loved performing in almost any venue, almost always in return for payment. He presented his dismissive view of Natan Alterman, whose "gothic" and "romantic" poetry never refers to modern or contemporary reality: instead of a pistol he writes about a sword, and instead of electric lights there is a repeated motif of a candle, and all the other timeless trappings. Similarly, Amichai talked about his linguistic revolution with regard to the poetry of the previous generations (Bialik, Alterman), whose language was so lofty and unnatural in his eyes.

NEW FORM, NEW MESSAGE – AMICHAI BURSTS ONTO THE HEBREW POETRY SCENE

Amichai began publishing poems in newspapers in the summer of 1949, at the end of the War of Independence.[4] His first book, *Now and in Other Days,* was published in 1955 by Likrat. Likrat was the name of a group of young poets who rebelled against the writing style and literary views of the preceding generation of Hebrew poets, whose most prominent representatives were Avraham Shlonsky, Natan Alterman and Lea Goldberg, who were all born in the first decade or so of the twentieth century. The poetic outlook of that generation was shaped by Russian culture, which at that time was itself partly influenced by French symbolism. Amichai, like Natan Zach, who became an eminent poet in his own right and was the main spokesperson of the Likrat group, was as a child formed in German culture. English was the first foreign language they mastered. This enabled them to infuse other influences into their work, contributing to the creation of a new style in Hebrew literature. Symbolism and its spirit of abstraction, far removed from the concrete and the everyday, with its refined and elevated register and regular meter, was now replaced by the influence of Anglo-American imagism (Ezra Pound, T. S. Eliot), which was "direct, concrete, exact, clean, dry, prosy, impersonal," as characterized by a spokesperson,[5] and was freed of the strictures of fixed rhyme, regular meter and symmetrical verse. Another poet who had a significant influence on Amichai was Auden, in terms of the use of spoken rhythms in poems, the quasi song-like organization of his poems (repeating lines at the end of verses), and borderline parody of classical forms such as the sonnet.

Amichai was also influenced by German expressionism (Else Lasker-Schüler, Georg Trakl).[6]

When *Now and in Other Days* came out, it was as though a bomb had been dropped on the Israeli public. Almost nothing in this book resembled anything published previously in terms of the style and structure of the poems, the language, or their aberrant worldview and hierarchy of values. Everyday language, spoken Israeli Hebrew, became a legitimate poetic mode of expression, the grammar of his poems was simple and familiar, and ordinary objects and events served as images: a car, the smell of gas, opening the refrigerator door, a newspaper lying beside a bed. Amichai's profoundly democratic outlook, where there are no hierarchies between people or in the world, led him to make daring comparisons between lofty things and simple, ordinary ones, between the sacred and the profane (see "Six Poems for Tamar"), by frequently creating a kind of superposition which Pound considered the bedrock of his own poetry. Some of his poetry during this period was written in rhyme and regular meter, but in others in free verse, without meter. The critics of the older generation considered his work to be heresy and the opposite of everything which in their eyes characterized national values and elegantly structured poetry.

However, the younger generation of that time perceived Amichai's poetry as an escape route from the Zionist ideology of the time which demanded of the individual to commit to the higher good of the collective. These norms may have been justified during the state-building years of the Yishuv. Amichai's poetry championed the legitimacy of the individual and validated the satisfaction of personal goals and the enjoyment of one's fleeting existence ("I Want to Die in My Bed"). After the protracted War of Independence which claimed so many lives, this message was an irritant for the political and literary establishment, but was taken to heart by the new generation. The initially narrow circles of Amichai's admirers quickly expanded.

HOW DID AMICHAI BECOME A CLASSIC, INFLUENTIAL POET?

What accounts for Amichai's success with broad publics in Israel and abroad? How did he become a cult poet, who is quoted and routinely recited at weddings and funerals, whose poetry is admired by both secular and observant readers, and whose poems have been translated and enthusiastically received in many countries and cultures – from the British Isles, to North and South America, from Germany to Eastern Europe, the Middle East and South-East Asia?

Beside the innovativeness and revolutionary nature of Amichai's poetry, there was a complexity in his poetic personality and his worldview that helped solidify his popularity in Israel. Over the years, Amichai was admired by broad segments of Israeli society who tended to lock horns elsewhere on ideological, educational, and political issues. This complexity may also help explain his worldwide popularity, which (in Hebrew poetry at least) may only have been equaled by Haim Nachman Bialik.

Amichai's upbringing, as well as certain cultural and biographical features, help account for this complexity in that they allowed him to combine what might appear to be incompatible or opposite directions. In a lecture to the Hebrew Writers' Association in May 1968 after the Six Day War he called himself a "double agent." This duality made him a revolutionary as compared to poets of the preceding generations (Bialik, Tchernichovsky, Alterman, Shlonsky), but also unlike his contemporaries such as Zach, Avidan, and later, Ravikovitch. Although these poets saw him as one of them, none achieved his stature in Israeli society or internationally.

Amichai's poetry associates three main intersecting axes: the secular-religious, contrasting Israeliness and Jewishness; individualism versus the bonds and commitments of society; and the universalism-nationalism axis. Tracing the biographical background of Amichai's unification of opposites can help to show why he was so significant for different publics in Israel and abroad, and how the embrace of these contradictions found expression in his poetry.

Secularism versus religion

Amichai – originally Ludwig Pfeuffer – was born to a highly observant family. Both his parents came from rural families in Bavaria and Hessen, as did all his relatives, so they were basically the first generation of city dwellers. When in his teens, his father went to Würzburg, a relatively small city with a Jewish community of 2,800 people, and became a worker and then a partner in his older brother's business. Amichai parents' variety of Jewish orthodoxy was German, rather than Eastern European. This meant that his father worked for a living and belonged to a Jewish community which saw itself as entirely German and belonging to the majority culture, which accepted the responsibilities of citizenship. When the First World War broke out, Amichai's father enlisted along with 400 other Jewish men of Würzburg out of a sense of obligation to the state, not militarism.

The quite observant Würzburg Jewish community was more like those in Eastern Europe (and primarily in Poland in the interwar period) than other Jewish communities in Germany, in terms of its relative insularity. Community institutions took care of nearly all the needs of its members. Ludwig-Yehuda went to a Jewish kindergarten and to a school where although the language of instruction was German, the morning was devoted to Jewish subjects, and general subjects were studied in the afternoon. As Amichai himself indicated in interviews, as a child and adolescent he lived his life almost completely without any contact with the non-Jewish environment. At school he also studied Hebrew, and learned the Jewish sacred texts - the Bible, Mishnah, Talmud - and of course prayer. Amichai liked to say that when he immigrated to Palestine, he already knew enough Hebrew to go to school and integrate easily into society. This may have been a slight exaggeration, but there is no doubt that he and his family were among the minority of immigrants from Germany in the 1930s who did not experience the Land of Israel as a foreign country and felt that their immigration to Palestine was a return to their ancestral home.

Amichai studied for a year in Petach Tikva, his bar mitzvah year. His parents then moved to Jerusalem where he attended a progressive-liberal religious school founded by Jews from Germany in the spirit of *Torah im derech eretz*, S. R. Hirsch's modern orthodox synthesis of devout observance and instruction in science and other secular topics. His initial sparks of creativity are apparent in the texts he wrote for his school yearbooks.

Sometime around the age of 15 he stopped being observant, hiding his decision from his parents. When in time he openly rebelled and became entirely secular, his father did not make him leave the house or mourn him (a traditional practice in such circumstances). Amichai's relationship to his father was complex. The bittersweet religious parting from his father is described in the poem "A Song of Lies on Sabbath Eve," which blends humor to capture how he and his father tried to deceive one another. As a boy he concealed the fact that he no longer attended prayer services, and in response his father lied to him in declaring on his deathbed: "I've gone to another life."[7] Nonetheless, Amichai embraced his father's humanism and anti-establishment attitude. This humanism, which was an important part of his self-image, emerges in one of his famous poems, "My Father Took Part in Their War for Four Years,"[8] and in a passage from the story "The Times My Father Died," where he describes his father doling out the last remaining water in his canteen to thirsty French soldiers who had fallen into German hands.

Amichai's father's humanity and gentleness permeated his family's everyday life. In a heart-rending poem, "A Letter of Recommendation," Amichai remembers going to *selichot* (prayers in the weeks before Yom Kippur) at dawn in the freezing cold in Germany: "I remember my father waking me for early prayers. / He would do it by gently stroking my forehead, not / by pulling the blanket off. // Since then I love him even more."[9] His father was known for dressing up for the Purim festival as a poor man, an Arab, or an *ostjude* (a Jew from Eastern Europe who immigrated to German-speaking countries). Amichai identified with these annual performances, and their veiled criticism of society.

Amichai had a dialectical relationship with religious texts, especially the Bible and prayers. In this respect he was more similar to poets of the preceding generations such as Bialik, Shlonsky and Alterman than to his contemporaries, who either had no religious education (like Zach), or whose ideological background and temperament led them to reject Jewish traditional sources (like Avidan, in his youth a Communist).

In terms of politics and ideology, he was antireligious and vigorously opposed to the political influence of the religious parties. But while he can be seen as being consistently secular, he nonetheless simultaneously sensed God's presence since without a spiritual emanation, something essential to his humanity would have been lost. In this sense he was very different from the other secularists of his generation, and even more so from later generations who did not grow up in a religious environment and whose secularism was not as multilayered, convoluted or paradoxical. In the poems "National Thoughts," "My Child Has the Fragrance of Peace," and "I Am Their Last" he comes to terms with a people who descends from a great continuous tradition, and has arisen from disasters threatening its extinction. In "I am Their Last," the speaker wants to enjoy a reprieve, not like the Biblical Job between past disaster and disaster sensed, but from tragedies yet to come. Although he is "like ashes that have forgotten what came before," perhaps reflecting Israelis as a collective who are all in a way Holocaust survivors, "my heart's visage still shows on my face"; i.e., his spiritual interiority is still apparent, and he longs for a place "at the end of the dark staircase" at the Cave of the Patriarchs, to merge, paradoxically, with a history he seeks to obliterate.[10]

Amichai thus gave his readers the sense that his secularism did not entail breaking the historical chain. This can be seen for example in his strong relationship to poets of the Middle Ages such as Yehuda Halevi and Ibn Gabirol in his first book, *Now and in Other Days*, and Shmuel Hanagid, "Like me, a man of mounds and a man of wars, / Who sang a lullaby to his soldiers before the battle."[11] He connected his world to previous eras and significant figures in the Jewish past.

Individualism and Nihilism versus the Social Bond and Public Commitment

Amichai conveyed the message that individuals and their legitimate needs came before those of the collective. He was educated in pre-state Palestine, at a time when political parties, and the political in general, were very much part of the life of the individual. His resistance to this trend may also have been rooted in his German culture. In high school he chose not to belong to a youth movement (although they were immensely popular among young Jews in Palestine at the time), and as an adult was never a member of any political party, although he strongly identified in early adulthood with the radical socialist Mapam and after that with the Alignment-Labor Party.

His individualism, as it emerges in his early poetry ("Not Like a Cyprus", "I Want to Die in My Bed") provoked the ire of literary critics and various "agents of culture," particularly the older ones. They blamed him for lacking values and mimicking Western culture. Amichai himself at that time wrote that he wanted to be "like a baby messy with food / I want to be dirty with the world's problems / All over my face,"[12] making it clear that he was not shirking his responsibility to the collective.

Younger critics at the time such as Dan Miron and Natan Zach emphasized his love for the main figures in his life, including his father and mother, a rare trait for his generation. He often wrote about his parents, much more about his father than his mother. In his youth he wrote what were to become famous poems to his mother,[13] as well as when he came back from his stay in the US, and later when she was on her deathbed; but his father was clearly the central figure in his poetry. Throughout his life, Amichai felt the need to clarify his complicated relationship with his father in terms of his father's religious observance and his own secularism, his father's faultless military service as compared to his rare experiences of combat, as well as his father's practical turn of mind as compared to his poetic and diffuse way of thinking. Amichai mostly dealt with these issues with humor, but there was also a certain amount of pain.

Amichai's closest friends also appeared in his poems, such as the poets Harold Schimmel, Arieh Sachs, and Dennis Silk. For many years they would meet every Sabbath, be rowdy and dance, and sometimes host important writers from abroad. This comradeship lasted from the early 1960s until their breakup in the 1980s, sparked by their reservations, perhaps tinged with jealousy, over his international success. All three considered that Amichi's success was bound up with his having cheapened his poetry by intentionally making it more superficial and accessible, so that it would be easier to translate and sell.[14]

Apart from his parents and close friends, two other figures appear in his poems. The first is Little Ruth, his childhood friend and neighbor in Germany'. One day in Würzburg, she was hit by a car while riding her bicycle and her leg had to be amputated. Her disability apparently disqualified her from emigrating to either the US or the UK and she was killed in the Sobibor death camp. Amichai remembered her his whole life, and a childhood picture of them together was always on his desk. His recurring references to her in his poems, beginning with his very earliest ones written in Egypt, express anger over the loss of a young woman whom he associated with an innocent, pure outlook on the world, his inability to save her, and a sense that she died in his place (a form of survivor guilt), as well as reveries about their life together if she had survived and come to Palestine.[15]

The second figure was Dicky, his company commander in the first months of the War of Independence. On paper, Amichai was a relatively experienced fighter by the time he went south with what would become the Seventh Battalion of the Negev Brigade of the Palmach in April 1948. In fact, he had had virtually no battle experience. When he was inducted into the Palmach he was 24, old in the eyes of the 18-year-old graduates of the scout movement with him in the battalion. His German punctiliousness and ways of expressing himself made him less appreciated in his organizational role as company sergeant major. Haim Laksberger, Dicky, had a somewhat similar past. He evidently noticed the social distress of someone who was not yet known as a poet, and made him his aide so he could help with company education, especially the "Cypriots," Holocaust refugees who had been in internment camps in Cyprus and had then joined the battalion. Dicky was killed along with 22 soldiers of his platoon in the catastrophic battle to retake the village of Huleiqat, which went wrong from its inception.[16]

The fact that Amichai returned to these figures, almost from the beginning of his poetic trajectory until the last decade of his life, suggests that he was deeply loyal to those he met in the various circumstances of childhood and youth. It strengthened the empathetic, intimate effect of his poetry and made him appealing to readers above and beyond their judgments of the quality of his poetry.

Nationalism versus Universalism

From the beginning, Amichai was seen as an antiwar poet. In a country that has fought for its existence in a series of recurring wars, it was considered heretical in the 1950s to ruminate on the heavy human and psychological toll of war ("I, who brought corpses down from the hills / Can tell you that the world is empty of mercy").[17] Even another well-known poem, "Out of Three or Four in a Room," with its broad existential concerns that uses images referencing a time of war ("Compelled to see the injustice between / the thorns and the fire on the hill [..] // And before him voices that are straying without packs, / hearts without provisions, prophecies / without water"), was seen as provocative.[18] However, the public knew that Amichai had served in World War II and the War of Independence. Amichai was never radical or a member of fringe movements. When the UN voted in November 1947 for the establishment of two states in Mandatory Palestine, which was met by non-compliance on the part of the Arab leadership, thus putting an end to the idea of a binational state which he supported, he took part wholeheartedly in the war to found a Jewish state and defend it.

Amichai's mix of sober Zionism and universalist humanism is perhaps best illustrated in his relationship to Israel after 1967, and especially his attitude toward the so-called "undivided Jerusalem," the city he lived in from the age of 13 until his death. Although Amichai was strongly in favor of a peace agreement with the Palestinians in the 1990s, and in general supported the creation of a Palestinian state, it was very difficult for him to abandon the idea of the undivided Jerusalem he had known in his youth. In poems he published almost immediately after the war, and which appear in *Now in the Storm* (1969), he expresses his wish to abolish the divide between Jew and Arab, and to create a bridge between the two peoples, based on the principle of complete equality. He describes himself standing across from an Arab shop which reminds him of his father's haberdashery which was burned down in Nazi Germany, and in an imaginary dialogue with the Arab shopkeeper he tries to explain the need for a Jewish state in Palestine as a land of refuge for persecuted Jews, not because of presumed rights to the land dating back to biblical times.[19]

Five years after the publication of *Now in the Storm*, and after Israel had fought the Yom Kippur War, Amichai published *Behind All This a Great Happiness is Hiding*, beginning with a poem cycle "Poems of the Land of Zion and Jerusalem." The cycle is full of wrath and impatience about Jerusalem, and differs considerably from the more placatory atmosphere of the previous book with its faith in the future. Was this change brought about by the extended wait for Arab states to take steps towards peace? Were Amichai's eyes opened after the Yom Kippur War to the meaning of keeping a large population in the West Bank under occupation without prospects of a solution? He had sudden longings for the small and intimate Jerusalem, the divided city before the Six Day War, perhaps because in the divided city there was something to long for; it had a sense of unresolved issues and tensions.[20] Prominent in this cycle is a poem that does not specifically talk about Jerusalem, but rather about the burden of memory, the memory of death and the dead, and the bitterness of exile, which the Israeli in him, through his education and the atmosphere surrounding him, is required to carry. In a compressed and aggressive series of anaphora, Amichai seeks to divest himself once and for all of the obligation to remember, and thus to shake off what he sees as the detritus of the past, and from history which is so good at castrating (as he puts it in another poem) and putting to death: "Let the flags remember, / those multicolored shrouds of history: the bodies they wrapped / have long since turned to dust." The "remembrancers", those who are overly attached to the national past, who cannot forgive or forget, are implicitly likened to "the beasts of the field and the birds of the heavens," who in the biblical vision are nourished on corpses. He is even ready to shake off the hold of the collective, sacred to Israelis, just so that he can finally rest ("Let all of them remember so that I can rest").[21]

However he still feels he must "love Jerusalem and recall / him who died for her on the Gethsemane Bridge" – the captain who fell in the Six Day War and in whose bloody belt was found a book of Amichai's poems, he "who was the land and the fruit of the land."[22]

PRIMARY AND SECONDARY SOURCES OF THE BIOGRAPHY

Literary sources

Amichai's prose – two novels, a collection of short stories, and some prose pieces not included in his books – and to a certain extent his poems, served here as sources for his biography, since they shed light on his personality, tendencies, and thoughts (explicit and perhaps implicit). In some cases these same sources also refer to actual events in his life.[23]

Certain figures have a recurring presence in his poems, such as Little Ruth, his childhood friend who was murdered in the Holocaust, and Dicky, his commander in the Seventh Battalion who fell in a battle that had been poorly prepared for. They constitute the foundation for his own self portrait. Even when he tried to conceal names of people, the disguise was minimal.[24]

His stage and radio plays are for the most part based on identifiable events, sometimes directly and in others more obliquely. The play *Journey to Nineveh* expresses his perplexity and confusion about his first marriage, which was on the rocks, and about the young State of Israel which had shattered his dreams and those of his generation by its faltering concretization. The radio play *Bells and Trains* incorporates the complexities of his relationship to Germany and Würzburg, his birthplace, through a depiction of an encounter in a Jewish old-age home. *The Class Reunion*, also a radio play, includes sketches of significant figures from his religious high school in Jerusalem who had a far-reaching influence on his life and spiritual world. The radio play *Come, My Beloved* comes to terms with the Jewish school in Würzburg, including an abusive teacher long after the community had been destroyed.

Archival Sources

Amichai's Interviews with Journalists

Amichai gave numerous interviews to the press, during which he discussed aspects of his life beginning with his Würzburg childhood, immigration to Palestine, service in the British army, in the Palmach and in the IDF, his work as a teacher, marriage to Tamar, their divorce and life with Hana, their children, and so on. He also often presented his views on poetry and literature, and sometimes on current affairs.

These interviews in Hebrew, English and German (interviews he gave to Spanish and Catalan newspapers were published in translation) constitute the building blocks of this biography, though they only provide partial insights. Despite their deviations from the facts, the interviews still shed light on the self-mythification and preferred self-image he projected. In a book with several biographical chapters on the young Amichai, Nili Scharf Gold is certainly right to note that he deliberately changed the dates of important life events or gave them different interpretations according to the interlocutor.[25] This was done essentially in order to present himself as a poet "born with the state." The interviews also reveal his increasing tendency to idealize his family background to adapt his story to his audiences. For example, Amichai told his American interviewers exaggerated details of his father's wealth, and described his family, which came to Palestine in 1936, as "one of the few families from Central Europe then in Palestine," at a time when tens of thousands of immigrants from Central Europe had in fact settled in the land of Israel.[26]

Letters

Amichai received many letters, some of which were formal, including a large number of invitations to give lectures or teach in Israel and abroad, read his poems at festivals as well as offers to publish in newspapers and journals. He also received frequent requests to authorize the publication of his works in anthologies in various languages, mostly in return for a handsome fee. Others were of a more personal nature and consisted of letters from friends, and many admirers who often also sought to interest him in their own work, distant family members who congratulated when he won an important prize, or when they heard rumors about his serious illness. For most of his life Amichai did not enjoy writing letters; sometimes he simply did not reply, or only very laconically, thus discouraging further correspondence. However, the letters he wrote and the responses he received from three significant people in his life are crucial to his biography.

Letters to Ruth Hermann (Zilenzeiger)

At the end of August 1947, a young woman left Haifa port for New York. She had been a fellow student of Yehuda Pfeuffer, whom she encouraged to change his name that year to Amichai. This was Ruth, who he had come to see as his lover and future wife. As a way of weathering his loneliness and frustration, which he expected to last a year until his beloved returned, he promised to send three letters a week, and did so for seven months, until they broke up (see Chapter 4). The more than 90 airmail letters he wrote to her are a treasure trove that reveal the young Amichai, the writer, teacher and fighter in the *Haganah*'s operations in Haifa and the environs. Ruth donated the letters to the Heksherim Institute at Ben-Gurion University in Beersheva through the Amichai researcher and friend of the poet, Nili Sharf Gold.

Clarice Kestenbaum's Letters to Amichai

In the summer of 1958, amid a marital crisis with his first wife Tamar, Amichai fell in love with the beautiful Clarice Kestenbaum, a medical student. After an impassioned affair with the poet, Clarice decided that Amichai was not suited to marital life with her and left the country to continue her degree in the US (Chapters 7 and 8). Amichai continued to beg her to come back to Israel: her replies were love letters, rich in content, revealing a courageous and highly talented woman, but firmly rebuffing his pleas. Unfortunately, Amichai's letters to her have been lost, but her letters to him were discovered in a room Amichai once used as a study. They were returned to her and thanks to her generosity, are now housed in the Heksherim archive in Beersheva.[27]

Correspondence with the Poet Ted Hughes and His Family

In the spring of 1967, during a stay in London on his way back to Israel, Amichai solidified his relationship with the poet Ted Hughes. This friendship had decisive significance for the development of Amichai's international career. Hughes was enchanted with Amichai the man and poet, and was convinced that he was one of the greatest poets of the twentieth century. Hughes encouraged his then life partner, Assia Gutmann-Wevill, who had been educated in Palestine, to translate some of Amichai's poems. He saw to it that the translations came out as a collection, in what was Amichai's first book of poems in English. Later, Hughes served as his editor and translator for two collections which paved the way for Amichai's international fame: *Amen* (with an introduction by Hughes), that includes the poems of *Behind All This a Great Happiness is Hiding*; and *Time,* an English version of most of the poems from Amichai's collection *Hazman* in Hebrew. Amichai also kept up a friendly, professional and business-like correspondence with Assia, his translator, and with Hughes' sister, Olwyn, who was a literary agent and kept Amichai in touch with publishers and media outlets in the UK. Hughes' letters, and those of Assia and Olwyn, are preserved today in the Amichai archive, whereas Amichai's letters to Hughes are housed at Emory University in Atlanta, Georgia.

Amichai's Notebooks / Working Journals

Amichai's repeated claim that he did not keep notebooks or working journals was only partly true. Although most of his working journals, as they are classified in the archive at Yale's Beinecke Library ("notebooks" in this biography), contain drafts of poems and passages from stage or radio plays (mostly in Hebrew, with a few in German and English), they also contain more personal notes such as plans for writing, descriptions of meetings with people, friends and acquaintances, his connections to his circle of intimates (his wives and children), visits to cultural institutions and trips.

Interviews conducted by the author with Amichai's acquaintances and family

Amichai's relative closeness to us in time was a clear advantage in that it allowed me to have conversations with people who knew him or who were his friends when he was young, including members of his family, friends and classmates from Ma'aleh high school, his students at the Geulah school in Haifa, comrades from the Seventh Battalion of the Palmach in the War of Independence, acquaintances from his time as a student at the Hebrew University in the early 1950s, his colleagues in the Likrat circle, and associates from his first years of teaching at the Luria school and night school for young employees. The psychiatrist Clarice Kestenbaum, a central figure in the novel *Not of This Time, Not of This Place*, and the subject of a number of important poems, and the psychologist Susana Huller, heroine of the Buenos Aires poems in *Not for the Sake of Remembering,* both spoke with me at length. I am especially grateful to Prof Robert (Uri) Alter from the University of California, Berkeley, who generously responded in writing and spoke with me at length when he visited Israel to receive an honorary doctorate (May 2015).

The closest family members were less willing to give interviews. Unsurprisingly, they were ambivalent, and were understandably concerned about dimming his luster in their eyes or creating what might seem to be a negative portrayal. Amichai's first wife, Tamar, refused to be interviewed; her brother, Gadi Horn, provided some missing information. Amichai's son from his first marriage, Roni, answered questions by email. I met his widow, Hana Sokolov-Amichai, once, and Emanuela, his youngest daughter, also once. The partial responses of members of his nuclear family to my enquiries were then completed by referencing published interviews with them in newspapers and radio shows.[28]

ACKNOWLEDGMENTS

The Judaic Studies Department of Yale University, New Haven, twice awarded me stipends for airfare and lodging to conduct research at the Amichai archive in the Beinecke Library and photocopy the material I needed. I thank the librarians for their help in gathering copious amounts of material. The Leo Baeck Institute of Jerusalem gave me a grant for writing the biography, and I was the recipient of a substantial grant from the Jewish Memorial Foundation, New York. I am most grateful to these three institutions.

I am indebted to Prof. Yigal Schwartz of the Hebrew Literature Department of Ben Gurion University of the Negev for his unstinting help, Ilan Bar-David, the Head of the Heksherim archive at the same university, Hila Tzur of Gnazim, and its Head, Adiva Gefen, the employees of the Israeli Center for the Documentation of the Performing Arts (previously the Israel Archive of Theater), and Dr Gil Weissblei, former head of the Archives Department at the Hebrew University.

My wife, Ginat, "the only one whose heart-light always accompanied me like a song", came with me on my trips to the US and Germany, where we visited Würzburg and the villages where Amichai's parents were born and raised. She helped me in sorting through the mountains of documents, letters and journal clippings in his personal archive at Yale University, as well as accompanying materials from the Gnazim archive.

My heartfelt thanks to all those who made this book possible.

NOTES ON THE NOMENCLATURE AND REFERENCE SYSTEM IN THE BOOK

Shortened forms of the titles of Amichai's books are generally used after the first mention (such as: *Not of This Time, Not of This Place – Not of This Time*; *Open Closed Open – Open Closed*). Published English translations of Amichai's poems are referred to in the endnotes with alternatives. The complete publication history in Hebrew does not appear; however, all poems in the Hebrew original are cited as they appear in the collected poems (*Shirei Yehuda Amichai*, Schocken, 2002, 5 volumes) as *Poems* [in Hebrew] vol., page. This edition brings together the thirteen volumes of poetry published in his lifetime, not including the three books of poetry for children and two other books in which new poems by him accompany drawings or photos: *Picture and Poem* (1970) and *Open-Eyed Land* (1992).

Materials from Amichai's personal archive are referred to by box and file; for example, box 13 file 254 appears as 13.254.

Interviews with Amichai and his family, usually by journalists, are referred to as "interviews". Interviews conducted by the author with family relatives, friends etc. of Amichai are referred to as "conversations".

NOTES

1. Idit Klein, Judith Rosenbaum and Tanya Schlam, "The Joy of the Struggle: A Talk with Yehuda Amichai," *Urim v'Tumim* 6:2 (Winter 1991): 27. The issue also came up in an interview with Omer in the context of the pro-Nazi pasts of poets he admired, "In This Burning Country Words Must Give Shade," *Proza* 25: 4 (September 1978).

2. Interview with Bina Barzel, "Writing is a Need – Like Loving and Eating" [in Hebrew], *Yediot Acharonot*, June 1, 1973.

3. In an interview with Eyal Meged during the 1980s he returned to the definition of his poetry as autobiographical: "Towards the end you become simpler" [in Hebrew], *Yediot Acharonot*, November 8, 1985.

4. Apart from a minor poem, published in 1945. He claimed he was pressured by friends to send it to a newspaper.

5. Frank Stuart Flint, *Poetry*, March 1913, quoted in Shimon Sandbank, Afterward to *Desire and the Object: An Anthology of Expressionist and Imagistic Poetry* [in Hebrew], (Tel Aviv, 2014), 241.

6. For more details, see Chapters 3 and 4.

7. *The Selected Poetry of Yehuda Amichai* (Edited and translated from the Hebrew by Channa Bloch and Stephen Mitchell, Berkeley, 2013), 138; *Shirei Yehuda Amichai* (Poems of Yehuda Amichai), 5 volumes, (Jerusalem and Tel Aviv, Schocken Publishing House, 2002). *Poems* [in Hebrew] 3, 334.

8. *Penguin Book of Hebrew Verse*, 568; other translations: *Selected Poetry*, 8; *Life of Poetry*, 23; *The Early Books of Yehuda Amichai*, trans. Yehuda Amichai and Ted Hughes, 48; *Poems by Yehuda Amichai*, trans. Assia Guttmann, 43; *Poems* [in Hebrew], 1, 57.

9. "Letter of Recommendation", *Poems* [in Hebrew] 3, 47

10. "National Thoughts," *Selected Poetry*, 57; *Poems* [in Hebrew] 2, 45; "My Child Has the Fragrance of Peace," *Poetry*, 90; another translation, *Life of Poetry*, 88; *Poems* [in Hebrew] 2, 23; "I Am Their Last," *Poetry*, 103; *Poems* [in Hebrew] 2, 59.

11. In the poem "Tel Gath," *Life of Poetry*, 409 (translation modified to reflect the resonance of the word *tel*, an artificial mound of archeological significance; may refer to tombs or strata of former civilizations); *Poems* [in Hebrew] 5, 11-12.

12. "Not Like a Cyprus," *Selected Poetry*, 12; *Poetry*, 30; another translation, *Life of Poetry*, 35; *Poems* [in Hebrew], 1, 98-99; "Poems about Myself," 3, *Poems* [in Hebrew] 1, 139.

13. See, e.g. "To My Mother," *Poems*, 40; other translations, *Life of Poetry*, 40; *Poetry*, 45; *Early Books*, 45; *Poems* [in Hebrew] 1, 131.

14. Amichai's warm friendships beyond the family are manifested in his tendency to write occasional poems for births, weddings, funerals, etc. of various friends and acquaintances, showing a cordiality and intimacy not found in other poets of his generation. Several poems of this sort were published in newspapers, but not in his books. Others were left as manuscripts with friends.

15. See in particular "Little Ruth," trans. Guttmann, Poetry International Archives, 2014.

https://www.poetryinternational.org/pi/poem/24211/auto/0/0/Yehuda-Amichai/Little-Ruth/en/tile; Poems [in Hebrew] 5, 69-70.

16. The best known poem about Dicky is "Rain Falls on the Faces of My Friends," which appeared in Amichai's first book, *Now and in Other Days* (1955). Later he related explicitly to Dicky in "Seven Laments for the War-Dead," written some fifteen years later, and in "Huleikat – The Third Poem about Dicky," from his penultimate book, *The Fist, Too, Was Once the Palm of an Open Hand,* and *Fingers* (1989).

17. For a detailed account of the reception of Amichai's poetry in the 1950s, see Chapters 7 and 8.

18. "Out of Three or Four in a Room," *Penguin Book of Hebrew Verse*, 569; other translations; *Selected Poetry*, 12 and *Poetry*, 29; *Life of Poetry*, 34; *Poems*, 6; *Early Books*, 14; *Poems* [in Hebrew] 1, 97.

19. Poem 5 of "Jerusalem 1967," *Selected Poetry*, 49, *Poetry*, 83; other translations, *Life of Poetry*, 81; *Penguin Book of Hebrew Verse*, 571; *Poems* [in Hebrew] 2, 13-14.

20. "I long for the serenity and for the old longing. / [...] lovers went up to it, testing, / like circus acrobats who try out the net / before they dare to jump. // The patches of no-man's-land were like placid bays." *Selected Poetry*, 111; *Poetry*, 208; *Poems* [in Hebrew] 3, 20-21.

21. *Selected Poetry*, 113; *Poetry*, 211; *Poems* [in Hebrew] 3, 30-31.

22. Poem 38 of the cycle "Poems of the Land of Zion and Jerusalem," *Poetry*, 213; another translation, *Life of Poetry*, 242; *Poems* [in Hebrew] 3, 30-31.

23. Cf. Michael Gluzman, "Dicky's Death: Amichai's Traumatic Text", *Jerusalem Studies in Hebrew Literature*, XXXI, 2020, 453-88.

24. "Poem of Friendship," *Poems* [in Hebrew] 3, 154-5.

25. On the issue of the self-mythification, if indeed there was any, see the debate between Kronfeld, *Full Severity*, 299, n.5 and Scharf Gold, *National Poet*, Chapters 1, 6.

26. Interview by Lawrence Joseph, *The Paris Review* 122, Spring 1992. Perhaps what he was referring to was the immigration to Palestine of his extended family from German-speaking countries. See Doron Weber, interview with Yehuda Amichai, December 18, 1987, 8 (unpublished).

27. In his novel *Not of This Time* Amichai drew on Clarice's letters to create the character of Patrice. In places he may actually be quoting from her letters in the dialogues.

28. "In Our Love," Tzipi Gon-Gross (moderator), Army Radio, April 19, 2001, with the participation of Roni, David and Emanuela Amichai; Yoav Birnberg, "Nostalgic" [in Hebrew] (interview with Ron Amichai), Yediot Acharonot, May 12, 2002; Ruth Reznick, "Yehuda Amichai's Son" [in Hebrew], Maariv, February 5, 2017; Sarit Fux, "It Is All Still Such a Whirlpool" [in Hebrew] (interview with Emanuela), *Maariv – Sof Shavua*, January 26, 2001; Yoav Birnberg, "A Long Poem to a Father and Daughter" [in Hebrew], October 19, 2001; Sagi Bin Nun, "The Muse [in Hebrew], *Maariv – Sofshavua*, February 5, 2012; radio interview by Tzipi Gon-Gross with Hana Amichai, "Books, Gentlemen, Books" [in Hebrew], Israel Army Radio, September 30, 2011.

Chapter 1

1924-1936

Childhood in Würzburg, Germany

GERMAN JEWRY AT THE TURN OF THE NINETEENTH CENTURY

Ludwig Otto Pfeuffer – Yehuda in Hebrew – was born in Würzburg in Lower Franconia, a beautiful, historic agricultural region of Bavaria, in southern Germany. Germany was a collection of principalities, dukedoms, and church states until the country was unified under the iron fist of Chancellor Otto von Bismarck. Over the course of the nineteenth century the Jews in all regions of Germany experienced a radical transformation in their ways of life, education, occupations, and no less importantly, self-definition.

Despite the restrictions imposed on them, as well as hatred and rejection by non-Jews which persisted even after their emancipation, German Jews made a consistent and resolute effort to integrate into German society, and to imitate its way of life. This was also true for observant Jews. The culture of the German Jews embodied the ideal of *Bildung*, a German notion of self-cultivation through philosophy, poetry and other components of high culture. Eventually it led them on a path quintessentially their own. Their heroes were Schiller, Goethe, and Lessing, the classical representatives of the humanist tradition.

One of the hallmarks of *Bildung* in the German-Jewish version was its unique merging of nationalism and individualism.[1] It has been argued that the uncertainties of emancipation attracted Jews to the ideas of equality and universalism associated with the Enlightenment, as well as to liberalism and the notions inherent to *Bildung*.[2] The marked tendency of German Jews to embrace liberalism, and their emphasis on culture can be seen as a response to the need to incorporate what they saw as the best of the German culture into their world and sensibilities. This was also the era when Zionist principles began to inspire segments of German Jewry. Martin Buber, whose writings dealt with the tensions between nationalism and universalism, viewed the Land of Israel (Palestine) as a future haven for a kinder and more moral humanity; "We want the Land of Israel for humanity," he noted in *Der Jude*. Similarly, the younger generation of German Jews in the Weimar period later sought to combine Zionism and socialism.[3]

This background helps account for the path followed by Ludwig Pfeuffer – or Yehuda Amichai, the name he chose for himself on the eve of the establishment of the State of Israel – when he disposed of his bothersome *tallit katan* and his pious skullcap, and threw himself wholeheartedly into the dominant mode of life in the secular and socialist Land of Israel. He did so through the perspective of a *Yekke*,[4] and in the spirit of the ideals that had forged his community of origin although he may not always have been conscious of their influence.

BAVARIA AND HESSEN, FAMILIES OF ORIGIN

The region known as Bavaria came together as an independent state when Napoleon invaded what was then the territories of the Holy Roman Empire in 1806. The Jews of southern Germany (the states of Bavaria, Württemberg and Baden) had their own religious culture and dialect (known as *Judendeutsch*, and later as Western Yiddish). In the first half of the nineteenth century, Bavaria had 50,000 Jews, 80 percent of whom were living in villages.[5] The Jewish teachers' religious seminary in Würzburg, (ILBA, *the Israelitische Lehrerbildungsanstalt*) was founded in 1864 primarily to train teachers to serve in the 150 tiny Jewish schools in these villages.

This continuing presence in small village communities during the nineteenth century helped maintained these Jews' strong religiosity.[6] Jews only began to reside in significant numbers in the towns and cities of Bavaria such as Würzburg, Munich, Regensburg, Fürth and elsewhere towards the end of the nineteenth century;[7] by 1932, already 85 percent of the 45,000 Bavarian Jews were living in the twelve largest centers.[8]

Towards the end of the nineteenth century, Giebelstadt, the village where Amichai's father was born and raised, had 800 inhabitants, several dozen of whom were Jewish.[9] Records show that the first member of the Pfeuffer family to live in Giebelstadt was Anschel, the great-grandfather of David, Ludwig Yehuda's grandfather. Yehuda's father, Friedrich Moritz, whose Hebrew name was Meir, was born on November 20, 1888, the youngest of three brothers and four sisters, to David and Clara née Rau.[10] David was a cattle merchant like most Bavarian Jews at that time, and seems to have had some farmland. Max, the second youngest, inherited the estate and dealt in cattle.[11]

Yehuda's mother, Frieda, grew up in the slightly larger village of Gersfeld, in the state of Hessen, bordering on southeastern Bavaria. Gersfeld totaled some 100 Jews and 1,500 Christians.[12] Frieda was born on April 8, 1895 to Meir Wallhaus, and Sara, née Katzmann. Her father was also a cattle merchant, like her future father-in-law. Gersfeld had a Jewish school, but the number of pupils had dropped so sharply that Frieda was most likely enrolled in the Protestant school.[13] According to acquaintances, she could speak basic Hebrew, enough to carry on everyday conversations.[14] She met Friedrich for the first time at his sister Paulina's wedding in 1912 to Frieda's younger uncle, her mother's brother. When Friedrich was conscripted to fight in the Great War, her family tried to find another suitable future son in law, but she remained faithful to him; he wrote frequently to her during the war and afterwards, while their wedding was being planned.[15,16]

In a number of interviews and in a short autobiography, Amichai described his grandfathers as being estate or large landowners.[17] In his article "My Judaism" (from a collection of pieces by Jews originally or still living in Germany, capturing the writers' takes on Jewish identity) he presents his grandparents on both sides as simple, unpretentious Jews, indistinguishable externally from their non-Jewish neighbors. "They had holdings, basically farms, cattle and fields, orchards and vegetable plots, horses and even a carriage, housekeepers and servants." Out of ethnic protectiveness, and perhaps also from German strictness, they considered religious observance of the *mitzvot* to be a given: "The Judaism of my parents' ancestors in southern Germany was naive and straightforward, simple, almost like that of a child [...] there was no interrogation of the past and no calculation with respect to the future [...] it was a pre-reflective Judaism, practical, without philosophy or science, without Geiger or Buber or Rosenzweig, unlike in Western and Central Europe."[18]

Amichai saw part of his poetic vision deriving from his maternal and paternal grandparents' simple, somewhat childlike form of belief, in that his symbols and images were often based on everyday activities and objects.[19] He felt that their close contact with the soil, farm animals and farm produce was the source of his own non-intellectual stance that made him so popular.[20] As a child he did not have complex conversations with his simple, uneducated grandfathers and grandmothers.[21] Surrounded by nature, he felt a direct connection between their farms and the biblical landscapes he studied at his Jewish school: "For me, Mount Sinai was next to the village where one of my grandfathers lived."[22] In his novel *Not of This Time, Not of This Place* he says that the Bible stories of the creation of the world, or the tale of David and Goliath all took place in Achfeld (a name echoing Gersfeld, but actually an imaginary fusion of his father's and mother's hamlets). This childhood experience was like those of such well-known Hebrew writers as Bialik, Tchernichowsky, S. Ben Zion and Berdichevsky. But unlike in classic Hebrew stories, his world of associations was also populated by heroes and episodes from non-Jewish history and culture: "I discovered, for example, the hill at Waterloo where, I imagined, Napoleon stood, and [...] as I went over these rural wooden bridges, and through grassy meadows and thin river mists, the bridges were those that Dante and his guide Virgil had crossed in the first circle of the inferno. Even the valley where David and Goliath fought was here."[23]

The biblical resonance of the beautiful locations surrounding the village was so strong that he was disappointed when he saw the actual Valley of Elah during his army training, "not far from the Har-Tuv of our time, [where] the duel between David and Goliath took place." It turned out to be smaller and less radiant than he imagined.[24]

FRIEDRICH AND FRIEDA, YEHUDA'S PARENTS

Friedrich Moritz, the father of Ludwig Pfeuffer, studied at the Catholic village school that had four classes.[25] He probably helped out in his father's business as an adolescent .[26] Christian Leo describes Friedrich as someone who had to fend for himself early in life. At age 15 he was an apprentice salesman in the Bavarian town of Hasfurt, like his older brother Sam, and at the start of 1906 he had already registered as a resident of Würzburg.[27] He moved often and found work as a traveling salesman for his brother's wholesale business that sold sewing notions to seamstresses and tailors (*Posamenteriegroßhandlung*).[28]

When World War I broke out, Friedrich was quick to volunteer for the German army, as did many Jews – 400 in Würzburg alone – who were afraid of being stigmatized as insufficiently loyal to the nation they so loved and admired.[29] He served until the end of the war, in the terrible battle of Verdun, on the Italian front and elsewhere, and was awarded two important decorations.[30] Amichai, who served in various military settings when he turned 18, frequently related to "the wars" fought by his soft-spoken and peace-loving father, particularly in the story "The Times my Father Died" and the poem "My father spent four years inside their war."[31]

In his acceptance speech for the Würzburg Cultural Prize, Amichai said that he kept his father's medals, including the Iron Cross, along with his own decorations from Israel's wars in a small box, which his oldest son Ron would play with. He conjectured that this box, which combined history and human fate, is what made him a poet;[32] he may have meant that the box embodied a poetic outlook where there are no hierarchical distinctions of any kind between high and low, exalted and mundane, holy and ordinary, or between society and the individual. The latter bears the sorrow of society, whereas society is not a inchoate mass, but rather is made up of individuals with faces like Dicky, Yonatan Yaḥil and Ḥubi who fell in Israel's wars, and who are remembered in his poems.[33]

WÜRZBURG: A COHESIVE JEWISH COMMUNITY

In Würzburg, where Ludwig Pfeuffer was born on May 3, 1924,[34] a little more than two years after his sister Rachel on February 18, 1922, there was a Jewish community of about 2,600 souls. The community revolved around its religious, educational and medical institutions at 21 Dommershulstrasse that housed a school (*Israelitische Volkschule*), a synagogue, and a hospital where the doctors were Jewish (though the nurses were Christian nuns). An old-age home was located close to the small synagogue that was built in the 1920s on the ruins of the old Jewish hospital.[35] It would play a key role in Amichai's brief but significant return to the town. An important institution at that time in Würzburg, which Amichai recalled with pride, was the ILBA, the Jewish seminary for teacher training on Bibrastrasse. It flourished as of 1924, when Germany's hyperinflation was once again under control.

The Jewish institutions were nearly all close to one another, and members of the community could spend the greater part of their lives in exclusively Jewish circles. In interviews, Amichai often emphasized that as a child the Jewish community was his frame of reference. There were few ties between the Jewish and non-Jewish communities, beyond practical affairs.[36] Nevertheless, when the narrator of *Not of This Time* presents a general overview of the town, he describes its medieval setting before it was destroyed at the end of WWII and rebuilt, not its Jewish community. However, the medieval walls of Würzburg never protected the narrator: "I found myself in a network of walls and ditches, remains from the late Middle Ages [...] fortifications inside fortifications, wall after wall, a pit and a moat. This is where the town of Würzburg begins, after which it opens up, where they walled in a broader space [...] it was like the spreading ripples around a stone thrown into water. I cannot really say that I too developed in this way. Soon I was thrown out beyond the town boundaries into a fearsome unwalled place."[37]

Like other Jewish children, Yehuda Ludwig lived in a dual culture. Their school plays performed for the festivals drew on Jewish tradition (Judah Maccabi, for instance), but no less on classical culture (Homeric and Germanic heroes). Amichai commented that his imagination was fueled by German songs as well as by Bible stories, untroubled by their incompatibility.[38] "We felt we could live with the others because we were so deeply different." However, when children from a German school attacked him and his girlfriend, he felt that the mask of "Hellenism" by being German and European had been ripped off: "We were not Achilles or Pericles again, but children on the run, escaping from gangs of young Nazis [...]."[39] In the 1980s and 1990s, when he was received in Germany with great honor, awarded prizes and invited to deliver talks and interviews Amichai emphasized – perhaps in a somewhat postmodern spirit – how his dual identity as Jewish and German, far from burdening him, was enriching.[40]

CHILDHOOD

Ludwig Yehuda was born at home, not in a hospital. "I nearly split my mother's belly,"[41] he wrote in the novel *Not of This Time*; perhaps he was a large baby. Both the imaginary reconstruction of his circumcision and the portrayal of Eschwege the *mohel* hint at Amichai's peculiarly strong sexual potency: "And down between my legs, still seen / The elegant, clean cut / of my circumcision, the work of Rabbi Reuven Moshe Eschwege, / Cantor and mohel, mighty and bald, a bull of a man / Who bends to me in grace and kindness to pluck / My pink flower in his sensitive hands."[42] His arrival in this world is described in terms of a physicality that is whole, where the circumcision is not interpreted as detrimental. In the descriptions of Eschwege, both in the poem and in the novel *Not of this Time* (where he is called Hildesheim),[43] the mohel's huge dimensions and his thundering prayers are seen by Amichai as a forerunner of his own unconventionality as a poet and his powerful sexuality.[44]

Ludwig Yehuda's parents were strictly observant in the spirit of their naive ancestors. This was more true of his father than his mother, who was less concerned about observing the *mitzvot*.[45] On a number of occasions Amichai said that as a child he was drawn to religious ritual: he liked religion, because it was not logical, and children love "what is not common sense" where the imagination can flourish.[46] Ritual can be a way to engage in fairy tales. These "religious games" endowed Amichai with a feeling of wholeness, which later as an adolescent gave him enough belief in himself that he could destroy this fantasized completeness. For him, ritual was the foundation for symbolic poetic thinking, and he felt sorry not to be able to pass on the traditional heritage to his children, and which might have turned them into poets as well.[47] In a 1985 interview with the writer Yotam Reuveni, he commented: "For any child who wants to become a poet, I would recommend having him grow up in a very religious household, or a Communist one. When a religion completely occupies your parents' existence, later on you might fight it, but you preserve its treasures."[48]

RELIGIOUS RITUAL

Clearly parents are not only objects of observation and imitation but also, and perhaps even mainly, material for fantasy. Amichai commented that as a child he saw his father as God, and his mother as God's servant ("my father was God and didn't know it"). In the poem "My Father, My King" Amichai makes a pseudo-logical connection whose first glimmers were perhaps already present in his boyhood, that if you can call God "father," then you can also call your father "God."[49] This reasoning eventually allowed him to engage in the daring associations of holy and secular, mundane and sacred, that are so characteristic of his poetic license. In the story "The Times My Father Died," he describes following his father as a child in the synagogue on Yom Kippur, fascinated by his appearance, by the back of his neck, cracked like an arid river bed in the Land of Israel, a land he had not yet seen. His praying father, dressed in white, looked like a ghost in a shroud. He died, or took leave of his life, during the *Aleinu* prayer, and then came back to life, shaking off death, once again to stand. He describes how jealous he was of women at prayer, prepared to faint and thus "be erased, withdrawing from everything, spontaneously, without opposition," in a process akin to inspiration or "prophetic influx." Hinting at his obsessive erotic interests, he describes the Torah scroll as naked, and the law undressed.[50, 51] In any case, the archaic prayers could not hold Ludwig Yehuda's attention for long, and were outpaced by his lively imagination that aspired to novelty and rebellion. As a boy, he loved to stand beside his father in the synagogue, even though most of the prayers bored him. There were only a few prayers recited on the High Holy Days that prompted reverie, such as the description of the priest in the Temple ritual, and the scapegoat being cast out into the wilderness to die.

His father kept him by his side in the synagogue, holding his hand with an iron grip, waking him up to go to *selichot* in the early morning by stroking his hair.[52] His mother is recalled more often in images of damp basements, along with the smell of laundry and purified pots and pans.[53] While wandering in Weinburg, the narrator (the "I") remembers: "When my mother bought new cookware , she went to the basement right away [...] she would lower the cooking pots and cups on a string with a handle, immersing everything three times.[54] Then I would help her close the heavy oaken lid. [...] To go down there and immerse kitchenware was one of my favorite things in childhood. The excitement, anticipation and the musty smell, and the echoing voices were for me, for my heart and my whole body, a great and mysterious experience."[55]

THE BELOVED AUNTS

Amichai clearly recalled "the ugliness of the dark corridors" of the very first house he lived in with his parents and sister, and "the smells of Henrietta's and her aunt's corner shop." The two women lived with them early on, because of the housing crisis during the period of rampant inflation in Germany. Henrietta's real name was Tekla Hähnlein; her elderly aunt was widow Ricka (Regina) Goldbach.[56] "When I was a boy I would often go to Henrietta's thinking (mistakenly of course) that I was always wanted, always invited and desired, that people always enjoyed me. Like all children, I thought that what gave me pleasure gave others pleasure too."[57]

On his journey to Weinburg (the stand-in for Würzburg in the novel) much later in life, he instinctively found his way to where the two women had lived. "The window was set in a small recess where Henrietta's aunt would sit and knit and tell me stories," he remembers. "Sometimes she would tickle me during the meal. When the cold knitting needle went down my shirt, it gave me great pleasure. In fact, it was at that time that I acquired an awareness of the world in proportion to the pleasure it gave me." This house of pleasure was so special and dear to him that "I would not even bring little Ruth to visit Henrietta and her aunt. Despite all the love between us, I wanted this place to be just for me."[58]

When reflecting on Henrietta's significance for him, visiting her in an old-age home thirteen years after the war, he wrote: "Her hair is wiry like an old broom. She sweeps away the dirt of life." "Her purity cleanses life, but she gets filthy in the process."[59] "Henrietta [...] stands for my mother." He seems to attribute this propensity to be soiled by purification to his mother as well; she is depicted picking through the innards of a fowl to prepare a feast for the Sabbath; protecting the world with her wings,[60] and shifting endlessly between an outpouring of protest at heaven and her domestic chores.[61]

The widow Goldbach died in 1936. The shop, run jointly by the two aunts then closed and Aunt Henrietta worked in a hostel for the Jewish homeless.[62] In September 1942 she was deported to Theresienstadt but survived along with a handful of other Jews from Würzburg.[63]

INFLUENCES ON PERSONALITY

His father's shop, where Ludwig spent much of his time as a boy, fueled his fantasies in which sexuality already had a hold. In the novel *Not of This Time* he describes returning to Weinburg-Würzburg to find that his father's shop had been replaced by the University's Institute of Psychoanalysis (a symbolic replacement in the story, which has no factual basis). As a child, the women's accoutrements sold in his father's shop were a rich source of metonymy for the female body, defining its curves and the barriers to penetration (see "Nipples, buckle, mouths, screws – all closed and strange," in "Farewell", and similar metaphors in other poems).[64]

In an interview, Amichai said that he had inherited his father's combination of seriousness and humor. He said, though, that he was more verbal than his father, as was to be expected given the cultural and educational disparity between them.[65] However, in an early story, "The Departure from Egypt," he described his father as a "reciter of parables" such as when he embellished the reading of the *Haggadah* with incidental stories and tales. "These stories and tales were about many things: as a soldier digging fortifications, incidents of good-humored clowning, things he had seen or memories from his childhood in his small Bavarian village." The impulse to tell stories also had a financial motivation: "My father was a travelling salesman, and sold everything a seamstress would possibly want [...] He would entertain his customers with stories and parables, and on that Seder night we also enjoyed this world of his." His father would "place little markers" on the pages of the Haggadah, "and they would help him recall his stories and interpretations he would use to comment on the Haggadah."[66]

Whether his father's loquaciousness was rare or frequent, it is clear that he had a creative streak which from time to time broke through the many religious prohibitions. This impulse prompted him to stand up for marginals and the rejected (East Europeans, the poor, Arabs), as well as his own lowly status in Jewish society as a travelling salesman and village peddler. "I think a lot of what I am has its roots in my father's sensibility: his sense of humor and his seriousness," Amichai commented to an interviewer.[67]

Alongside this tie to his father's warmth and occasional bursts of creativity (particularly during the festivals), Amichai always felt he had disappointed his father by not being more practical, and by being a dreamer. Whereas Amichai's father found it relatively easy to integrate military life, Amichai found it artificial and served in the army in response to the needs of the collective. In other words, for him, facing the dangers of battle was an artifice; it required him to "wear his father's face," and give up his own.[68]

AUNT BELLA'S KINDERGARTEN AND THE JEWISH SCHOOL

In interviews, Amichai expressed pride at having gone to a Jewish kindergarten operating on Montessori principles, and even devoted lines to it in his long autobiographical poem "Travels of the Last Benjamin of Tudela:" "You went to a Montessori kindergarten. / You were taught to love, to do things alone, with your own hands. / You were educated to loneliness. You masturbated, / wet dream of the day and wet dream of the night. 'I'll tell your father.'" And later: "Oh Montessori, Montessori, white-haired woman / the first [of the] dead I loved. 'Child, child!' Still / I turn in the street when I hear that called out / behind me."[69] On a few occasions he also said that he began to learn Hebrew in the kindergarten.[70] His pride was compounded by the fact that this was the first kindergarten to be run on Montessori principles.[71] In actual fact, the Montessori kindergarten in Würzburg, which opened in 1929, was not Jewish, and naturally Hebrew was not taught there. The only Jew involved in the founding and pedagogical orientation of the kindergarten was the assimilated, stiff and unattractive Lotte Haas, according to another Würzburg Jewish child, similar in age to Yehuda.[72, 73]

Little Ludwig, then four or five, like nearly all the Jewish children of Würzburg his age, went to Bella Kohn ("Tante [Aunt] Bella's") kindergarten.[74] At that time the Montessori method, which encourages self-directed activity, hands-on learning and collaborative play was attracting attention in the German education system, as opposed to the book-centered intellectual orientation of conservative education, and Tante Bella's nursery school to some extent used Montessori techniques. This would seem to be the source of Amichai's apparent confusion when he remembered learning to do things for himself, which was one of the principles of the Montessori method.

At the age of seven, in the spring or summer of 1931, Ludwig began studying at the Jewish school in town, which in 1921 had become part of the state system. Amichai often recalled the high standards of this school in Würzburg, and emphasized how he learned living, spoken Hebrew alongside Biblical Hebrew and a little Mishnah. He stressed that this was an ordinary German school, financed by the state, but for Jewish pupils alone.

The reasons for the quality of his education were partly political. Before he turned nine, the school began to fill up with Jewish children who had been forced out of German schools when Hitler came to power and Jews were expunged from the ranks of "Aryans" in the state education system. Since Jewish teachers were also expelled,[75] it meant that the school could hire quality teachers, who although they had no real connection to Judaism, were highly educated and took a progressive approach to education.[76] In that threatening reality, the approach to spoken Hebrew was reevaluated, and the link to the real Land of Israel reaffirmed, beyond teaching the descriptions of the imagined landscapes of the Bible and prayer. The study of contemporary Hebrew – in its Sephardic pronunciation as used in the Land of Israel – was introduced when *aliyah* had become a serious alternative for many.[77] Similarly, course time was dedicated to learning English, a language that had not previously been taught in elementary schools, in response to the distinct possibility that children might suddenly become refugees in Mandate Palestine or an English-speaking country.

In general, winds of innovation and openness swept through German education in the 1920s, a system whose modus operandi had been characterized by conservativism and rigidity. Montessori's influence on early childhood education was part of this search for new directions which were also manifested in the growing awareness in Jewish schools of the importance of the arts, and the related need to devote time in the curriculum to drawing and music.[78] School plays, one of which would later be significant in Ludwig's life, were seen as important opportunities for students to express their emotional sides. The growing shadow of the persecution of German Jewry became a further stimulus for creativity.

However, not everything in the school was as festive as Amichai attempted to convey to his interviewers.[79] Discipline there was rigid: there were "rules that couldn't be broken" – something that was all the more clear to Yehuda when he compared the school in Germany to the one in Petah Tikvah, where he first lived in Israel.[80] Although there were fewer examples of corporal punishment at that time, in part because of laws voted in Germany during that decade (1922), at least one teacher at the Jewish school, Moritz Hellman, who became the principal in 1933, was a believer in the "old method," and would strike pupils with a rod, for example when they could not solve math problems.[81]

LITTLE RUTH AND HER FAMILY

Throughout kindergarten and his school years in Würzburg, and to some extent for his entire life, Ludwig Yehuda was preoccupied with Ruth Hanover, the daughter of the rabbi of the town (and district) and his ailing wife, Clara. Amichai first met Ruth when he was four, when the Pfeuffers moved to Alleestrasse (today St. Benediktstrasse) in 1928. Ruth and Ludwig walked to the Jewish kindergarten and back home together every day, and later to school. Ruth was etched in Amichai's memory as combining intensity and purity. He noted in interviews that sexuality in childhood was connected to "games" with boys, whereas with Ruth he felt simple childish affection and mutual concern.[82] This girl/young woman would later appear over and over again in his poetry, particularly in his later works , and occupied a central role in the thoughts and fantasies of the protagonist-narrator of *Not of This Time*.[83]

Ruth's father, Siegmund Shimon Hanover, became rabbi of the town in 1920, after the death of Nathan Bamberger, who had served as rabbi and head of the teachers' seminary for 40 years.[84] Hanover was a fan of detective novels, a witty deliverer of sermons, and active promoter of community projects such as a book club and Jewish-Christian encounters. He also allowed women to vote in community institutions.[85]

Amichai described Ruth as follows: “We went together to kindergarten, and together to school, and as peaceful legends of peaceful peoples put it: these two were meant for one another [for their entire lives].”[86] They were a kind of society unto themselves, an elite, regarding the human reality around them from afar.[87] When depicting Ruth to a ballet teacher he met as an adult in Würzburg, Amichai described her as assertive, a person who followed the rules but also aimed for self-realization: “Her small, feminine chin, her cheerful braids, and her snub nose, and her freckles, and her hair strictly parted along the center of her skull, as was the style of ballet dancers.”[88]

THE DRAMA OF THE ACCIDENT

The terrible drama that separated Yehuda and Ruth, but which also connected them deeply and eternally, occurred after a childhood argument that turned into a tragedy. The direct connection between the argument and the tragic incident is unclear, and seems to be more the product of an overly sensitive imagination. Yehuda Ludwig was supposed to play the lead role in the school Hanukah play, until Norbert (in the novel, Siegfried), a classmate, challenged him for the part. Norbert was the son of the strict principal. “We got into an argument about who was to get the role of Judah Maccabi, and I did not relent and kept my dignity.”[89] “On that morning the argument broke out again among teachers and pupils over who would get the part of Judah Maccabi: redheaded Siegfried, the son of the principal, or me? [...] Beside the wooden balustrade of the school, which was now a girls’ dance academy, Ruth tried to get me to relinquish the role proudly – ‘throw the role in their faces,’ she told me; but I didn't give up. We parted in anger.”[90]

Ruth, who was furious, invited Hans Laredo, the son of wealthy parents (in the novel, Franz and sometimes Heinz) to be her date to the school Hanukah party.[91] They became closer and he lent her his bicycle.[92] “She rode Franz’s bike to irritate me,” concludes the narrator of the novel. It was deep winter and the icy road was dangerous, all the more for an inexperienced rider. Ruth was caught between two cars, “and a fender seriously injured her leg.”[93]

“At first, when Ruth got out of hospital, I would carry her book bag to and from school.”[94] She was still using crutches, while waiting to get her artificial leg, and her classmates would gather round her, out of love perhaps mixed with pity and shock.[95] When the prothesis was attached, "it was as though the wooden leg had become a robust oak, giving her its power.” But in fact, the leg was clumsy and uncomfortable. Ruth, who was twelve years old and a budding adolescent, was undoubtedly very troubled by her appearance, and afraid she would not be lovable or desirable as a woman, or would be considered an unproductive member of society. "One day in the palace garden, beside the pool where a stone nymph sat [...] Ruth asked me: 'what does the future hold, do you think?' I remember that I was in shock. I told Ruth what I had heard from grownups, that no physical handicap today was really a problem, and that in the twentieth century someone missing a leg could have a decent place in society. Ruth heard me out, and her voice [a sign of her maturity rather than any faith in what he was saying] was quiet like the water flowing beside the nymph in the pool. 'Of course! No problem. How could I ask you a question like that!' She was twelve then. We got up and I left her and headed towards the rest of the palace garden [...] From that day, we never spoke about her handicap, but I dimly felt that something had come between us [...] She had stopped being a little girl. After the amputation of a leg, the body matures the human being."[96]

RUTH AND LUDWIG FACING GERMAN SOCIETY, BEFORE AND AFTER 1933

Antisemitism and the determination to harm Jews existed prior to 1933 in hate speech, physical attacks, and in laws restricting their livelihoods, and nowhere more powerfully than in Bavaria and Würzburg. Local journalists, Catholic and otherwise, had been inciting the populace against Jews since the 1890s.[97] Jewish children frequently had stones thrown at them by children from the neighborhood school and the *Realgymnasium*, or were taunted with chants such as "Jewish pig, Isaac, go to Palestine!" After Hitler rose to power, the violence became blunter and more brutal. Looking back, Amichai thought that religious antisemitism had become political.[98]

Before leaving for the Land of Israel, teenage Ludwig had a humiliating experience, whose cruel impact would remain with him his whole life, together with the feeling of terrible powerlessness and wounded masculinity for someone who was supposed to protect his girlfriend and fight back. In both interviews and his writings, Amichai returned repeatedly to the story of the gang of Hitler youth who violently insulted handicapped Ruth and himself as they were returning home one afternoon.[99] "They knocked [Ruth] down, the Nazi youth, and they knocked me down too. [...] We were separated some week later when my family left for the Land of Israel. I thought it was the end of the world, as only children can feel the end of the world, or its beginning." Later, on the journey from Europe, when looking out a train or hotel window, he would drift into a reverie: "I saw Ruth's face, as it was when she had turned to me when we were lying on the ground, and the Hitlerjugend youth were on top of me, and I heard how one of them kicked her, and her artificial leg gave off a metallic sound of hoops and buckles and leather."[100]

Because almost no one in Amichai's family was murdered in the Holocaust, he cherished Ruth's memory not only for the childhood purity he associated with her, but also as a victim of the Holocaust. This was his very personal, individual way of mourning a world that had gone up in smoke.

THE EXTENDED FAMILY GOES TO PALESTINE

Amichai often emphasized the religious quality of his parents' Zionism,[101] which was concretized by the events of the era. The haberdashery run by his father and older brother failed economically after the boycott of Jewish businesses throughout Germany which was instigated in April 1933. Uncle Max and his family in the village were harassed by non-Jewish animal traders. Ludwig's father had non-Jewish acquaintances, probably comrades in arms during WWI, who expressed their sympathy. They tried to persuade him that Hitler and the Nazis would soon be gone.[102] The last straw was when Friedrich Meir, Ludwig's father, saw the bodies in the Jewish hospital of two Jewish men from the village who had been beaten to death by the Nazis. Friedrich, who belonged to the ḥevra kadishah (burial society), went home in shock, and his children, who as was then the norm, did not take part in parental decision-making, puzzled out what had happened from overhearing his frequent whisperings with their mother.[103] "My father then began to disband the business, selling his stocks of buttons, thread, and zippers."[104] His father's willingness to emigrate to the Land of Israel was also eased by an inheritance bequeathed by a childless family member living in the United States. This inheritance would help sustain the family many years when Friedrich's business initiatives in Israel did not succeed.[105]

Although this legacy allowed his father to emigrate to the Land of Israel as "a person of means,"[106] the family left Germany without the certificate issued by the Mandate authorities to enter the country. The journey to the port of Trieste in Italy, via Switzerland, was one of constant anxiety. In Trieste, under the fascist government of Italy, Ludwig Pfeuffer envied "the fascist youth with their beautiful black uniforms" and their show of strength, similar to the Nazi marches in Würzburg. All the while "my father ran between travel agents and the English consulate, urged on by the need to escape."[107]

The story of the extended family, which seems to have journeyed to Palestine as one, would with time be narrated in such a way as to strengthen the sense that this was not the flight of refugees: it was not a story of escaping with their lives, aiming for the first shore that would accept them, but a conscious *aliyah* motivated by ideological commitment, along with spiritual and moral readiness to settle the land and wholeheartedly integrate there.

NOTES

1. See George Mosse, *German Jews beyond Judaism* (Bloomington, 1985), 46. Mosse defines Weimar culture (1919-1939) as an "intra-Jewish dialogue." Ibid, 38.

2. David Sorkin, *The Transformation of German Jewry*, 1780-1840 (New York, 1987), preface and first chapter.

3. Based on Guy Miron, "Zionism and Jewish Nationalism in Germany" [in Hebrew], in Allon Gal (ed.), World Regional Zionism: Geo-Cultural Dimensions [in Hebrew], vol. 1 (Jerusalem and Beersheba 5770 [=2009/10]), 304, 310, 312.

4. *Yekke* - Yiddish-Israeli slang for a Jew of German-speaking origin. The term has connotations of punctiliousness and a sense of social decorum.

5. Walter Kaufmann, "A History of the Jewish Teachers Seminary," in Max Ottensoser & Alex Roberg (eds.), *ILBA: Israelitische Lehrbildunganstalt, Würzburg 1864-1938* [partly in German], (Detroit, 1982), 27.

6. Yaakov Borut, "Religious Life among the Jews of the Towns and Villages of Western Germany un the Weimar Period", in Oded Heilbruner (ed.), *Weimar Jewry* [in Hebrew] (Jerusalem, 1994), 92.

7. Christian Dexelmüller, *Jüdische Kultur in Franken* (Jewish Culture in Franconia), (Würzburg, 1988), 30-31.

8. Max P. Birnbaum, "The Union of Communities of the Bavarian Galilee [in Hebrew]," in Avraham Margaliot and Yehoyachim Kochavi (eds.), *History of the Holocaust – Germany*, vol. 1 [in Hebrew], (Jerusalem, 5758 [=1998]), 423.

9. H. Gapner, *Giebelstadt in alten Ansichten*, Band 1 (Giebelstadt in old photos, vol. 1); J. Sprock-Pfitzer, *Die ehemaligen jüdischen Gemeinden im Landkreis Würzburg* (Former Jewish Communities in Würzburg District), (Würzburg, 1988), 61-63.

10. The eldest child was Samuel Amson (Samson, perhaps), born in 1876. Four girls followed: Regina, Malchen (Amalia), Marianna, and Paulina. Eighteen months before Friedrich, Max was born. The Giebelstadt archive, and various certificates in the Würzburg municipal archive.

11. Reiner Strätz (ed.), *Biographiches Handbuch: Würzburger Juden* 1900-1945 (Biographical Lexicon of Würzburg Jewry 1900-1945, 2 Teilen, in German) (Würzburg, 1989), vol. ii, 440.

12. Ingrid Wiltmann, *Nur Ewigkeit ist kein Exil* (Only Eternity is not Exile), [in German], Möhlin, 1997), 95.

13. Conversation with Avivah Sauer, widow of Yigal, Amichai's nephew. June 22, 2015.

14. Conversations with Avivah Sauer, and with Dubi Zahavi, husband of Amichai's niece, Hanna. July 2, 2016.

15. Würzburg culture prize acceptance speech, June 1981. Quoted in Roland Flade, Würzburger Jüden (The Jews of Würzburg), [in German], (Würzburg, 1987), 416-418; also mentioned in later interviews: with Omer, "In This Burning Country",

4-11; with Liraz Pank, "Even Poets Watch the World Cup" [in Hebrew]), Rosh 1,July 6, 1990 12.

16. Private collection of the Sauer family.

17. Amichai, "Mein Judentum (My Jewishness, in German)", In Hans Jürgen Schulz (ed.), *Mein Judentum.* Stuttgart-Berlin, 1978, 20-35.

18. Cf. experiences described by Herbert A. Strauss, *In the Eye of the Storm* (New York, 1999), 6.

19. Amichai, "Mein Judentum", 24. See also an interview with Reuveni, "Yehuda Amichai: This Is the Place" [in Hebrew], *Yediot Acharonot,* May 17, 1985.

20. Cf. his interview with Wiltmann, 92; and with Rachel Hollander-Steingart, "In My Heart is a Museum", *The Jerusalem Post,* September 28, 1981.

21. Jewish cattle dealers in the region, and probably beyond, had a bad name; to more cultured Jews, they were an object of scorn for their "uncouth expression and unfairness" at the market. Article in *Algemeine Zeitung des Judentums*, March 7, 1913.

22. Omer interview. Elsewhere he recalls the hill in Würzburg as site of his confusion of biblical and German landscapes.

23. *Not of This Time*, 590. All references to this novel are to the Hebrew original unless indicated otherwise. The English translation is abridged and adapted.

24. Yehuda Amichai, "Every Man is Born a Poet," 2. Draft for a speech, Amichai archive.

25. According to documents in the village archive. Cf. description of a meeting with a village priest who "taught my father and uncle [...] when they were at school." *Not of This Time,* 592.

26. In a postcard dated October 25, 1901 to Friedrich when he was still in the village, he is addressed as *Ökonomessohn,* "the son of the estate manager." Postcard collection of the Pfeuffer family, the Heksherim Archive, Ben-Gurion University of the Negev.

27. Christian Leo, *Zwischen Erinnern und Vergessen* (Between Remembering and Forgetting, in German); Würzburg, 2004; Idem, "Die deutsch-jüdischen Wurzeln Jehuda Amichais" (Yehuda Amichai's German Jewish Roots), in *Zwischen Krieg und Liebe*, edited by Renata Eichmeier and Edit Raim, Berlin, 2010, 33-60.

28. In a number of places Amichai indicates that his father was a travelling salesman, for example "Therefore I Am Now Rich," *Poems* 3, 139 (no translation).

29. Out of 400 Würzburg Jews who were drafted or volunteered for the war, 40 were killed. Twelve thousand German Jews were killed in WWI. On the Jews of Würzburg, see Christian Dexelmüller, "Tausend Jahre Juden in Würzburg – eine wechselvolle und tragische Geschichte" (A thousand years of the Jews of Würzburg – a tragic history with many upheavals), [in German], in Christian Dexelmüller & Roland Flade (eds.), in *Ruth hat auf einer Schwarzen Flöte gespielt* (*Ruth Played a black flute*), (Würzburg, 2005), 32. Amichai's maternal uncle, David Wallhaus, who was born in 1893, served in that war, and froze to death in the Carpathian Mountains. The first poem of the "Three Photos" cycle by Amichai is dedicated to him, *Poems* 1, 134 (no translation).

30. Leo, "German Jewish Roots," 19.

31. "The Times My Father Died" (translated by Joseph Shachter) in *The World is a Room* (translated by Elinor Grumet et al.) (Philadelphia, 1984), 185-197; "My father spent four years inside their war," From the cycle of poems "We Loved Here," in *The Selected Poetry of Yehuda Amichai*, trans. Bloch and Mitchell, 8; *Poems* 1, 57.

32. He received the prize in 1981. The main part of the speech appears in Flade, *Jews of Würzburg*, 416-418.

33. Amichai's identification with the oppressed and excluded may reflect something of his father's thought. It is probably no coincidence that the cycle "We loved here," which starts with his father's anti-nationalist vision, ends with "the handicapped and unemployed / are songbirds on poets' trees / instead of cuckoos and nightingales" (Sonnet 22), and "men wear their first love / and not signs of battle and war" (Sonnet 23) (trans. MJ); *Poems* 1, 72-73.

34. The Hebrew name given him by his parents at his circumcision was of one of his mother's ancestors, the first to be identified – Yehuda Walhaus, born in 1770. His mother's maternal grandfather was also called Yehuda (Juda), according to family trees drawn up by Zigard Walhaus, 80.2044, and Ruth Kobliner Katzman of Kibbutz Sde Eliyahu (kindly provided to me by Avraham Zilber of Sde Eliyahu). The name Ludwig, by contrast, was more common on his father's side.

35. Strauss, ibid, 2. See also Leo, "German Jewish Roots," 55.

36. Interview in English, conducted at Yale University, with Geoffrey Hartman and Benjamin Harshav, 3.11.94, for the Fortunoff Video Archive for Holocaust Testimonies. HVT-2679; Omer interview, "In This Burning Country."

37. *Not of This Time,* 508. See also Leo, *Between Remembering and Forgetting*, 145.

38. Amichai told Aryeh Arad, in an interview on Israel Army Radio, that this was also true for the other children at his school. Arad interview, March 3, 1969 [in Hebrew].

39. *Not of This Time*, 561.

40. "Die Last doppelter Identität?" (Is dual identity a burden?) Text of a handwritten speech. 15.700.

41. *Not of This Time*, 215, 216.

42. "Song of Circumstance" [trans. MJ]; *Poems* [in [Hebrew] 3, 92. See also in "The Jews": "You don't know me and I don't know you / But we are the Jewish people, / Your dead grandfather and I the circumcised and you / the beautiful granddaughter / With golden hair: we are the Jewish people." *Yehuda Amichai: A Life of Poetry 1948-1994* (translated by Benjamin and Barbara Harshav), (New York, 1994), 463; *Poems* 3, 92. See also Moshe Yitzhaki, "You Don't Know Me" [in Hebrew], *Haaretz*, March 29, 2013.

43. *Not of This Time*, 403. Eschwege, like Hildesheim, is a place name. The town of Eschwege is in the state of Hessen, the region where Amichai's mother was born and raised.

44. He would sing liturgy written in the classical style to popular tunes. Singing hymns set to secular music written by non-Jews was also found in Hasidic circles.

45. Later, when Amichai visited her, on a brief furlough from the army on Yom Kippur 5709 (1948), she served him food, telling him that "God who is making

wars, cannot order us not to eat". The moment is recalled in one of his poems, and in interviews.

46. Over the years, when asked to describe his childhood, Amichai would play up the amusing and funny sides of religion as he saw it as a child. Yosef Bar Yosef interview, "Cold Lightning Doesn't Move Me" [in Hebrew], Bamachane, February 26, 1986.

47. Amichai, "Mein Judentum."

48. Reuveni interview. However, in the same interview, he compares compliance with religious laws in adulthood to the application of the rules of football to the whole of the human race.

49. "My Father, My King," *The Poetry of Yehuda Amichai* (edited by Robert Alter, various translators), (New York, 2015), 95,

50. "The Times My Father Died," in *The World Is a Room*, 187.

51. The Torah, in its narrower sense, refers to the Five Books of Moses. They constitute the Sefer Torah, the scroll read aloud in synagogue.

52. This image is found in the poem "A Letter of Recommendation", in *Selected Poetry*, 101. *Poems* 3, 4. Amichai returns to this experience in a number of interviews.

53. *Not of This Time*, 352-353.

54. Immersion in a mikvah, a ritual bath, of new utensils bought from a non-Jew, to complete their transfer to Jewish ownership.

55. *Not of This Time*, 351.

56. Leo, "German Jewish Roots," 37.

57. *Not of This Time*, 242. In an interview with Corinna Benning, Amichai depicts Henrietta as having looked after him and his sister, and describes them visiting her together. Broadcast on Radio Bavaria, reproduced in Leo, *Between Remembering and Forgetting*, 247-257.

58. Ibid., 236-237.

59. *Not of This Time*, 345.

60. "God's Hand in the World," Poetry, 24; Poems 1, 80.

61. "To the Mother." Poetry, 35; Poems 1, 131.

62. Leo, "German Jewish Roots," 42.

63. Leo, ibid., 43. His relationship with the aunts was also the subject of a late poem, "Throw Pillows", *A Life of Poetry*, 452; *Poems* 5, 118.

64. "Farewell", *A Life of Poetry*, 50; *Poems* 1, 219.

65. Interview with Larry Joseph, "The Art of Poetry: Yehuda Amichai", *Paris Review* 44 (Spring 1992), 5. https://www.theparisreview.org/interviews/2095/the-art-of-poetry-no-44-yehuda-amichai.

66. "The Departure from Egypt," *In this Terrible Wind* [in Hebrew], first edition: Sifriat Poalim, 1961; renewed edition: Schocken 1973, 247-8.

67. Ibid.

68. *Not of This Time*, 295-296, 351-352.

69. *Poetry*, 110-111; *Poems* 2, 119. The referent of "the first of the dead I loved" is not clear. Maria Montessori died in 1950. Perhaps he meant the principal of the kindergarten.

70. Amichai said that he learned Hebrew prayers in this kindergarten: Omer interview.

71. The first kindergarten in the world to be run on Montessori lines was indeed Jewish, but was in Vilna, not Würzburg.

72. An article by Lotte Haas on the Montessori method "The Method of Freedom in the Montessori Educational Method" [in German], appeared on January 3, 1931 in the *Würzburger General Anzeiger*. I am grateful to Roland Flade for the material from this newspaper. On the Montessori method, see Rita Kramer, *Maria Montessori: A Biography*, New York, 1988, 115-122.

73. According to Har-Gil, he was the only Jewish child in the kindergarten. Unlike Amichai, who said that he was learning Hebrew there, Har-Gil said that in first grade at the Jewish school, he heard Hebrew songs without understanding a single word. Schraga Har-Gil, *Alte Liebe rostet nie* (Old Love does not Rust, in German), (Würzburg, 2004), 57-64.

74. Strauss, *Eye of the Storm*, 11. Strauss did not like the kindergarten teachers, and thought they were oppressive. He only later realized that the kindergarten was run on progressive lines. See also Flade, *Jews of Würzburg* [in German], 156.

75. Yosef Walk, "Jewish Education in Nazi Germany," in *History of the Holocaust – Germany,* vol. ii, edited by Avraham Margaliot and Yehoakim Kochavi, 607-608 [in Hebrew]. Joseph Walk, *Jüdische Schule und Erziehung im Dritten Reich (Jewish Schools and Education in the Third Reich*), [in German], (Frankfurt am Main, 1991), chapters 1-2.

76. In the Omer interview, Amichai said that at the school in Würzburg he received "the best of progressive education."

77. Nili Scharf Gold, *Yehuda Amichai: The Making of a National Poet*, Boston, 2008, 36-37; Walk, "Jewish Education", 624-628. Officially, The Department of Education of the National Representatives of the Jews of Germany (*Erziehungsausschuss der Reichsvertretung der Juden in Deutschland*) decided to teach Hebrew solely with the Sephardi pronunciation in 1936.

78. Walk, "Jewish Education," 628.

79. In the Hartman and Harshav interview, for example.

80. Joseph interview, 4.

81. Strauss, *Eye of the Storm*, 14; Arad interview [in Hebrew].

82. Omer interview, and others. For more on relations with friends and games, see *Not of This Time,* 559. The parks in Würzburg remind the "narrating I" of the ditches where as children he and his friends engaged in sexual play – perhaps mutual masturbation. Ibid., 269.

83. The period of composition of *Not of This Time* is discussed in a later chapter. On Amichai's references to Ruth in his poetry, see Chapter 3. The childhood picture showing him and Ruth hugging under a tree was always on his desk. Omer interview; "In our love" [in Hebrew], program on Israel's Army Radio, April 19, 2011. The photo is memorialized in the poem "All These Make a Dance Rhythm": "her one hand / on my shoulder, and the other one free, reaching out from the dead / to me, now." *Selected Poetry*, 132; *Poems* 3, 292. See also Hana Amichai, "Little Ruth is my Private Anne Frank" [in Hebrew], *Haaretz*, August 8, 2010.

84. On Nathan Bamberger see in *Biographical Lexicon*, vol. i, 71-72.

85. Flade, *Jews of Würzburg,* 234, 187.

86. *Not of This Time*, 512.

87. Ibid., 561.

88. Ibid., 369.

89. Ibid., 558.

90. Ibid., 370. In one place, a different, almost opposite version appears. He imagines Ruth, although not the Ruth of childhood but the spirit of the dead Ruth, "speaking in such a serious voice, saying: 'Don't give up on the role in the play. You and not Siegfried must get the part of Judah the Maccabi. Don't give up, even if his father is the principal of the school!", ibid., 299. In the end, the Hanukah party was cancelled because of Ruth's accident. Letter from Amichai to Ruth Herrmann, December 7, 1947, the Heksherim Archive.

91. Inconsistencies in the names of characters may stem from the disorderly way the manuscript was submitted to Schocken publishers. Dan Miron, the editor, put an enormous amount of work into organizing the material, but there are inevitably loose ends. Although it is tempting to see the inconsistencies in names as a sign of the book's postmodernism, this would be difficult to prove.

92. Hans Gunther Laredo was the son of the wealthy art dealer Oskar Laredo, a descendant of the only Moroccan family in the town. According to one source he was born in 1921, and thus was older than Ruth and Ludwig. *Biographical Lexicon*, vol. i, 327.

93. *Not of This Time*, 311.

94. *Not of This Time*, 232-233. In another version, he helped her learn to walk at the beginning, guided by a physiotherapist. Pank interview, 13.

95. *Not of This Time*, 295.

96. Ibid., 311.

97. Flade, *Jews of Würzburg*, 163-166.

98. Joseph interview, 3. In *Not of This Time*, Maximillian's school, perhaps with bitter irony, is called the Pestalozzi School, after the great educational reformer.

99. *Not of This Time*, 85-86.

100. Trans. MJ.

101. Over the years, his growing self-mythification and enshrinement of his father prompted him to state in an interview with Benning on Radio Bavaria that his father decided to go to Palestine "immediately" (*sofort*) as soon as Hitler came to power. Corinna Benning, broadcast on Radio Bavaria, May 4, 1998, reproduced in Christian Leo, *Zwischen Erinnern und Vergessen* (Würzburg, 2004), 247.

102. Lawrence Joseph, "The Art of Poetry: Yehuda Amichai", *Paris Review* 44 (Spring 1992), 3; Omer interview, "In This Burning Country," 5.

103. He was the honorary treasurer, according to one interview, but in a later rendition is depicted by his son as the head of the *ḥevra kadishah.*

104. *Not of This Time*, 438.

105. Scharf Gold, *National Poet*, 45.

106. The term was *ba'al hon*, designating individuals who possessed £1,000 sterling, which made them and their close family eligible for *aliyah* (immigration to Israel) without belonging to any pioneering movement.

107. "Venice Three Times," *In This Terrible Wind* [in Hebrew], 287-288.

Chapter 2

1936–1942

Teenage Years in Petach Tikva and Jerusalem

THE YEAR IN PETAH TIKVA

In hindsight, Amichai saw his parents' decision to immigrate to Israel rather than the United States, Western Europe or Latin America – the preferred destinations of many Jews who left Germany in those years – as critical to the discovery of his calling.[1] In the United States, he would probably have become a lawyer rather than a poet.[2] In Israel the spirit of the Bible is still present and a source of inspiration. In Jerusalem, he wrote in an autobiographical article, "you tread the stones where the prophet Isaiah walked, and in the Sharon, it's as if you roam the villages and vineyards where the lovers of the Song of Songs sought each other out."[3]

In his opinion, however, what was decisive to his formation as a poet was not just the transition to the Land of Israel overflowing with biblical and historical references. Rather, the linguistic shift from German to Hebrew as his first language, the language of the classroom, daily life and thought shaped the trajectory he might well not have taken in another language. In Israel, poetry is both one's daily bread and the "compact prayers [...] that you can take with you everywhere."[4]

Until his dying day, and despite transformations in public trends and literary taste that to some extent challenged his optimistic outlook, Amichai continued to believe that "as a small people, we are definitely in the major league of literature [...] This is a country that reads literature."[5] He felt destined to be a poet, first in the Yishuv and then in the new State of Israel where he felt that poetry was a basic necessity of life,[6] a means of expressing joy and partial solace for the pain and loss that came with continuing war.[7]

For the extended Pfeuffer family, leaving Germany was final and absolute, with no second thoughts about one day returning. No one from the extended

Pfeuffer-Walhaus clan, which exceeded 1,000 in the 1980s according to Amichai's estimates, ever went back to settle in Germany.[8] Yehuda's father, Friedrich Moritz, sent as many of his possession as he could to Palestine, including large heavy pieces of furniture, which arrived after months in the hold of a ship.[9]

When did the family immigrate to Palestine? No one is more reliable than the young Yehuda Pfeuffer. Next to his still somewhat childish picture in the Fourth Grade Yearbook of 5696 [1936] of the Maaleh school, he writes: "Came to the country in Tammuz 5696."[10] Two years later, next to his picture now clearly a teen, he notes: "We came to this country in July '36, and I studied in Petach Tikvah at the Netzah Israel school.[11] In 1937 we moved to Jerusalem, and I was enrolled in the fourth class of the Maaleh school." The semi-autobiographical poem "The Travels of the Last Benjamin of Tudela" also has the family arriving when the narrator is 12 years old, at the beginning of the Arab Revolt, which would leave its mark on his life and give him a sense of never-ending war:

You ate and were filled, you came
in your twelfth year, in the Thirties
of the world, with short pants that reached down to your knees,
tassels dangling from your undershawl
sticky between your legs in the sweltering land.
[...]
But even then I was marked for annihilation like an orange scored
for peeling, like chocolate, like a hand-grenade for explosion and death.[12]

Friedrich Moritz's brother and sister and their families had settled in Petach Tikva perhaps a year or two earlier, paving the way for Yehuda's parents.[13] Petach Tikvah was one of the leading destinations for German immigrants at that time.[14] The municipality realized that having welcomed German Jews, the town needed to contribute meaningfully to finding them jobs and easing administrative hurdles such as helping them open businesses and benefit from reductions in municipal taxes.[15]

Amichai recalls that his father purchased a plot of land in Petach Tilkva because he planned to be a farmer (*Landwirt*).[16] This decision was not only consistent with the Zionist ideology of settling the land and engaging in agriculture, which most immigrants identified with, but also derived directly from the family's background: Yehuda's grandparents were "rural Jews, with large farms in southern Germany. Petach Tikvah, where we settled, was a completely natural continuation. A house within a fine grove, wells, the sound of a pump."[17] "We would go barefoot, but most exciting was walking through the groves to the sea and to the young city of Tel Aviv."[18]

The memory of Petach Tikva remained etched in Amichai's mind as a fleeting, spectacular, but only partially fulfilled promise, in which he would become the ultimate dweller in the Land of Israel, the new Jew, as this character was thought of in his formative years. Like many young people living in Palestine at that time, as an adolescent he identified with the ideas of socialism and cooperative agricultural settlement. The poem "The Old Ice Factory in Petach Tikvah," written almost 40 years after Amichai left the settlement, is related to this in a subtle way, while taking a broader philosophical view. He writes in the poem of an intimation of lucidity, of normal maturity, which came to him "behind the dark cypresses [that separated the groves from one another] [...] 'You live / Only once.' // I didn't understand then / and now that I understand, it's too late." As a child, he was too young to perceive the message of normality, of eating and drinking and seizing the moment for there is no other life. Writing at the the age of 50, it was too late to follow this principle, now that the inner life of a poet and poetic revelation took precedence.[19]

As an adult, Amichai was at pains to point out that as a child who had received a Jewish religious education (and who had lived almost exclusively among Jews in the city in which he was born), it was not hard for him to adjust when he came to Palestine. "I studied [in Petach Tikvah] in a religious school, Netzah Israel. I had no difficulty integrating. I knew Hebrew and immediately made friends."[20] In his opinion, integration was problematic for those who had been assimilated Jews in Germany, who no longer identified or felt they were Jews. For these immigrants, their new life in Palestine came as a shock. By contrast, similar to other immigrants with strong Jewish roots, he felt that going to Palestine was like coming home. In this respect they more closely resembled immigrants from Eastern Europe, for whom the visions of the Bible were fueled by some of their childhood fantasies as pupils in the *cheder*,[21] while praying in the synagogue alongside their parents, and in later years, in Hebrew secondary schools or in various Jewish-Zionist frameworks.

The Arab Revolt became a tangible presence when the family journeyed from Haifa to Petach Tikvah, and in the year in which he lived in the settlement. The train that took the family from Haifa to the Rosh Ha'ayin station, where they would take a bus or car, was forced to stop by rioters throwing rocks.[22] Yehuda's father, uncle, and older cousins had to do guard duty.[23] Entering Jaffa was forbidden. Typically, given Amichai's inclination to put a positive gloss on things, he wrote that there was no fear, only a need for caution.

The Jewish school in Würzburg was strict, and the rules were not to be broken.[24] By contrast, in the religious Netzah Israel school Yehuda and his sister attended in Petach Tikvah, "there was hardly any discipline." Boys and girls studied together. Classes contained pupils of different ages, since many stayed back a year, and so even before his bar mitzvah, Amichai's classmates included brawny pupils sporting moustaches who were a year or two older.[25] As a polite child, and a Yekke, he was amazed to see Moshe Auerbach, the bearded principal, dragging an unruly pupil out of the classroom under his arm like a slaughtered calf, when all other attempts at imposing discipline had failed.[26, 27]

Yehuda's father insisted on maintaining the German-Jewish community's religious traditions including its prayer ritual. Together with a group of other German immigrants in Petach Tikvah, he founded the Mekor Hayyim synagogue, headed by a rabbi from Cologne, Rabbi Pinhas Wolf.[28] Amichai celebrated his bar mitzvah in this synagogue. He would later claim, both seriously and in jest to his audiences, that the Torah portion for the Sabbath of his birthday - the double portion of *Tazria-Metzora* in the book of Leviticus - was fatal to his connection to religion. How could anyone keep on being religious after having to read passages about leprosy and boils all in the right cantillation?[29]

Since Yehuda's father had to support his family, he submitted a request to the municipal council, in the name of Yaakov Pfeuffer (his brother Max's son), to engage in ritual slaughter for the sausage industry. According to Amichai, this was a partnership between his father, his uncle Max, and "one of my older cousins.[30] They opened a small sausage factory of sorts." His father travelled on donkey to sell their products to groceries." In various interviews, where he briefly mentioned his father's business initiatives, Amichai would wryly observe that this is how he found out what sausages are made of.[31] This business venture in fact eventually collapsed.

After a year in Petach Tikvah his parents decided to move to Jerusalem, "so that [the children could] receive a more Jewish education, in the European sense of the term."[32] Nevertheless the year in Petach Tikvah appeared to have eased the inevitable upheavals that beginning anew in Palestine necessarily entailed. In Petach Tikvah he spent a great deal of time in the countryside which was similar to the landscapes he he had come to know during vacations at his grandparents' home. In his new home in the Land of Israel he could give unfettered rein to his imagination, identify with the boisterous behavior of the children around him, before the move to Jerusalem and the return to the Yekke orderliness that was both similar and very different from what he knew in his birthplace.

THE MOVE TO JERUSALEM

As is frequently the case with poets, the place where his family took up residence in Jerusalem seemed to Amichai fateful and symbolic.

> "We lived in a very pretty neighborhood, Neveh Bezalel, that was right on the border between Nahalat Ahim, Nahlaot, and Shaarei Hesed, that was a little less

extreme than Mea Shearim, but with a Haredi center. So we were in the middle - this nice neighborhood was between down-to-earth Nahlaot, with its Mizraḥi joie de vivre, and the sullen severity of the religious extremist Ashkenazim [...].[33] I think that the place where a person grows up has an influence: between an appetite for life, the joy, the color of Mediterranean life on the one hand, the Ashkenazi sadness that persisted the Diaspora on the other, this was decisive for the way my life unfolded."[34]

He said in an interview that his father tried once again to establish a factory, but failed. "He didn't become rich. We lived simply, but comfortably."[35] The family lived among German Jews in the Rehavia neighborhood or nearby, thereby avoiding ethnic conflicts and rejection.[36]

THE FATE OF LITTLE RUTH

While Yehuda thrived, soaking up the experiences of freedom in the Jewish community in Palestine, intoxicated by the fragrances of the new land, the grip of solitude and death tightened on Little Ruth, his childhood friend from Würzburg. The disparity in their maturity was even more pronounced when they were 13-14 years old: her intelligence, the loss of her mother, and the amputation had made her grow up faster than normal, while he was still a child. "She continued to write, because the situation there was really bad."[37] She told him, both bashfully and proudly, about the girls in her class whispering that "Ruth has a boyfriend."[38] In one of her last letters she asked him pointedly: "Would you marry me with only one leg?"[39] At different stages of his life Amichai gave a different answer to this heart-wrenching question. In 1971 he told interviewer Aryeh Arad that "although in the meantime I had fallen very, very much in love with another girl [Ruth Falk], if she [Little Ruth] had come, I would have married her instead of joining the British army."[40] This would have undoubtedly changed the entire course of his life.

At the beginning of 1939, Ruth's father, Rabbi Hanover, was imprisoned in the Buchenwald concentration camp. The Nazi authorities made it clear to him that he had to leave Germany.[41] Britain, to which the couple initially turned as a transit point, refused to accept their disabled daughter.[42] Her older sister Rosi and her stepsister "Big Ruth" made their way to Palestine after spending time in a program sponsored by the religious Zionist youth movement Brit Halutzim Dati'im (the Alliance of Religious Pioneers).[43] Ruth was sent to Holland, where she initially stayed with relatives, and later with a number of other families. She did her utmost, using her considerable abilities, to improve her knowledge of the languages of the countries where she might have immigrated – English, Hebrew, and Spanish – trying to work and "be useful."[44] Yehuda's father, an emotional and good-hearted person, apparently made strenuous efforts with Jewish Agency officials to enable Ruth, with her amputated leg, to enter Palestine. His efforts bore fruit too late, when the transports of Dutch Jewry to the death camps were already in full force.[45]

Ruth Hanover's cultured personality and effervescent character emerge clearly from her letters to her family. On July 2, 1939, she wrote to her sister Rosi, who was already in Palestine:

> "I study now 4-5 hours every day, in addition to school [...] I was at a concert on Sunday. The orchestra was large and excellent [...] Have you heard anything about a certificate [authorizing entry to Palestine]? I haven't totally given up hope of hearing Toscanini in September in Jerusalem. I must learn Hebrew, but I've run out of steam."[46]

A note of despair crept into her next postcard along with a description of her activities and achievements:

> "I really don't know what to do about Palestine. Nor can I hang myself [...] You have to hear how elegantly I speak Dutch and English [...] Why can't I get out? Father writes that I don't know enough Hebrew. Is this true?"

Three months later, she wrote to her stepsister, Big Ruth, who had immigrated to Palestine together with Rosi, that she had been transferred to yet another family, "nice, sympathetic people, but very simple, not educated." School lessons were at a low level, especially since, as a refugee from Germany, she was placed in "a class lower [than her true level] [...] I am [...] the terror of the teachers, because I think and express my ideas, and they're not used to it [...] I didn't join the Mizrachi movement here, because it's worthless. Everything here obviously lacks purpose and depth, which is perhaps what they call a normal life." In late March 1940, on the eve of the Nazi army's invasion of Holland, she wrote to Rosi that she doubted she would be able to be reunited with her parents (her stepmother and father) in America, "especially since the relations between us weren't any great shakes [...] On the other hand, you can't imagine how happy I would be to come to Palestine, despite all the difficulties."

On May 29, 1943, a postcard was received from the Red Cross signed by Abraham de Jong, who reported (in English) that Ruth had been living with them for some months. "She left on May 18, in good health and high hopes." It emerged that De Jong (later Avraham Yinon, a superintendent in the Israel Ministry of Education) was conveying what had been dictated by the Nazi authorities. Ruth was put on a transport to the Sobibor death camp, and she was almost certainly murdered the same day in the gas chambers, possibly after humiliating treatment and torture during the transport.[47] Or perhaps she was shot, as was the practice with the disabled.

In an interview in 1969, Amichai said that "Ruth is with me," and hoped that he had been able to "ingest" her, so that she would always be with him.[48] He himself said, and his children confirmed after his death, that a childhood picture depicting him and Ruth hugging under a tree was always on his desk.[49] The poems sent by the soldier Yehuda Pfeuffer to Dov Sadan, one of the editors of the *Davar* newspaper on April 1, 1946, included a piece entitled "Second Lament," with the subtitle, "From the poem cycle "'The Annals of a Jewish Girl in This Time.'"[50] This poem (dated 1945/46 in the margins), begins: "Once I dreamed that you were saved and came to Palestine; / I would teach you, as a child, to walk and talk / To walk strongly and to talk forgotten words: / Joy and sea, man and beast. // A little, I would describe to you our lives." This almost certainly envisions Ruth's rescue and an imaginary journey that he would take with her, as a new immigrant, if she had come to Palestine: he would teach her the wisdom of the Land of Israel, with its new Jews, who are close to nature.

Every few years, throughout almost his entire life, Amichai invoked her memory in a poem, either by implication or directly, but primarily in his novel *Not of This Time*. In the poem "The Clouds Are the First To Die" she is mentioned among those condemned to cruel and certain death, including Amichai himself, who was wounded in the hand in the War of Independence and could have been among the so many soldiers who fell: "Little Ruth, and also those / who are not marked by numbers," that is, those whose death is completely random.[51] Her image is evoked again in the poem "Hanukkah," without mentioning her by name;[52] and in the sixth section of "Poems of the Hot Wind":[53]

And all the sleepers were swallowed
in the serpent's maw of death.
[...]
Little dead Ruth
gets up from her bed
covered with glass shards,
half of her is her dream, half is my dream,
passing through enemy lines.[54]

MUSIC AND BOXING LESSONS

Ludwig/Yehuda started taking violin lessons in Würzburg at the age of nine, when he was probably not old enough to appreciate the musical experience or willing to practice for hours:

> "When I was nine they gave me / A half-sized violin and half-sized feelings."[55] His father started his music lessons again in Jerusalem, actually forcing them on his son, "like every Jewish father," according to Amichai.[56] One of his poems indicates that this time his father apparently addressed him as an adolescent: "'Learn to play the violin, my son. When you are / Grown-up, music will help you / In difficult moments of loneliness and pain.' That's what he told me once, but I didn't believe him."[57] This time the lessons were much harder than in Würzburg: "My father sent me to a violin teacher, some woman in Jerusalem. She was a very beautiful woman, of German origin. For me she was an old woman – 24 years old [...] She would sit in front of me and would shout at me, because I wasn't very talented."[58]

While he was struggling to meet the uncompromising standards of the teacher, the "old witch," the conservatory where she taught decided to start a children's orchestra. "The conductor was Thelma Yellin, a well-known cellist and a great educator.[59] She conducted all sorts of children who today are better known in the banking field." The orchestra performed in the Edison movie theater "in between performances." Yehuda was shunted aside to the edge of the stage; "I was constantly afraid of falling off. In the end I lost the rhythm because I was so scared of falling, so I just pretended to play and everything went fine."[60]

This would not be the end of Amichai-Pfeuffer's exploits as a performing musician. He continued to play violin to his fellow students, either as a soloist or in ensembles, for at least two years. In the tenth grade he performed for his class on the recorder. He realized that as a mediocre violinist at best, he would just try his and his neighbors' patience; but as a listener, music would occupy an important place in his life and would be a source of consolation and tranquility until his final hours.[61]

Besides music, Amichai engaged in athletic pursuits, and not merely for health reasons. In Jerusalem, where very few knew how to swim, Amichai excelled at swimming, and once even saved a classmate from drowning.[62] Somewhat surprisingly, he also took boxing lessons from a German giant called Horst Schade. Schade had been a Communist activist in Berlin, was married to a Jew, and was a seasoned street fighter against the Nazis. When Hitler took power he and his wife fled to Czechoslovakia, where Jewish friends helped him obtain immigration certificates to Palestine. In Palestine and Israel he made a living as a boxing instructor (later for the IDF).[63]

Amichai described Schade as both scholar and warrior, a combination that appealed to him as a new Jew, someone who could defend himself but was also cultured and knowledgeable. He told Ingrid Wiltman, who collected the life stories of German Jews who immigrated to Palestine in the 1930s, that Schade was "an expert middleweight boxer," who "taught me boxing, though

I learned much more than this from him. He was an exceptionally learned person. I learned with him about Rilke, and about Else Lasker-Schüler."[64]

THE MAALEH SCHOOL: FORMATIVE YEARS

The Pfeuffers could not have made a better choice of school for their son and daughter than the Maaleh school on Habashim (Ethiopia) Street in Jerusalem, close to King George Street. It was "a small experimental and elitist school, expensive and good," according to Netanel Lorch, Yehuda's classmate and a future high-ranking army officer and diplomat.[65] The school was a product of the educational thinking of German Jewish immigrants brought up in the framework of *Torah im derech eretz,* R. Samson Raphael Hirsch's fusion of modernity and orthodoxy.[66] The founders and administrators of Maaleh were guided by Hirsch's basic principles of "joining the holy and the mundane, where Judaism leaves the confines of the study hall to enter economic, social, and cultural life," "training the Jew for civil and social activity within a modern state," and the integration of the European cultural heritage, especially German, into Jewish education.[67] Their approach, however, was even more pluralistic: "The Maaleh educational policy sought to integrate Judaism, Zionism, and humanism." Many hours were devoted to literature, art, and music. A critical approach was taken to general and Jewish history.[68]

Yehuda Pfeuffer's classmate Aharon Ariel told me that the school was primarily founded in order to teach pupils (as the traditional *Ethics of the Fathers* puts it) "to know how to answer [a heretic] ," in this case the non-religious Jew. They studied the New Testament as part of the foundations of Jewish culture, while devoting years to the teaching of Ahad Ha-Am (who thought of Palestine as a spiritual center for the Jewish people, not necessarily connected to traditional Jewish observance).[69] Ahad Ha'Am was regarded as a bridge between Judaism and modernity, between nationalism and universalism. The teachers, however, totally failed to achieve their fundamental goal: not a single pupil in Amichai's class remained religious.[70] When Dr. Pinchas Blumenthal, the legendary homeroom teacher of Yehuda's class outlined his credo to his former pupils on his 65th birthday, he sounded more like a Conservative or Reform Jew than an Orthodox Jew of his time: "In Judaism, one has to select and supplement. Select – to emphasize what's important, the main things; and supplement – with humanist principles."[71] Yehuda's class was small, with a majority of girls. The fifth grade yearbook (for 14-15-year olds) declared that it was "the country of Amazons," and after fluctuations in size, the class stabilized with 13 girls and seven boys. The children of German immigrants from religious homes predominated, since the spiritual-educational tendency of the school was well suited to their background, but there were also pupils from Poland, and Sephardim (in the original sense of descendants of Spanish Jews, from old families in Palestine), who were generally from the middle classes, most probably looking for a connection to a more modern, broad-minded Judaism. Another example of the school's pluralism was its acceptance of a non-Jewish pupil, the daughter of a mixed marriage, whose parents had immigrated from Germany in those years.[72]

Amichai claimed that he first discovered world literature, and Freud thanks to Blumenthal.[73] "The truth is that they hardly taught Hebrew literature in the Maaleh school. We studied Bible, Talmud, Mishnah, and general knowledge. But we didn't study Hebrew literature."[74] Reading Shakespeare and Tagore was apparently not seen as a threat to the pupils' faith, unlike the critical poems and stories of Hebrew writers from the second half of the nineteenth century and the first decades of the twentieth.[75]

Despite the barbs that pupil Yehuda Pfeuffer directed towards his homeroom teacher Dr. Blumenthal in the class yearbook, Yehuda and his classmates all perceived him as exceptional. Blumenthal, a Berlin native who had earned a law degree in Cologne, and received his doctorate in 1933, immigrated to England and supported himself with menial jobs until he received a scholarship to study education at King's College. In 1935 he went to Palestine and taught in various schools, before being appointed homeroom teacher and English teacher at Maaleh.[76] Amichai considered him to be a key figure in his life, someone who had found the ideal middle road between religion and humanism, to a great extent like his father. Blumenthal had been raised in the spirit of German liberalism, which had fused with Eastern European socialism to produce the kibbutz, then regarded by most of the Jewish community in Palestine as an exemplary way of life.[77] He introduced Yehuda to world literature (Dostoevsky, Kafka), and taught him to savor burgeoning adolescent love to the fullest.

Yehuda Pfeuffer was an active member of his class council in his first years at Maaleh, and contributed extensively to the class yearbook. Although these could be considered his first known works, Amichai saw them as simply having "social" significance, since he always insisted that he only discovered poetry, and his calling in literature much later. The class four yearbook for 5698 (1937/38) contains a skit he wrote entitled "Early Prophets," describing family life in the biblical period. It hints at his later prowess and daring use of biblical verse in very mundane contexts Amichai's signature infusion of biblical language into the everyday involved the complete secularization of the verses which were solely meant to entertain, a trait also found in the composers of Hebrew maqams of Christian Spain, but also in the humorous pieces by Dan Ben-Amotz in later years. A narrative poem in English, "The Hair," portrays the encounter of an incarnation of the Jewish holiday of Purim with a brutal Nazi officer, who blocks its passage at the border as it comes to gladden the Jews of Germany.

In the introduction to the class five yearbook of 1938/39,[78] the editorial board thanks Blumenthal for his support, and discusses difficulties in preserving class cohesiveness due to the "events in our land" and "crises in the social life of the class." For Yehuda, it was a momentous year for other reasons: Ruth Falk, who had come to Palestine from Germany, enrolled in the class. Nonetheless, he also mentions the deterioration in the situation of German Jewry, Germany's annexation of Austria (the Anschluss) in March 1938, Kristallnacht, the widespread and organized actions against German Jews in November of that year, and the outbreak of the Second World War in September 1939. In 1940 the "first of Iyyar party [falling on May 9 that year] was dedicated [...] to a series of lectures on the political situation of the countries occupied by Germany."

ALIENATION FROM THE RELIGIOUS WAY OF LIFE

Morning prayer was mandatory at the Maaleh school, but "at the age of 14 it no longer interested me [...] But I so loved my parents that I lied here and there. I always wore a head covering at home." He maintained that he talked to his father about his non-religiosity/ religious matters, things/the arguments [between them] went "without threats and without shouting."[79] In this interview when he was 60, Amichai explained that his hostility to religion was a way to completely dedicate himself to Zionism, which he viewed as inherently opposed to Jewish belief in the coming of the Messiah.[80] On occasion Amichai stated that his rejection of religion was not the result of a principled intellectual struggle, but rather was a reflex response of repulsion and boredom. He insisted that he did not rebel against his father, but was simply averse to observance of the commandments and prayers.[81] He likened his arguments with his father about the order of the universe to a struggle with God.[82] In another interview, he claimed that his main reason for becoming secular was that he hated being forced "to do things."[83] "I was bored by all these commandments, and I saw no point to them"; observance wasted precious time.

What remained was mainly the language of the Bible and prayer as a basis for formulating penetrating truths, a cocktail of polemic and a source of play. In the novel *Not of This Time,* written in the early 1960s, he says that the verses of the Bible are "like a pacifier": "I recently adopted a practice of talking with myself in biblical verse. This calms me. What others said in their distress and despair - calms me."[84]

LAST YEARS OF SCHOOL: BEGINNINGS OF WRITING AND A PASSIONATE LOVE

In sixth grade Pfeuffer was still the life of the party in his small class of 13 pupils. According to the yearbook, he was tremendously interested in radio. The whole class put on "*The Country of the Body* [...] adapted by Yehuda" (Sixth Grade Yearbook, page 14). This might have been the basis for an early poem entitled "Government."[85] To celebrate Hanukkah, the class took on the roles of the Olympian gods (perhaps because of the ancient struggle against the Greeks). Amichai chose to be Poseidon, the god of the sea (page 16). The day after the Shavuot holiday (June 8, 1940), the class went on a trip to Solomon's Pools. "Unfortunately, only those in the class who knew how to swim could go " (21). This would seem to be the trip Amichai recollected with a tinge of melancholy at the party held in Blumenthal's honor in 1973, years after the suicide of Naomi Michael, his classmate who had been the main mover in organizing the class's social life.

> "The water was very cold. Some really didn't know how to swim. Naomi Michael almost drowned, and David and I jumped in and rescued her. It's sad – we rescued her, but [...] several years later, as an adult woman, she couldn't rescue herself."[86]

Further on in the yearbook an article by "Y. P." discusses a particularly sensitive and significant topic at that time : the youth movement. In various interviews, Amichai explained that he did not join a youth movement because he felt no need to, since his class, under Blumenthal's guidance, was already one:

> "They took us to Bnei Akiva.[87] At that time they were leftists, open-minded individuals, who established kibbutzim, the exact opposite of what they are today. They took us to a moshav for a week, during the Passover vacation, and I immediately saw that it was not for me. I didn't like them telling me what to do."[88]

Obviously, a youth movement did not suit his personality, despite his belief at that time in national and social ideals. He also attributed his reservations about political or quasi-political frameworks to his father:

> My father was very religious, but he was extremely suspicious of religious wheelers-and-dealers, or anyone who made a living out of religion. I inherited this from him. This accounts for my distrust of leaders and my unwillingness to join the youth movement of any specific party."[89]

When Ruth Falk, a new immigrant from Germany, entered Yehuda's ninth-grade class she did not know a single word of Hebrew, so he offered to help her with her homework. Ruth attracted the attention of all the boys in the class.[90] Love inspired Pfeuffer to keep a diary, a pastime that would occupy him to a lesser degree in the future. At that time it was in German, "which was something of a soul language for me."[91] In the beginning, the diary was a way of talking to Ruth ("this love was conducted mainly in German").

> "I waited many months before I got the chance to talk to her. At the end of the seventh class,[92] she asked to borrow a book from me to read. A few days later, she said, "Come on over and get your book, I've finished reading it." She was alone at home [...] We stood on the porch facing Jerusalem. I put my hand in hers, and I put my head in her hair, like you wrap a fragile object in cotton batting so it won't break on the journey. Then I put my soul in hers, like water into water, and my soul was no longer to be seen. I said, your skin is warm and fragrant."[93]

When David Ehrlich, a journalist, read this to the 83-year-old Ruth, she laughed: "Well, this is already the writer. But the beginning is correct. I remember that I really wanted the book, but the truth is that I also wanted a connection with him." In a story entitled "The Class Meeting," Amichai describes times with Ruth (the character of Miriam), on the verge of erotic fulfillment, against the backdrop of the German advance on Palestine (between the summer of 1940 and November 1942):

> We always sat in the air raid shelter, and even when we sat in the field [...] I discovered that Miriam was wearing silk underwear, but was embarrassed by it, since at that time young girls wouldn't wear fine, luxury underwear [...] We talked about books and music. The words came as camouflage for what we really wanted to say. Our hands were more straightforward."[94]

Afterwards, when sitting across from her at the home of his friend Ottensoser: "Music was on the radio, and the late afternoon sun was in her hair. We were gilded in an ancient tomb. When did we come back to life?"[95] During a train ride, perhaps on a class trip:

> Once I traveled with Miriam on the train from Tel Aviv. We sat facing each other, and my hair touched hers [...] At the Arab village of Yatir, she suddenly said to me, "pick me a blossom from the yellow bush!" [...] I got off and chose a branch. The train began to move. I tore the branch off and jumped onto the steps [...] We knew that we would see each other in the evening in the valley [...] The face of my face and the face of my palms already knew her, but what about the rest of my face? She told me that at times my true desire could be seen underneath my apparent desire."[96]

Their relationship apparently became so intense that 18 year-old Yehuda told his parents, as perhaps Ruth also did, that they were planning to get married. "I thought this was the only way to formalize the relationship; but our parents took a stand rightly enough and said no." Upset and unsure of what to do, Amichai went to Blumenthal's apartment to ask him for advice. "He was involved in our problems, our first loves, and in picking up the pieces". In Amichai's story "The Class Meeting," Blumenthal (cast as the character of Veilchenfeld) gives his student some apparently contradictory advice: "Love her, love her. Give yourself over to the wonderful feelings [...] Let the love develop. Always seek perfection. Don't reach the height of love because you are liable to destroy the gentle beginning."

When the students met years later at Blumenthal's retirement party, Amichai stressed the extent to which his teacher's words of warning against engaging too rapidly in youthful sexual passion, and how much the value of restraint had been decisive. "I discovered a beautiful sort of romantic love. We eventually got to the more ordinary form of love a bit late, but with profound human emotion, without which there can be virtually no spiritual life". Thus, the main issue was not the character of Ruth but sex before its time, which might have sapped the poetry welling up in him.

The year 1942, when Yehuda entered 12th grade, was a horrific time in the history of the world, and in particular for the Jewish people and the Jewish community of Palestine. This was the year the German army invaded Russia and mounted its devastating offensive against Stalingrad, while the German Africa Corps swept across the western deserts of North Africa guided by the military acumen of Field Marshall Rommel. The Jewish community was gripped by the fear that Axis troops would conquer Palestine. The Palestine Final Fortress Plan drawn up by the Mandate authorities and the Haganah's Plan of the North were both designed to prepare infrastructure to evacuate most of the Jews of Palestine to Haifa and the hills of the Galilee to "a protected area where resistance would be feasible."

This climate of tension and fear helps explain why the Vaad Leumi directed the school system to end the 1941/42 school year early, and to ease the requirements to pass the high school matriculation exam. Yehuda Pfeuffer's required essay entitled "My Life History," which he submitted to the admissions committee of David Yellen Teachers' College, states: "I completed my course of study in 1942, and was awarded my diploma from the Education Department of the Vaad Leumi."[97]

His grades were far from impressive, despite the easing of standards. His best grade was in Talmud. Even in Bible and English, subjects which he liked and where he excelled, his work was judged only satisfactory. His grades in chemistry and science were unexceptional. It is not unusual for poets or writers in general, even those with obvious intellectual abilities, to get poor grades. Perhaps Yehuda was too love-smitten to be bothered by such minor issues as science and mathematics.

NOTES

1. 1 Yoav Gelber, *New Homeland* [in Hebrew] (Jerusalem, 1990), 55-57, 614; Doron Niederland, *German Jews: Immigrants or Refugees?* [in Hebrew] (Jerusalem, 1996), 32-43.

2. Interview, Doron Weber, December 18, 1987, 29 (unpublished). He made similar remarks to Esther Fuchs, *Encounters with Israeli Authors* (Massachusetts, 1982), 88-89.

3. Yehuda Amichai, "Memories from Israel," *Diversion* (May 1986), 174. In numerous interviews Amichai described Israel as a place where "people frequently buy books of poetry" as an existential necessity; e.g., with Haim Nagid, "I Think This Country Is a Paradise for Poets" [in Hebrew], *Maariv - Literary Section*, May 15, 1977, 37; Naomi Gal, "Yehuda Amichai: Poet of War - and Love" [in Hebrew], *Yediot Acharonot - Literary Section, November 9, 1981, 4.*

4. Interview, Enrique Krauze, "Las vetas del pasado," *Vuelta,* 165 (August 1990), 38-39.

5. Interview, Nurit Baretzky, "Private Property" [in Hebrew], *Maariv - Sof Shavua magazine,* April 4, 1986, 12-13.

6. *Yishuv* – the umbrella term for the Jewish community in Palestine during British mandatory rule in Palestine.

7. Weber interview, 2.

8. Interview, Ayelet Negev, "I'm a Happy Person" [in Hebrew], *Yediot Acharonot -7 Leilot* magazine, March 25, 1994, 62.

9. "The shipments had already arrived in Jerusalem with all the furniture and rugs from the house in Germany. Many pieces of furniture were sold, and I'm sorry about them to this day [...] My father managed to bring some of his money from Germany." Interview, Yosef Bar-Yosef, "Cold Lightning Doesn't Move Me" [in Hebrew], *Bamachane*, February 26, 1986, 32.

10. Corresponding to 1937/8. The fourth year of a gymnasium corresponds to the eighth grade in Israel or the US today.

11. The yearbook was a sort of collective diary of a class or youth movement group. I thank Naomi Zeevi-Blumenthal, the daughter of Dr. Pinchas Blumenthal, the homeroom teacher of Yehuda's class, for allowing me to read the yearbooks.

12. "Travels of the Last Benjamin of Tudela," *The Selected Poetry of Yehuda Amichai*, translated by Chana Bloch and Stephen Mitchell, 60-86, at 60. "Tassels dangling from your undershawl" refers to the tsitsit, ritual fringes worn by religious Jewish boys and men.

13. "We lived the first year in Petach Tikva. Our uncles lived there, and they rented a house for us." Bar-Yosef interview, "Cold Lightning," 32.

14. Gelber, *New Homeland* [in Hebrew], 251, 327. Petach Tikva was then a *moshava* – an agricultural settlement where land is privately owned.

15. Council meeting, June 3, 1933, File 1512, Minutes 51; *Historical Archive of Petach Tikva*, Minutes 53, with thanks to the archive staff.

16. Geoffrey Hartman and Benjamin Harshav, interviewers, Yehuda Amichai Holocaust testimony, *Fortunoff Video Archive for Holocaust Testimonies*, November 3, 1994.

17. Baretzky, "Private Property," 29.

18. In an interview by Hartman and Harshav he estimated the distance to be 10 kilometers (about 6 miles).

19. "Poem 27," in *The Poetry of Yehuda Amichai*, edited by Robert Alter, 248.

20. Bar-Yosef interview, "Cold Lightning" [in Hebrew], 32.

21. *Cheder* – Jewish religious elementary school.

22. Hana Sokolov-Amichai, "Jehuda Amichai - Die Jugendjahre in Palestina/Eretz Israel," in Eichmeier and Raim (eds.), *Zwischen Krieg und Liebe* (Berlin, 2010), 101-42, at 107.

23. Strätz, *Biographical Lexicon*, vol. 2, 440.

24. Interview with Lawrence Joseph, "The Art of Poetry: Yehuda Amichai," *Paris Review 44* (Spring 1992), 4.

25. Interview, Amnon Ahi-No'omi, "The Brawny Ones Refused to Leave the Classroom" [in Hebrew], *Yoman Hashavua*, December 11, 1983. See also the description in the diary published by Amichai, "Diary" [in Hebrew], *Moznaim 1*, 29 (June 1969), 20.

26. Yekke – Yiddish-Israeli slang for a Jew of German-speaking origin. The term has connotations of punctilliosness and a sense of social decorum.

27. For more on the school, see Baruch Oren (ed.), *The Netzach Israel School at Eighty* – 1909/10-1989/90 [in Hebrew] (Petach Tikva Municipality, Petach Tikva, 1991).

28. Ahi-No'omi, "Brawny Ones" [in Hebrew]/ The synagogue was located in the session chamber of the Petach Tikva council.

29. Amichai wrote in his published diary: "I recited this wearying and nauseating Torah portion almost in its entirety, and also the Haftarah [additional reading from Prophets]. At home I delivered a discourse that Rabbi Wolf had prepared for me" (20-21). In his poetry: "My Bar Mitzva chapter / was double too: delivery-leprosy, telling / of skin diseases / vivid with sore colors." ("The Travels of the Last Benjamin of Tudela," *Poetry*, 109-39, at 126).

30. Joseph interview, 4.

31. Hartman and Harshav, Holocaust testimony.

32. Bruno Rottenbach, *Zwischen Würzburg und Jerusalem* (Wüirzburg: Gesellschaft für christlich-jüdische Zusammenarbeit, 1981), 12; Hartman and Harshav, Holocaust testimony; Joseph interview, 5.

33. Probably by "Mizrahi" Amichai meant Sephardi Jews and Jews from Arab countries.

34. "Poet Sings to His City" [in Hebrew], Israel Army Radio, Yoel Rappel (moderator), May 28, 1976.

35. Bar-Yosef, "Cold Lighting" [in Hebrew], 32.

36. Hartman and Harshav, Holocaust testimony.

37. Interview with Liraz Pank, "Poets, Too, Watch the Soccer World Cup" [in Hebrew], *Rosh 1* 117 (July 6, 1990), 13.

38. Interview with Aryeh Arad, "One from a City" [in Hebrew], Army Radio, September 5, 1989; interview with Dalia Karpel, "Hoping for a Nobel" [in Hebrew], *Ha-Ir*, November 3, 1989, 23-24, 89.

39. As related to Ayelet Negev, "The Secular Prophet" [in Hebrew], *Yediot Acharonot - 7 Leilot magazine*, April 3, 1998, 43.

40. Arad, "One from a City" [in Hebrew].

41. Edith Raim, "Verfolgung und Exil der jüdischen Familie Hanover aus Würzburg" (Persecution and Exile of the Hannover Family from Würzburg), [in German], in Renata Eichmeier and Edith Raim (eds.), *Zwischen Krieg und Liebe*, 65-98, at 78-80, 82-83. Amichai reconstructed in his imagination what happened to Ruth and her family on the night of the Nazi pogrom (Kristallnacht). See *Not of This Time* (Hebrew edition), 367.

42. Nili Scharf-Gold, *National Poet*, 155-56.

43. The aim of the *Brit Halutzim Dati'im* movement, founded in 1928, was to immigrate to Palestine and found the cooperative settlement of *Ze'irei Mizrachi* (the young guard of the Mizrachi religious Zionist movement).

44. Letters from Ruth Hanover, in Yehudit Katzman-Kobliner and Avraham Silber (eds.), *Family Letters* (Yad Eliyahu: n.p., 2013), Part II, 529-66. Translated into Hebrew by Ruth Katzman-Kobliner.

45. Scharf-Gold, 155-56. The promises he was given might have been empty from the outset. Friedrich Pfeuffer's letters to the family members dispersed throughout Palestine reveal his love and concern for his extended family; see *Family Letters*, Part Two, 613-17.

46. The postcard is addressed to "Rosi Hanover, care of Pfeuffer, 17 Metudela St., Rehavia, Jerusalem" (*Family Letters*, Part II, 530).

47. According to the letter from Rabbi Hanover to Ruth Katzman-Kobliner, May 22, 1946; Raim, "Verfolgung und Exil," 92.

48. Arad, "One from a City" [in Hebrew].

49. Tsippi Gonn-Gross (moderator), "With Our Love" [in Hebrew], Army Radio, April 19, 2011 (interview with family members).

50. For more on this series of poems, see Raquel Stepak, "What Are Amichai's Poems Doing in the Davar Newspaper's Censor's File?" [in Hebrew], *Haaretz*, September 25, 2014.

51. Poems [in Hebrew] 1, 128-29. "Marked by numbers" might refer to the numbers tattooed on prisoners in Auschwitz. It was not clear to Amichai, either when the poem was first published in 1958 or apparently later, which camp Ruth was murdered in.

52. First published under the title "Hannukah this Year," *Lamerhav - Masa*, December 16, 1960, 1, during the period in which the novel *Not of This Time, Not of This Place* was taking shape, and collected in *Poems* [in Hebrew] 1, 303-4.

53. First published in "Six Poems of the Hot Wind," *Davar*, April 9, 1971, 21; *Poetry*, 193; *Poems* [in Hebrew] 2, 350.

54. Ruth is portrayed several times in *Not of This Time* as "covered with glass shards". "Passing through enemy lines" (*Poetry*, 193) perhaps alludes to the Jewish girl who is tortured in I. L. Peretz's "Three Gifts."

55. "Half-Sized Violin," in *Selected Poetry*, 142-44; *Poems* [in Hebrew] 4, 120.

56. For more on Amichai's musical tastes, see his monologue in Liora Nir (moderator), "A Propitious Time" [in Hebrew], Army Radio, October 7, 1974.

57. "My Father in a White Space Suit," *Selected Poetry*, 100; *Poems* [in Hebrew] 3, 55.

58. Nir, "Propitious" [in Hebrew].

59. Thelma Bentwich-Yellin (1895-1959) was a noted cellist, soloist, and a member of a popular trio of female musicians. After a visit to Palestine, where several family members had key roles in the British Mandatory administration, she decided to remain in the country, and dedicated herself to a career in education.

60. Nir, "Propitious" [in Hebrew].

61. Ibid; Helga Dudman, "Disembodied Voices," *The Jerusalem Post*, October 4, 1974, 23 and Amichai's comments in various interviews on the meaning of music in his life; conversation with Esther Hacohen-Narkis, August 5, 2015.

62. Amichai's comments on the evening in honor of Dr. Blumenthal's 65th birthday, when Blumenthal, Amichai, and other former students gathered in 1977 to celebrate their teacher's birthday. I am grateful to Naomi Zeevi-Blumenthal who loaned me the recording and for other details she shared with me about her father and students.

63. Conversation with Aharon Ariel (Engel) on February 16, 2016. Amichai himself wrote in his notebooks: "I was in the Christian cemetery in the German Colony [in Jerusalem]. It was open because they had painted the fence. Horst Schade – boxing teacher and guide for poetry. Sidney Seal – the drunken director of the Conservatory. Ghosts from my childhood" (notebook entry from April 1994, or possibly 1995).

64. Ingrid Wiltmann, *Nur Ewigkeit ist Keil Exil*, 94-95. Amichai mentioned in this interview that his friend had published a book, *Ein Engel war mit mir* (Zurich: Steinberg-Verlag, 1949).

65. Netanel Lorch, *The Day will Turn: A Sort of Autobiography* [in Hebrew] (Tel Aviv: 1999), 40.

66. Doron Niederland, "From Frankfurt to Jerusalem: The Unique Path of the Horeb School in Religious Education in the Land of Israel" [in Hebrew], *Dor le-Dor* 25 (2005): 81-121.

67. Following Niederland, "From Frankfurt to Jerusalem" [in Hebrew], 86-87.

68. Debora Weisman, "Girls' Education in Jerusalem during the Period of British Rule" [in Hebrew] (PhD., Hebrew University, 1994), 49-54, 101-4.

69. Interview with Aharon Ariel. In certain respects, the Maaleh school was more open, with a more universalist approach, by comparison not only to other religious schools, but also to ordinary secular schools. This is the impression from a school committee's report on history curricula in high school (Weisman, *Girls Education*, [in Hebrew], 101).

70. The issue of Amichai's classmates becoming nonreligious is discussed in an article by David Erlich, "Class Meeting: The Class of Yehuda Amichai" [in Hebrew], *Haaretz- Mussaf*, July 10, 1987, 19-23, and in various interviews with Amichai.

71. Recording of the party for Dr. Blumenthal (1977) [in Hebrew]. This humanistic orientation was rooted in the explicit aim of Jewish education in Germany to thoroughly curb any manifestation of hatred of the other, the stranger, apparently out of a desire to oppose the widespread image of Judaism as withdrawn, and hostile to the non-Jew. See Joseph Valk, *The Education of the Jewish Child in Nazi Germany* [in Hebrew] (Jerusalem, 1976), 28.

72. Convesation with Aharon Ariel.

73. Hartman and Harshav, Holocaust testimony.

74. Dan Omer interviews Amichai, "In This Burning Land" [in Hebrew], *Proza* 25 (September 1978), 4-11, at 5. Weisman states that Hebrew literature classes at the Maaleh included both medieval poetry and modern literature (*Girls' Education*, 101). Amichai, however, who loved medieval poetry, did not mention that this period was studied in school. (Haim Nagid, "Tchernichovsky Who?" [in Hebrew], Literary section, *Yediot Acharonot*, October 1, 1993, 32-33).

75. Cf. Niederland, ("From Frankfurt to Jerusalem," 104-5) on the curriculum of the Horeb school system.

76. For sources on Blumenthal's biography, see: "Autobiography" [in Hebrew], in "Additions," Sixth Grade Yearbook; conversation with his son, Elhanan Blumenthal, May 26, 2015.

77. Rachel Hollander-Steingart interviews Amichai, "In My Heart Is a Museum," *The Jerusalem Post*, September 28, 1981, 5.

78. Ninth grade in today's Israel.

79. Pank, "Poets, Too" [in Hebrew], 13. Interviewed by Ayelet Negev ("I'm a Happy Person" [in Hebrew], 62, 98), he claimed that he had stopped being religious at the age of 15.

80. Similarly, the interview with Lawrence Joseph suggests that opposition to religion was then in the air. Amichai connected this with "the beginning of the socialist movement in Palestine" ("The Art of Poetry", 5). Most of the pioneering Zionists had abandoned religion, and he saw himself as following in their footsteps.

81. Rochelle Furstenberg, "The Poet Revolutionary," *Jerusalem Report*, December 1, 1994, 44.

82. With respect to becoming secular as a teen, see "A Song of Lies on Sabbath Eve," *Selected Poetry*, 138; another translation: *The Great Tranquility*, trans. Glenda Abramson and Tudor Parfitt (New York: Sheep Meadow Press, 1997), 47; *Poems* [in Hebrew] 3, 334.

83. Hollander-Steingart, "In My Heart," 49.

84. *Not of This Time* [in Hebrew], 509. The English edition of this novel, transl. Shlomo Katz (New York: Harper & Row, 1963) is a selective and adapted translation of the Hebrew work.

85. See Sokolov-Amichai, "Jehuda Amichai" [in German], 134. *Poems* [in Hebrew] 1, 20-21.

86. Recording of the party for Dr. Blumenthal. The class trip to Solomon's Pools is also mentioned in an article that Blumenthal contributed to the Sixth grade yearbook, 25-28 [in Hebrew].

87. A religious youth movement.

88. The *moshav* was Kefar ha Ro'eh. "Our class was itself a group, we were [called] "blue" [in English in the Hebrew interview], and we had no need for a youth movement, whether Jabotinsky or Ben-Gurion. This may have been a way of remaining slightly on the sidelines, being cautious, viewing everything with reservations and doubts [...] this gave us the means to be critical in that period [...] we did not realize that someone could be critical from the inside " (Pank, *Poets, Too* [in Hebrew], 13). Amichai's classmate Netanel Lorch had different recollections of the experience in Kefar ha-Ro'eh (*The Day will Pass* [in Hebrew], 41). A *moshav* is an agricultural, cooperative settlement, less collectivized than a kibbutz.

89. Lorch, *The Day will Pass* [in Hebrew], 5.

90. Conversation with Aharon Ariel (Engel). Cf. what Ariel told David Erlich, "Class Meeting," 20. In "The Class Meeting" Amichai describes Ruth's golden hair "like the sun preserved for a long time in a dark ancient box" (in his collection of stories, *In This Terrible Wind* [in Hebrew], 11).

91. Omer, "In This Burning Land" [in Hebrew], 5.

92. Amichai was 17.

93. "Class Reunion" [in Hebrew], *In This Terrible Wind*, 11-12.

94. Ibid., 12-13.

95. Ibid., 13. This image of lovers' intimacy like mummies in an ancient tomb, appears in the sixth poem in the cycle "We Loved Here": "In the long nights our room was closed off and / sealed, like a grave." *Selected Poetry*, 9.

96. "Class Meeting" [in Hebrew], 17.

97. *Va'ad Leumi* - the Jewish Zionist assembly under the mandatory government in Palestine, with little authority outside of education.

Chapter 3

1942–1946

Military policeman and soldier in the British Army

DISCOVERING THE PARADOXES OF LIFE THROUGH LITERATURE

Amichai's parents had little formal education; both were brought up in the rudimentary society of cattle dealers. Nevertheless, Amichai often noted that his parents were enlightened and cultured: there were books in German and Hebrew at home, and they were interested in theater and music.[1] In a wide-ranging late interview he recalled that his father "wrote little things sometimes, little feuilletons in newspapers just for fun. He published them in Germany. A few things. Quite sentimental things, but very, very sweet things. And he was a great letter writer [...] He was a good orator. He knew how to speak."[2] At the same time he insisted that he came from a family where no one had anything even remotely to do with literature or art.[3] The image he cultivated in interviews and at readings was that as a teen he did not give a moment's thought to becoming a writer or a poet. When asked at the end of the 1960s when he first wanted to become a poet, he replied: "I never wanted to be a poet. Writing poems, stories – it just didn't interest me."[4]

Although Amichai tended to describe himself, especially in his later years, as "not an intellectual," and in old age even refrained from reading prose, it is clear that books and the discovery of literature played an important role in his life.[5] When asked to name his favorite literary heroes when he was an adolescent, he mentioned three characters from European fiction: two from works by Thomas Mann– Tonio Kröger, from the novella of that name, and Hans Castorp, from the novel *The Magic Mountain*. The third hero was Andrei Bolkonsky, from Tolstoy's *War and Peace*, a very popular work in Israel at that time.[6]

These three works all deal with the appeal of death in general, and in particular death in war, as well as war as a way to negate death, to defend oneself against it, and the thin line between love and death. These themes are all present in *The Magic Mountain's* treatment of Hans Castorp's stay at the sanatorium, and in different ways in the other two books. Tonio Kröger's feelings of loneliness as a sensitive young man may have captivated Amichai, as suggested in one of his well-known early poems "Out of Three or Four in a Room" that describes an individual who is "compelled to see the injustice between the thorns," and the exhaustion and loss of hope endemic to human lives.[7] He may have shared Andrei Bulkonski's feeling of obligation to his compatriots and to the collective, and a readiness to enlist to fight for them.[8]

"A FINE YOUNG MAN": ENLISTMENT AND WORLD WAR II

In the autumn of 1939, the Yishuv experienced a respite from attacks by the Arab population. The British government, which had shown relative restraint and tolerance of the attacks, murders and arson of the Great Arab Revolt, could not now contain a second front at home. It came down hard on the rioters, and put an end to the rebellion in almost a one blow.

From the point of view of the Haganah, the unofficial military arm of the Yishuv, the period of the rebellion was an opportunity to gain strength, though it was still far from being able to face regular armies. The Yishuv leaders asked the British government and the Mandate authorities in 1938 to authorize the formation of "a Jewish military force in the Land of Israel that could take responsibility for the security of the Yishuv and defense of the land," once it was properly trained and had an officers' corps.[9] Faced with the challenge of the war against the Axis powers, a volunteer force within the regular British army seemed "the right path towards developing the Yishuv's military power."[10]

In April 1941, voices in Yishuv organizations were already calling for "partisan warfare" in the eventuality of a German invasion. Meanwhile, the British military command proposed the formation of a large military police force to defend the country, an important part of which would be a naval branch. The Haganah leadership, which predicted that a German invasion would be by air and sea, was favorable.[11] There was intense fear of a war of annihilation, that would destroy the soft core of the Hebrew Yishuv in the Land of Israel. The danger was anticipated from the Nazi occupying army, but also from the local Arab population, which if backed up by Iraq, Syria or Jordan, would no longer be deterred by fear of the British army, if it was defeated by the Germans as they advanced through the Middle East.[12]

Unsurprisingly, there were fierce disputes in the Yishuv leadership (*Mapai, Hakibbutz Hameuchad*)[13] over enlisting in the British army or "self-enlistment" in the *Haganah* or the *Palmach*, the corps that would emerge from it.[14] Russian failures at the beginning of Operation Barbarossa (the German invasion of the Soviet Union) and Japan's entry into the war on Germany's side at the end of 1941 made the picture even darker, and the British authorities in Palestine began to plan in earnest to build "the last stronghold in the Land of Israel," in case the German army under Rommel invaded the country (either from the north or the south).[15] In March 1942, despite the first glimmers of hope after the Russian front was stabilized that winter, there was panic in the Yishuv. The National Council which also oversaw the Jewish school system in the country, decided cut short the school year for students in year twelve and organize early and easier matriculation exams so that these students could be drafted quickly.

Amichai and his classmates were mostly taken up with youthful pursuits: they did not fall under the sway of the great fear of their parents and their generation;[16] in the 1990s Amichai liked to say that he experienced first love while he was serving in the British army.[17] He was most likely referring to his love for his classmate Ruth Falk, which became open mutual affection in their last year at school, after which their relationship strengthened, as suggested in his at least partially biographical story "The Class meeting," Nevertheless, Amichai recalled that in 1941 he was indeed "terribly anxious," because "we all knew what would happen if the Germans entered Palestine."[18]

The high school graduates, seen as an elite among the much larger cohort of adolescents, assembled in "Ein Harod's amphitheater."[19] In "Memories from Israel" Amichai describes hundreds of students sitting together after the speeches, as they talked about the future "in the holes of olive trees between Ein Harod and Tel Yosef."[20] Amichai and the young people of his generation may indeed have felt an intense, primal connection to the ancient biblical landscapes. Their talk turned to war and love. The Land of Israel was small and one "could frequently feel the great stage director's hand – whether it was the hand of God, history or fate – stirring together loves and wars, hills, fields and memories."[21] Along with the spiritual elation of experiencing history, there was also the longed-for excitement of sexual experience, fueled by the presence of many young people in a landscape so resonant with the past, the joy of release from school and its rigid framework, and the powerful tension inspired by the unknown future: "On the sweet and protected bed of danger,[22] / like a log on a streaming current [...] with my eyes that were then stars / for the first and last time. // [...] with this falsehood, with this sweet nothingness [...] full and emptying and filling / like blood donations / to a stranger, then flowing on to somewhere else."[23]

Who was this wondrous lover? Ruth Falk? A brief encounter at a gathering? He writes of his eyes "which were then stars, for the first and last time," hinting perhaps at eyes that had experienced sex for the first time, that would never return to their initial purity, or that first, primal gaze.

A MOTLEY CREW: THE MARITIME GUARD

"The next morning all kinds of conscription offices opened, along with committees to decide where each person should be sent. There were three possibilities: the British Army, the military police, and the *Palmach* [...] Initially I was sent to a special unit established in '41."[24] On various occasions Amichai gave a humorous account of his role in the "naval guard" – his military police unit or "brigade". The unit was set up by Yishuv organizations in coordination with the Mandate authorities, and was "totally improvised. They anticipated a German invasion from the sea, and therefore dreamed up a unit called the Coast Guard [...] it was unprecedented chaos."[25] He refers partly in jest and partly with melancholy to his service in this unit in an obscure line in the poem "God Full of Mercy":[26] "I who was Salt King by the sea," a kind of pillar of salt, stuck to the spot like a scarecrow. On Tantura beach, not far from an Arab village of that name, where there was also a police outpost, they gave him a club or "an Italian carbine, seized in East Africa."[27] His job was to run – later on he and his crew were equipped with whistles – whenever he saw a German ship approaching to alert authorities to the danger. Apparently this was local *mukhtar* (head of the village) who would then notify the police.

On leave, or in the evenings when he had no guard duties, Yehuda would get together with Ruth Falk in encounters that became increasingly tempestuous. In "The Class Meeting", it is difficult to determine where autobiographical description ends and febrile imagination begins. In the story, he and the character of Miriam, modeled on Ruth Falk, went on dates that gradually became more intimate:[28] "I was in the British army and had to guard the coast, watching for submarines [...] Miriam was then in one of the *hachsharot* [training gatherings] in the south of the country."[29] "We didn't talk much, but our thoughts romped inside [...] we went down to the sea [...] the next week we sat beside the lifeguard tower. Later we undressed to go into the waves [...] the waves were our curtain. I caressed her shoulder and the inside of her thighs." After wandering between cafes, hesitating about going to a hotel, they went back to the beach. "My clothes were mixed up with hers [...] at first we spoke in whispers. Then we hugged in the sand. Sand clung to her light hair and my hands knew everything, but did not learn. Even my body knew but didn't learn"; perhaps suggesting that they had sex but only on a level that did not lead to a fuller understanding of each other. The narrator himself hints at the meaning: "Learning only happens when someone sits alone. The wise are cautious with their words and their bodies." This may explain his eventual breakup with Ruth Falk. It is possible that the whole episode of the encounter by the sea was simply an allegory, conveying the love of eager bodies whose souls remain distant strangers. "Miriam's breasts were unprotected and soft between my hands," but her mind was "shut inside a hard shell" preventing her lover from reaching its depths.[30]

Meanwhile, the intense battles in East Africa took a dramatic turn: The German army soundly defeated the British at Tobruk, on the border of Libya and Egypt, on June 20, 1942; 35,000 British soldiers were taken prisoner. Field Marshal Bernard Montgomery was appointed commander of the African theater of war. Montgomery blocked a further attack on Rommel, sensing that time was on his side, mainly because of the bombers and Sherman tanks wending their way from the US. This stalling of the German army under Rommel which left it low on arms and without reinforcements, began in early July 1942, and culminated in his defeat at the Second Battle of El Alamein in November, which ended the Axis threat to Egypt and the Middle East.

The Zionist leadership were busy consolidating whatever munitions they had managed to steal from the British in their effort to make the Yishuv militarily stronger.[31] In February 1943, with the final routing of Rommel at Tunis, it became clear that the chokehold on the Yishuv and with it the threat of invasion by the German army had been removed. Amichai was discharged from the coast guard unit, or requested discharge, and spent several months in limbo.[32]

SERVICE IN THE CARTOGRAPHY COMPANY OF THE BRITISH ARMY NEAR CAIRO

In a document entitled "A History of my Life," which the demobilized soldier Yehuda Pfeuffer would later send to the admissions committee of the teacher training college at Beit Hakerem in the summer of 1946, certain pieces of information emerge about this period that are usually omitted from accounts of his life. This document states that he served in "the military coast guard" for six months and "in the winter of the same year I was discharged. At the beginning of 1943 I audited courses, over several months, at the Hebrew University – without having to enroll – and in the early summer of 1943 I went to one of the kibbutzim in Beit Shean," perhaps to complete the year of service which national organizations required of school graduates in those tense years.[33] The unidentified kibbutz in this document was almost certainly Hamadia, founded in 1942 (after maintaining a presence there in the days of "tower and stockade"[34]), and which in its first years faced multiple hurdles, including a shortage of water and Bedouin harassment. Almost 40 years after his stay at the fledgling kibbutz, Amichai published a poem of longing for that time and his own stormy passion, called "Hamadia."[35]

Much later when Amichai's teenage daughter was a recruit at "Camp Tsrifin" – known in the Mandate period as Sarafend – at the end of a pre-army course, Amichai was reminded of the training exercises he took part in there after joining the British army, in October 1943.[36] The 19 year old Pfeuffer could have joined a unit of the British army in Europe, but instead was transferred to Egypt after an intervention by the Haganah, "because the Haganah was interested in having people in North Africa."[37]

The British military authorities attached considerable importance to surveying and drawing up maps, and in the first years of the war created a company for this purpose, "one of the important, and classified, units of the British engineering corps."[38] At first it was completely off-limits to foreign citizens, but after the capture of field survey platoons in battles in Greece and Crete, there was a shortage of suitable British soldiers, and in February 1942 skilled Jews from the Land of Israel began to be conscripted.[39] In general the British had a particularly good relationship with Jews who enlisted in specialized fields such as cartography. "There was a real military need," and the view was that conscription of this sort would not complicate things with the Arabs.[40] Yehuda Pfeuffer was placed in Field Survey Company 524 of the Royal Engineering Corps, probably in the stores unit, Field Survey Depot 2.[41] From the beginning it is likely that he was not designated for any professional task since his high school education only made him eligible for a technical position in this prestigious unit. He did know a little Arabic from high school as a student of Irena Garbel.[42]

The soldiers in the field survey company and the stores unit were all from the Yishuv, and they were assigned to the Tura camp located between Helwan and Cairo.[43] Eventually, Amichai was sent to Ma'adi.[44] "At Tura there were a number of large caves used as shelters, workshops and warehouses."[45] There was a big hole, "an invitation for a thief";[46] and the "thieves" – Haganah people or those working for them who were eager to get their hands on the weapons and ammunition needed for the Yishuv in a time of emergency – made good use of it to take weapons from the store to increase their arms cache. Life in Egypt had another advantage for the Jewish "Palestinian" soldiers: while their service was indeed required, and here and there some of them were given menial tasks around the camp, their day was generally extremely relaxed and not at all under pressure. This allowed them to spend their time in different ways, to develop intellectually or professionally, as well as to contribute to the security needs of the nascent state.

"In Egypt, unlike in the Land of Israel, signs of war were not in evidence. There was not a blackout or food rationing, because Egypt was considered neutral in that war."[47] Amichai and his comrades did not experience the war in any direct way ("I didn't get to fight"); rather he felt that he was on an "adventure," framed by the awareness that it was all for the newborn state.[48] He would only be plunged into the traumatic dimension of war later, in the battles for the War of Independence.

Amichai enjoyed but perhaps also suffered from this surfeit of free time. On a questionnaire he filled out in the summer of 1946 when applying for the Beit Hakerem teacher training college he notes that "I was sergeant in charge of education in my military unit, and I gave lessons on language and Bible and literature; I gave Hebrew lessons in the *Hehalutz* ["the pioneer"] movement in Cairo."[49] However, these activities apparently did not weigh on him very much either. His army buddy in the unit, Gedaliah Kraut, used the time for violin practice, and eventually became a professional violinist in one of Europe's main orchestras.[50] For Amichai, his two years of close proximity with the pyramids became associated with his favorite musical works.[51] The free time allowed him to go on outings with friends he made in the unit, to concern himself with matters of love, and above all to read literature that made inroads into his soul, and from which poems flowed, perhaps surprisingly to him as well, only to be interrupted from time to time by his official missions. He also took part in smuggling weapons and illegal immigrants, particularly at the end of this period.

He had a short love affair that lasted a day and a night, almost certainly in the port city of Alexandria:[52] Amichai describes the affair in a poem which he sent to the editors of the *Davar* newspaper, and which remained unpublished and unknown until it was unearthed in the Labor Movement's archives a few years ago.[53] Was this a young Jewish woman, happy to mix with soldiers from the Land of Israel, the courageous new Jews?[54] Or was the woman perhaps a prostitute, as the line "she whom I acquired" suggests in the poem?[55]

To find a place to be alone, they entered the port zone, where soldier Pfeuffer had authorization. She passed as his wife, and after some searching they got to "my vehicle," probably the truck that took him to Alexandria with other soldiers on some errand. A drama then unfolded near the car: "the other drivers" began to congregate "because they heard a woman's voice" and "her voice charmed everyone." When the others left, "we didn't sleep a wink all night [...] / we were wild in our desire, I ripped her dress [...] / oh I was hungry for her body and I forgot every limit I had set for myself while abroad." After "we rested [...] we spoke about the war and the stars and the ways of men, / about God and death." In the morning "I drove with her to the quay [...] the crane came, stretched out its arm from on high and grabbed my car, and lifted it onto the deck." The lover – or perhaps the client – had resigned himself in advance to a one- night stand, and tries to make his beloved see the symbolic act of the hoisting away of their temporary abode as decisive, a closure dictated by reality.

DISCOVERING HIS CALLING IN THE DESERT SANDS

Passing loves and excursions in the fascinating land of the pharaohs, which had been ruled by corrupt King Farouk since 1936, were merely a backdrop or stage set for the profound processes Yehuda Pfeuffer would undergo between the ages of 19 and 22. Various types of pressure (boredom, abundant free time) and chance occurrences such as a mobile library getting stuck into desert sands seemed like a "message from heaven", bringing him closer to his calling as an original creator, a pathfinder for the generation whose main literary figures came of age in the first years of the State, and as one of the world's foremost poets of the second half of the twentieth century.

In an unusually frank interview with a close friend, the journalist Dan Omer, Amichai described his discovery of literature in the military camp near Cairo, "facing the pyramids" and above all Hebrew literature, which was largely avoided at the religiously-oriented school in Jerusalem he had attended.[56] "It began there [in "His Majesty's army"]. A great desire for literature came over me [...] I spent two years in Egypt. There was no war there, and I was mostly involved in smuggling guns [...] In those days I took advantage of the library in the Jewish soldiers' club in Cairo.[57] I began to read methodically, all the Hebrew literature, from Feierberg to Shai [=Shmuel Yosef] Agnon. Every book I could get my hands on, I read. This is how I got through most of the literature of the *Haskalah*." This was a way to be enriched by the language and depth of associations with the Bible that the literature of the *Haskalah* (Enlightenment period in Hebrew literature) stretched to the fullest, extracting what was found there to describe modern reality and ideological conflict. In a lecture published as an article, "Agnon and I," a large part of which is devoted to a description of his discovery of Agnon's writings during his British army days, Amichai stressed that this addiction to reading was only given free rein on "my short days off [...] Sometimes I took the books with me to Cafe Groppi [...] or to the ugly huts in the camp. I read everything Agnon had written up to that point." Amichai's prose, but above all his first stories and the novel *Not of This Time* illustrate the extent to which he absorbed Agnon's style, including Agnon the modernist in the stories "Adjacent and Seen" and other works that represent the irreducible complexity of human lives.[58] "Apart from Hebrew literature, I read a lot of general literature: Herman Hesse, Dostoevsky, Thomas Mann, James Joyce – and others. I read a massive amount of prose."[59]

At the same time, he was also writing poetry – perhaps not systematically, but with a vague sense of needing to be involved in creative work as a form of expression and self-definition. His first published poem is entitled "At the End of the Holiday" which was sent to the Hebrew weekly *Hagalgal* at the urging of comrades in his unit.[60,61] The weekly, edited by the writer Dov Kimchi, was the printed companion to the launch in 1936 of an official radio station in Israel/Palestine that broadcast in English, Arabic and Hebrew.[62] The headline above the poem reads " Poems by our soldiers wherever they are," and the poem is signed "Soldier Yehuda Pfeuffer." Presenting himself as a soldier in the British army would certainly have increased the poem's chances of being published. There is no real drama in it to justify the story it tells, and its final chord sounds slightly hollow. Nevertheless, the future Amichai can be seen in the contrast forming the core of the poem which opposes a leave for a soldier during the war as "holy," and the obligation to the nation which is "secular." Similarly, his identification of the "scent of hair" – the fragrance of his beloved – with the Havdalah spices hints at the way Amichai would "secularize the holy," by placing the holy on a material footing. In formal terms, Amichai adhered to the basic structure of the classic sonnet, but took liberties with its rules, an early illustration of Amichai's poetic credo of the late 1940s and 1950s.

Amichai also began to read modern British and American poetry as the result of a serendipitous incident. "One event in Egypt had an extremely important impact on my life. It was in 1944, I think, we were somewhere out in the Egyptian desert. The British had these mobile libraries for their soldiers, but of course most of the British soldiers, [who were from the lower classes and pretty much uneducated] didn't make much use of the libraries. It was mostly us Palestinians who used them – there we were, Jews reading English books while the English didn't. There had been some kind of storm and one of the mobile libraries had overturned in the sand, ruining or half-ruining most of the books. We came upon it and I started digging through the books and came upon a book, a Faber anthology of modern British poetry, which I think came out in the late thirties. Hopkins was the first poet, Dylan Thomas the last.[63] It was my first encounter with modern British poetry – the first time I read Eliot or Auden, for example, who became very important to me. I discovered them in the Egyptian desert in a half-ruined book. This book had an enormous impact on me – I think that was when I began to think seriously about writing poetry."[64] Two years after this interview, Amichai talked about the same event, and named the four poets - Eliot, Auden, Hopkins, Dylan Thomas - who were the most significant to him in the anthology. He talks about them as though speaking to equals, not merely as being influenced by them: "Until then I had never written poetry. When I read the book, I felt like a chef going to a well-known, high class restaurant, and saying to myself:

I can do this as well as they can."[65] What did Amichai find in this anthology that turned him from the class clown, who perhaps saw his youthful experiences of writing as little more than a joke, to a poet fashioning a new generation, whose poems would in time, with their emotional directness and simple appearance, charm poetry lovers from India, China and Japan to the United States and Argentina? The anthology seems to have released an inner ocean that was raging inside. He discovered that poetry could be relevant, close to life and actual existence, and free of burdensome formal constraints. The urge to write took hold.[66]

"Direct, concrete, exact, clean, dry, prosy, impersonal – these are the qualities imagism aims to achieve."[67] This remark hints at what Amichai discovered in Auden and Ezra Pound and helped fashion his poetic style. Pound argued for the need to abolish the difference between prose and poetry, stating famously that imagism aimed to "raise poetry to the level of prose." This is certainly valid for Amichai, who could have felt this in the poems he read. Another important principle that Amichai learned from Pound was "superposition" or the "open analogy" between images such as between faces in the Paris metro and flower petals on a wet branch. However, Amichai developed superposition in his own way. The comparisons across domains in his poetry are daring, but the figurative similarity between terms is more open and easier to sense than in Pound or T. S. Eliot.[68] Similar to Pound and Eliot, Amichai made numerous connections to ancient and classical texts. In Pound and Eliot this is often achieved through direct quotation, but remains implicit in Amichai.[69]

For the young Amichai, the major poet in the anthology was the cynical, ironic Auden who introduced the rhythms of speech to poetry, who mastered the structure of the classical poem while also playing with it. Auden appears to have been a mentor for Amichai who gave him a springboard for his own tendency to undercut and overthrow traditional forms, but also to preserve some of them, at times loosely in a way bordering on parody.[70] The influence of Dylan Thomas, the romantic, whose associations are often wild and angry, is more recognizable in the prose Amichai began to write in the mid-1950s.[71] Amichai may have identified with Thomas as a rural figure, and with the pristine remote landscapes which reminded him of his childhood environments, as the opposite but also the complement to Auden's pronounced urbanity.

PFEUFFER FLEETINGLY AS JAMES BOND

Amichai was probably only discharged from the army in spring or summer of 1946.[72] In more than one interview he indicated that his main contribution "to helping the nation" in Egypt took place during the last year of the war, and in the year that followed .[73] Weapons smuggling, and the illegal aliyah from Egypt of young Jews were then at their height. In interviews and lectures Amichai frequently hinted that he took part in these operations, but never spoke openly about them even in a lecture he gave in the 1990s.[74]

Perhaps there were not so many secrets to reveal. In his story "The Departure from Egypt,"[75] the main character is involved in the illegal immigration to Palestine of sixty young Jews, initially disguised as scouts, and then as soldiers of His Majesty the King. This mission indeed took place, though not on Passover in 1945, but a year later, when he was on his way home from the army, or during his last leave.[76] As with the gun-running episode, Amichai's imaginative reconstruction shows him playing an important role in a complex operation in which in fact many others were involved. No less typical of Amichai is the romantic interlude between the male narrator and a female figure at the center of events in a plot that has the trappings of a spy movie, as he himself describes it, where an eroticism suffuses the characters as they become closer through their shared exploits.[77] "When I got to Cairo I waited in a Greek cafe. I ordered something and opened a newspaper to its full breadth on the table. A man I did not know came in, circled me twice [...] At last coming close, he deposited a note between the sheets of the spread-eagled newspaper. Afterwards, I opened the note, which specified a time and a place. We went to the place, walked up to the pyramids [...] Diana appeared. She came towards me, raised her brown eyes and set out the details of the plan [...] I conveyed the instructions from the Haganah."[78] The two of them go back to Cairo together, and sit in Cafe Groppi. Dina the faithful Zionist is sorry not to be among the new immigrants and also complains that Amichai – or the character narrating – will not stop using "Diana," her non-Hebrew name he prefers because it recalls "the Greek goddess of hunting."

The very next day he meets Diana in Cairo, "dressed in a scout uniform," he dressed as the scout leader. "We went to Bab al Hadid, a big railway station. There already waiting for us was a group of sixty scouts, members of the *Heḥalutz* dressed up in preparation for the illegal aliyah."[79] After travelling an hour and a half they disembarked, where they now changed costume: instead of scouts, the frightened Jewish youth became "British soldiers," "each with a forged passport."[80] The teens practiced dealing with possible questions from the military police.[81] "We got up at dawn and went to the railway station. We boarded the train and dispersed into all the carriages," while the guides from Palestine served as "translators between the police and the perplexed youth being questioned."

"In the morning the train reached orchards whose fragrance was strong like love"; in fact, the settlement of Rehovot, two days before Passover. At nightfall, the young travelers who had sneaked into the country would be in danger of being arrested for breaking the curfew. "Group after group left the train at different stations and disappeared between the orchards and the houses. I did not see them again."[82] As he saw it, participating in this operation added a significant contemporary page to "the pictures in my little old-fashioned Haggadah," that was part of his childhood ancestral legacy.[83]

THE POEMS WRITTEN IN EGYPT

Just before leaving Egypt, on April 1, 1946, Amichai took the brave step of sending a sizeable group of poems to Dov Sadan, a well-known literary critic, a member of the *Davar* editorial board and longtime editor of the newspaper's literary supplement.[84] As the different titles and subtitles of the poems show, this was a selection of poems that Amichai seems to have written while in Egypt. The letter to Sadan indicates he was afraid the content would not be appropriate for the demands of the moment or the period in general.[85] He attributes his focus on his own experiences to his youth and perhaps also to his restricted horizons: "Soon I will be twenty-two years old. I enlisted when I was eighteen, a fact which will perhaps help you see why the poems are about me, my feelings and my loves."

Despite the immaturity and innocence verging on childishness of some of the poems (for example, "On the Path," perhaps from the beginning of his military service in Egypt), the poems are striking for their independence and authenticity. His literary sources of inspiration are not obvious; Amichai, even when he stumbles, is himself. One of the poems, "Now, Now" (signed 1944), is particularly crucial for understanding the principle behind the *ars poetica* Amichai developed over the course of his career: everything is analogous, anything can be compared to anything; there is no hierarchy in an analogy, so that if divine x is equal to human y, then y is also equal to x. Amichai talks about discovering the unity of being, the unity of experience, and the unity of humanity – especially women, that part of humanity that particularly interested him: "Now, now I see / the likeness in all young women [...] // Soon they will fall into my hand, / ripe fruits from the tree of knowledge." Indeed, the fruit would soon fall into his hand as a writer.

NOTES

1. Pank interview. Amichai's father insisted that he learn to play a musical instrument, as was characteristics of a bourgeois German home.
2. Weber interview, 9-10. See chapter 1.
3. Joseph interview, 5.
4. Arad interview [in Hebrew].

5. For example, in the Wiltmann interview: "Anyway, I am absolutely not an intellectual. That involves a certain way of facing reality, a stance towards everything. Poetry is a good mixture [...] of intellect and feeling."

6. Baretzky interview.

7. *The Penguin Book of Hebrew Verse*, ed. T. Carmi (Harmondsworth, UK: Penguin, 1981), 569; *Poems* 1, 97 [in Hebrew]. Carmi's book is bilingual Hebrew and English, and is presented and annotated in English.

8. Cf. Dan Miron's discussion of "Open-Closed-Open" in his book *More!* [in Hebrew] (Tel Aviv, 2013), 259-279, which analyzes the "cognitive infrastructure" of Amichai's works, and deals with the poet's struggle between the tendency to withdraw when preoccupied with his own experience, and the need to break out of this self-containment and engage meaningfully with others, with the public.

9. Yoav Gelber, *"Masada": The Defense of the Land of Israel in the Second World War* [in Hebrew] (Ramat Gan 1990, 12-13); Howard Sachar, *A History of Israel*, Alfred Knopf, New York, 1979, 234-5.

10. Gelber, "Masada," 14.

11. Ibid., 30, 50-54. Gelber argues that the British were preparing for a German invasion from the North, while the *Haganah* expected it to come from the West, from the sea. Ibid., 58.

12. On a number of occasions Amichai emphasized that the Germans' ability to occupy and advance in the Middle East depended on the strong support of "the Arab leadership in Iraq." For example, "Memories from Israel," 320. In the Joseph interview he stresses the Mufti of Jerusalem's ties with Mussolini and Hitler.

13. *Mapai* (the Land of Israel Workers Party) was the dominant party in the Yishuv and, for the first 30 years of Israel's existence, including its later incarnation as the Labor Party. *Hakibbutz Hameuchad* (the United Kibbutz Movement) was one of the three large groupings of Kibbutzim in Palestine and Israel. In the pre-state Yishuv, it acted independently, but later was affiliated to radical socialist Mapam (the United Workers' Party) and after splitting with this party aligned with the more nationalistic *Achduth Ha'avodah.*

14. Palmach - Jewish paramilitary units that carried out missions before and during the War of Independence. A person who served in these units was a *Palmachnik* (fem. *Palmachnikit*).

15. Gelber, Masada, 40.

16. David Ehrlich, "The Class Meeting: Yehuda Amichai's Year" [in Hebrew]," Haaretz Supplement, July 10, 1987.

17. Interview with Kobi Nissim, "They Always Threw Stones at Her" [in Hebrew], Al Hamishmar - Hotam, May 6, 1992. See similarly, Joseph interview, 6.

18. Joseph interview, ibid.

19. Omer interview, 5. In another interview Amichai talked about the outing near the Tel Yosef spring.

20. See previous note.

21. "Memories from Israel", 173-175, 320, 322.

22. A play on words on "Jewish Agency beds" – *sochnut/sakanot* (agency/dangers).

23. "1942. A Year of Man and Not of Wine [in Hebrew]," trans. MJ.
24. "Memories from Israel".
25. Omer interview, 5.
26. *Poetry*, 26; *Poems* [in Hebrew] 1, 86.
27. On Italian carbines, see "The Class Meeting," *In This Terrible Wind* [in Hebrew], 25-26.
28. See Chapter 4.
29. "The Class Meeting," 24. This also corresponds to the biography of Ruth Falk, who at that time was on a religious kibbutz, probably Yavneh, on a year's alternative army service, according to Erlich, "Amichai's "Class Meeting", 32.
30. "Class Meeting," 25-27.
31. Gelber, Masada, 69.
32. "When the Germans were defeated at Stalingrad and El Alamein, fear subsided and the unit was disbanded. We were free for a few months, and then in summer, 1943 I joined the British army." Bar Yosef interview.
33. "A History of My Life." Document submitted to the Teacher Training College as part of his candidacy for the soldiers' course. Archive of the David Yellin College of Education, Beit Hakerem, Jerusalem. For more on this period, see Yoav Gelber, *Volunteering and its Role in Zionist Policy*, 1939-1942, 4 [in Hebrew] (Jerusalem 1984), 293.
34. Method of quickly constructing the rudiments of settlements in the late 1930s, under conditions of armed hostility.
35. *Poetry*, 335; *Poems* [in Hebrew] 4, 119. The complete Hebrew title is "Hamadiya, zichron hamudoth", a play on words on name of the kibbutz and "sweet times" (or "sweet womanly organs").
36. Interview with Negev, "The Secular Prophet" [in Hebrew], *Yediot Acharonot – 7 Yamim*, April 3, 1998. See also a series of interviews by Chava Razily, "The Poet's Image [Tchernichovsky] in the Eyes of the Young Generation [in Hebrew]," *Davar*, October 2, 1963.
37. Harshav and Hartman interview. In the Bar Yosef interview he indicates that he served in the British engineering corps "on instructions from the *Haganah*."
38. Hanoch Patishi, *Underground in Uniforms* [in Hebrew] (Tel Aviv and Haifa, 2006), 115.
39. Ibid. An overlapping description of the reasons for setting up the unit was provided by Asher Solal, "A History of the Hebrew Cartographic Company 524," in Moshe Paz-Ner, ed., *Soldiers' Stories of the Hebrew Cartographic Company 524* [in Hebrew], (1990), 11.
40. Gelber, *Volunteering and its Role*, 4, 283-284.
41. Dov Gavish, *Land and Map* [in Hebrew] (Jerusalem, 1991), 239.
42. Joseph interview.
43. Amichai called the place "the Tura caves," and describes them as facing the pyramids, south of Cairo. "Agnon and I" [in Hebrew], *Yediot Acharonot*, December 17, 1978.
44. According to Rahel Stepak, the unit was originally stationed at the Abassiah camp near Cairo. "What Do Amichai's Poems have to do?" [in Hebrew], *Haaretz*, September 24, 2014, 2.

45. Patishi, *Underground in Uniforms*, 116. Cf. Amichai's description in his story "The Aswan Dam", *In This Terrible Wind* [in Hebrew], 226.

46. "The breach invites the thief" is a proverb found in the Babylonian Talmud, Tractate Succah 26: a.

47. D. Schmidt, "Some Historical Notes," in Paz-Ner (ed.), *Soldiers' Stories of the Hebrew Mapping Company 524* [in Hebrew], 1990, 19.

48. "The excitement began in 1945 when I smuggled arms for the Haganah." Hollander-Steingart interview, 49. See also Joseph interview, 6.

49. File of Yehuda Pfeuffer [in Hebrew], Archive of the David Yellin College of Education.

50. "A Propitious Hour."

51. "Suddenly I heard a passage from the Haydn quartet. Since then, the quartet is associated with the pyramids [...]. There are things that won't ever again protect you." "A Propitious Hour."

52. Amichai's visit to Alexandria while in the British army is alluded to in the long quasi-autobiographical poem "The Travels of the Last Benjamin of Tudela": "I remember Alexandria: Number 66, Sisters Street. / General Shmuel Hanagid on his horse [...] riding round the round Abyssinian Church." *Poetry*, 126; *Poems* [in Hebrew] 2, 140. Sisters Street was in fact "Seven Sisters' Street," named after the nuns who ran a hospital on that street. While the British Army was in Egypt, and in particular during WWII, the street had many night clubs and houses of prostitution. It was considered a major commercial artery in the city.

53. The episode is described in the poem "From the Stories of One of the Soldiers in a Foreign Port" [in Hebrew], from *Cairo poems* published by Stepak, "What Are *Amichai's Poems*."

54. See Ruth Kimchi, *Zionism in the Shadow of the Pyramids* [in Hebrew] (Tel Aviv, 2009), especially chapters 3 and 4.

55. "From the Stories of One of the Soldiers in a Foreign Port."

56. "Almost no Hebrew literature was taught at Maaleh school." Omer interview, 5.

57. Amichai even names the street where the club was located: Adli Pasha, one of Cairo's main streets. The famous Cafe Groppi, mentioned in the interview, is still operating today, and Amichai hints at the presence of many foreign journalists there. "Agnon and I" [in Hebrew]. See also Kimchi, *Zionism in the Shadow of the Pyramids*, 162-163.

58. Amichai acknowledged this direct influence on his prose and attributed it to the absence of other models of Hebrew fiction.

59. Omer interview. *Haskalah* – the Jewish Enlightenment, which began in the second half of the 18th century with Moses Mendelssohn and his circle in Berlin, Germany, and later spread to Galicia, Austria, and then to imperial Russia. Modern Hebrew literature mainly emerged there.

60. *Hagalgal*, January 17, 1945.

61. The magazine was a companion to the new radio station *Kol Yerushalayim* (in Hebrew), and was published by the Government Information Department of the British Mandate.

62. David Melamed, "The Story of the Hebrew Weekly entitled *Hagalgal*" [in Hebrew], *Haaretz*, August 26, 2016.

63. This time Amichai was quite accurate, which reinforces the sense that this was a formative event. He was referring to *The Faber Book of Modern Verse*, edited by Michael Roberts, first printed in 1936. The first poet in the anthology is indeed Gerard Manley Hopkins. Dylan Thomas's poems appear almost at the end of the anthology.

64. Joseph interview, 6. But in an interview with Beser he said that during his time in the British army "I didn't dream of writing poetry." Yaakov Beser, *Poets Talk about Themselves* [in Hebrew] (Tel Aviv, 1971), 51.

65. Negev Interview, "I'm a Happy Person".

66. In an interview with Glenda Abramson, Amichai defined the essence of what was common to the two poets he most admired: "I admire Auden – his poetry of the late 1930s and early 1940s – and Eliot, because they both wrote about things, objects, children, animals." Glenda Abramson, "Yehuda Amichai: A Kind of a Lay Prophet," *The Jewish Quarterly* 35: 1 (129), 1988, 10.

67. Frank Stuart Flint, quoted in Shimon Sandbank, *The Desire and the Sun* [in Hebrew] (Tel Aviv, 2014), 241.

68. A good example in Eliot is the opening of "The Love Song of J. Alfred Prufrock:" "Let us go then, you and I, / When the evening is spread out against the sky / Like a patient etherized upon a table;". When Amichai compares people on a bus, hanging on to the rings attached to the ceiling, to people at prayer, the comparison may be conceptually stunning and iconoclastic, but the image makes sense in visual terms and is easy to accept.

69. This is achieved in a kind of ongoing dialogue with the Bible and prayer, and to a lesser extent with verses from other traditional sources. For the most part, Amichai can be considered to have expanded the Hebrew poetic tradition which began in the Spanish Middle Ages and continued with Bialik, Alterman and other poets in their generation, for which he did not necessarily need the example of Pound and Eliot.

70. As in sonnet cycle "We Loved Here" (see chap. 2).

71. In Amichai's conversation with Stan Rubin and Earl Ingersoll he states that what attracted him to Thomas and Eliot was the "music" of Thomas (particularly the rhythm of the poetry, and perhaps also the prose) and his "childhood memories." In Eliot he found "biblical rhetoric" and "irony and humor, particularly in his early writing." "A Conversation with Yehuda Amichai," University of NY, 1984; unpublished), 4. 17.741. See also interview with Haim Chertok, *We Are All Close*, New York 1989, 57.

72. Notes of Amichai for his lecture in English, "Every Man is Born a Poet"; unpublished.

73. Hartman and Harshav interview. In the Hollander-Steingart interview, 49, he also says that he "never got to fight" during the war, and for him the "excitement" began in 1945 with arms smuggling.

74. A talk to mark the publication of a book by Uzi Narkiss, *Soldier of Jerusalem* [in Hebrew] (Tel Aviv, 1991; English translation: London 1998).

75. *In This Terrible Wind* [in Hebrew], 247-255.

76. For more on the episode of bringing *olim* (immigrants to Israel, then Palestine) on the "Passover train" in 1946, see Kimhi, Zionism in the Shadow of the Pyramids, 507-510.

77. "It proceeded like a spy movie", as he describes it himself in "The Departure from Egypt" [in Hebrew], *In This Terrible Wind*, 253.

78. Ibid., 253-254.

79. The reference is to *Hehalutz He'ahid*, which on the initiative of *Haganah* emissaries from the Yishuv, united the main scout movements of Jewish youth in Egypt.

80. See Kimhi's description, ibid.

81. "The Departure from Egypt", *In This Terrible Wind*, 255.

82. The new immigrants were integrated into various kibbutzim. See Gelber, ibid.

83. In his notebooks dated February-March 1957 (File 413), probably from the time when he was writing "The Departure from Egypt," he cites "an old story of Horn's" as the source of this piece. Horn was Tamar's father.

84. Sadan was the editor of the supplement until 1944, and then became an editor at Am Oved publishing house (see Getzel Kressel, *Encyclopedia of Modern Hebrew Literature* 2, 471; in Hebrew) (Tel Aviv, 1965). Rachel Stepak, who published the poems that Amichai sent to Sadan, together with passages from his letter to him, thought that Amichai hoped that Sadan would recommend him to the current editor. Stepak, "What Are Amichai's Poems."

85. Dov Sadan archive, Archives Department, the National Library of Jerusalem. ARC. 4* 1072.

Chapter 4

July 1946–April 1948

Teachers' College and the Beginning of Amichai's Teaching Career

TEACHER TRAINING

Amichai came home from the army in mid-July 1946.[1] His father and mother were already considered elderly by the standards of the time. His father was 58, without a regular income, and was apparently not in good health. Amichai needed to decide on his next steps. Various Yishuv organizations including the Jewish Agency (founded in 1929 and active in fostering *aliyah*),[2] the *Histadrut* (The General Organization of Workers in Israel), and the National Council, which was responsible for the education and other systems, created a professional training framework to set up new settlements, and provided housing for discharged soldiers. "The *Va'ad Leumi* (National Council) offered courses, funded by the British, for war veterans," Amichai noted.

The German-born painter and potter Herbert Applebaum convinced Amichai to go to teachers' college and use teaching as a source of income, thus avoiding the constraints of possible 'capitulation to the establishment'.[3] Another reason for choosing the teaching profession, perhaps closer to the truth, emerged in an interview he gave as part of a wide- ranging piece about the history of the David Yellin Teacher Training College.[4] Amichai mentioned that he had considered studying law, which would have been typical of a bourgeois son.[5] However, the law courses at the Hebrew University on Mount Scopus were not intended to prepare students for the legal profession, but rather to form a cadre of scholars. Teaching was thus "the only way to make a living. It was axiomatic that the best young people would go into teaching."[6]

In the 1940s, high school graduates who were accepted to David Yellin College only needed to complete a 2-year curriculum to qualify as teachers. Students without high school diplomas were required to spend one year at a preparatory school (*mechina*).[7] Candidates discharged from the British army, however, could take a 14-month intensive course beginning in May 1946.[8] Starting this special course late was advantageous to Amichai in one way: it was an excellent excuse to ask Ruth Hermann, a good-looking, impressive student, to lend him her notebooks from the classes he had missed.[9]

The curriculum at the College covered the theory of education, the history of education, and teaching methods for reading, writing and arithmetic. The main final exams were in essay writing, pedagogy and grammar.[10] In the material distributed to students in the accelerated course and to students taking other courses at that time, alongside the writings of Johann Heinrich Pestalozzi (1746-1827) on the educational importance for a child of a connection to nature, was a quote from the Teachers' Union council (1903): "Only now have we begun to live naturally, now that we have come to the land to learn freedom and resurrection."[11] "Freedom and resurrection" also had a universal ring. The courses at the College reflected a new progressive ideology in the philosophy of education: sparking passion for learning in the student, and avoiding the use of coercion based on punishment, fear and disrespect. The assigned books and reading lists included Georg Kerschensteiner's (1854-1932) *Idea and Character Education*, and Pestalozzi's *How Gertrude Teaches Her Children*.[12] Kerschensteiner criticized the tendency in teacher education in previous eras to mold pupils' character.[13] Pestalozzi viewed rationalist education with contempt and advocated relating to the whole child.[14]

Amichai and his fellow students were also exposed to modern pedagogical notions through Dr. Benjamin Brenner's cautious lens. Brenner, their advisor and coordinator, published a pamphlet arguing that pleasantness and enthusiasm were the core of the learning process.[15] In Amichai's letters to Ruth Hermann written during the year he taught in Haifa, he sometimes mentions teachers at the College who were particularly important to him, her, or both of them. Interestingly, he does not mention teachers who were a source of spiritual or intellectual inspiration, but rather those who focused on the practicalities of teaching. He praised instructors who had taught him efficient ways of explaining vital concepts to students, how to structure lessons, and ways to enforce discipline. The teacher he most often mentions is Dr. Benjamin Brenner, who had a "practical sense," as Amichai put it in a letter dated October 23, 1947.[16] In a letter to Ruth (October 23), Amichai applauded Brenner's realism, in particular as regards issues relating to a large school such as Geulah where he was teaching, and which did not provide much latitude for experimentation. Rather, the goal was to maintain a stable framework and instill good habits: "In a school of 1,000 children the main concern is to inculcate good habits, set a pattern for entering and leaving the classroom, lunch time, the system of punishment. All these are of the essence (how right Brenner was!)".

POLITICAL LEANINGS AND EXPRESSION

In a number of interviews Amichai describes the time spent at the College as a reprieve between wars. This reflects the feelings of many Israelis of his generation and those that followed.[17] His feelings for music intensified, both as a listener and concertgoer, as shown by the presence of music in his love affair with Ruth Hermann. There was also political involvement, at least as Amichai saw it, and his engagement in the *Haganah* was indeed the closest he ever came to political activity (see Chapter 3). In his view, belonging to the *Haganah* was tantamount to being part of the mainstream Yishuv. He considered the so-called Revisionists (right-wing Zionists), to be illegitimate outsiders, along with the local anti-Zionist Palestinian Communist movement.[18]

His letters to Ruth Hermann in 1947-8, and in some later letters, show the extent to which he adhered to the ideology of Radical Zionist Socialism by being a *Mapamnik*, which in his case was strengthened by a Marxist analysis typical of the leaders of this movement. The *Mapam* only became a political party in January 1948, and Amichai would report to Ruth on its founding with the enthusiasm of someone who considered it to be the fulfillment of his dreams.[19] His impassioned identification with the new party shows clear echoes of the issue that preoccupied Amichai during the interwar period: his opposition to the partition plan to split Palestine into Jewish and Arab political entities. The idea of a partition, as formulated in the Biltmore Program, which under David Ben Gurion's leadership at the Extraordinary Zionist Conference of American Zionist organizations in New York in May 1942 began to gain traction in the Yishuv, was taken up by the United Nations Special Committee on Palestine (UNSCOP) in May 1947 and was hotly debated by the Jewish public. Amichai, similar to the stance of the radical Leftist politicians, wanted a binational state. He was opposed on principle to partition, because it meant giving in to the schismatic argument between the two peoples, and putting a tiny country with artificially created borders at permanent risk of the loss of its security and wellbeing.[20]

Nevertheless, when the chips were down (the United Nations passed a resolution in November 1947 in favor of the partition of the Land of Israel and the establishment of two states) Amichai became more favorable to the partition plan and the idea of separation between the two people given the resolute Arab hostility, and the need to follow through on founding the State of Israel.

RUTH HERMANN – BEGINNINGS OF ULTIMATE LOVE

In addition to earning his teaching certificate and his involvement in preparations for the emerging state, slim, serious fellow student Ruth Hermann was in Amichai's sights. Born in 1923, her father Leo was from a small German-speaking town in Bohemia (later part of Czechoslovakia). He was the editor of the Zionist Federation of Germany's weekly, the *Jüdische Rundschau*, and was a member of the Zionist Executive. After some years in London he emigrated to Palestine with his family in 1927 to become the secretary of *Keren Hayesod* (the Jewish National Fund, a fundraising organization established in 1920 aimed at Jewish settlement in the Land of Israel). Ruth's mother was Lola née Wahl, a native of Lvov-Lemberg, who had been educated in Berlin.[21] Ruth's older sister, Hadassah, settled on Kibbutz Maoz Haim in the humid Beit Shean Valley, married there, and raised a family. Her younger brother by two years, Gabriel (Gabi), was thought of as a prodigy in physics, as well as being a talented pianist. When Ruth graduated from the Gymnasia Rehavia high school in Jerusalem, and after a year studying the humanities at the Hebrew University, she joined the more than 3,000 Jewish women who enlisted in the British ATS (Auxiliary Territorial Service), a women's corps mainly deployed in Egypt and Palestine.[22] Like many recruits, both male and female, joining the army in the summer of 1942 was not only motivated by idealism but was also a way to postpone a decision about what direction to take in life.[23]

As Ruth tells it, Yehuda Amichai (then Pfeuffer), fresh out of the army, made her acquaintance at a party just before he started taking classes. He asked for her notebooks to catch up on lessons he had missed by enrolling late, and she willingly obliged. Nili Scharf Gold's rendition of Ruth's story suggests that Amichai fell in love with her almost immediately. His shyness prevented him from direct expressions of emotion; rather he let her know his feelings circuitously through indirect words of courtship.[24] A long shadow hung over their developing relationship: for much of her time serving in the British army, Ruth had a boyfriend who was one of the *Mem-Gimel*, the Hebrew acronym for the 43 Haganah members taken prisoner by the British while on a commanders' course in October 1939 and sentenced to five years in the Acre jail.[25] The man's name, in all probability, was Avraham Pushinsky.[26] Ruth met him at a party after his release from jail (early, along with others) prior to February 1941. He was nine years older, an age gap she found alluring. Years later, and with the perspective of a marriage to another man that worked out well, Ruth still described Avraham to Scharf Gold as the love of her life.

According to the latter, the split that eventually separated them, after more than two years of a stormy relationship, had its roots in ideological differences. However, this interpretation, as good as it is for the plot of a romantic novel, is not grounded in reality. As a member of the *Haganah*, Avraham was on the same side of the political spectrum as Ruth. If they did have ideological differences, these would have been about how close the relationship with the British should be, and what support should be given to them during WWII. Possibly a more prosaic reason for their estrangement is that 18 months of imprisonment (and possibly being tortured during the British interrogations) crushed Avraham's spirit. The love affair with him had been exciting, but it was difficult for him to return to life, and to function at work.[27] Ruth, a young middle-class woman at the outset of adulthood, may have felt that the relationship was going nowhere.

Amichai was aware of Avraham's presence in Ruth's life. The love triangle plays an important role in the long poem "In the Public Garden," whose initial version dates back to Haifa in 1947. Amichai also knew that Ruth had had other relationships (letter to her, October 10, 1947). Nevertheless, as his love for her grew, he believed that her "legacy" of lovers had simply made her a more complete person and would enrich his relationship with her ("All this was yours. It all left you as you were before, but you grew and were enriched." Ibid.).

Ruth and Amichai's relationship gradually became closer. Hanukkah of that year at the College seemed like a turning point to him. Six months of a relationship in a new key began, albeit not as perfectly close as he expected. Often, they would study for classes or tests together, as frequently as every day, mostly at Ruth's home on Ramban Street. Her home was secular, open and more permissive than that of his observant parents.[28] Ruth recollected that at the start she tried to curtail the friendship by having a third person be present at the same time, but this defense was short-lived. Apart from the time they spent at her parents' home, and to a lesser extent at the home of his parents, who would certainly not have allowed him to have sexual relations before marriage in their house,[29] they frequented the famous Atara Cafe (November 26, 1947). Amichai made mostly unsuccessful efforts to introduce Ruth to the world of classical music so beloved to him (the following year he wrote to her: "I suppose that by the time you come back, you'll know how to be a music lover. And if we go together to a concert, I won't have to ask you whether it bores you" (December 17, 1947).

Two events at the College allowed them to gauge just how much interest and enjoyment they would have by spending extended time together. The first was their class outing to Haifa, soon after Hanukkah, to observe classes in the city schools under the guidance of Dr. Brenner. In a letter from Amichai to Ruth exactly a year later he recalls the surge of love that indicated a new, more promising stage in the development of their sensitive relationship: "Tekele, I went past that steep place where we walked a year ago, when we were living at Rothenberg House [the student dormitory] ... it was like a prophecy within us ... and you talked with me about how chance can become destiny, for our meeting was by chance, and instead of me it could have been someone else, and only chance brought us together at our time of need" (January 28, 1948).[30]

An even more dramatic turning point, this time an opportunity for real couplehood, took place during their stay in the Binyamina settlement a month or six weeks after that walk, as one of the pairs or trios of students who were assigned to different places in the country to acquire teaching experience. A year later, on February 28, 1948, while working as a teacher in a school in a high-risk area in Haifa, Amichai wrote to her: "Exactly a year ago, we were in Binyamina. ((It was a time of flowering for us both, and we laid the foundation between us. Spring was everywhere [...] gentle hills covered in rich vegetation. The scent of oranges and orange blossoms. And we were happy, you and I." "How rich our lives are!" (October 3, 1948).

BINYAMINA – A WAY-STATION

The experience in Binyamina that Amichai chose to describe in retrospect was what happened to them on the first night in their rented accommodation.[31] "We studied together, were apprentices in Binyamina, and there, in the dead of night ... English paratroopers circled the little inn, since they knew that a young man and woman had come from Jerusalem, and they were sure they had caught the leaders of Etzel (National Military Organization). They got us out of bed in the middle of the night and only let us go when they had ascertained that we were in fact the good sort of Jew from the Haganah."[32] In his opinion, this experience finally brought them together and crystallized their decision to link their destinies.[33]

A number of unpublished poems entitled "Binyamina 1947" – the "Binyamina Poems" – six sonnets that Amichai wrote while he was there, or more likely in the following months, give a good idea of the couple's experiences. The metamorphosis of his relationship with Ruth during the two weeks or more in Binyamina, including being caught in heavy rain and hail which became the background to Sonnet IV ("The hut has turned blue! The door squeaks when she opens it. / We are inside: hail on tin, a racket"), a meeting with "an old woman mumbling about the past," his attempt to teach Ruth how to play the recorder and to draw her (Sonnet VI)[34] were perhaps less important than the poetic event of writing the sonnets in which Amichai immortalized the time spent with Ruth there with more lightness and assurance than seen before in his writing. In their relationship he continued to be the interested one, the one anxious about whether she would reciprocate, and how long her only partial commitment would last. By contrast she doled out her enthusiasm, while enjoying his generous love, his unique talents and friendly humor.

The "Binyamina 1947" sonnets convey the general influence of the poetry of the early Lea Goldberg (*Green-Eyed Spike; On the Blossoming*[35]), together with the innovativeness later associated with Amichai's poetry, which so supported Israel as it recovered from a catastrophic war. This innovativeness and audaciousness are expressed through his directness and prosaicness, his legitimation of the everyday, and his way of extracting symbolism from everyday occurrences, which the poet pursues with stethoscopic sensitivity (as in the anticipated link up of the railway and the highway in Sonnet III). They capture his daring trademark: making analogies between the threatening and the humorous, such as his comparison of lovers to the dead by playing with the verb "to rest" (Sonnet IV).[36] Perhaps he only had to allow himself to be himself, for example when he describes buying items in the local store, and experiences of overindulgence; in his letters to Ruth recalling their time together, eating is prominent. On January 16, 1948, for example, he wrote: "For some reason I remember the little restaurant at the school [...] in the afternoon we ate there, small plates and portions. And we sat on little chairs and we were so big beside the children."

Ruth and Amichai enjoyed spending time together during holidays with his family including his sister who lived in Tel Aviv with her husband, Benjamin Sauer (Zauer), an English teacher, and their young daughter Hannale, or with her family including her sister Hadassah who lived on Kibbutz Maoz Haim and was married to German-born Yona Wolf, and already had two children, Moshe and Navot. Both in Tel Aviv and on Kibbutz Maoz, the children were the main attraction. Like other poets, Amichai saw children as having a natural affinity with poetry and creativity. The man who became renowned for his poetry and a sought-after speaker would begin many talks with the words "everyone is a poet," and illustrate this by references to children who astound by their linguistic creativity, their original visions. When he wanted to convey to Ruth an amusing image of the hugeness of his love, he described a gesture he had observed in children: "If I was a child like little Yael [the painter Applebaum's daughter] or little Navot, I would open my arms wide and declare: this is how much I love you, big-time, a lot!" (14-15 October, 1947).

Seven months had gone by since the "soldiers' class" sojourn at Rothenberg House at the end of January 1947, which had led to the deepening of Amichai and Ruth's relationship, and her departure for New York at the end of August. For Amichai, these seven months were rich, filled with movement towards a great and sure light, summoning him to an enduring connection with Ruth. He was so certain of her perfect compatibility with him, and his spiritual sense and public ideals, that he naively believed nothing could destroy such shared devotion.[37] He saw this half year of closeness with Ruth as having contributed to his emotional and intellectual life beyond anything he had experienced during his army years.[38]

HAIFA – SEPTEMBER 1947 TO APRIL 1948

Ruth's Departure

When Amichai and Ruth had both completed their intensive teacher training in the summer of 1947, they had to decide where they would go next. Whether because there was a surfeit of teachers in Jerusalem, or because he wanted to get away from his parents, Yehuda Pfeuffer applied to the Geulah school in Haifa and was accepted as a teacher for grade four. The principal Shraga Nafcha asked him to change his German name to a Hebrew one, in the spirit of the Hebraization then in fashion among the Zionists in Palestine. Ruth and Yehuda came up with Amichai together. Looking back, he thought it was a perfect name, in harmony with the spirit of the time and his ideological commitment to Zionism (he sometimes put this in terms of military defense) and socialism.[39] According to what Ruth told Scharf Gold, in view of his doubts that the name might be "too pretentious," she told him that the name was right for the great poet he dreamed of becoming. Amichai vehemently denied that he had any thoughts at that time of being involved with poetry,[40] a denial that does not coincide with the facts.

Ruth, who was born in England and served in the British army for more than three years, spoke good English and grew up in a German-speaking household, so the choice of a career as a language teacher was a natural one. Reflecting back on that time, when a much older woman, she told Scharf Gold that she went to New York after seeing a newspaper ad for the Jewish Theological Seminary announcing preferential admission for students who were "war veterans," and those who had already done teacher training. However, judging by the evidence in the letters Amichai sent to Ruth from the day she set sail, it is doubtful whether she really knew where she was going or what she would do in New York. What is clearer is that she sought to escape Amichai and his absolute certainty as to the enduring nature of their love, his conviction as an intellectual and poet immersed in imaginative thinking.[41] Amichai was invested in dreams, convinced that he had found the ultimate conversation partner with whom he could rise above the prosaicness and triviality of bourgeois life, with its narrow horizons and sparsity of poetry.[42] Meanwhile she was sailing to a world where she would quickly find a more stable and ordered life than she could expect in the Land of Israel on the eve of war alongside a young and ambitious poet whose future career was still uncertain.[43]

Amichai and his Students

Amichai began to teach at the large Geulah school which had nearly 1,000 pupils[44] and was located in Hadar Hacarmel, Haifa. This school was considered to "serve a medium income social stratum and above."[45] For the doctor and writer Yitzhak Kronzon, a native of the neighborhood who studied at Geulah at that time, the area was "home to an ascetic and homogenous community of East Europeans, members of *Mapai*. Most of the men were industrial workers, and everyone was crowded together into rented apartments, for the most part two or three families to one apartment [...]. The children all spoke better Hebrew than their parents. Most did not have grandparents, because everyone had been murdered in the Holocaust."[46]

Class 4/2, which was assigned to Amichai, had 25 girls and 16 boys.[47] Perhaps because the school board recognized his diverse talents, or because as a new teacher he could be pressed upon, he was required to teach drawing and singing on top of the other subjects taught by year four teachers (letter dated September 9, 1947), and soon after gym and nature (September 17 and 20). "My gym classes are very successful," he reported to Ruth. "I am also teaching nature. To begin with, I didn't want to, and now I am happy I took it on. This way I will teach myself!" He also taught English in year six. "The children love me [...] Since I have a good word for everyone at the break [...] discipline comes to them naturally". This is how he summed up his first two months of teaching. When a class was particularly difficult, such as when he taught English, he did not raise his voice and did not impose punishments, but simply closed his book and waited, on one occasion for two hours. "I let them vent their energy, and later gained a camp of supporters [...] today they are quiet and good" (September 5). At a PTA meeting one of the mothers pleaded that her son was sensitive and that teachers needed to "speak to him gently." Amichai's response was that if he was gentle with him in a class of 43 pupils, "it would be at the expense of others." Mothers did not, he thought, understand the school's "*socio*-educational role [his emphasis]. "For them, the main thing is grades. In my opinion, the main thing is social education, getting along together, waiting in line" (November 1-2).

Amichai's relationship to his pupils combined the strictness of a teacher who wanted to do his work conscientiously and keep his students on a short leash, and a poet who saw the children as peers with whom he identified. He felt that laughter was the bridge between them: on one occasion when he criticized them for some failing, they laughed. He loved their laughter when they watched a performance: they express "laughter without malice, without irony" (September 5). Relating to their creativity, or at times the lack of it, helped him learn about artistic creation, and continued to serve him over many years in readings and interviews (for example, darkness and difficulty as a rich and nuanced source of narrativity). Amichai knew from his experiences as a boy in a German Jewish school that when you give children a composition to write, they tend to use borrowed expressions and even copy whole passages from the work of older children. In his opinion, his students wrote more freely and authentically than the norm because they were drawing on their exceptional experiences which included Arab attacks and Jewish revenge, their fathers' activities in military defense, a bullet that had gone through a home (December 21).[48]

Relationships with Other Teachers

A duality developed in his relationships with the other teachers that enabled him to survive as a poet with an inner, creative life, while giving those around him the sense that he was not arrogant or unfriendly. Amichai enjoyed spending time with the other teachers, but felt he was essentially an outsider who enjoyed observing, reflecting on why those around him behaved as they did, and drawing conclusions: "We were a nice community. Humor informed everything. Mutual understanding. We talked over mugs of steaming tea. Tekele, there are days when everything you see is a poem, every utterance sounds like a proverb or a rhyme."

Amichai liked going to staff meetings (for the whole school, and for the year four teachers; November 26, 1947), and even found them useful. He led the school scouts, and was proud of the Hanukkah show he wrote, which was a hit.[49] The teachers, particularly the young and single ones, had a social circle, and Amichai at least initially joined in, but quite quickly tired of it, since he was very conscious of his otherness. "I will try to escape gradually, because I have lost interest [...] Perhaps you have spoiled me, with your character, your way of talking" October 14-15). He felt even more distant from a mixed group of teachers and students at the Technion that met for the Sabbath. These meetings were hosted by "one of Ora [Haklai]'s friends [...] who was finishing the Technion this year as an architect. She is very talented, a painter [...] has a beautiful room, with atmosphere. Sculptures, books. She plays Beethoven sonatas. We recited poems and I fought for modern poetry. I didn't succeed even a bit. They prefer romanticism in poetry, the melancholy moon. [...] In the evening they came to me. [...] In the end it became idiotic and couple after couple began playing around and making out. It made me moody. A petit bourgeois society! Why can't they be simple? This morning I cleaned my rented room, because [what happened] disgusted me. I have nothing in common with them. It's good that we aren't like that" (November 9).

Attitudes Toward the Public Sphere and Politics

Despite his strong sense of uniqueness, Amichai's relationship to the public sphere and his ties to Israeli society were still wholehearted. In a letter dated

November 13, 1947 he describes paying his membership/medical care dues at the *Histadrut* office, which apart from being a trade union, oversaw the public healthcare system, and had important state-like functions even after statehood. "Right from the beginning I encountered a good polite attitude," he reported sincerely, without cynicism, happy that the clerk had found his card. "A great raucous happiness. The happiness of being safe, and a warm feeling of being known in a large society [...] it's the sense of sociality that embraces us in public places, in the street, at meetings."[50] "Yes, Tekele, from day to day I see more clearly the greatness of the everyday, the poetry that remains constantly greater than exceptional poetry, than the marvelous [...] the everyday is more marvelous, for it fashions our image out of thousands of little stones [...] thousands of small habits construct the big habit."[51]

He wrote to Ruth, with the naiveté that could surprise readers of his later poetry, that "if there is a state, it makes sense to be here. The country, the Yishuv and the enormous immigration will need us" (September 3). When he delineates his vision of their future as a couple, he writes innocently about the ideal of their integration into the state-in-the-making and the new society. "Here I am in Haifa, the beautiful and industrious city, laying the foundations for us. [...] Dear, the country needs us, whether partitioned or not. There will be difficult times, internally and externally, and we will be brave, righteous and good. [...] In our story, which is being written in a great and steady hand, it now says [...] 'and so she went to America. She was afraid of the strange land, and loved the little country, and within her, she began to plan her way home'" (September 25).

It was not easy for Amichai to give up his vision of a binational state. On September 17, after a visit by the popular educator Blumenthal, he wrote to Ruth: "The majority in the country is for partition. I too have changed my opinion somewhat and I agree". His moderate, anti-militarist political stance came to the fore when he expressed his horror at the Arab states' assault on the country, while also disagreeing with the belligerent declarations of the *Mapai* leaders (such as Golda Meir, at that time the Head of the political bureau of the Jewish Agency; letter dated October 10). He was afraid of the militarist nature of the Jewish state in the making which would continue to rely on the sword (October 16).

His judgment and analysis were unequivocal and bore the *Mapam*-Marxist signature of a clear-cut division between good and bad, both in terms of countries and social classes. On January 1, 1948 he wrote to Ruth: "The coming months, until the summer, will bring difficulties, sacrifices and destruction. It looks like America will betray us, as could have been seen from the start". A little later he says: "Sometimes I see with symbolic clarity" how "the line comes straight from the shining streets of New York to the positions held here [perhaps by the Mandatory government] [...] and I know [...] the Arab in the street is not to blame, but the effendi, and the British Colonial Office" (February 1, 1948).[52]

While applauding the representatives of the Soviet Union and the Vice President of the United States, Henry Wallace, who called for a less intransigent policy towards the Communist powers, Amichai saw the Western states, the US and Britain, as "evil powers," "reactionary in all their forms" (February 23). "America has betrayed us most despicably. Russia is the only one staying true to its original position. And this position is what will finally bring about the triumph of world Communism. The dawn of each new day shows that this doctrine is the true one, and the vitality of its popular spirit." A month later (March 21) he wrote to Ruth that "anyone familiar with Marxist thought knows that this betrayal [of the US with regard to the plan to establish a Jewish state] was entirely inevitable." He saw the dominating hand of imperialist America over the world in the UN.[53]

Involvement in Haganah Missions and the Army

In any case it was clear to him, even before the UN resolution of November 29, that he had to take part in the defense of the Yishuv as a citizen and volunteer in the field corps, which involved giving up his weekends to take part in Haganah partisan activities.[54] Despite his qualms about ruining his Sabbath he enjoyed "the crawling and jumping," and the training atmosphere made him feel youthful (November 23). On December 11, he could already report to Ruth that for the first time in his life he "[...] had a part, albeit small, in an attack." A number of Arab houses, from which our convoys had been fired on, had been destroyed [...] After one gets over the nausea and shock of the first times, one does everything calmly and quietly" (February 23).

Sometimes there were reconnaissance missions. Carrying a grenade belt and a rifle with 100 rounds was very tiring, but "it is a better method of defense. The older soldiers man the positions." Sometimes they encountered Arab reconnaissance units, and "you can imagine what happened then" (March 12). Despite all his reservations he felt exultation when immersed in the heat of battle, and that same night he enjoyed the soldier's feeling of satisfaction on returning to base, to hot tea and smiling young women (March 6). Nevertheless, he did not see himself as having any military talent, and had no aspirations. In a letter dated January 12 he relates that the leaders of the local Haganah asked him to take on a role parallel to that of colonel in the army and that he had wiggled of it with difficulty, since they threatened to view him as a deserter if he refused.

The Hamerkaz School

Amichai put himself in the line of fire and at great risk by agreeing to leave the class he loved at the Geulah school (January 23) to teach at the Hamerkaz

(Central) school downtown, in a neighborhood close to an Arab locality. Parents in this school's catchment area came from lower socioeconomic backgrounds than those who sent their children to Geulah. The men were mainly dockworkers.

When he got to the school to replace a pregnant teacher who was afraid to go on teaching at a school under fire, it was already "a school made up of six different schools, an emergency school. From day to day, fewer and fewer pupils dared come to class." On March 5 he describes how he came to the school along with a handful of children, only to see it had been half destroyed by a car bomb; "but we steeled ourselves and continued" by studying in people's apartments (March 10).

Amichai's letters from this time depict the terrible reality of fear and murder of Jews and non-Jews in the neighborhood near the school. When a shell landed in the schoolyard, an armored vehicle came to extricate him and the children (March 19). Nevertheless, as a teacher Amichai knew how to derive a lesson from these terrible circumstances. Against the backdrop of the imminent closure of "our little damaged school, now moribund," the children in his small class (just eight at this point) found a pool of blood of a British soldier who had died by Arab fire. "One child commented: 'My teacher, here is the blood of the Englishman. It's the same as our blood!'" (undated letter, March 27 or 28).

Fire of Love, Blaze of Creativity

Amichai was deeply in love, and so happy to have found Ruth as the embodiment of his physical and spiritual wishes. He loved her so much so that he did not stop her leaving him to pursue her education in distant America. Just as he expected a partner to respect his freedom, so he had to respect hers and let her develop in her own way (March 11, 1948). However, his letters to Ruth, three a week over eight months, until she sent him the bitter news of their separation, show that he was inwardly divided. Every so often he would come up with what seemed compelling reasons for her to come back to him sooner or later: the state of war in the country that would require every member of the Yishuv to be there and help, his greater wherewithal to set up a stable home, or the beauty of Jewish social solidarity in Palestine despite all the difficulties and suffering, but he also understood her desire to move forward and to experience a new reality.[55]

To a great extent, Amichai's letters are a kind of writing workshop. He is fully engaged in writing experiments; the letters are threaded with lines of poetry that he knows or that he and Ruth know together; almost exclusively German and English poets. The only Hebrew poet mentioned is Bialik (March 25). Nevertheless, these letters only document a portion of the long and more or less continuous development of Amichai's beginnings as a poet.

It is no coincidence that the poems and translations in these letters are not included in Amichai's books. Sometimes the poems are embarrassingly unsophisticated; they have been sweated over, and seem like the work of a beginner who has yet to fully master the language or exploit all the subtleties of poetic techniques. The real poetry in these letters lies in their prose. A strong wind catches radiant sails when he appeals to Ruth, or describes his experiences in general. In the poems he is still the sorcerer's apprentice, rather than an accomplished magician.

As someone for whom poetic inspiration comes from the inside, he borrows freely from the poetry of the past and from the revolutionaries of his time. The poems he quotes are the library he imagines he would share with Ruth which would set them apart from the complacent secular bourgeois household with its routines (November 28). The famous phrase in Shakespeare's Julius Caesar enables him to express the relationship to death that may be waiting for him in future wars: "Cowards die many times before their deaths" (March 21). To explain the difference between "doers" and "thinkers" he defines himself as "in the middle, between Fortinbras and Hamlet": Hamlet is someone "who tries to push himself to a drunken act, in an attempt to leave behind his analytic mind and foresight," while Fortinbras, who in Shakespeare's play goes blithely to conquer a largely insignificant territory, is "a joyful man of deeds, a young commander" who loves action for its own sake (January 19).[56]

However, the modern poets he quotes or translates are more than passing expressions of his mood. Talking about their poetry and thought most likely enabled him to situate himself as a poet, explain the nature of his writing, and clarify where he stood as a creator. He was engaged in revealing the innovative structure and hidden code of his poetry. The poet he cites the most often is Rilke (he was either unfamiliar with the expressionists Lasker-Schüller and Trakl at that point or showed no interest in them). On November 28 he copies out Rilke's famous poem Autumn Day (*Herbsttag*), which begins with the words "Lord: it is time" ("Herr, es ist Zeit") and whose last verse, "Who has no house now, will never build one / Who is alone now, will long remain so" he thought appropriate to Ruth at the beginning of her stay in America.[57] He awkwardly translates Rilke's *Liebeslied* (Love Song) for her. For him Rilke was a guide: "Great people like Rilke see childhood as containing everything, the source and key to the human" (December 17, 1947).[58]

He translated Auden into Hebrew but T. S. Eliot seems to have been more important to him. He defines his core identity as a poet in the spirit of the opening lines of "The Wasteland", "April is the cruelest month, breeding Lilacs out of the dead land, mixing Memory and desire, etc.," and reflects on them: "A wonderful picture: a blend of memory and desire. It stirs within me as if in the breathing earth. Memory and love against a background of this war we are fighting." In a letter two weeks later he analyzes Eliot's poetic style to explain the nature of modern poetry, and Imagism in particular which he sees as its main representative (March 23): "When Eliot describes the character of a woman, he doesn't talk about her directly but shows her environment, her room, part of a conversation he can characterize her by, her dress [...] a person living his life is like the thread on which pearls are strung."

Amidst all these influences and references to poets, storytellers and dramatists (H. C. Anderson, Kafka, Shakespeare and others), Amichai was growing in his own exuberant but deliberate way. His notes to his poems and the poems themselves show the conscious process he engaged in to produce a form and structure that would be his own. The importance of the Haifa period is related primarily to defining his writing habits; for example, his famous notebooks where he wrote down lines that came to him, the fruits of inspiration: "I have a small, tiny notebook, where I write everything that comes to me, everything I see and which makes an impression [...] over the years some of the words have become poems" (September 17), and in his reflections on his poetry and his approach to it. These are perhaps more significant than the poems themselves. In the same letter where he talks about the little notebook, he defines his artistry as deriving from an entirely unique approach: he sees Ruth and himself as "realists," for whom life is not a succession of feelings but "a mosaic of pictures, happenings, and events in which the big ideas and emotions are reflected." In terms of Amichai's own esthetic, his "realism" can perhaps be more accurately described as "thing poems" (*Sachlichkeit* or *Dingedichte*), as in Rilke's poetics.[59]

During the first month after Ruth's departure he sent her many poems. Despite the torment of separation, formal experimentation emerged as very important to him, primarily perhaps to test how far his literary license could go, as an individual educated in the classic poetics of regular versification and meter. The week after she left, on September 6, 1947, he sent her two poems: "On the Day of Your Departure" and "The Dream." The former comes across as prose-bound, inattentive to the music. Never the less it contains something of the future Amichai in a moment of symbolism where he makes something exceptional out of an everyday thing: a mirror removed from a coffee house leaving "just a black stain" in its place. "The Dream" is a sonnet, a little more sophisticated formally, which centers on a minute observation of a hanger which appears "suddenly, as if [spread open by the] wind, a hidden hand, / the closet gaped open." Despite the reality of his lover's departure some time before, "one hanger will still move as if you had just removed your dress."[60]

In the months that followed he sent fewer poems to Ruth, but these showed more focus. On November 11, 1947 he sent a poem to her, perhaps the conclusion of a longer work, "*Hade'iya*" ("Gliding,") that he may have wanted to submit to a competition.[61]

Although it does not have traditional poetic rhythm, it has an inner one:

> I walk and walk./ Walking away from her the whole time singing her song,/
>
> Though she forgot the song some time ago, [...]/[...] I gather up the tatters of torn letters/ [...] I hoard ceased and forgotten loves / Cultivating them like bacteria in in the laboratory."

Although the poem has some original analogies, such as the comparison of forgotten loves to a microbial culture, the poem on the whole is diffuse.

Amichai seems to have aspired to maximal freedom in writing, and a release from the conventions he found stifling. The way to consolidate independence, and to free what is hidden in the soul, was through the use of word play that involved associating sounds rather than rational content, which led to unexpected connections and surprising analogies. A typo in a newspaper article about an attack on a kibbutz – "Two of the *musicians* fell" (instead of "two of the *defenders*:" *menagnim* instead of *maginim*) gave him "the urge to go on with this wonderful idea. The defenders are musicians. This conflation of death and grenades with playing the piano or the brown noble-bodied violin" (February 20).[62]

Seeds of the Future in Letters and Poems

The first version of the long poem "In the Public Garden," which was published by Achshav in 1959, was already in draft form at this time.[63] The poem summarizes his relationship with Ruth up to that time, with all its torments and quandaries, by turning it into an existential parable about the modern human condition with its profound loneliness, awareness of death and attachment to Eros as a solution. Amichai presents Eros in this poem both spicily and with humorous distance (for example, a butterfly snared in a woman's dress).

His main poetic perspectives, and the motifs that would reappear in his famous later poems first appear in his aerograms to Ruth. He was already employing a concept of time which would figure in all his subsequent poetry. In a letter to Ruth dated February 6, 1948, he wonders how one can grasp time, and how it can be situated. He writes that the origin of time is perhaps outside the circle of life "and only the dead arrive at this source of times." He characteristically concretizes the abstract while at the same time turning the concrete into something strange and mysterious, intangible and not directly accessible.

On March 7, 1948 he tells Ruth about his search for inner sources to deepen his poetry. Immersion in childhood experiences is what seems to have induced him to shake off intellectualism, abandon "grand and philosophical thinking" and instead "go and ponder and play inside [...] because the great spring is upon us" (undated, March 27 or 28, 1948). This echoes his earlier letter that prefigures the well-known poem "Not Like a Cypress."[64] "How great is this wonder of sensing, feeling one's participation in one's surroundings. I am beginning to put down roots: not [as] one big root, but thousands of tiny, miniscule roots," he writes. In the same letter where he renounces "grand and philosophical thinking," he mentions the number of Jewish dead killed in battles and Arab attacks. "Our country is small, and there is hardly anyone without family and acquaintances [who have fallen]. We don't have an 'unknown soldier.' The absence of each is felt." This primal reaction, a direct response to the horrifying extent of bereavement in the War of Independence from its very beginning, would not be expressed in a poetic form until the Six Day War and the death of one of Amichai's former students in the poem "We Have No Unknown Soldiers."[65]

Coming to Terms with the Breakup with Ruth

Ruth, however, was following her dreams in another direction. Perhaps from the outset she was looking for a comfortable life in the US, and simply cultivated the illusion that she would return. A family member from Palestine who knew about her trip introduced her to a German Jewish friend, Eric Wolfgang Zielenzeiger, who had survived the war in Holland. He was the son of a senior civil servant in the German government before Hitler's rise to power. While Amichai was showering her with letters of spiritual abundance and the treasures of his love, and she every so often sent letters to feed the fire burning in him, even including poems, in November 1947 she had met Eric, who was working for a wealthy German banker.[66] By February she was engaged to him, but did not tell Amichai until early April (her letter from February was still "so sweet and friendly and natural in its love and assurance," as her brokenhearted lover put it). Did she delay the announcement to avoid hurting his feelings? Or perhaps she decided not to tell him until she was sure the marriage would indeed take place?

Amichai's letter of April 11, 1948 responding to the bitter news, expresses terrible shock along with an understanding of Ruth's decision, and an attempt to see her point of view, thus showing unexpected altruism in a young man so invested in an "absolute" love and the belief that he had found the one destined for him. In contrast to the somewhat childish rage in the poem he wrote about Ruth in later years ("That whore [...] left me alone with my new name"),[67] he martialed all his psychological sensitivity to understand and justify her decision: if they had gotten married less than wholeheartedly, and with less than complete faith, they would have made each other miserable. His heart ached that he had not tried to dissuade her from going to the US, which had had no real purpose in the first place. However, he had not wanted their relationship to involve any kind of coercion on either side. As he saw it, when she told him the year before that she would agree to be a writer's wife, perhaps she had not been completely honest. He had three resources to draw on to cope with severity of the blow: his creative work, his activity as a soldier for the nascent state, and his blazing ideological commitment to establishing a just socialist society.

Amichai Goes into Battle

When the Merkaz school shut down entirely before the Passover break,[68] he expressed the hope, in a letter to Ruth on March 21 "that they will allow me to fully participate in the fighting forces and that I will be a simple soldier." He wanted to be a full time soldier, since teaching during the day and military missions at night were exhausting. He was not afraid of dying, he told her, but feared for his writing which was on the threshold of maturity, since death would truncate it before it reached "perfection."

Two letters dated June 6 and 7 but almost certainly written two months earlier[69] show how far his expressions of acceptance of Ruth's leaving him – and even encouragement for her new life – stemmed from a deliberate effort to preserve the standards of an enlightened and egalitarian masculinity, and did not express his inner feelings. The first letter reads as though there had been no announcement of separation and full acceptance of it on his part: "Recently a new idea came to me – that you will one day reappear. And this idea [...] has taken root." At night he sometimes dreamed of her return "in the hours of rest between actions" (April 6). In his love for her, that never for an instant loosened its grip, he found "that confluence of vitality and tradition, of reality and ancient legend that informs my emotions and my poems." He was so immersed in his emotions that he even thought about finding an apartment where they could live, and wrote "it is not difficult to find a place of work now. See then how everything is ready for you. And if I don't hear otherwise, I will go on hoping for you every day" (April 7).[70] Since believers always wait for the Messiah.

NOTES

1. "A History of My Life" [in Hebrew]. Document remitted to David Yellin College.

2. According to Yoav Gelber, in June 1944 the Jewish Agency set up a special department for demobilized soldiers. *Volunteering*, 4 [in Hebrew], 294.

3. Amichai talked at some length about his relationship with Herbert Applebaum in a diary that was published in *Moznaim* 29:1, June 1969, [in Hebrew], 22. Elsewhere, he described his keen interest in firing pottery with Applebaum, and said that a large part of his love of literature and poetry had come from him; "Monologue of a Lone Wolf" (in Dan Omer's column) [in Hebrew], *Haolam Ha'ze*, June 30, 1976.

4. Yotam Benziman, "A School for New Teachers" [in Hebrew], *Kol Ha'ir*, December 10, 1993, 97-101.

5. In another interview he said that if his parents had emigrated with their children to the US instead of Palestine, he would certainly have become a lawyer and not a poet (see Chapter 2).

6. Benziman, "A School" [in Hebrew], 100.

7. "Information and Instructions for Students at the David Yellin College 5707 [1946-7]," [in Hebrew]. Collection of Matanya Rosen, Archive of Jewish Education, University of Tel Aviv.

8. This information was found in an English permit given to Ruth Hermann by the dean of the college, Dr. Israel Mehlman, November 19, 1949. Personal file of Ruth Hermann, David Yellin College Archive.

9. Amichai applied for the course in June, 1946. Ruth Hermann had already begun in May, just a few days after her release from the army. For more on her lending her notebooks to Amichai, see Scharf Gold, *National Poet,* 191.

10. Collection of Matanya Rosen, Archive of Jewish Education, University of Tel Aviv. This information pertains to the 5708 (1947-8) academic year, but it is likely that it was similar to the year before.

11. David Yellin College Archive, 19.1, 105-2.

12. These are recalled in Amichai's letters to Ruth Hermann, written during his year of teaching in Haifa, in which he frequently refers to their experiences in class the year before at the college. Letter dated October 22, 1947 and others.

13. Georg Kerschensteiner, *Idea and Character Education*. This book appeared in Hebrew translation in 1929.

14. Johann Heinrich Pestalozzi, *How Gertrude Teaches Her Children*, trans. Lucy E. Holland and Francis C. Turner (London: Swan Sonnenschein and Co., 1894), 18-19. The Hebrew translation was published in 1927.

15. Benjamin Brenner, *The Lesson* [in Hebrew] (Jerusalem, 4704 [1943-4]), 7.

16. Benjamin Brenner (1898-1982), the younger brother of the writer Joseph Haim Brenner, went to Palestine in his youth and studied at the David Yellin teacher training college in Beit Hakerem. After earning degrees in Germany and at Columbia University in New York, he returned to teach at the college.

17. "While in the intensive course, I had a friend, a violinist [probably Gedaliah Kraut], who was studying at the conservatory, and so I entered the world of music. It was a wonderful year." Omer interview "In This Burning Country" [in Hebrew], 6.

18. Joseph interview, 5, 7. He described Begin and his followers in the same way in this 1992 interview.

19. Letter dated January 28, 1947. There is remarkable similarity between the formulations of the new party's manifesto and Amichai's remarks in letters to Ruth

(statements about a global struggle against "capitalist-imperialist forces of reaction", viewing the English-speaking powers as the heirs of Hitler's treatment of the Jews) and what historian Eli Tsur calls "a principled negation of the solution of partition" while accepting it "in reality." Eli Tsur, *Landscapes of Illusion* (Beersheva, 1998), chapter 1 [in Hebrew]. See also Anita Shapira, *Israel*, chapter 8.

20. Letters to Ruth dated September 16 and November 23, 1947.

21. She met the Zionist activist Leo in Berlin. Ruth's younger brother described the "Czech" nature of his father as a softer and slightly more easy-going version of the familiar yekkeness.

22. Later in other countries as well.

23. "Personal problems were set aside. I enjoyed the freedom and independence. Everything was so interesting and different," wrote a recruit in the same framework, in her memoir. Tzili Brandstatter, *A Shadow of my Own* [in Hebrew] (Tel Aviv, 2003), 41.

24. Scharf, Gold, *National Poet*, 194-5.

25. Interview with Ruth's brother, Dr. Gabi Hermann (November 11, 2016), which confirmed that this man was one of the 43 (for more about this group of commanders and its imprisonment, see Shabtai Teveth, *Moshe Dayan: Biography* (London, 1972), 104-115). His efforts to dissuade Ruth from continuing to serve in the British army, if indeed he did try, were connected to the deep divisions in the Yishuv between those who enlisted in the *Haganah* and its military arm – the *Palmach* – and those who joined the British army. Ruth's lover doubtless felt all the more hostility towards the latter after his arduous and humiliating incarceration.

26. This is based on the list of the accused at the trial, *Davar*, October 26, 1939, 1 [in Hebrew].

27. The information about Avraham's condition comes from a conversation with Gabi Hermann, Ruth's brother, who lived with her in those years. Ruth told her sister's son, Navot Matan (Wolf), that Avraham was a coarse, "crude" man. Conversation with Navot, May 16, 2017.

28. This was also how Ruth's brother saw it. See also Scharf Gold, *National Poet*, 197-200. Amichai noted the presence of her brother, a student at the university, in her parents' home in a letter dated September 14, 1947.

29. Scharf Gold deduces from what Ruth says that Amichai's parents opposed her relationship with their son, but this was not the case, as shown in his letters to Ruth: before she left for New York they asked him to send her their regards (September 9, 1947), and relations were good between his parents and hers (January 9, 1948). The Pfeuffer couple, who were simple and unpretentious people, would not have been opposed to their son's marrying the daughter of a senior establishment official, the former editor of a major Jewish newspaper.

30. This trope of turning chance into destiny was close to Amichai's heart, and appears in his poems from that time; it remains unclear where the young Amichai took it from. He may have been familiar with the philosophy of Martin Heidegger, perhaps by way of Hugo Bergmann's articles in the weekly *Hapoel Hatsair*. "Tekele" is Amichai's nickname for Ruth.

31. In her book, Scharf Gold gives the name of the family who hosted them.

32. Eilat Negev interview, "Secular Prophet," 43.

33. In a later version, as told by Ruth to her nephew Navot Matan at one of their meetings in New York, they were making love when British policemen burst into the room. She "spoke up, cursing like a truck driver," in language that she had learned in the Egyptian desert during WWII, which perhaps helped get them freed. Conversation with Navot Matan, May 16, 2017.

34. See a letter dated September 17, 1947: "I went past Binyamina. The hill is still there, the hill where we sat under the fig tree [...] its trunk was split, and I tried to teach you the recorder. Until the wind came bringing a light rain and we went down laughing."

35. Lea Goldberg, *On the Blossoming*, trans. Miriam Billig Sivan (New York, 1992).

36. See his letter from the Haifa period describing the time in Binyamina: "It was our last day. The grass was verdant and springy, and the dead rested, sleeping close by. Everything around was humming and trembling and ripening." (October 18-19, 1947).

37. Ruth was asked many years later about the poem containing the line, "the British [...] locked us up for a sweet togetherness" ("'The Rustle of History's Wings,' as They Used to Say Then," *Selected Poems*, 129) when he [Amichai] wanted to marry her. She answered with a chuckle: "From the beginning." "Did you love him?" She responded: "At the beginning, no. But later I was happy rejoicing with him".

38. "You write that we've only known one another for half a year. But what is time. I spent three years in the army, and half a year with you, and you know which of these carries more weight." (October 5, 1947).

39. In a poem he wrote many years later, in great anger, about his relationship with Ruth: "For five shillings I changed the Jewish name of my ancestors / to a proud Hebrew name that matched hers" ("'The Rustle of History's Wings,' as They Used to Say Then," *Selected Poems*, 129). Amichai gave different versions for this change. He told Sarit Yishai that "I changed my name in 1946; after I was discharged from the army I was going with a young woman from the ATS. We had a very nice love affair, and decided to stay together forever. At that time everyone wanted to forget the Diaspora, and we decided to choose Hebrew names. We were full of enthusiasm for defense and socialism. So we chose the name Amichai [My people is alive]. […] But what did God do? After I changed my name, we broke up " (*Haolam Ha'ze*, March 28, 1983 [in Hebrew].) In an interview with Corinna Benning, he was more accurate about the time: two months after the name change, "we separated and I was left alone with the name;" in other words, it was the summer of 1947 (Benning interview [in German]), 248.

40. Scharf Gold, *National Poet*, 206; Benning interview, ibid.

41. When the two met many years later, Amichai was proud of the many women he had conquered, but claimed that if she had married him, he would have been faithful to her.

42. We see as much from his letters, explicitly stated and between the lines. In one he compares future couplehood with Ruth to the relationship of the couple from whom he was renting a room: at the beginning they had a book about sex, then one about raising children, and eventually, no books at all (October 19, 1947).

43. According to what the older Ruth told her nephew Navot, her main reason for leaving the country was weariness after years of serving as a truck driver in the British army, and the desire for a little rest. Interview with Navot Matan, May 16, 2017.

44. This meant working two shifts. Minutes no. 1 of the teachers' meeting at Geulah school, 1948 [in Hebrew]. History of Education Archive, University of Tel Aviv, 1.47/316. I am grateful to Alona Mendelson and Ella Trumenshleger at the archive for their help and the photocopying.

45. Yosef Yonai, "The Schools in Haifa and Tel Aviv During the War," in Mordehai Bar On and Meir Hazan (eds.), *Citizens at War* (Jerusalem and Tel Aviv 2009), 103 [in Hebrew].

46. Yitzhak Kronzon, email to the author, May 17, 2016. See also his story "The First Day at the Geulah School," in *See the Land at a Distance* [in Hebrew] (Tel Aviv 2010), 127-130, where several characters from the school staff who knew Amichai appear.

47. Minutes of the school for 5708 [=1947/48] [in Hebrew], 9.

48. In many lectures and remarks after he became a popular and sought-after poet in Israel and internationally, Amichai claimed that people tend to express positive experiences in vague terms, while suffering and pain bring out descriptions full of concreteness and vitality even in people who are not literary-minded.

49. He confesses he was flooded by the memory of the Hanukkah party at the school in Würzburg, that was cancelled because of Little Ruth's accident that day.

50. The image recalls his well-known poem "Not Like a Cypress," Poetry, 30.

51. Similarly, after a visit to Jerusalem on Rosh Hashanah, he describes and identifies with a new year's greeting notice in a newspaper (*Hamishmar*, the first incarnation of *Mapam's* newspaper *Al Hamishmar*) placed by the kibbutzim: "I was on a kibbutz where I have an acquaintance from the army, I know it from afar [...] it has a family feeling, in this Yishuv of ours." To indicate the personal connection he felt to every enterprise and institution in Palestine which published greetings in the newspaper he writes: "I use its light bulbs, I shave with its soap [...] I am a member of the Histadrut" (September 14).

52. On February 18 he wrote: "I am full of deep faith in our alignment with the progressive world against the reactionary forces [...] to the extent that I follow American journalism, I see that the persecution of progressive forces there has reached ludicrous proportions. Fear of Communism unites the petty bourgeoisie and the money moguls."

53. On January 14, 1948 the US imposed a weapons embargo on the Middle East, a decision endangering Jews more than Arabs, who had alternative sources of arms. On March 19, 1948 the US backtracked from its support of the partition plan. See Heller, *The United States*, 22.

54. The field corps was set up by the *Haganah*. Unlike companies in the *Palmach*, they were composed of citizens who continued to work and devoted their free hours to defense. In the city of Haifa (excluding its outer districts) the field corps had 500 part-time soldiers at the end of 1947.

55. Although Amichai's letters to Ruth appear to express complete honesty and a pure heart, he may not have been entirely faithful to his New York lover during

the Haifa months. In later years he suggested that he had affairs with other women during that time. In any case, when *Maariv* published a photo of him with a young woman, apparently taken on the eve of November 29, the day of the UN vote, Amichai's explanation implied that they were just good friends who spent time together. Manuscript of an article by him sent to Rubik Rosenthal, 34.1178.

56. He would continue to use the Hamlet metaphor in his best-known play *Journey to Nineveh*, against the backdrop of a crisis in his relationship with Tamar.

57. Rainer Maria Rilke, *The Poetry of Rilke*. Bilingual Edition, translated and edited by Edward Snow, introduced by Adam Zagaiewski (Farrar, Straus and Giroux, 2014), 212.

58. Prof. Efrat Gal-Ed of the University of Düsseldorf; personal communication.

59. See Shimon Sandbank's discussion of Rilke's influence on Amichai, "'Turn, Stand, Tarry': Rilke, Amichai and Looking Back," in *The Voice Is the Other* [in Hebrew] (Jerusalem and Tel Aviv, 2001), 90-98.

60. More than ten years later Amichai published a sonnet based on "The Dream," but with modifications that were much closer to the mature Amichai (*LaMerhav – Masa*, 24.1.58).

61. The meaning of the title and its pronunciation are not clear: is it hade'iya – in the sense of floating or perhaps daya, a kite (the bird).

62. In the same letter he even says: "I wrote several poems about this typographical error."

63. Scharf, Gold discusses this in *National Poet*, chapter 9, but she tends to overlook the significant differences between the poems as they appear in the letters and the book.

64. *Poetry*, 30; *Poems* [in Hebrew] 1, 98-99.

65. In memory of Yonatan Yahil. *Poems* [in Hebrew] 2, 28. https://www.eng.chagim.org.il/Literature/We-have-no-unknown-soldiers.

66. The details about Eric Wolfgang Zielenzeiger and his relationship with Ruth were documented in his son David's emails to me, February 6, 2015 and October 5, 2017. "Spice broker" according to the description in the poem in the following note, was a later line of business.

67. In the poem "'The Rustle of History's Wings,' as They Used to Say Then," *Selected Poems*, 129; *Poems* [in Hebrew] 3, 299-300.

68. On the atmosphere among students in elementary schools in Haifa at that time, including child refugees who had been forced to leave kibbutzim in the Jordan Valley and were now living on the school grounds, as seen by a student at Geulah school, see Yitzhak Kronzon, "Like a Steel Wall," *Haaretz*, November 5, 2016 [in Hebrew].

69. The first letter, an aerogram, is postmarked April 6. The second letter, written on ordinary paper, does not have a postmark.

70. Although dated June 7, it was almost certainly written April 7, given the mention of the passage of a convoy to Jerusalem "yesterday" after ten days of total siege. This would have been the Givati Brigade's Operation Nachshon on April 5-6.

Chapter 5

April 1948–Summer 1949

The War of Independence; Marriage to Tamar

SOUTHWARD WITH THE BATTALION

By the Passover break, the *Merkaz* school had shut down completely, and Amichai already knew that "in two weeks I will have to leave my teaching in Haifa to be a full-time soldier, not just part-time as I have been up to now" (letter to Ruth, April 7, 1948). He was not nervous ("the atmosphere among us is excellent, a quiet tension"), and even found the inner resources to copy out a poem for Ruth he had written that recalls the period when she was wavering between her stormy love for Abraham and starting a relationship with him: "The question is entirely simple: / will you cross the empty yard / so as to come to me, / or remain afraid."[1]

On the night of April 21, after the British army retreated from many parts of Haifa, the local *Haganah* and the Carmeli Brigade took over the city, bringing the Arab attacks to an end. Amichai's skills, along with those of others from the *Palmach* reserves, were needed in Battalion 7, which was preparing to go to the south of the country as essential reinforcements for the Negev Brigade. The latter was formed after the Second Negev Battalion had reached full strength. It was then decided to establish a territorial brigade which would defend the new sparsely populated settlement projects in the Negev, and fight for the borders of the area that would constitute roughly 60% of the state.[2] The Negev Brigade, the only brigade in the *Palmach* assigned permanently to one area, came into being in December 1947 under the command of Nahum Sarig, a member of Kibbutz Beit Hashita associated with the centrist *Hakibbutz Hameuchad* movement. Sarig was a legendary much-loved figure .[3] The Givati Brigade, commanded by Shimon Avidan (Koch), fought alongside the Negev Brigade in the battles in the south, although there were lapses in coordination between the two commands .[4]

Amichai described how men and women of Battalion 7 gradually joined its ranks as it wended its way south to its base. The battalion drew its members from various reservoirs at each halt .[5] In late April and also in early May, he and several others were sent to a camp near the Okaba razorblade factory in Rishon LeZion where they underwent training, including shooting practice, using the wall of the Rishon cemetery.[6] Further reserves were recruited from the Givat Brenner and Kvutzat Schiller kibbutzim, where there were *hachshara* (training) groups of 18 year olds and even younger.[7] These adolescent recruits were members of scout movements and *Hashomer Hatzair* (the left-wing youth movement) who had taken their final high school exams and graduated early in compliance with the National Council's Education Department directive to bolster the military effort.[8] The Cypriots, as they were called, arrived a little later. As Amichai described them: "These strong young men, who had been liberated from the Nazi camps and immigrated illegally, members of pioneer youth movements, were excellent material for the *Palmach* Battalion."[9]

THE BATTALION FINDS ITS PLACE; THE BATTLE OF ISDUD

Amichai was 24, considerably older than most of the other soldiers, and certainly those on *hachshara,* fresh from year 12, but different as well from the "Cypriots," who were Holocaust survivors. Although he had his British army service under his belt, he had not experienced the heat of battle. At that time, he was not known as a poet;[10] he was seen as "clumsy," and a Yekke at a time when Yekkes had yet to become the elite in Israeli society, and his Hebrew was somewhat different from the Sabra norm, despite his years in the school system. He served in company headquarters, under Yehuda Klein, in an organizational role as company sergeant-major (officially with the rank of sergeant).[11]

The battalion was camped initially in "the deep wadis beside kibbutz Ruhama." These wadis were concealed and provided good protection.[12] The guerilla actions by the battalion were primarily meant to signal the existence of a large Jewish force that could overwhelm the regular Egyptian army which had invaded the Negev (estimated at 20,000 soldiers, along with artillery and planes). When the State was declared on May 15, around 3,000 men and women, including members of local kibbutzim would face off against the Egyptian army.[13]

The most important battle in Amichai's life, by his own account, took place in the village of Isdud on the night of June 2-3, 1948 where units from the Negev Brigade fought alongside the Givati Brigade. The newly formed

Israeli air force intervened for the first time. Despite the severe losses sustained by the IDF in this battle, the abundant errors, and the many fallen soldiers (14 from Battalion 7, 50 altogether, including those of the Givati Brigade), it was considered a turning point in the War of Independence, since it brought about a change of strategy in the Egyptian command. On a radio program in which Amichai described the course of the war in the south, he said that Nitzanim, where the soldiers withdrew from Isdud, was more critical to him than Jerusalem, because the battle of Isdud stopped the Egyptian expeditionary force from overrunning the country.[14] The poem "Since Then" returns to the retreat to Nitzanim, and describes how he carried the body of his dead friend, believing he was still alive.[15] Years later he integrated the fierce symbolic significance and post-traumatic consequences of these events in this poem:

> I carried my comrade on my back. / Since then I always feel his dead body / Like a weighted heaven upon me, / Since then he feels my arched back under him, / Like an arched segment of the earth's crust. / For I fell in the terrible sands of Ashdod / Not just him.[16]

UZI NARKISS BECOMES COMMANDER OF THE BATTALION; AMICHAI'S FRIENDSHIP WITH DICKY; DICKY'S DEATH

Historians consider that one of the reasons for the failure of Israeli forces at Isdud was the poor coordination during battle on the part of the battalion commander.[17] He was replaced by Uzi Narkiss, who had been on the Jerusalem front in the Harel Brigade. Narkiss appointed Meir Pa'il (Pilevsky) as his deputy. At the time, Amichai formed a close friendship with battalion signaler Esther Hacohen. Esther was the daughter of David Hacohen, later a Knesset member and ambassador, son of the writer Mordehai Hillel Hacohen, a memoirist who immortalized the years of Hebrew renaissance in Russia and daily life in Palestine during the World War I. Amichai and Esther's friendship was founded on a love of classical music, as depicted in the opening of the story "Dicky's Death":

> "I ran hand in hand with the girl over the trenches and into the ditches. In the coming days, a pipeline would be laid in them. But for now, we ran there [...] It wasn't easy to make progress: a leap here, a pit there, a twisted ankle – and the oncoming night would make it harder on us [...] Why did we run, the girl and I, on the day of a ceasefire in a Negev surrounded by enemies, cut off from the north and from the sea? We wanted to get to the half-ruined house from which

the melody of Schubert's quartet was drifting. *Death and the Maiden* – the two of them, like us, at large in the world."[18]

This lively good-looking signaler impressed the new battalion commander from the moment he first set eyes on her.[19] Uzi made Esther battalion secretary, and she later became his wife.

After the battalion left Ruhama to camp at Wadi Majnun outside Kibbutz Dorot,[20] the new infantry company commander, Haim Laksberger, known as "Dicky"; i.e. 'chubby' in German, a member of Kibbutz Givat Brenner, took notice of Amichai. Dicky, born in Berlin, was four years older than Amichai.[21] One of the first to join the *Palmach*, he was attached to the "German division", and served in the Jewish Brigade in WWII. Except for short periods on the kibbutz, during one of which he got married, and where his only child was born at the end of 1947, he was totally dedicated to service, and most of all to military defense. As a Yekke it was very difficult for him to adapt to the chaos of the Palmach, and the general lack of discipline of his soldiers.[22] This seems to have been what prompted him to make Amichai his informal aide, in the hope that he would help him acquire greater authority, especially in overseeing order and cleanliness.[23,24] Amichai would later say that Dicky was completely wrong in his personal assessment: despite his German background, Amichai was disorganized.[25] However he seems to have helped Dicky with educational work with Holocaust refugees, whose mindset was so different from those born or educated in Palestine.[26] The commander housed Amichai in his tent: "Dicky [...] / who was four years older than I and like a father to me / in times of anguish."[27] Their friendship amazed the soldiers, many of whom has little esteem for Amichai. In any case, right or wrong in his judgment about Amichai, Dicky gained immortality through his poems.

Amichai often commented that Dicky's enduring commitment to the fate of the Yishuv prevented him from savoring the intimate pleasures of life. Ada, Dicky's daughter, was born in December 1947. When Dicky capitalized on the last days of a ceasefire to slip through enemy lines to get to Givat Brenner to see his baby daughter, it was the first time he had seen her.[28] "On the following night he returned and immediately began planning the maneuver."[29] The villages of Huleiqat and Kaukaba controlled the road to the Negev. "At Huleiqat the system of Egyptian fortified positions was among the strongest in the country."[30] These two villages had been captured by the *Palmach* on the eve of the Egyptian invasion but had been retaken by the enemy; it was now decided to take them again as part of 'Operation Death to the Invader', which was planned for the night of July 17-18, just before the second UN ceasefire was to take effect.[31]

It was decided that the attack on Huleiqat would be undertaken by a company of jeeps, a company of regulars under the command of Dicky, a mortar unit, and two units recruited from residents of the area, under the assumption that the fighting would not be difficult. The recruitment of inexperienced kibbutzim members, among them Italian immigrants and Holocaust survivors, amplified the impending tragedy.[32] Not all of those heading out for battle knew one another, and there was no reliable information about the Egyptian forces. The unit under Dicky's command was exposed to fire, and all its 21 members were killed. Another unit, under Solel Cohen, with Amichai as one of its number,[33] retook a minor position. Members of two squads later claimed that "they hadn't heard the order to attack over the sound of the battle, and opted to wait."[34]

The bodies of the fallen were not initially found, despite attempts to find the dead and wounded the following night.[35] Three months later a mass grave was discovered, after a bombardment of the area. The bodies of nine men from Battalion 7, 13 from local kibbutzim, and the accompanying medic could not be identified. Dicky's body could only be identified from dental records from Givat Brenner. Amichai recalled Dicky frequently in his poems in a loving and grateful way, perhaps tinted by guilt feelings he was the first to admit for having survived the battle uninjured while Dicky fell along with so many others.[36] The operation was a fiasco as a result of bad planning, and pressure to go into battle with inappropriate leadership and inadequate intelligence.[37]

Apart from the story entitled "Dicky's Death," which was first published as a kind of eulogy,[38] Amichai returned to the figure of his commanding officer and friend in the immortal poem dedicated to him, "Rain on the Battlefield," which appeared in his first book along with other war poems. Like a number of other figures in his life, particularly Little Ruth, Dicky was incorporated into Amichai's biography, and became part of his public profile. Writing about Dicky strengthened a central trope of his poetics; namely, that life and poetry are indistinguishable in verses written by an individual who needs to be unburdened of sorrows and joys, poet or not. Such occasional poems are usually addressed to or are about the writer's nearest and dearest friends or about his enemies.

Over time, Dicky became less of a real presence and more the locus of reflections about the meaning of memory. In the fifth poem in the cycle "Seven Laments for the War Dead,"[39] Dicky is described as having been hit by a bullet in the stomach, but when Amichai writes in the poem, "Dicky was hit. / Like the water tower at Yad Mordechai. / Hit. A hole in the belly. Everything / came flooding out," he is fundamentally writing about how the memory of both the dead and the living is extinguished and rekindled, falls away and reemerges in the minds of those who knew and loved them:[40] "But he has remained standing like that / in the landscape of my memory / like the water tower at Yad Mordechai."[41] In the poem "Huleikat – The Third Poem about Dicky," which is included in the "Anniversaries of War" cycle, he combines biography with exhortation, the intimate and heartfelt with the recurring dynamic of transient human lives: "Remember that even the road to terrible battles / always passes by gardens and windows / and children playing and a barking dog. // [...] and don't forget that the fist, too, // was once the palm of an open hand, and fingers."[42]

When the battalion was sent to Be'er Ya'akov, near Tzrifin, for rest and recuperation, Amichai went to Givat Brenner to see Dicky's widow, and took Dicky's satchel with him.[43] In their conversation, she clearly struggled to detach herself from the terrible pain of losing her young husband by repeatedly trying to divert the discussion from troubling questions about the reasons for his death to life on the kibbutz and its development, work and education.[44]

FATIGUE IN THE BATTALION; LATER OPERATIONS

At the end of August 1948, members of the brigade were sent north, to Be'er Ya'akov, to regroup after their failures, and mourn the many dead and wounded sustained in an attempt to retake the Iraq-Suweidan fortress. This failure nearly decimated Battalion 7.[45] They were replaced in the south by members of the Yiftach Brigade.[46] The next phase in the defense of the Negev was to complete its conquest and secure its future to nullify proposals by Count Bernadotte, the UN emissary.[47] Operation Yoav, or Operation Ten Plagues, was an attack on October 16 by a battalion of the armored brigade, a battalion of regulars from the Negev Brigade, and Battalion 7 on the village of Iraq al-Manshiyya.[48] Most of the soldiers were unfamiliar with their new equipment (which in many cases turned out to be faulty), and there were numerous communication failures among the Polish Holocaust survivors, ex-members of the Red Army, and those educated in Palestine who only knew a smattering of Yiddish or English. These factors played a significant role in the failure of the mission, which Amichai later recast in somewhat humorous fashion.[49] After a hasty retreat, Amichai was among those who reached Kibbutz Gat. Others, according to the bitter commentary of Battalion Commander Narkiss, fled as far as Hadera or even deserted.[50]

The misfortunes of Battalion 7 – the dead and wounded, and the lost battles – were redeemed somewhat when they captured Beersheva during Operation Horev. Nahum Sarig needed to work hard to convince Yigal Allon, the commander of the southern front, to divert forces from Gaza to Beersheva.[51] The conquest of Beersheva seemed to be a solvable problem that would potentially restore the shattered confidence of the Negev Brigade, which was plagued by losses. The gamble paid off, and the town was quickly taken by two companies of regulars from Battalion 7 between October 20 and 21, with relatively few losses.[52] After the conquest of Beersheva, Issachar Shadmi was made commander of Battalion 7. He went on to lead the battalion in future missions with other brigades, including Operation Lot to establish a corridor between Beersheva, and Sodom and Kurnuv, the continuation of Operation Horev to force the Egyptian army to retreat from Israel's borders, and Operation Uvda to take control of the southern Negev as far as Eilat. At that time Amichai was a service conditions officer at headquarters.[53]

CONTACT WITH LEA GOLDBERG, AND FIRST SIGNIFICANT PUBLICATION

Beginning in March 1949, the Palmach brigades were dissolved and made part of the IDF (the Negev Brigade was disbanded in May).[54] Soldier Y. Amichai, who was on active duty, felt that this was the right time to write a letter to the poet Lea Goldberg.[55] Although Goldberg was not yet considered one of the leading poets of her generation, she was nevertheless a significant presence on the literary scene as a poet, an editor at Sifriat Poalim, the publishers of the *Ha'Shomer Ha'Tzaïr* movement, and as a theater and literary critic. Amichai was surely aiming to convince Goldberg help him enter the holy of holies that was *Sifriat Poalim* and the literary magazine of the journal *Al Hamishmar*, both then major literary venues.[56] He may have also felt a special connection to Goldberg: they shared a background in German culture, and the appeal of classical forms, particularly the sonnet.[57] He may also have been attracted by her use of a "softer," feminine symbolism than that of her contemporaries Alterman and Shlonsky. Amichai's interest in Goldberg and his decision to contact her followed a pattern noted in studies by the Russian Formalists in the 1920s and 1930s that poets of younger generations relate to and are influenced by marginal and relatively spurned poets of previous and earlier generations.[58]

In his letter to Goldberg, Amichai says he was sent her collection of poems "From My Old House," published in 1946, by "someone very dear to him [Ruth Hermann perhaps]. I often read it, in lulls in the fighting or in the gloomy emptiness of the Negev, and it did me good."[59] He states that he is 25 years old and has been "writing now, more or less continuously, for four years." He distances himself from other poets who were "fighting comrades [in the Palmach, such as Haim Gouri and "Ayin Hillel" – Hillel Omer] [...] who have published: because for some reason I did not want my poems to go the same way as theirs." Perhaps he meant that stylistically he did not want to follow in their footsteps.

Amichai enclosed four poems in the letter: "Two Poems in the Isolated Negev," which are annotated "Ruhama, March 1948" (the date cannot be right, and he probably meant May of that year), and "Two Poems to

Delilah,"[60] written, he says, a week before. There is a considerable disparity between "Two Poems from the Isolated Negev" and the other poems enclosed, "Two Poems to Delilah." The poems composed at the beginning of his stay in Ruhama are rather childish, bordering on banal, and recall the poems sent to Sadan in 1945, and not the best of them at that. "Two Poems to Delilah" are already more evocative of the "great" Amichai, or at least anticipate the beginnings of Amichai's many-layered plurivocality. He alludes here in complex ways to the biblical story of Samson: the honey that Samson scooped out of the carcass of the lion he split open is found by the male character and probably the speaker of the poem "deep in you" (the beloved), but this deep-lying honey, with its supposed softening and sweetening properties, causes the man to "split you with his love", which is suggestive of the violent pursuit of love of the early Amichai (and to some extent also later). The beloved, the object of desire, is ripped "from yourself" just as the gates of Gaza were ripped "bars and all" from the ground.[61] This violent uprooting is necessary for the female character because without it she cannot go beyond herself and achieve erotic union.

Roughly three months after the letter was sent to Lea Goldberg, the literary section of *Al Hamishmar* printed three of Amichai's poems. These poems are somewhat reminiscent of "Two Poems to Delilah," but the stark brightness of the Delilah poems has become a different, remote kind of illumination, more suited to the convoluted and non-linear perspectives of Amichai's poetry. The two lovers – the "we" of the cycle – pursue knowledge and understanding in a way typical of young people; they want to know what makes for a worthy life, and their goals.[62] They live with a sense of the greatness of their time, wanting to learn from everyone, including simple people ("we wanted to learn above all from others"), but everyone they meet has their own questions about the right way to live ("'give us teachings,'" they said). In the end, this sought-after knowledge is only found beyond life, in death ("we don't know, we're still alive"), unlike Mount Hermon which do know, but is "white and dead." The poem ends with an apparently contradictory message manifesting Amichai's deep plurivocality: the very power of knowing may lead to the conclusion that further movement is worthless, but stasis is itself death. As soon as a water turbine stops making electricity, it is "suddenly quiet, after the turbulence, / and that was death, inability."[63]

FIRST WRITINGS: BIOGRAPHY AND AUTO-POETICS

Amichai was frequently asked whether he had written poems (or other pieces) during the war and would emphasize that he had not at that time, or in the throes of love.[64] He generally claimed that he only wrote – or began writing – at the end of the war. Sometimes he made this claim as part of his friendly sparring with Haim Gouri, who returned from outreach work in Europe in July 1948 and was appointed deputy company commander under Avraham "Bren", Adan, in Battalion 7 by Yigal Allon. Amichai would often praise Gouri the poet, although he may not have been entirely sincere. Gouri, certainly when he was writing his first books *Flowers of Fire, Wedding, Poems of the Seal,* was influenced by the poetry of Alterman and Shlonsky, who represented everything Amichai wanted to avoid. In a late interview he called Gouri "the *Palmach* poet," and said that "we loved his poetry."[65] At an evening honoring Gouri, six months before Amichai died, he lavished fulsome praise on Gouri, in a voice weakened by illness: "When he came to us, he gave the whole Negev Brigade the spirit of poetry in war. He was a poet who actually spoke on behalf of everyone. I remember that we all loved 'Here Lie Our Bodies.'"[66] Amichai may not have been expressing his true feelings. However, perhaps during the war, before the horizons of his poetry had finally taken shape, he identified with Gouri's poetry.[67] As death approached, he may have indeed concluded that despite all his reservations, "we belong together, like two hands and two feet," and came to see Gouri and himself as two complementary faces of the spirit of their generation at the inception of the State.[68]

When Amichai was asked to present his war poems on the radio in November 1973, soon after the Yom Kippur war, he reacted angrily that "the very fact that I am suspected of having an immediate poetic response humiliates the man in me, the soldier, and the poet too [...] Things take a lot of time [...] A poem is a very slow process, and we need to accept that."[69] As with the poetics of restraint and emotional refinement developed by Natan Zach, Amichai also maintained that a good poem is written when the storm of emotion has subsided.[70] At times, however, Amichai acknowledged that he did write between battles. In wartime he saw writing as a way to "preserve one's own thoughts," an occasional practice that was not necessarily aimed at publication or sharing: "Between battles I wrote what were almost small testaments, small legacies, last wills, feelings I could keep and carry with me."[71]

Intentionally or otherwise, Amichai had difficulties saying when he began to write seriously. In an interview with Larry Joseph he said that he had thought at first that others were doing a good enough job of expressing what he felt, but "in the late forties" he began to consider writing himself. In the same breath he said: "I began to write poems in the early fifties. I was attending the Hebrew University." With the support of Prof. Halkin, a literature teacher at the Hebrew University, Amichai published his poem "Other Evenings" in the journal *Gilyonot* which was edited by Yitzhak Lamdan in the spring of 1951. In other words, he dated the start of his publishing career to the time when the literary establishment recognized him, despite the fact that the poem he published in *Gilyonot* was quite weak (he did not include it in his books), and although he had already published in *Al Hamishmar*.

We know today that Amichai wrote and translated poetry – apparently quite regularly and frequently – as of 1943 or 1944,[72] but more than once preferred to attribute his first writings to psychic frailty or depression brought on by the wars: "I needed the words to keep me going," he told Harshav and Hartman, after completing his tour of duty in the War of Independence.[73] Ten years prior to this interview he made a similar comment: "Seven years of wars and loving. And so in a primitive way I realized that there are two things in life: war and love. And that they have to be together."[74]

MEETING AND MARRYING TAMAR HORN

Tamar Horn, born in 1929, whom Amichai married towards the end of 1949,[75] was the daughter of a doctor, entrepreneur and partner in the Tzori pharmaceutical factory.[76] Gadi, Tamar's brother, states that she first met Amichai at their parents' home in Tel Aviv on Hayarkon Street. They were neighbors of Amichai's sister and brother-in-law, "their doors literally facing one another". Amichai's letters show that he visited his sister every now and then, since at that time they had a good relationship.[77] However, in a letter to Ruth Hermann dated October 12, 1949, Amichai says his first encounter with Tamar was when she was a secretary in the office of Brigade Commander Sarig in October 1948, apparently towards the end of the battle of Iraq al-Manshiyya, when he was among those who retreated from the atrocious fight. In the novel *Not of This Time, Not of This Place* he describes Ruth, the character based on Tamar, as someone he "met in the war in the sandy sunken valley." "Later she visited him in the Dajani Hospital in Jaffa, while he was recovering from a leg wound."[78]

That October, Amichai had been out of the army for three months.[79] He had begun teaching at a primary school in Jerusalem, and planned to go to the university,[80] apparently with the encouragement of Tamar's family, when he unexpectedly received a rare letter from Ruth Hermann-Zielenzeiger. In his reply he told her about the presence of Tamar in his life, and its significance for him: "You won't be surprised if I tell you that in exactly another two weeks I will take Tamar to be my wife, a woman who has already been my woman for a year. Who is Tamar? You will surely know her from the kind of literary writing you shared with me from time to time. She is one of those created so that poets will sing of joy and not only of quandaries." After describing his first meeting with her at battalion headquarters, he adds: "All this happened a year ago. Since then we have been on many trips, from Galilee to Eilat on the Red Sea [...] A lot of honeymoons, and now we will tie the knot. She's 19.[81] Once you told me that I would end up marrying a girl. Here we are quite simple. Two plants sprouting in war. We have a kind of passion, a kind of smiling wisdom and quiet planning."

His description of meeting Tamar, her character, and their relationship just before their wedding prefigures what would subsequently transpire. Tamar was a beacon of light in the dark underbelly of the war. Although he writes about her with great enthusiasm and hopes of happiness, there are also hints of renunciation, and acceptance from the beginning of something missing in terms of his high ideals. Unlike his letters to Ruth that were filled with talk of deep, mutual intellectual understanding and reaching a shared creative goal, his description of Tamar is more evocative of hopes of tranquility, comfort and happiness within achievable limits.

When Amichai tells Ruth about his relationship with Tamar and says that "we have a kind of passion, a kind of smiling wisdom and quiet planning," he is testifying to the restraint that had come with maturity and experience. In his poems written during his first years with Tamar there is a tone of acceptance. He ends the sonnet "Military Operation," in his second book *Two Hopes Away* (1958) with the line "But the border guards of possibility / permitted us to enter their domain."[82] There are intimations in the poems he wrote during their time together (between 1949 and 1958, and again after a separation, from 1960 to 1963) that his leonine appetite for intellectual wholeness, freedom, and his imagination that broke with normative bounds, remained unsatisfied, struggling as he was to momentarily "furnish with grace/ Even a lion's maw."[83] Even the jet plane that closes the famous poem "The Smell of Gasoline in My Nose" – that "makes peace in the sky for all, / For us, and all those who love in the fall,"[84] signifies, in light of the images in Amichai's letters, a peace of the resigned, a fabricated harmony between despondent lovers. The jet, as shown in his letters to Ruth, is an image of sober maturity, in which disappointments are digested and kept to oneself: "being an adult is to think, speak and be like a jet, uncomplicated and bright."

In the letter quoted above, written two weeks before his wedding, there is a hint, in language that is still soft and containing, of the problems that will later emerge between them: her unease about his egocentricity that points to her inability to accept his uniqueness, and his needs as a poet intent on his work and on goals that are out of the ordinary.

UNENDING ROMANCE?

Almost a year after Ruth's surprise letter to him, hinting at problems in her marriage and hinting perhaps at reviving their relationship,[85] Amichai sent her one of his own, on August 2, 1950. He tells her about his difficulties, this time, his growing awareness that perhaps he had chosen badly and allowed life to sweep him too far from what he had hoped to build. The letter starts by discussing an impending war – most probably the Korean War opposing the US and the Soviet Union and later China.[86] It is clear however that Amichai was more engaged in the war of his own life and was trying to be rescued by love: "Perhaps we can hope that we two will be Noah and weather the flood." This is how he writes to a woman whose marriage he had accepted nobly and maturely more than two years earlier. "Ruth, it just isn't true that a person is of only one mind; one part of me remains with you. Take good care of it, big girl."

This April 1950 letter precedes one written in August 1950, but seems in fact to complete the later series of letters to Ruth: "Dear Ruth, with this we will finish our 'second meeting' of four letters. This meeting was full of friendship, straightforwardness and maturity, tinged perhaps by sadness. Let's not write anymore to one another. Our connection does not depend on letters or even on meeting. If life brings us together, all well and good. If not...".

However, this chapter in his life with Ruth Hermann was not over. When Ruth donated Amichai's letters to the Heksherim archive at Ben Gurion University she refrained from including one he wrote her while on reserve duty at Sarafend-Tzrifin on August 3, 1951. It was written in answer to one she sent him in Tel Aviv, probably to his sister's address. What is amazing about it – and which amazed the letter writer himself – is the strength of his feelings for Ruth, which had not abated three years later and after two years of marriage to Tamar. "I never thought it would be possible to love across light years of distance and place." "I will take you with me inside, and though I will drink from you, you will not be depleted in me, you will go on being within me." Although he did not feel it was necessary to make plans to end his marriage, he saw the possible future relations between them as an "oasis."

Almost a year after the death of Ruth's father Leo Hermann, Amichai sent a letter congratulating her on the birth of David, Ruth and Eric Zielenzeiger's first son. He shares an arresting image from his inner life: "The past often stands to one side, like a sad animal, and watches what we do, remaining quiet." He says that after moving a number of times, and being evicted from their last apartment, he and Tamar bought a three-room apartment on 14 Mitudela Street that was spacious enough in those days to be considered close to luxurious. Amichai, then on summer vacation, was using his time to catch up on his university coursework, and sometimes, with the power of a patiently contained incubation process, as he put it, "words come to the surface and float, and then life becomes abundant, rich and ripe." He goes on to quote the famous adage in *King Lear*, "ripeness is all."

NOTES

1. This is the first version of one part of "In the Public Garden" [in Hebrew]. The later version is in *Poems* [in Hebrew] 1, 191.

2. For a general background about the War of Independence, see Martin Gilbert, *Israel: A History London 1998)*, chapters 9-14; Sachar, *A History of Israel*, chapter 13; Anita Shapira, *Israel: A History* (Massachusetts, 2012), chapter 7. For more detailed descriptions of the battle for the Negev (south of Israel), see Sachar, ibid, 339-353; Shapira, ibid, 166-170.

3. Amichai would show his fondness for Sarig in his final book, *Open Closed Open*. Lines from the poem are engraved on Sarig's headstone (1914-1999). See Yuval Barkai, "His poems of bereavement present the war in all its horror and nakedness" [in Hebrew], in *Hadash Baemek*, September 29, 2000.

4. According to Sarig, in an interview with historian Anita Shapira, handwritten manuscript [in Hebrew]. Anita Shapira Archive, National Library, 1933 Arc 4° 1 51. For more on Sarig as the Negev brigade's commander, see Anita Shapira, *Yigal Alon, Native Son: A Biography* (Philadelphia, 2008), 214-5, 245-6.

5. Amichai, "Journey in the Map of the Past" [in Hebrew], *Bamachane*, January 2, 1962, 10-11.

6. *Mareh Makom*, program on Israel Army Radio, edited by Sarale Doron, June 10, 1988. The cemetery firing wall is also mentioned in Amichai's story "Dicky's Death" (*The World is a Room*, 113).

7. These young people underwent a training period with the Palmach while living on a kibbutz where they worked half of the time, and trained the other half. This was also preparation for founding their own new kibbutzim.

8. The records in the information center of the *Palmach* Museum give a more exact and detailed picture than can be gleaned from Amichai's recollections, but concur in the essentials.

9. Amichai, "Journey in the Map of the Past", 10.

10. Hanka Yisraeli-Halperin, secretary of the company, recalled that Amichai wrote "limericks for the Negba comrades on *hachshara*" (postcard from her on Kibbutz Bar'am, to Amichai [1994], 13.628), and that he wrote a poem for her when she injured her leg (conversation with Hanka, September 6, 2015). These were not preserved.

11. Conversations with Hanka Yisraeli-Halperin (previous note), Esther Hacohen-Narkiss (February 24, 2016), and Avraham Benkel (June 19, 2017), who were among the young people on training with Amichai in Battalion 7.

12. Amichai, "Journey in the Map of the Past."

13. For other estimations of the power relations between the Egyptian invading force and the two Israeli brigades, see Benny Morris, *Righteous Victims: A History of the Zionist-Arab Conflict*, 1881-2001 (New York, 1999), 227-228.

14. Mareh Makom. Cf. Morris, *Righteous Victims*, 229-230.

15. *Poems* [in Hebrew] 3, 269; Amichai, *The Great Tranquility: Questions and Answers*, translated by Glenda Abramson and Tudor Parfitt, 1. Another translation, *Life of Poetry*, 310. Cf. a passage in Amichai's journal (notebook May 1988-June

1990), where he talks about sensing the living dead: "Saul [the King]and his sons fell on their swords, so we fell on our souls. Some of us died immediately, most of us go on twitching and dying for another 60 or 70 years."

16. See also Amichai's late treatment of the Battle of Isdud in part 3 of the poem cycle "In My Life, On My Life," from *Open Closed Open*, in *Poetry*, 478; *Poems* [in Hebrew] 5, 245.

17. According to one historian, the soldiers of Battalion 7 did not take part in this battle; they lay in the sand waiting, and when the order was given to retreat "they began fleeing for their lives in total disarray. Armed Arab inhabitants of Isdud saw the rout and came out to harry stragglers." Moshe Givati, *On the Road of Desert and Fire* [in Hebrew], 104-113.

18. "'Dicky's Death," *The World is a Room*, 111-112.

19. Uzi Narkiss, *Soldier of Jerusalem*, 86.

20. The records of Kibbutz Dorot mention welcoming the battalion on June 19. Dorot, June 19, 1948 [in Hebrew]. The battalion got to the kibbutz some days earlier, after its failed attack on the Iraq Suweidan garrison on the night between June 10 and 11.

21. Sources in the Palmach Museum: Memorial Book; Stories from Givat Brenner [in Hebrew]; membership card of Haim Laksberger.

22. "Dicky loved educating Hanka and all the trainees. Like a father, he would teach them not to yell, to be clean and decent, how to dine politely." "Dicky's Death," *The World Is a Room*, 115.

23. Over the years this role evolved into the position of first lieutenant, in Amichai's own description on the radio program *A Small Anthology*, on Voice of Israel, November 13, 1973; but Amichai never held that rank.

24. "Dicky's Death," *The World Is a Room*, 114.

25. Interview of Amichai with Avirama Golan, Educational Television, 2000 .https://www.youtube.com/watch?v=9BoF_nqh_WU

26. Perhaps the line, "Like me, a man of hills and a man of wars, / Who sang a lullaby to his soldiers before the battle" (referring to Shmuel Hanagid, the Hebrew Spanish poet and general of the eleventh century), hints at this educational role. *A Life of Poetry*, 409; *Poems* [in Hebrew] 5, 11.

27. "Huleikat – The Third Poem About Dicky," *Selected Poems*, 179; *Poems* [in Hebrew] 5, 14.

28. "Dicky's Death," *The World Is a Room*, 116; article by Eilat Negev, "The Face of My Comrade" [in Hebrew], *Yediot Acharonot*, September 22, 2005.

29. "Dicky's Death," ibid.

30. Israel Carmi, *In the Way of Warriors* [in Hebrew] (Tel Aviv, 1964), 322.

31. On the whole affair, see Ardon Cohen, Michael Cohen, and Amos Mendelsson, *The Negev Brigade in the War of Independence* [in Hebrew], (Tel Aviv, 2011), 206-207; Givati, *On the Road of Desert and Fire*, 178-184.

32. See especially Tali Lipkin-Shahak, "The Lost Battle" [in Hebrew], *Maariv*, February 3, 2006, 13-17.

33. Interview with Dalia Karpel, "Hoping for the Nobel" [in Hebrew], *Ha'ir*, November 3, 1989.

34. Givati, *On the Road of Desert and Fire* [in Hebrew], 183.

35. Avraham Benkel of the scouts' division of the regiment, personal communication, June 9, 2017.

36. In the interview with Hollander-Steingart, "In My Heart Is a Museum," he talks about the natural guilt feelings of those who were still alive after battles, and compares this to Holocaust survivor guilt.

37. Brigade Commander Sarig was in the hospital after a car accident at the time, and the battle was planned by his deputy, Haim Bar-Lev. Opinions are divided about the shortfall in planning and information. In their book *The Negev Brigade* [in Hebrew], Cohen, Cohen and Mendelson do not take the position that there were significant failures in planning.

38. It was published in *Mibifnim* (From inside), the literary quarterly of *Hakibbutz Hameuchad*, the kibbutz movement to which Givat Brenner belonged.

39. *Selected Poetry*, 92-96; Poetry, 221-225; *Poems* [in Hebrew] 3, 107.

40. On this, cf. Dan Miron, "Safeguarding the Vessels and their Repair: A Discussion of Now and in Other Days," in his *Facing the Silent Brother* [in Hebrew] (Tel Aviv, 1992), 271-314; Miron, "Open Closed Open;" "Revolutionist with Father" in his *More!* [in Hebrew] (Tel Aviv, 2013), 259-279.

41. *A Life of Poetry*, 410.n

42. *Selected Poetry*, 180.

43. "Dicky's Death," 118. There is a structural similarity between the description of his meeting with Dicky's widow and with the cooper of the Rishon LeZion winery, Yitzhak Erlich's father, in the late poem "Yitzhak's Last Kit Bag," *A Life of Poetry*, 386; *Poems* [in Hebrew] 4, 172-173. Yitzhak Erlich fell along with Dicky in the Battle of Huleiqat. When in May 1992 the poem was republished for Memorial Day in *Maariv*, Yitzhak's niece, Lea Rashkovsky, responded with a letter drawing on the poem to describe "the fermentation [...] that will never cease" in her family over the years after the death of her uncle. 10.463.

44. Further details can be found in an article by Eilat Negev, "The Face of My Comrade" [in Hebrew], *Yedioth Acharonot - 7 Days*, 22.9.2005.

45. For Amichai's perspective, see his interview with Eilat Negev, "The Secular Prophet" [in Hebrew], *Yedioth Acharonot - 7 Days*, 3.4.1998.

46. Carmi, *In The Way of Warriors* [in Hebrew], 324.

47. Shapira, *Israel – A History*, 166-170.

48. Today the industrial zone of Kiryat Gat is located on the site of the village.

49. Hartman and Harshav interview.

50. Narkiss, *Soldier of Jerusalem*, 64-67. In the English version of his book this 'desertion' is referred to more allusively. Amichai also rescued a wounded soldier in this battle. Personal communication, Menachem Regev from Kfar Warburg, October 10, 2015.

51. Meir Pa'il, who at the time of Operation Yoav was Deputy Battalion Commander of the Staff Department of the Negev Brigade, was present at the meeting between Sarig and Allon. See *Me'irke - Chapters of Life and Articles* [in Hebrew] (2014), 48-49.

52. For a description of the battle, its background and consequences, see Narkiss, *Soldier*, 69-70. On the atmosphere in the brigade on the eve of the conquest of

Beersheba, and the actual taking of the city, see Haim Gouri, *Until the Break of Dawn* [1950], in *The Imprint of Memory*, vol. 1 [in Hebrew], (Jerusalem and Tel Aviv, 5775 [=2014/5]), 51-59.

53. Amichai attributed his position to the shrapnel wounds he sustained, but this may not be accurate. In any case, in a list of ranks from first private to first sergeant major for Battalion 7, Brigade 12 (the IDF designation for the Negev Brigade) dated June 2, 1949, Sergeant Yehuda Amichai appears as a staff sergeant. Archive of IDF and Security Branches. I am grateful to Michael Cohen for this document.

54. On the disbanding, see Shapira, *Allon*, 251-256.

55. Gnazim Archive, 274 5644 /1 [in Hebrew].

56. Motti Neiger, *Publishers as Cultural Mediators: The Cultural History of Hebrew Publishing in Israel* [in Hebrew], (Jerusalem, 2017), 379-396.

57. For more details, see Gideon Tikotzsky, "'At Desolate Moments of My Life, I Read It, and It Was Good for Me'" [in Hebrew], *Ot* 1 (Autumn 2010), 217-219; as well as his *Light Along the Edge of a Cloud* [in Hebrew] (Tel Aviv, 2011), 141-143.

58. See Victor Erlich, *Russian Formalism* (The Hague, 1955), chap. xiv.

59. Apart from Goldberg, Amichai mentioned Sh. Shalom (Shalom Shapira), another outsider in the Alterman and Shlonsky generation, and particularly his book *Face to Face*, as a possible influence. Interview with Alex Zahavi, 'Poetry as Comfort' [in Hebrew], *Davar*, May 7, 1976. Amichai also indicated his special love for Tchernichovsky, Bialik's "second" ("More beloved than anyone," in a poll conducted by Haim Nagid, "Tchernichovsky Who?" [in Hebrew], *Yediot Acharonot*, October 1, 1993).

60. When Lea Goldberg died at the beginning of 1970, he affectionately recalled in a poem the book that had given him comfort in difficult hours: "In the Negev battles her little book / From My Old Home was always in my kit bag. / Its pages were torn and stuck together / with Band Aids, but I knew / all the hidden words by heart / and also what was revealed." "Leah Goldberg Died," *Poetry*, 185; *Poems* [in Hebrew] 2, 290. See Tikotzsky "At Desolate Moments." In 1976 a small book of Goldberg's poems was published in English translation by Amichai's friend Robert Friend, with a short forward by Amichai. Here he again recalls his time as a soldier in the War of Independence, carrying her slim volume in his knapsack. Yehuda Amichai, foreword to Leah Goldberg, *Selected Poems*, translated and introduced by Robert Friend (London 1976), 9.

61. Judges 16:3. King James translation.

62. They study "the destiny of lovers, of nations" from the burlesque novel *Till Eulenspiegel*, written by the 19th century Belgian author Charles de Coster. The book describes the King of Spain's cruel suppression of the Protestant rebellion in the Low Countries.

63. See Miron, *Facing the Silent Brother* [in Hebrew], and idem, *More!* [in Hebrew].

64. Larry Joseph interview, 7.

65. Harshav and Hartman interview.

66. "Here Lie Our Bodies" was written on January 17, 1948 when Gouri, who was in Budapest at the time, was told about the convoy of 35 soldiers who were killed in an ambush on their way to the Etzion Bloc to relieve the kibbutzim there.

67. See the quote from Amichai's letter to Goldberg, above.

68. Gouri himself described the profound generational difference between himself and Amichai (even though Amichai was only a year younger) in an example he would often return to, conveying the twinge of jealousy he experienced on first reading Amichai: "When after several days I reread this poem ["I see you standing by the wide-open fridge door, revealed / from head to toe in a light from another world"] I thought about this illuminated woman. An ordinary woman involved with everyday living. Her face is not lit by the mythical candle, by a gothic or pastoral light [as in Alterman], or even by a Palmach campfire [that we would find in Gouri's own poems] [...] but by the quiet matter-of-fact light of the domestic fridge, the tiny almost bourgeois light. [...] 'And That Is Your Glory' point[s] to an innovation in style and spirit – as if an era is beginning. Time's up and something different is emerging." "The Reverse Fridge Method: On Yehuda Amichai" [in Hebrew], *Maariv*, April 5, 1985; republished in Gouri's *On Poetry and Time* [in Hebrew], vol. 2 (Jerusalem, 2008), 292-5.

69. *A Small Anthology* (radio show) [in Hebrew], Voice of Israel, Radio 1, November 13, 1973.

70. "When the feeling dies down, the true poem speaks," Zach noted (*Collected Poems* [in Hebrew] 1, 295). As Wordsworth maintained: "Poetry takes its origin [...] from emotion recollected in tranquility."

71. Larry Joseph interview, 7.

72. See Chapters 3 and 4.

73. See his response to Yigal Sarna's question, in Sarna's article "People of War," *Yediot Acharonot – 7 Days*, May 5, 1989, "when did your war first become a poem?": "It took about four years, first in the 1950s, when I just decided to think about everything that had happened to me, and the thoughts got formulated as words in a kind of personal therapy."

74. Interview with Sarit Yishai, "Writing Poems Is Like Chewing the Cud" [in Hebrew], *Haolam Haze*, March 28, 1983.

75. "Announcements of Marriages Registered with the Offices of the Rabbinate [...] in Tel Aviv" [in Hebrew]. Among the entries: "Yehuda Amichai ben Meir (Pfeuffer) from Würzburg, Jerusalem and Tamar Horn from Kassel, Tel Aviv." *Hatzofeh*, September 28, 1949. Tamar came to the country with her parents when she was three or four.

76. Conversations with Gadi Horn, May 16, 2016, and May 28, 2016. In Gadi's opinion, his sister only had a very short career in the army. He thinks Amichai's description of the encounter taking place against a backdrop of war and battles was the fruit of his poetic romanticism.

77. In any event, Rachel Pfeuffer saw herself as the matchmaker, and felt very guilty when Amichai left Tamar, and later divorced her.

78. *Not of This Time* [in Hebrew], 349.

79. The Palmach Regiment, functioning now as part of the IDF, began disbanding in spring 1949. The Negev Armored Brigade existed until autumn 1949, but Amichai was not connected to this part of the regiment. See Shapira, *Yigal Allon*, 251-57.

80. According to the letter cited here, dated October 12, 1949 and sent from 15 Shatz St., Jerusalem.

81. Tamar was born in 1929, so she was then nearly 20.

82. *Poetry*, 23; *Poems* [in Hebrew] 1, 78.

83. "I saw you could live and furnish with grace / Even a lion's maw, if you've got no other place." From "I want to Die in My Own Bed," *A Life of Poetry*, 37; *Poetry*, 34; *Poems* [in Hebrew] 1, 118.

84. *A Life of Poetry*, 11; *Poems* [in Hebrew] 1, 25.

85. Ruth's letters to Amichai did not survive. We only know of their content from his reaction to them, in this case his letter dated October 12, 1949.

86. The new State of Israel found itself involved in the decision that the government had to make to openly support with the United States. See Joseph Heller, *The United States, the Soviet Union and the Arab-Israeli Conflict, 1948-67* (Manchester, 2012), 22-23.

Chapter 6

1949-1955

University Education, the Trip to the US, Amichai's First Book

AN AMBIVALENT RELATIONSHIP TO WAR AND SOLDIERING

In his short story "Battle for the Hill" Amichai writes that "In wartime [...] boys are promoted to the rank of adults and ripen too quickly.[1] Whoever breaks, breaks, and those who return no longer have the patience to sit and await their turn like those pitchers.[2] They want to be useful and functional right away. They want a coat of glaze before they are even dry. Later, when the cracks begin to appear, they will be irreparable." Amichai came out of the War of Independence psychologically wounded and seemingly defeated. In his famous poem "From Then" he wrote:

> "I fell in the battle of Ashdod / In the War of Independence. / My mother said then, He's twenty-four years old, / And now she says, He's fifty-four, And lights a memorial candle [...] // Since then, my father died of pain and sorrow, / And my sisters got married / And named their kids after me, / And since then my home is my grave, and my grave – my home. [...] // And since then I compensate myself for my death / With love and dark feasts."[3]

Although the details in the poem are not autobiographical, it does hint at inner destruction, and a need to overcome, if not depression then a gnawing sadness, by means of "love and dark feasts." Similarly, a prose piece he wrote some ten years after the War of Independence describes the need to engage in intense sexual relations to dispel his corrosive feelings.[4]

Throughout his life, Amichai appears to have maintained an ambivalent relationship toward war and everything associated with it: life in the army, in particular being in the company of men, proximity and handling weapons and other military equipment, the threat of death and injury. In a journal entry, perhaps a draft of a poem which is hard to date but certainly relates to the experience of the War of Independence, he writes out of bodily, sensory revulsion, not necessarily out of an antiwar ideology: "I hate / the world of men at war. / Wet iron, / Stones instead of pillows / [...] / Ugh! / Ugh!"[5] Perhaps this disgust at the male world of military life explains why he would flinch at the touch of men, and preferred the company of women, to the point of wishing he were a woman to be able to utter the blessing "who hath made me according to his will. And his will is woman."[6] He was no less ambivalent about the *Palmach* identity that clung to him as a result of enlisting and serving in unfortunate heroic Battalion 7 of the *Palmach's* Negev Brigade.

Nevertheless, it was important to Amichai to emphasize his military past. He liked to recall that he was 'lightly wounded' in the War of Independence;[7] he even allowed interviewers, and those introducing him to audiences at various venues, particularly in the US and Germany, to state he had participated in five or six wars, and to situate him in the tradition of soldier-poets, or poet-warriors. Despite his justifiable reservations about belonging in literary terms to the *Palmach* generation, and his disgust with the mores and "legacy of the *Palmach*,"[8] he was drawn to his fellow soldiers who fought during the War of Independence, and liked to associate with them. This may be because he, like most Israelis at the time, saw these men and women, who had fought body and soul to establish the State, as an elite.[9] However this attraction was also replete with conflicts related to his desire to expose the inaction of part of Israeli society, and the hypocrisy of many during the War and after it: "He planned to get drunk one evening with several comrades from those days and suddenly jump up, pound on the table and shout: 'Lies, lies! All the stories about the War of Independence are nothing but lies! And he would keep shouting, that only very few took part in actual battles and that most of the people lived at the expense of the few and that there had been [little] volunteering."[10]

THE STATE IS BORN BUT THE MESSIAH DID NOT COME

The emotional reaction to the establishment of the State for those in the country is perhaps best described by sociologists: "The story of Israeli society is one of flawed fulfillment. Israel's development has been accompanied by high expectations for the achievement of collective goals which were inspired by an ideology shared by the vast majority of the population and the dominant elites. While some of these collective goals, at the outset, entailed a strong utopian component, others could not be achieved without mobilizing considerable resources [...]. Under such circumstances, the social system became overburdened with competing collective tasks."[11]

The literature and journalism of the time clearly expressed the disappointment and frustration of the old-timers, those born in the country or who had immigrated while still young, with the concretization of the age-old Jewish dream, or the younger, political Zionist dream to achieve an independent State.[12] In a well-known poem, written 30 years after the founding of the state, Amichai expressed the pride and distress of his generation: "When I was young, the whole country was young. And my father / was everyone's father. When I was happy, the country / was happy too, and when I jumped on her, she jumped / under me. The grass that covered her in spring / softened me too [...] and when I sank / she began to sink with me."[13]

Various factors contributed to this profound disappointment among old-timers and "natives": the poverty and depletion of the young country after a terrible war in which thousands of its young people died, the paucity of resources and infrastructure, despite the Yishuv's investment and building over the decades preceding the establishment of the State, rationing of food and other essentials in the first decade of the State to accommodate the waves of *aliyah,* which more than doubled the population of Israel in a decade, and the miring of government institutions in cronyism, along with an inflexible and alienating bureaucracy. The most troubling issue, however, was the absorption of the vast waves of immigration from Europe (mostly Holocaust survivors) and the Arabic-speaking world, which created enormous economic, educational, and cultural challenges for the State and its long-time inhabitants.[14]

Amichai and the cultural elite in the first decade of the State also considered that they were threatened by another dark cloud associated with Israel's relationship with the world. At that time, tensions between the Soviet Bloc and the West, and in particular the US and its allies in Western Europe, was intensifying. Fear of annihilation if nuclear war between the superpowers were to break out was widespread, and occupied the thoughts of numerous intellectuals in Israel and the rest of the world. Israel at that time was hesitating between allegiance to the East or the West, for ideological and political reasons. Efforts to ease the plight of Russian Jewry encouraged Israeli leaders keep channels with the Soviet Union open in the eventuality that it would allow Jews to emigrate .[15]

This was the turbulent period in which Amichai the poet and writer emerged. The previous five years had been spent experimenting with various forms of poetic expression, including the translation of his favorite poets (Morgenstern, Rilke, Auden).[16] Amichai had in fact espoused his destiny as a poet and writer ever since his stint in the British army map division outside Cairo. Thus, it would be a mistake to see Amichai as a late bloomer.

However, his public breakthrough was indeed relatively late and dated to the summer of 1949, when he was already 25. The birth of the State seemed then to miraculously coincide with the appearance of a crystallized poetic gift and originality.[17]

THE DEATH OF AMICHAI'S FATHER AS A THEOLOGICAL AND POETIC POINT OF DEPARTURE

In the last year of his life, when he knew his days were numbered, Amichai told David Ehrlich, the journalist and owner of the literary café and restaurant Tmol Shilshom, how his father had died in his arms from a sudden heart attack in 1951 at age 62, in very ordinary circumstances: he had just noticed a cat on the roof of the house.[18] However, his father had suffered from health problems for quite some time.[19] Amichai's relationship with his father was part of his complex psychic economy, and his father is present, sometimes centrally and sometimes more on the sidelines, in dozens of poems written throughout Amichai's life. In a number of interviews Amichai claimed that his intense preoccupation with his father, much more than his mother, was due to his father's early death, since his mother died at 88 (in 1983).[20] This explanation is consistent with his view that absence is the source of poetry, and perhaps of creation in general. Clearly, however, his father's early death is not the only reason, and perhaps not even the main one, for his frequent appearances in his poems.

Amichai saw his mother as an eternal optimist, always protecting her loved ones against negativity.[21] In one interview he describes her as a flexible woman, ready to waive religious prohibitions in certain exceptional circumstances. During the War of Independence, he was given leave on Yom Kippur (5709, 1948). "I came to see my parents at the synagogue. We parked the jeep a little way away. My mother insisted that I come home with my comrades, and she cooked for me. On Yom Kippur! And she was a very religious woman. She said: 'God who makes wars cannot prohibit us from eating.'"[22] Her desire to protect and support her family, to the extent that she would argue with God about His ways in the world, emerges in the poem "To Mother": "Like an old windmill / two hands always raised to shout to the sky / and two lowered to prepare sandwiches. // […] At night she puts all the letters / and photos side by side, // to measure with them / the length of the finger of God."[23]

His father's personality was more complex. Amichai's father was very proud of him for serving in the army and fighting for the Land of Israel. From this perspective they were not in conflict. Neither did he ostracize or mourn his son after he became secular (as was typical in Eastern European Haredi culture). Nevertheless, their arguments about keeping the commandments were bitter and long-lasting and according to Amichai, his father was very disappointed at his decision to become non-observant.[24] He often spoke – and wrote in poems – about his father's patience and good nature. However, during Yehuda's childhood and early adolescence, Friedrich attempted to impose the mitzvot. In an interview with the poet Howard Schwartz, Amichai suggested that leaving religion was a natural process of maturation; just as in adolescence one leaves childhood behind, he realized that his father had faults, and that he also saw the flawed nature of the world, which contradicted the idea of divine providence.[25] He sometimes claimed that the disagreements with his father were a dialogue within himself, and did not create disharmony; they could still communicate.[26] However, when the interviewer Schwartz asked him if he felt that his father "still whispers in his ear," he laughed and said, "it's more that he tugs on my ear."

His relationship with his father remained in limbo. His father's good deeds flowed from "the rivers of his hands," as he put it in an early poem.[27] Friedrich Meir Pfeuffer did not hate or persecute anyone; perhaps the only people he despised – an abhorrence he passed on to his son – were civil servants or agents of religion and the government, who he saw as out for themselves rather than working on behalf of the community.[28] In the eyes of his son the poet, his father's relation to war and his compassion for the defeated enemy were a model to be emulated.[29] He was beloved, but also represented traditional Judaism, whose beliefs and practices were so problematic for the poet.

Amichai related how as a child, perhaps because his mother adored his father, he tended to equate his father with God. He seems to have thought that if one addresses God as "Our Father our King" (Avinu Malkeinu, an iconic prayer on Yom Kippur), one could call one's father God. His father was his personal god, and this was perhaps the equation at the root of Amichai's daring similes, the most striking feature of his poetry. This basic equation enabled him to infer that all things can be compared to one another: heaven to earth and earth to heaven, the holy to the mundane and the mundane to the holy, the exalted to the lowly and the lowly to the exalted. Behind these parallels was a profoundly democratic vision, no less theological and ontological than political. In Amichai's world there is no supreme being; all existences are equal.[30] In an interview for *Contact* weekly, he developed the idea that it is no coincidence that people have "two halves, two of everything" such as eyes and nostrils. This doubling gives perspective and allows for comparison, and thus a valid understanding.[31] In other words, the parallelism whose importance Amichai occasionally compared to the invention of the wheel is actually the prototype of thought or at least one of its central mechanisms.

ELEMENTARY SCHOOL TEACHER IN THE 1950S AND 60S

In the 5710 academic year (1949-1950), Amichai became an elementary school teacher in Jerusalem, and some years later also taught at an Evening School for Working Youth to supplement the household income. In an interview in 1973, he noted that "when I began writing, I was also a teacher. I wasn't pampered. I worked two jobs in an elementary school."[32] One year, 1956-1957, right after receiving his teaching certificate, he also taught at Gymnasium Rehavia, but did not remain in this position long, perhaps because of discipline problems.[33] During this time or a little later, he taught at the Luria school, which opened in 1955 in an apartment building at the end of Palmach Street, which was walking distance from his home.

What we know about his life as a teacher and his feelings about work come mainly from what he wrote in his stories, as well as some scanty archival material, and a conversation with Malachi Beit-Arié, emeritus professor and former Head of the National Library.[34] As Beit-Arié remembers it, Amichai, the only male on the teaching staff, was given the tough classes, and the failures, such as the children of refugees from the Old City. Most sources agree that Amichai taught class eight, and also taught arts and crafts, such as drawing to other classes .[35]

In 1955 and perhaps earlier, he began teaching at the Evening School for Working Youth. In the story "Ballet in Jerusalem,"[36] he describes the unappealing school atmosphere: the pupils are tired after the day's work; much of what he says "fails to make an impression on the young people and is like chaff in a field."[37] He felt both stressed and stimulated by the young people around him. The pupils, on the verge of adulthood, are described as caging him in, besieging him with questions, but when they leave him alone and keep their distance, he feels empty and weak. He was interested in the female pupils, and according to one of his stories, "Battle for the Hill," when he encounters one of his ex-pupils, there is an erotic tension. In the story he is asked to report to his unit before the Sinai Campaign. "Along the narrow walled pavement, a former pupil of mine knelt to fix her shoes [...] She looked pretty in the beam of the flashlight [...] As she sat, her body seemed to fill out. Not so my thoughts, which were pointed [...] 'I don't understand you,' she said [...] 'Now I'm grown up and pretty, and I sit before you [...] and my thighs are full.'"[38]

He also felt pressure in the staff room. Amichai states that his famous poem "Out of Three or Four in a Room," which is often seen as about people in wartime ("Compelled to see the injustice between the thorns and the fire on the hill. // [...] Behind him the words. And before him, / voices that are straying without packs, / Hearts without provisions, prophecies without water", with further imagery of banishment and displacement,[39] was actually "written in the staff room. There was a teachers' meeting in Katamon at the Luria school, and I went to the window and looked out to see the view of Beit Hakerem." His comments in "God Has Pity on Kindergarten Children" in which the subject of war seem even more present and self-evident, are no less surprising since Amichai states that it is not a war poem at all. It was written on a crowded bus from Tel Aviv to Jerusalem, as he was rushing to get to his teaching job at 8 AM. The crowded bus, "the fear before the week's work [...] this is what gave birth to the poem."[40] This does not mean that these poems should be interpreted as being about the experiences of a teacher under pressure at work. However, their immediate source of inspiration should caution the reader against attributing far-reaching meanings and global significance to Amichai's poetry.

STUDYING AT THE HEBREW UNIVERSITY

Tamar's parents found it difficult to accept that their son in law would simply have a career as a schoolteacher, since they were also concerned about who would take over the factory. The issue of succession plagued the three founders of the Tzori business.[41] The Horns wanted Amichai to study chemistry or pharmacology, which were altogether outside his interests and aptitude; but he felt under pressure to advance his prospects, and decided to register at the Hebrew University in the Hebrew Literature and Bible Departments, probably at the beginning of the 1950-1951 academic year.[42]

Amichai was not a typical college student for that era. He was a little older than most, and married. Dan Miron, who was also a student at that time, noted that there were other relatively mature students, including the poet Haim Gouri in their classes (Gouri was studying Hebrew Literature and French), but Gouri was "a perpetual adolescent" in appearance and behavior. Amichai was a levelheaded adult, and earned the affection of others with his soft and easygoing personality.[43] Some years later, in honor of the 60th birthday of his distinguished teacher of Hebrew literature at the university, the poet, novelist and researcher Shimon Halkin, Amichai described his misgivings about going to the university.[44] Sitting in class felt like a return to childhood after his adult experiences, "but I finally forced myself [...] and so it was that, at an age when others remove the scaffolding of their lives, I began to raise new scaffolding behind which I hoped to alter the structure I had become familiar with."

A quarter of a century later, when Amichai was talking about his favorite places in Jerusalem on the radio program "A Poet in His Town,"[45] he presented his university days in a very down to earth way : "When a man of 26 or 27 goes to study – and if he is already married – there's already no question of just hanging out and enjoying things. You go to class, take exams and that's it." However, judging by what he wrote in honor of Halkin, this period meant much more for him than just taking exams toward earning a degree. "I, who already wanted to immerse myself in a field where there are few achievements, saw that my world was expanding and developing. I sometimes had a feeling of happiness."[46] The encounter with at least two of his lecturers was a source of influence and inspiration. One of these was Halkin, who was born in a city in White Russia and immigrated with his parents at age 15 to the US. Although he earned his degrees there in English literature, like many Litvaks[47] he saw Hebrew as key to his cultural identity, and made it the language of his oeuvre. In 1949, having lived and worked in Palestine for several years during the 1930s, he was made Head of the Hebrew Literature Department at the Hebrew University, when Prof. Joseph Klausner retired. Halkin cut a troubled figure, perennially wavering between his vocation as a writer and his duties as a professor and researcher, and pained by the faint response to his poems and prose, which were considered difficult and accessible to only a few.[48]

As a creative writer, Halkin took an interest in students who tried their hand at writing literature. After Amichai started going to Halkin's lectures at the suggestion of friends,[49] he approached him one day after class. Halkin recognized him as someone who kept "texts with diacritical marks added, as is characteristic of published poetry" in his pockets. This led to a closer connection, and with his professor's endorsement, his poem "Other Evenings" was accepted for publication in the literary magazine *Gilyonot* which was directed at the time by Yitzhak Lamdan.[50] "I got a lot of encouragement from the conversations in his office, which was like a wondrous cave of books." Amichai considered Halkin to be "the creator for whom literature was a matter of life and death."[51] Nineteen years later, in laconic words of tribute on Halkin's 80th birthday, Amichai described the publication of the poem in *Gilyonot*, which was known for its conservative literary tastes, as a dramatic moment in his life: "It was no coincidence that Halkin awoke me to a more conscious creativity, and one of my first poems was published in Lamdan's *Gilyonot*. The day I got Shimon Halkin's approval for being a real poet was a day of great celebration."[52] Halkin selected a poem to his taste, one with a prose-bound heaviness reminiscent of his own style. Amichai's enthusiasm may in part have been due to being received by old-school mainstream writers.[53]

Another teacher who had a strong influence on Amichai, which would be more recognizable in later years, was Haim (Yefim) Shirmann, born in 1904 in Kiev, who completed his secondary and college education in Germany. Shirmann's appearance was somewhat outlandish and his lecturing style was dry, according to a student and classmate of Amichai's, the future professor Benjamin Hrushovski-Harshav.[54] Shirmann's research approach was "descriptive," which seemed thoroughly unsophisticated to Harshav, who was then beginning to specialize in New Criticism. Still, the encounter with the classic poets of Spain, who Shirmann introduced to his young rebellious students, was highly significant for Amichai's poetry, and for his classmates' understanding of the continuity in Hebrew poetry across the generations.[55] Shirmann's descriptive method had an advantage from their point of view: it was free of ideology, which literary critics of the time often interjected into their discussions, to the disgust of Amichai and his friends. This dislike did not, however, necessarily apply to the then prevailing ideology per se. In any case, they preferred Ibn Gabirol, the proto-existentialist. and Shmuel Hanagid, the sheer pessimist, to the "Zionist" Yehuda Halevi.[56]

In Amichai's third year at the Hebrew University, in 1954, he submitted a seminar paper to Shirmann entitled "The War Poems of Shmuel Hanagid." The essay was graded "very good," despite Shirmann's view that it was "not written according to a unitary method [...] nevertheless, the writer's literary and psychological analyses testify to an independent approach."[57] Luckily, Amichai preserved this assignment in his archive. It clearly shows the roots of his particular sensitivity to Hanagid's fate, personality, and original poetic perspective.

Shmuel Hanagid's influence on Amichai was fourfold (the latter two relate to medieval Hebrew poetry in general as a source of inspiration). The first is formal: the quatrain, four rhyming lines, often found in Hanagid's poems, even though there is, strictly speaking, no form in HaNagid corresponding to what Amichai began to write in 1957. The second is structural-meditative in that a poem takes an everyday concrete experience as the springboard and point of origin, and then internalizes it, giving the trivial occurrence symbolic or contemplative implications. Many of Amichai's poems embody this structure, where there is a transition from an everyday event to contemplation of its context and significance for the observer or the broader context. Three examples from his early books are illustrative of this influence: "I waited for my girl and her steps were not there. / But I heard a shot – soldiers / training for war. / Soldiers always train for some war" ("I Waited for My Girl and Her Steps Were Not There"). "On the radio they're reading the news – / but in our hearts it's all old stuff" ("Lovers in Autumn");[58] and the poem "Out of Three or Four in a Room."[59] The third type of influence emerges in poems dealing with personality and fate of poets of the Middle Ages (Ibn Gabirol, Yehuda Halevy). The fourth type is his use of terms typical to Hebrew medieval poetry, such as *nedod*, *zman*, and *ne'urim* in their classical rather than contemporary meanings.[60]

THE LIKRAT CIRCLE AND THE PUBLICATION OF AMICHAI'S FIRST BOOK

Amichai's years at the university resulted in significant acquaintance and involvement with literary circles, and ultimately a long-awaited breakthrough in the reception of his poetry. From time to time a group of literati would meet at Yehuda and Tamar's apartment. These included Benjamin Hrushovsky (later Harshav), educated at Hebrew and Yiddish schools in Vilna, a Holocaust refugee who went to Palestine, enlisted in the *Palmach* and took part in the controversial battles for Latrun;[61] Ruth Weinbren, later Nevo, then a young immigrant from South Africa, for whom reverberations of the Holocaust had stirred a dormant Jewish identity; and the immigrant US English literature teachers Shalom Yaacov Cohen and Robert Friend.[62] Under Ruth Nevo's guidance, the group read Eliot's "The Waste Land" in 1951 and 1952.[63]

Harshav later discovered that Tamar had preserved two hundred poems of Amichai's in a closet. "Amichai's responsibility was to write, and hers was to safeguard what he wrote," as Harshav put it humorously. "I took a few poems of his, including "The U.N. Headquarters in the High Commissioner's House in Jerusalem," which seemed to me at the time too prosy and current, and we published it in *Likrat*".[64] Harshav was in fact referencing a poem published in *Likrat* 3, after the journal had already published poems by Amichai, beginning with the second mimeographed booklet. He thus somewhat erroneously saw himself as responsible for Amichai's being discovered and with the latter's association with the *Likrat* group.

Natan Zach, who would later be a leading poet in the state generation and who quickly took over Harshav's role as leader of the Likrat circle, described how Amichai joined the circle, and emphasized the personal connection between them. Zach originally interested him in publishing in the journal put out by the group, and apparently also encouraged him to bring out his book with the group's new publishing company. They first met when Zach heard that Amichai had received a prize for a poem in a competition held by the university.[65] It should come as no surprise that Zach and Amichai hit it off so well given their Yekke background, their cultural common interests, and their receptivity to the same poetic currents.[66]

According to his son Ron, Amichai tried to publish his first book of poems with one of the publishing houses connected to the Labor movement.[67] But Avraham Shlonsky, the managing editor of *Sifriat Poalim,* thought that Amichai, the "new immigrant,"[68] did not know Hebrew well enough and was only parodying classical poetic forms. Amichai may have remembered the icy reception he received from the literary supplement of *Lamerhav* journal when the editors rejected a poem he sent them on the grounds that it lacked an optimistic message.[69] Apart from the first poems published by *Al Hamishmar* thanks to help from Lea Goldberg, three further poems that came out in the same paper in 1951, and the poem appearing in *Gilyonot* on Halkin's recommendation, his only published work in newspapers and journals before his book came out was in *Likrat* and one poem in *Mevo'ot*, which was run by the *Mapai* political party.[70] The poem, "Now That the Water Presses Hard," may have been accepted in *Mevo'ot* for its relative simplicity and clarity.

Zach, who initiated *Likrat's* publishing operations by bringing out books by himself and several other members of the group, pushed Amichai to let *Likrat* handle his book. Amichai had already accumulated hundreds of poems, of which only a tiny fraction had been published. A source of funding for the book's production was found: Tamar's father, one of the owners of the Tzori pharmaceutical company, agreed to contribute 500 liras with the proviso, which was perhaps not difficult for Amichai to comply with, that it would not include a poem in praise of Stalin composed upon his death.[71]

There is no doubt that Zach shepherded the publication process of Amichai's book with love and meticulousness,[72] but the extent of his involvement in its editing and its final form is unclear. Harshav indicated that Zach shortened Amichai's poems drastically, which seemed to him verbose and unfocused;[73] in particular he cut "Rain Falls on the Faces of My Friends," which originally included lines that detracted from its main thrust.[74] Harshav and Zach's version had a considerable influence on Dan Miron when he described Zach as making "drastic edits" to the book *Now and In Other Days*, which involved rejecting most of the poems Amichai submitted to him and shortening those that remained."[75, 76]

Amichai tended to see Likrat more as a social framework than a literary circle, where he was at most a "passive member."[77] When he tried to characterize the poets of the statehood generation whose nucleus was composed of the members of Likrat, he claimed that their uniqueness lay in their biographic and stylistic variety, in contrast to the rather uniform backgrounds and upbringing of the poets of the *Palmach* generation. He himself was unique in that his preteen years were spent in the Diaspora, and because of his observant background. As he himself put it, his father passed on a "treasure" which he made use of, even though he was not himself observant.[78]

In any case, he was reluctant to go along with the emphasis Zach placed on creating theoretical foundations for the poetry of the statehood generation. It was important for him to describe himself as an "unaware" poet, writing the way a simple person writes, out of emotional excitement and suffering. Thus, when comparing himself to members of the Likrat group, Amichai rather disparagingly stated that they were always writing manifestos, while he wrote poems.[79] In fact, his rebellion against the poetics of Alterman, Shlonsky and their generation was a conscious one, and in lectures and interviews he would often return to his differences with them. Alterman in particular was at antipodes to everything that he sought to achieve in poetry, so that even Bialik, who was more of a grandfather than a father, was closer in his eyes to the ideal: "Alterman [...] wrote about his daughter – but this was a generalized daughter, just as the mother was a generalized mother. In Bialik, in poems about his parents' deaths ["My Father," "Widowhood"], you see real parents, not symbols, not generalized."[80] In the only lecture by Amichai that I attended, he spoke about Alterman's Romanticism, which prompted him to write about the sword instead of the pistol or rifle, unlike his own poetry, where every-day familiar objects appear. The poetics he shared with Zach and other prominent figures of the group (including Avidan, who joined later), is clear: writing in language tending towards the unembellished and the mundane that deals with topics from the world of the individual, distancing from major national issues bound up with ideology, and attempting to shake off the dominance of biblical or traditional verse.[81]

A YEAR IN THE US WITH TAMAR

In the 1950s, only the affluent in Israel could travel abroad. Yehuda and Tamar, who chose not to have children in the first 11 years of their marriage because they wanted to "make the most of life,"[82] took a year off from their jobs, and lived in New York from the late summer of 1954 until the spring of 1955.[83] Amichai entrusted the manuscript of *Now and In Other Days* to Zach, almost certainly after approving the corrections and changes suggested by Zach, before embarking with Tamar on the cargo vessel Rimon. This was the cheapest way of getting to the US. The captain only agreed to allow them on his ship if they disembarked at the first port they reached, and so they left the ship in Maine.[84]

The poems "Three Sonnets from the Voyage" and "A Room Beside the Sea"[85] suggest something about Amichai's, and perhaps Tamar's frame of mind on the way to New York. The poems mainly convey the couple's need for the world to let them be and to disconnect from the web of responsibilities entangling them in Israel (Sonnet 3). In the sonnet "A Room Beside the Sea," there is a sense of fatigue, frustration ("a citadel of self-restraint on two legs") and perhaps also the couple's continuing impasse, where the problems between them remain unsolved even on this long holiday ("And afterwards I again spun doubt / into a flag [...] / and watched how it flapped).[86]

Something about his first "American period" and the couple's journey home via Europe can be gleaned from his stories entitled "In This Terrible Wind," "An Evening of Poetry" and "A Poet's Landscape" (the latter two are closer to journalism). An event from this time is also described briefly in the novel *Not Of This Time*: the narrator's chance encounter with the *mohel*, the man who performed his circumcision and served as a cantor of the synagogue in Würzburg.[87] The title story, "In This Terrible Wind," shows how he dealt with the distress arising from his own personality, and perhaps also from something wanting and broken between him and Tamar. His curiosity and lively desire are expressed in what was perhaps an imaginary relationship he forms with a young woman in "Fun City," an amusement park. He tells her about Israel, and about his childhood in Germany, and how in childhood he was able to sense the essence of the soul. The story ends with a description of a sexual encounter with the woman on the beach, her clothes torn from her in the wind, similar to the clothes ripped off in one of his first poems about his relationship with a prostitute in Alexandria.

THE VENERATED AUDEN READS

In the middle of a New York winter ("it was a winter's day, and it was only by chance that there wasn't snow") he encountered a poet who had already played a significant role in the crystallization of his poetics: Wystan Hugh Auden. However, this no less importantly confronted him with his lost youth, and the dreams of justice and redemption, which he had abandoned with the sobriety of maturity.[88] Accompanying him that evening was Lottie, a New York nurse, who was almost certainly Jewish, and according to the narrator of "An Evening of Poetry" had been his friend-lover in Jerusalem when he was around 18, after graduating early from high school: "We were beside one another like two dominos. But we knew that the other side of each of us was different, and connected to far and distant things." Perhaps there is a real basis to the story, and he had this type of relationship during his time in the Coast Guard or in the period of transition after it.[89] The other person who attended the poetry reading with them was Lottie's life-partner, a cynical engineer working on "electronic brains", more or less the first computers. He prophesized that "one day it will be possible to write poems using an electronic brain. How? They will take all the words and combine them in all the possible permutations."[90]

That evening bore into the narrator "like a drill mixing up what was past with what was present," as he recalled reading Auden's poems in the army camp outside Cairo. Here in New York, he felt an essential thread connecting him to the love and faith of his youth, and to the time he first encountered the best of British and American poets, in the anthology of modern poetry chanced upon in a British library on wheels near Cairo. However Amichai, who looked up to Auden and absorbed his influence in a number of ways, felt that the great poet was not at his best that evening, and in any case was not the lyricist he had come to know more than a decade before.[91] Like lovers who attempt to ward off disappointment by looking for the excuse that will exonerate the beloved: "I told myself: he is certainly not reading his true poems, but is keeping them to himself. When he saw the curious public, the hippies and the bored intellectuals, he hid his true poems and read these poems of mockery and parody, to entertain them."

He felt that Auden had aged, in mind and body. When Lottie asked him how he knew this, since he had never seen him before, he tells her: "But I've read his poems." His reception of Auden's poems during WWII conveyed to him the very embodiment of youth. Auden's early poetry, which he discovered from the anthology, expressed an ideal: it was "comforting [...]. Good poetry has to be calming, like a nursery rhyme, lulling one to sleep, providing comfort, regularly repeating serene lines, ending quietly. A warm home [...], a mother's apron, a father's hands." "Bucolics," a poem cycle written two or three years earlier, which Auden read that evening,[92] was not bad in his view, "but I wondered inwardly what Auden was making of himself, and so I didn't laugh like others in the audience."[93]

It is not clear whether when listening to Auden, he read himself into him or whether there really were parallels in their lives. As the short story tells us, he too, like the poet addressing the audience that evening, had dreams of fighting on the Republican side against the monarchists in the Spanish Civil War. Auden indeed went to Spain, but recoiled from the violence of the Republicans and their debasement of religion, and went home.[94] As the narrator sees it, participating in the Spanish Civil War could resolve an inner conflict: one could be a soldier and fight in the pursuit of world peace. The picture he gives of Auden that evening comparing him to a child pulling a toy car on a rope and continuing to drag it around even after the car is broken, may have applied to him too. If he immersed himself in a bourgeois life of limited aspiration, there was a danger that his poetry would be undermined and lose its primal authenticity.[95]

TO ENGLAND AND WALES: PILGRIMAGE TO THE GRAVE OF DYLAN THOMAS

After a seven or eight month stay in the US, Yehuda and Tamar left at the beginning of April and headed to London.[96] The goal was a pilgrimage to the Welsh village where the lyric poet Dylan Thomas had lived in adulthood. Amichai wanted to physically experience the landscapes where the poet lived, the poet whom Amichai had first met, like Auden, in the selection of poems in the Faber anthology. Thomas had died a year and a half earlier in

New York at the age of 39, of causes apparently related to alcoholism and inappropriate medical treatment. During his short life he astonished readers with his wild and richly associative poetry. Thomas was also known as an excellent performer, often reading his own poems and those of others before public, mainly in his final years.

In response to a request for information, Amichai received a letter from the administrator of the Welsh county of Dylan's home town, giving details about Thomas' village and the address of his mother, "resident of the county town of Carmarthen, not far from the poet's village." Amichai was appalled by the town with hotels whose names all involved puns on pork, people loitering in pubs, the pictures on the walls of cockfights. In the morning light the town looked different, not "grudging" and full of "beer fumes and the smell of cock's blood."[97] Thomas' mother welcomed them cordially as arrivals from the Holy Land. There was no need to encourage her to recollect. "Her voice was fresh and her speech well-formed and crystalline, conveying clear and exact pictures." When a few days later he heard a recording of Dylan Thomas reading, "the similarities of the speech of mother and the son, and his imagery, became clear to me." Perhaps he was thinking also of himself in relation to his parents: "The qualities of the parents, who are still ordinary, are developed and become genius in the son."

The couple then moved on to their main destination, the village of Laugharne, where Thomas lived with his wife and children until his death. Thomas also spent considerable time in London working mainly as a radio scriptwriter (including his best-known radio play, *Under Milk Wood*). "And even though we come many years after the discovery of Copernicus, I thought that here in Thomas' village was one of the ends of the Earth, one of the far reaches of my life." "Many generations have lived out their lives in these rooms, among books [...] without thinking at all about the fact of their deaths." Although Amichai and his wife had no clear destination when wandering around the village, they kept to their initial plan to sense out the poet's adult environment.[98] "A map of Dylan Thomas' poems led us on our walks," among other places to Fern Hill, made famous by the wonderful eponymous poem by Thomas. Amichai saw a similarity between Dylan Thomas and his own writing: an event occurring during the writing of a poem becomes part of the poem (in the case of Thomas, the screeching of seagulls).[99]

At the end of their stay in the village he felt that he had "fulfilled my intention" to perpetuate the memory of Thomas in his heart, by reading Thomas' poems in Jerusalem. There were multiple parallels here as well: "There was some reciprocity between me and the landscape, and sometimes it sang to me in a voice harmonizing with my life."[100]

NOTES

1. "Battle for the Hill," in *The World Is a Room*, 19.

2. The metaphors of clay vessels were inspired by a friend of Amichai's, the potter and painter Herbert Applebaum, who had considerable influence on him

3. *A Life of Poetry*, 310. https://pij.org/articles/212/three-poems.

4. "At the Inn, on the Way to the Battlefield" [in Hebrew], *Lamerchav – Masa*, September 21, 1960.

5. 35.1235.

6. "Travels of the Last Benjamin of Tudela," in *Selected Poetry,* 66; *Poems* [in Hebrew] 2, 125-126. In the story "The Orgy," Malka, seemingly the ex-lover of the narrator, tells him: "You've already tried to switch with my body; you entered me, but only a little part of you penetrated. You'll never be able to be me" (*The World Is a Room*, 129).

7. Talk given in honor of the publication of Uzi Narkiss' book, *A Soldier of Jerusalem*, 32. 34.1191. In *Not of This Time* [in Hebrew], 349, too, he recalls a wound of this sort and hospitalization in Al-Dajani Hospital in Jaffa, where Tamar visited him.

8. This is expressed in the novel in a number of ways. Minzer, the painter, makes fun of the atmosphere and songs at *Palmach* gatherings (*Not of This Time*, 102). In the poem "The Young David," David's loneliness contrasts with the typical *Palmach* types: "The noisy ones in their armor [...] / thumping on shoulders, shouting hoarsely. / And someone cursed and others / spat." *Poems* [in Hebrew] 1, 147.

9. See his article "A Divided Soul" [in Hebrew], *Yediot Acharonot*, December 26, 1997.

10. "Love in Reverse," *The World Is a Room*, 151. The story is set during the celebrations of the first decade of the State of Israel, in 1958.

11. Dan Horowitz and Moshe Lisak, *Trouble in Utopia* (Albany, N.Y, 1986), 231.

12. Harshav writes about the state of mind of young people when the State was founded, in terms of the ways they responded to bureaucratic overreach, protectionism and the policy of austerity: "Any all-embracing ideology was suspect. The hypocrisy of public expression was revealed for what it was." The warping of the Communist ideology and the news of Stalin's state-terrorism and mass-murder regime also contributed to this sense of despair. Benjamin Harshav, "Personal Reflections on Amichai – Poetry and the State" [in Hebrew], *Alpayim* 33 (2008), 121-139.

13. *Selected Poetry*, 116; *A Life of Poetry*, 279; *Poems* [in Hebrew] 3, 214-215.

14. For the perspective of a friend and member of Amichai's circle, and his future English translator, see Harshav, "Personal Reflections"; idem, "On the Beginning of Israeli Poetry and Yehuda Amichai's Quatrains," in his *The Polyphony of Jewish Culture* (Stanford, Ca., 2004), 175-182.

15. On the political struggle in the new State of Israel in relation to the conflict between the major powers, see Heller, *The United States, the Soviet Union and the Arab-Israeli Conflict*, chapters 1-2.

16. Letter from Amichai to Lea Goldberg, Gnazim Archive 5644/1. See also Ticotsky, "At Desolate Moments" [in Hebrew], 215-226; Elad Zeret, "Between Amichai and Goldberg" [in Hebrew], *Yediot Acharonot – 24 Sha'ot*, December 21, 2014, 10-11.

17. Nili Scharf Gold discusses Amichai's creative output before the War of Independence, based on his letters to Ruth Hermann. Scharf Gold, *National Poet*, chapters 8-9. However, her book was written before the publication of his poems from Egypt.

18. Interview with David Ehrlich, June 12, 2017; Negev interview, "I am a Happy Man."

19. Letter to Ruth Hermann in which he discusses his father's poor health, February 16, 1948. In the story "The Times My Father Died," *The World Is a Room*, 192-193, the character of the father is hospitalized with serious heart problems, but recuperates at home. Amichai's father died a few weeks after he was discharged from the hospital.

20. Esther Fuchs interview, in her *Encounters with Israeli Authors* (Micah Publications, 1982), 90. In an interview with Joseph Cohen, after describing the bitter arguments he had with his father when he stopped being observant, he explains that: "The memory of my father is vivid, for he died at the height of his powers. My mother, by contrast, slowly became an old woman, so I got used to her ageing gradually." Joseph Cohen, "Yehuda Amichai," *Voices of Israel* (New York, 1990), 36.

21. "Battle for the Hill," *The World is a Room*, 11. The protagonist's mother is described there as "my mother who used to calm us by saying about everything that it was nothing. If it was a blistering hot she said: "Just another summer day". When it hailed she said, "How pleasant the air is, so mild and fresh! It's good that it's not too dry. It's good there is no drought".

22. Edna Evron interview, "National Poet? That's All I Need!" [in Hebrew], *Haaretz*, October 22, 1999. Amichai states that this took place on Yom Kippur 5708 (1947), but this is clearly an error. On Yom Kippur 1947 the War of Independence had not broken out and he was not a soldier.

23. "To the Mother," *Poetry*, 35; *Poems* [in Hebrew] 1, 131. According to Boaz Arpali, "the finger of God" is God's involvement in the world, and measuring its length can be interpreted as assessing the extent of justice stemming from God's involvement. Arpali, "Words 'Not of This Time, Not of This Place'" [in Hebrew], *Hasifrut* 29 (December 1979), 45. See also the portrait of his mother in the poem "Autobiography in the year 1952," *Life of Poetry*, 7.

24. Joseph Cohen interview, 36. His father would speculate why the Jews had kept their faith throughout all the years of the Diaspora, but now that they were in their own land, many were abandoning an observant way of life. Amichai would answer that in the Jewish community in the land of Israel, and then in the State, there was no need to prove one's Jewishness, which was natural and taken for granted.

25. Howard Schwartz, "A Way to Reality," *The Jerusalem Post*, February 17, 1978.

26. David Montenegro, "Yehuda Amichai: An Interview", *American Poetry Review*, 16: 6, November-December 1987, 20.

27. "My Father," *Poetry*, 16.

28. In his first play, *No-Man's Land*, Amichai expressed hostility to officialdom and his view that bureaucrats were superfluous. This short play was first performed at the Zavit Theater in 1962. It was published in *Bells and Trains* [in Hebrew] (Schocken, 1992; Expanded edition: 1992), 49-77.

29. As described in the first poem of the cycle "We Loved Here" (*Selected Poetry,* 38) and in Amichai's most frequently translated story "The Times my Father Died", in *The World Is a Room*, 185-197.

30. See Dan Miron's discussion in a similar vein, "Revolutionist with Father," in *More!* [in Hebrew], 291-292, 294-295; as well as Amichai's remarks in an interview with Anat Levit, where he sheds some light on the association between his poetics and his ideology: "God is found everywhere. All laws carry the same weight. Either everything is holy or everything is profane. I don't believe in hierarchy. I don't accept it in political life, and certainly not in intellectual life." Anat Levit, "To Sing the Small Love Song" [in Hebrew], *Iton 77*, 72-73 (January-February, 1986), 24-25.

31. Aloma Halter, "Poems, Prayers and Psalms," *Contact*, July 26, 1991, 11.

32. Interview with Bina Barzel, *Yediot Acharonot*, June 1, 1967. Amichai provides a fabricated date for the inception of his writing of 1949, at the end of the war.

33. Personal file of Yehuda Amichai in the archive of Gymnasium Rehavia. I am grateful to Dr. Jules Amouyal, literary studies coordinator at the school, for giving me access to Amichai's file.

34. Conversation with Malachi Beit-Arié, April 13, 2015.

35. As much is suggested in a letter from principal Hadassah Brill, concerning a brawl where a student got hurt during an art lesson with Amichai, "near the Saint Simon monastery." January 20, 1961. 7.340. More on the atmosphere at the school can be found in Amnon Birman's reminiscences of his conversations with Amichai: "The school was visited by the police at least weekly." Birman, "Yehuda Amichai" [in Hebrew], *Kol Ha'ir*, September 29, 2000.

36. First published as "The London Ballet in Jerusalem" [in Hebrew], in *Lamerchav-Masa*, July 13, 1956. Collected in *In This Terrible Wind* [in Hebrew], 177-184.

37. Ibid., 177.

38. "Battle for the Hill," *The World Is a Room*, 30. Something similar appears in the story "Eat and Drink" [in Hebrew]. In the story "Small Pleasures of Summer" [in Hebrew] (*In This Terrible Wind*, 238-246), he describes the same sort of tension and interest – which he keeps to himself – about a 17-year-old student at the school (245).

39. Carmi, *Penguin Book of Hebrew Verse*, 569.

40. Interview after the publication of his *The Hour of Grace* (1982) or *From Man Thou Art and Unto Man Shalt Thou Return* (1985), source not clear. Descriptions of writing under pressure and stress are recurrent in Amichai, and he talked explicitly about such experiences as sources of his poetry; e.g., in his responses to the survey "Writers Tell About Their Works" [in Hebrew], recorded and edited by Ida Zoritte, *Lamerchav-Masa*, May 8, 1958.

41. Interviews with Clarice Kestenbaum, Amichai's lover in the late 1950s, New York, September 4, 2015, and Gadi Horn, Tamar's younger brother (May 28 and August 16, 2015), confirm this general account.

42. Amichai's college registration forms could not be found in the university archive. Nevertheless, a number of documents bearing on the period when he taught at the university have been preserved including his time in the theater department, though mainly at the Rothberg International School for Overseas Students. According to one form he filled out, he studied at the Hebrew University from 1950 to 1954. On other occasions he indicated that he also studied there in 1955, when he was starting his masters' degree.

43. Radio interview with Dan Miron. Miron describes him as "dressed in a suit"; "a bourgeois figure, very pleasant, with a fine countenance, a warm voice, friendly. He has already published poems, but did not behave like a poet 'superior to common people.'"

44. "Students Write About Their Teacher – Halkin's Students on His 60th Birthday" [in Hebrew], *Lamerchav-Masa*, November 13, 1959.

45. Israel Army Radio, May 28, 1976. Program edited by Joel Rappel.

46. "Students Write About Their Teacher."

47. The Litvaks were Jews from what is today Lithuania, White Russia and the northeastern part of Poland, and had their own specific culture, customs and Yiddish dialect.

48. This was the spirit in which Alex Zahavi, a student of Halkin's just a few years later, described Halkin in the special edition of the literary supplement of *Yediot Acharonot*, November 10, 1978, dedicated to Halkin at eighty. Halkin's short portrait is also based on my mother Shulamit Silman-Bassok's recollections, who was Halkin's student and close associate in the 1960s and 1970s.

49. The seminar room was "long and narrow like a train carriage" and crammed with students, according to Amichai. "Students Write About Their Teacher" [in Hebrew].

50. *Gilyonot* 25 (11 Iyar, 5711) [Spring, 1951]: 350 [in Hebrew].

51. "Students Write About Their Teacher."

52. *Yediot Acharonot*, November 10, 1978.

53. Over time Halkin seems to have become envious of Amichai, and took a hostile stance. Clarice Kestenbaum's letter to Amichai dated August 21, 1960 hints at this. The lovers' correspondence was in English. Heksherim Archive, Ben-Gurion University of the Negev.

54. Harshav, "On the Beginning of Israeli Poetry," 180.

55. Tova Rosen also addresses this in her article "'As in a Poem by Shmuel Hanagid' – Between Shmuel Hanagid and Yehuda Amichai" [in Hebrew], *Mechkarei Yerushalayim besifrut Ivrit* 15 (5755 [1995]), 85.

56. Perhaps Harshav attributed his own feelings and reactions to Amichai.

57. 35.1230.

58. *Poems* [in Hebrew] 1, 22.

59. Carmi, *Penguin Book of Hebrew Verse*, 569; *Poems* [in Hebrew] 1, 54.

60. Nedod – wandering (Mod. Hebrew)/separation of lovers (medieval); z[e]man – fate/time; ne'urim – youth/ frivolousness, recklessness.

61. Harshav, "On the Beginning of Israeli Poetry."

62. Letter from Amichai to Ruth Hermann-Zielenzeiger, October 12, 1949. Friend, a lecturer at the Hebrew University of Jerusalem and an English poet, who

was openly gay, befriended Amichai and would later become his initial English translator.

63. Harshav, "Personal Reflections" [in Hebrew], 128-129.

64. Ibid, 123.

65. Natan Zach, *From Year to Year It* [in Hebrew] (Tel Aviv, 2009), 11. In the interview with Omer, "In This Burning Country" [in Hebrew], Amichai said that Harshav was the first member of the Likrat circle to see his poems.

66. In an interview Zach said that he visited Amichai at his home and "he showed me his poems. They were written in children's exercise books – lined exercise books." Perhaps the anecdote was his way of capturing a certain innocence about Amichai, particularly his lack of pretentiousness, even after he had poems published.

67. Ron Amichai, email.

68. Conversation with Dan Miron.

69. Interview with Montenegro. Megged vehemently denied this in a letter which appears in Amos Levin's book *No Line* [in Hebrew] (Tel Aviv, 5744 [1983/84]), 31.

70. "Now That the Water Presses Hard", *Poetry*, 21; *Poems* [in Hebrew] 1, 77. Three other poems, "I Told You It Would Be So and You Didn't Believe" (*Poetry*, 21) and "Two Poems in Remembrance of My Father" were published in the *Achsanya* journal, which was edited by Shlomo Grodzenski in Sivan 5715 (Summer 1955), at the same time as the publication of his first book *Now and In Other Days.*

71. As related by Amichai, responding to a survey conducted by Yoav Birnberg, *Chadashot* (holiday supplement) [in Hebrew], March 1, 1988.

72. According to Moshe Dor, *Coals in the Mouth* [in Hebrew] (Tel Aviv, 1995), 101.

73. Harshav heard "a rumor" that Amichai's poems were subject to significant editing by Zach, and that this, in Harshav's opinion, helped fix "Amichai's familiar style, made up of two tendencies: the rolling monologue along with fine and condensed imagism." "Personal Reflections" [in Hebrew], 129.

74. According to Menachem Perry, who cited Zach at a conference on Amichai's poetry at Yale in 2007. See Perry, "In the Face of the Dead: The New Poetics of the Young Yehuda Amichai," in Pastor Fido [in Hebrew], Ziva Shamir and Menachem Perry (eds.) (Tel Aviv, 2016), 196. See also Zach's to journalist Naama Lanski, "Protest Poem" [in Hebrew], *Yisrael Hayom - Weekend Supplement*), March 8, 2011.

75. Dan Miron, *Facing the Silent Brother* [in Hebrew], 275. In his book about the Likrat circle Amos Levin writes that he understood from Zach that he had "edited and arranged Amichai's first book of poetry." Levin, *No Line* [in Hebrew], 44, 80-81. Over the years Zach retreated from this sweeping account, which had prompted the view that he had to a significant extent fashioned the book.

76. Naama Lanski, *Protest Poem* [in Hebrew]; Conversation with Zach, October 25, 2014. Hana Amichai addressed this topic several times in literary journals. See in particular Hana Sokolov-Amichai, *For the Sake of Remembrance* [in Hebrew], *Achshav* 73-74, (Autumn-Winter 2013-2014), 32-33.

77. "Monologue of a Lonely Wolf" [in Hebrew], *Haolam Ha'ze*, June 30, 1976; Interview with Michael Miro, "Writing is the Fruit of a Wonderful Laziness" [in Hebrew], *Pi Ha'aton*, April 1978, 6.

78. Comparing himself to James Joyce. Birnberg interview [in Hebrew].

79. He told Edgar Reichmann that as far as he was concerned there was not a conscious rebellion against the Alterman-Shlonsky generation, and mentioned members of his generation who were "fully aware," in other words, overly concerned with theoretical issues of poetics; thus expressing his distance from Zach. From his perspective, "a real artist does what he does because that's the only way he can do it." "Yehuda Amichai Talks to Edgar Reichmann," *The Unesco Courier*, October 1994, 6.

80. Eyal Megged interview, "Towards the End You Become Simpler" [in Hebrew], *Yediot Acharonot*, November 8, 1985.

81. See Gershon Shaked, "The Early Amichai and His Early Literary Reference Group", in *New Tradition* (Cincinnati, 2006), 144-172. Cf. Natan Zach, "The Stylistic Climate of the 1950s and 1960s in Our Poetry" [in Hebrew], *The Poetry Beyond Words*, 165-171 (Tel Aviv, 2011). Amichai addresses this issue in his novel *Not of This Time*: "The quote [i.e. allusion to Jewish traditional sources] chokes everything I do. The quotes come like a cancer and destroy the cells of my activity" [in Hebrew] (218). What chokes him is not the biblical passages, which he knows how to engage with, but the new classical Hebrew literary language of the Hebrew Enlightenment and Renaissance of the 19th and early 20th centuries. This language was imbued with scriptural reminiscence and essentially lived off its rich repository.

82. As they put it to Tamar's parents. Conversation with Gadi Horn.

83. The timing of the end of their stay in New York can be ascertained from their trip over Easter to London, and then Wales, on their way back to Israel ("A Poet's Landscape" [in Hebrew], *In This Terrible Wind*, 197.)

84. Conversation with Amichai's friend, the poet Harold Schimmel, September 23, 2014.

85. One of the sonnets is in *Selected Poetry*, 21; the three sonnets in Hebrew are in *Poems* 1, 159-162.

86. Though this is one of Amichai's lesser-known poems, it is discussed in a journal article published in the US. Rina Lee situates it in the context of the trope in Amichai of standing at a window, and seeing this as a state of irresolution, "a struggle between the will of the world and inner will – or lack of it." Lee, "On One of Yehuda Amichai's Sonnets" [in Hebrew], *Bitzaron*, Shvat-Adar 5733 [1973], 111-115, 120.

87. Reuven Moshe Eshwege appears in the novel as Hildesheim (206, 242). Amichai recalls him in a number of poems.

88. "An Evening of Poetry" was first published seven or eight months after Yehuda and Tamar's return to Israel. *Lamerchav-Masa*, December 2, 1955.

89. A woman of this name is mentioned in the context of his sister Rachel's wedding in the summer/autumn of 1942, when he met with "Ruth Falk and her future husband, who came to study," almost certainly at the Hebrew University. Amichai's journal. 36.437.

90. "An Evening of Poetry" [in Hebrew], 214.

91. Auden's poems in the Faber anthology that the soldier Yehuda Pfeuffer discovered fortuitously in the Western Desert did not have the learned and academic tonality of Auden's later poetry, which was manifested at the reading.

92. In the story, Amichai listed the individual poems in the cycle: "Winds," "Woods," "Mountains," "Lakes" "Plains," and "Streams," as well as translating parts of them. For a description of the series, see Jason Fuller, *A Readers' Guide to W. H. Auden*, London 1970, 218-222.

93. "An Evening of Poetry" [in Hebrew], 218.

94. M. H. Abrams (ed.), *The Norton Anthology of English Literature*, fifth ed., vol. 2 (New York, 1986), 229.

95. In his article "Stories - In This Terrible Wind," Baruch Kurzweil argues that what Amichai says about Auden in the story applies in fact to Amichai himself: He is a child pulling a toy on a string; the toy has been torn off, but he goes on pulling the string as though something is still there. The article is included in his book *In Search of Israeli Literature* [in Hebrew] (Ramat Gan, 5742 [1981-1982]), 221-230.

96. Something of the couple's considerations as to whether to stay together despite their difficulties may be hinted at in one of the quatrains appearing in the group of poems "In a Right Angle: A Cycle of Quatrains": "The driver asked. We answered. All the way. / His shoulders said, if that's what you want, okay. / [...] / Our lives were stamped to the last stop: one-way." *Selected Poetry*, 28; see also the selection in Harshav and Harshav, "from 'At Right Angles: Hebrew Quatrains'," *A Life of Poetry*, 41-44; *Poems* [in Hebrew] 1, 177-178.

97. "A Poet's Landscape," *In This Terrible Wind* [in Hebrew], 199-200.

98. Amichai's account suggests that they spent some time in the village: "On one wonderful and clear morning I stood in front of Thomas' house", implying that this was one of several mornings.

99. According to Amichai, "sometimes all kinds of foreign elements – chance occurrences in my surroundings – enter the story line of the poem and are absorbed into it" (Zoritte, "Writers Tell" [in Hebrew]).

100. "A Poet's Landscape," *In This Terrible Wind*, 209.

Chapter 7

1955–1958

Responses to his Book, First Award, Separation from Tamar, the Stormy Affair with Clarice

RETURN TO ISRAEL; CRITICAL RECEPTION OF *NOW AND IN OTHER DAY*

Close on the heels of Yehuda and Tamar's return to Israel, in April-May 1955, Amichai's first book *Now and in Other Days* came out in a frugal gray cover. Later, when asked how he felt about the publication of his first book, he struggled to clarify his frame of mind at the time. He was already a mature man of 31, scarred by his experiences in the war and chastened by various disappointments. Still, "Looking back, it was very exciting, for me and for the whole group [the *Likrat* circle]."[1]

One can better understand the storm around Amichai's poems if one takes into account the atmosphere of the time. Aside from the formal innovations in his poetry, his writing constituted an enormous challenge to the values championed by the Israeli society of the time that was imbued with Zionist ideology and polarized around political questions concerning the role of governmental institutions, now the State had actually come into being. However, there was general consensus that the needs of the collective took precedence over the wants and interests of the individual. In the book's closing poem cycle, "We Loved Here," Amichai combines distillations of his amorous relationships (with Ruth Falk, Ruth Hermann, his wife Tamar, and perhaps others) with reflections that were scandalous by the standards of the time on the status of the individual with regard to social and political circumstances demanding self-abnegation and constant sacrifice on the part of each member of the Jewish community of personal pleasures, and a willingness to make the ultimate sacrifice. "Behind headlines, giant and wide / The two of us hide" (sonnet 20):[2] the lovers are hidden from view behind the noisy headlines debating public issues.

Today's readers may be troubled to discover just how much critics of that generation lacked the ability to separate moral and value judgments from esthetic judgments of a literary work on its own terms. The bogeyman haunting that generation – on left and right of the political map – was "nihilism."[3] Nihilists scorn all ideals, distance themselves from morality and are contemptuous of the core values sacred to the era. Hedonists, a close relative of nihilists, opt for the more elementary every-day and self-centered pleasures of life over devotion to any ideal or commitment to the public good and society.

In a review of Amichai's book in *Masa*,[4] the writer Matti Meged made deliberate efforts to clear Amichai of any suspect trace of pessimism, cynicism or nihilism. He stressed the importance of childhood memories in the poems and their role in adult perceptions: "As an adult, he is not only able to recall his world, but beyond the actual act of remembering, and despite the sadness, to endow that world with love and faith". He cites lines and passages that authorize an optimistic interpretation: "Despite a persistent thread of sadness in the poems (or perhaps actually because of it), he is an optimistic poet."[5]

The two most searching articles were written by young critics: Dan Miron, then 21, a frequent contributor to the magazine of the Progressive Party, *Zmanim*, and Natan Zach, a friend and admirer of Amichai and the editor of *Likrat*. While Miron was not eager to praise Amichai's poetry, he did find the poems in *Now and in Other Days* to be "the most mature so far published by the Likrat group." He thought that some of Amichai's similes "lacked an experiential basis [...] to the point that whole passages contain only [...] logical combinations."[6] Nevertheless he compared Amichai favorably to "other *Likrat* writers" since he "situates himself in the world as it is." Despite his negation of collectivist norms, Amichai maintains his unwavering faith, rare in poets of the period, in the power and goodness of human relationships between father and son, man and woman.[7]

Natan Zach was quick to publicly respond to the book, which he himself had edited, and like Miron, suggested that the uniqueness of the poet lay in being "a believer in love".[8] Zach somewhat exaggerated the account of Amichai's "positivity," perhaps seeing him as his opposite. He thought that this absolute relation to love was Amichai's way to escape loneliness, "the most common feeling in modern poetry." Other than love, the absolute values in his life included "the father-son bond, and, access to poetry itself."[9] "There is hardly a poem of Amichai's which does not gather what is natural into the human […] the world is the human […] and the human pervades everything." "The micro-cosmos is perceived in the dimensions of the macro-cosmos and loses its sense of the uncanny."

Zach drew attention to the novelty of Amichai's language: it was "free of flowery expression, it is every-day, in the rhythms of speech, without being dull and prosy." Amichai did not say more than what was required; neither did he "condense" when this was unnecessary. A forceful example is the short poem "Rain Falls on the Faces of My Friends."

THE SPECIAL IMPACT OF AMICHAI'S POETRY

Perhaps the best indication of the intensity of the "Amichai effect" in Hebrew poetry at that time was the ongoing engagement with his poems. A year after the book came out, *Al Hamishmar* published a review by David Eren, a discerning and independently-minded literary critic who was born in Austria and was a member of Kibbutz Gat. He wrote that "Amichai is conquering a broad readership with his originality and because he listens to and responds to the spiritual needs of a whole generation." Eren argues that the old hackneyed poetic tropes (birds, stars, the sunrise) appear in Amichai "in immediate and harmonious proximity with his own inventions": "birds return, without knowing why, / new cars passing by on the road," or "pigeons sitting on a ledge, and only the heart remains far inside."[10]

Tenth-year students from Municipal High School 4 in Tel Aviv wrote to *Masa* asking Amichai "to explain" his "Seven Quatrains," that appeared in the supplement on February 22, 1957.[11] These students' request shows the level of interest in poetry among young people of that time in general and Amichai's in particular. The poet's response, while humorous, reveals some of his world and his implicit poetics although not in terms of the quatrains, which constitute a unit. To explain his approach to poetry that tends to "glance rapidly at an abundance of pictures instead of one," he related a childhood misdemeanor: "When I was a boy, I would sometimes ring all the bells at the entrance [of the apartment building] and then run away," so he could hear the fragments of speech, and see what could be seen for fleeting moments, no more than a delivery man or a tax collector might, but enough to stir the imagination, and engage his senses full force. In his response to the letter Amichai dwells on the basic composition of his images, which intentionally bring together the sensuous and the abstract. The nexus of their encounter in the poem, he emphasizes, is the zone between them. "They are the points between which one can draw one straight line [...] this line is the poem."[12]

ECHOES OF THE SHLONSKY PRIZE

In July 1957, Amichai won the first of his important series of awards, honors and doctorates. The award in the name of Avraham Shlonsky, who at that time was at the height of his literary activity and social impact, had been created two years earlier and was meant to constitute a kind of left-wing counterweight (associated with *Mapam*-the Hashomer Hatsair Kibbutz movement) to the Brenner and Bialik awards, which were seen as politically biased.[13] The prize of 1,000 Israeli liras was to be awarded once a year on May 1.[14]

The choice of Amichai as the recipient of the award sparked controversy among leading critics, but constituted a breakthrough for him, since up to then he had been known to only a small circle of readers.

On the eve of the award ceremony, after the recipients had already been announced, Shlomo Zemach, a critic who had been brought up in the poetry of the revival generation,[15] published a long article, entitled "Tree-trunk and leaf-fall." It discusses "a book by Yehuda Amichai, from the camp of the young." He argues that Amichai was imitating poetry from "foreign vineyards;" i.e. Anglo-American imagism,[16] which was old-fashioned and no longer acceptable even in its culture of origin. "Imagism was once a great thing, and timely. The declaration that there is no abstract poetry of ideas, and its language has no grammar other than the world of things, objects, bodies in their poetic perception [...] shook the soul with sudden awe stemming from the realization of the affinity and fellowship of unlikes [...] but with the passage of time, this devotion to things became a frozen formula."[17]

In a short piece in *Al Hamishmar* entitled "Unto Iron," the poet and critic Lea Goldberg responded to the critique.[18] Although at that time she had only read Amichai's first book and a few poems published in newspapers and magazines, she was able to capture an essential component of Amichai's poetry. She argued that there was a dialectical relationship between the poets of the State generation including Amichai and the poetry that preceded them: "This is a generation that does not want to be bound by the shackles of ready-made forms [...] or give up what has been achieved in the living poetic language, but wants to develop it in a new way." She acknowledges that this orientation "also draws on the experience of foreign literatures of our time and those preceding it (in Amichai's poems, Rilke and the new English poetry)." She cites the first sonnet of "We Loved Here" ("My father spent four years inside their war...") as an example of this dialectic at work "in his acceptance and spurning of the inheritance at one and the same time," and sees Amichai as succeeding in conveying the reality of the First World War "using the expressive means of a new generation." "I don't know if there is another example, anywhere in the new Hebrew poetry, that renders such an accurate depiction of the grief and courage of the young generation, which so profoundly understands the past and is nevertheless committed to its own present."

A short while later, *Davar*, the same paper that published Zemach's article, carried a piece by Shlomo Grodzenski,[19] which like Goldberg's article was published after Amichai had received the Shlonsky Award.[20] Grodzenski addressed the claim that Amichai lacked mastery of the Hebrew traditional sources (mainly the Talmud), arguing that the absence of a conscious repertoire of biblical verses worked in his favor. His poetry was all the more consistent for taking its point of departure from spoken Hebrew. The fact that Amichai was influenced by poetry in other languages was neither a sin nor unusual among classic Hebrew poets; the only difference was the influencing culture. Furthermore, Amichai never wrote for an auditorium of people; his poetry was intimate, showing "a flowing and spontaneous affinity for love (for his father, for his mother, for a woman), unsentimental delight."

COUPLEHOOD WITH TAMAR, INCHING TOWARDS THE BREAKUP

On the personal level, Amichai's life was about to be tossed about like a ship in a storm. In their apartment on Metudela Street, Amichai and Tamar lived a petit-bourgeois life, with its practiced and meticulous routine. Nevertheless, their lives were subject to stresses and pressures. Tamar worked as a secretary and he taught in various schools. There was certainly beauty in their relationship in the first years, in particular the full and intense eroticism that Amichai had longed for after "all the rare birds with beautiful plumage" had flown away ("My Mother Baked the Whole World for Me"). He had come to terms with reality and the limits of the possible: "But the border guards of possibility / Permitted us to enter their domain" ("Military Operation").[21] While Tamar is memorialized by name in the series "Six Poems for Tamar," she is present in a number of other poems in *Now and in Other Days* as well as in some collected in *Two Hopes Away*. Both books are dedicated to her, the second perhaps not wholeheartedly. Amichai argued in an interview that the poems addressed to Tamar were "birthday poems,"[22] the kind of verses read at family festive gatherings. However, the power and frankness of the poems contradict this declaration, which was probably made to placate another woman in later years. "You had a laughter of grapes: / many round green laughs. // Your body is full of lizards, / All of them love the sun. // Flowers grew in the field, grass grew on my cheeks, / everything was possible" ("Six Poems for Tamar", poem 2). "You're always lying on / my eyes. // Every day of our life together / Ecclesiastes deletes a line of his book" (poem 3). Lines like these found a place in the holy canon of secular readers, in that they communicate a thrill of delight at the fulfillment of desire, intensified by Amichai's antinomian counter-reading of traditional Jewish sources: "Near my bed, the rustle of newspaper wings. / There are no other angels."[23]

Amichai himself said of a well-known poem from his first book, "Both Together and Each Apart," that it was written at a time when he and Tamar (he does not refer to her by name) were having problems finding an apartment, trying without success to put a roof over their heads without always having to move on.[24] The poem talks about an experience at the root of his poetry, which made him an existentialist prophet in Hebrew poetry. He referred to the vulnerability of loving; in other words, the dangers inherent to its ephemerality, the war lying in wait "behind the hills" to come and crush love beneath it, and the experience of holding on to love and the joy of desire as a replacement for religion, a source of comfort in a godless world ("no angel who will come to redeem"; "My love turns me like a salt sea, it seems, / Into sweet drops of autumn's first rain").[25] There is here an echo of the speaker's private fears as he struggles to defend and strengthen what in his world was fast becoming fragile and unsteady.

In the story "Small Summer Pleasures" he describes their apartment including the hidden fissures and cracks threatening its collapse: [26] "Our balcony was at the back, facing a yard surrounded by balconies and windows [...] one day builders appeared in my apartment [...] Ours was a rooftop apartment. It came to a disagreement between the outside wall and the inside wall [...] the builders came, and the plasterers and the whitewashers, and broke our apartment open for all to see." He seems to feel like someone in disguise by living in bourgeois tranquility, able to make himself at home even in the lion's jaws, as in the poem "I Want to Die in My Own Bed," but living removed from the capacity to express the truth inside, and from the creativity necessary to his freedom. Nonetheless, despite the decline of feeling and the smothering of love's happiness, there was reconciliation with the experience of couplehood, albeit with few expectations. In the colorful language of the story, at the end of the season when the pool was empty, "I went back as I came, through the field of thorns, and then feelings of truth did come, but the water flowed so slowly that one doubted if the pool would ever fill."

The "Six Poems for Tamar" in Amichai's first book are echoed in "Poems for a Woman" in his second book, *Two Hopes Away.* They were almost certainly written for Tamar as well. Like the earlier cycle, they are intensely passionate: "The womb's wind blew for us everywhere. / We always had time" (poem 2); "If you open your coat, / I have to double my love" (poem 5); but there are hints of feelings of loss and confinement: "My hopes are widows [...] // Our loves wear the uniforms of orphans" (poem 3); "The moon, fastened with a chain, / keeps quiet outside. // The moon, caught in the olive branches, / can't break free" (poem 6).[27]

In the story "Battle for the Hill" he describes the couple's difficulties communicating as a trap preventing serious talk. Although this is related to the wartime situation, it is implied that this kind of problem is lying in wait even in ordinary circumstances. On a return home from his army unit for a night, perhaps without a permission, "I debated whether to wake my wife or let her sleep. Opportunities to talk are few. Always the stillness before the noise, and always the noise before the stillness. In the noise we cannot hear one another. In the stillness we cannot talk for fear of being overheard."

In another story, "The Bar Mitzvah Party," Amichai reveals something of his and Tamar's social life when he describes the fictional couple's visit to a German-Jewish family to celebrate their son's bar mitzvah. Unlike them, this family comes from Prussia, in northern Germany where Berlin is located: "Twenty-five years earlier they had all immigrated to Palestine. The elderly parents and their married sons came from northern Prussia and their speech was sharp and a little derisive". The story shows him feeling uncomfortable and out of place in their house, even if outwardly he knows how to be an amicable guest. He does not know why he was invited to the bar mitzvah, and the story is replete with antipathy and anger towards the company his wife obliged him to meet. This is the tone used to describe a woman friend of Tamar's who vacillates between different men, and the array of gifts on display for the son's bar mitzvah that include scout equipment and "black-banded te'fillin [...] and a book about other people's heroic deeds. And Bialik and Tschernikovsky and two pictures by Van Gogh [...] and encyclopedias that never get opened. And a toilet kit [...] and envelopes with his name printed on the back." The gifts of the Hebrew classics correspond to a need to belong. The confused cultural identity of the hosts and their guests reminds him of his family of origin, and the lack of acculturation into Hebrew-Israeli culture of the Yekkes in general, and their persistent alienation from native Israeli society riles him.

Perhaps as a way to escape from domestic awkwardness, Amichai flirted with Jerusalem bohemia, which was not entirely his style. In the story "Terrible Spring" he paints a picture of life among the patrons of Jerusalem's Café Ta'amon, a scene he was caught up in, whether as a frequent customer or as an observer. Right at the beginning of the story he hints at the inauthentic and essentially false image of his life: he holds a "large paper bag" of "Purim costumes that I wanted to return to their owner." After exploiting the symbolic resonance, he writes: "It would soon be Passover [...] The angel of death passes over us and we name a holiday after him. Sometimes life passes over a man and he fails to live."[28] Things are stated even more sharply in the novel *Not of This Time*: "When did this great turn in Joel's life begin? That turn which leads to the abyss or to the great freedom?"[29]

HIGH SCHOOL TEACHING, WORK AT THE HAYIM GREENBERG TEACHERS' COLLEGE, THE SINAI CAMPAIGN

In the 1956-57 academic year, after earning his BA and beginning his MA (as recorded on the form he filled out for the Gymnasium Rehavia), Amichai went to work as a literature teacher at a high school, for the first time in his life.[30] He did not do well as a high school teacher, and did not remain there for more than a year. His students at the time tended to comment that "we didn't connect with him."[31] As a poet who had developed a unique poetic language, was he equipped to communicate with his young students? Did his way of explaining things seem strange to them? Did they perhaps take advantage of his easy-going manner? There were certainly discipline problems.

That year Amichai received a letter of congratulation from Zevulun Tuchman, the principal, for the Shlonsky Award. Tuchman applauded him using the Zionist formula for praise of the time: "This award is a mark of great achievement, and a sign to encourage you to continue on your momentous path. Our poetry is the poetry of the redeemed Zion." This was almost certainly Amichai's swan song in the institution, after which he went back to teaching at Luria elementary school.

The following academic year, 1958-59, he took on a second teaching job at the Hayim Greenberg College of Diaspora Teachers in Baka'a, but this time he came into his own. According to a form he later filled out after being accepted for a teaching post at the School for International Students at the Hebrew University, he taught literature at Greenberg, which in fact was Hebrew as a foreign language at an advanced level.[32] His friendly, lenient and anti-establishment attitude ("he took every opportunity to speak out against officialdom, against the *Mapai* government"), and his anti-academicism ("a Hebrew teacher who hated grammar") enamored him to these twenty year-olds and up.[33] Most were graduates of Jewish schools in Latin America and the US who had come to Israel to experience its ways of life, and become better acquainted with a language they had mastered to differing extents.

However, the most significant events of his life at that time did not take place at school. In the autumn of 1956, the nascent State of Israel was confronted with a threatening Egyptian rearmament program under the government of dictator-president Gamal Abdel Nasser. In September 1955, Egypt acquired modern arms from Czechoslovakia, a sale encouraged by the Soviet Union, fedayeen terrorist attacks were perpetrated against Israel from the Gaza Strip which was under Egyptian (and later also Jordanian and Syrian) rule, Egypt was blockading the Straits of Tiran, and Nasser nationalized the Suez Canal. The Israeli government, joined by French and British forces, decided to attack Egypt. The purpose was to thwart Egyptian plans to destroy

Israel, and to open the Gulf of Eilat to Israeli shipping.[34] The Sinai War itself began on October 29-30, 1956, and ended on October 31 - November 1 with a victory for Israel. After the IDF took over the Sinai Peninsula on November 5, the operation to open the Gulf of Suez began. Israel was eventually forced to cede military control of the Sinai, but its strategic and diplomatic standing in the world was strengthened considerably.[35]

In this web of circumstances, how did Company Sergeant Major Yehuda Amichai of the Jerusalem Brigade, charged with overseeing organizational matters in his unit, deal with his logistical tasks and coordinating the call-up of reservists? Quite a lot about his state of mind and behavior during preparations for the Sinai Campaign in autumn 1956 can be gleaned from "Battle for the Hill," a story which, though surrealist in style, has realistic and biographical underpinnings.[36] The story describes the situation on the eve of the Sinai Campaign, when Israel was engaged in a large false flag operation designed to appear to be preparing for war with Jordan.[37] The narrator emphasizes his fear of death: "I stepped outside. I passed a hard wall. I wanted to press myself against the terrible wall of history, like Rashi's mother.[38] I wanted to find myself a niche safe from an intransigent history" (47). He appears to believe he may not survive the battle,[39] and is afraid that "half the company would be mowed down" (29). There was indeed a plan to send the Jerusalem Brigade to Sinai, though it was eventually rescinded. Amichai's company, composed of relatively older reservists, was suddenly removed from the terror of taking part in the war. The story describes their hurried training and then being discharged by their company sergeant major to return to their ordinary jobs (37). Apart from getting ready for war, he was very taken up with wooing or responding to the possibly imaginary advances of a young woman of seventeen, whom he described elsewhere as "the one who would often sing in the bath, and go to the parties of the American navy."

At the time of the deployments of the Sinai Campaign and during the war itself, at the end of 1956, Tamar, referred to in the story as "my wife," was still very present in his life. He sought out a way to escape her, but also looked to her for support, somewhat like a weak child needing a hand. According to the story, "when I came downstairs it was already night and my wife was waiting for me. How did she know I was here? Her hair rustled and thorns rustled and the smell of burning was in the air, and her eyes were black as if after a terrible fire. I told her: 'Come, let's go and wake people up.'" (17). "My wife" even accompanies him to a gathering of reservists. Then she leaves without him:

> After a conversation with his commanding officer, the narrator excuses himself on a pretext and hurries home. "My wife was not there, so I stood by the window" (24). After looking at his surroundings, he lowers his head, "like a flag at

half-mast. Only then did I spy the slip of paper, left for me by wife [...] 'I'm at Mother's, come.' I marveled that the slip should be faded and yellow like a Dead Sea Scroll," – perhaps a hint at the ageing and yellowing of their relationship – "for the note had been written only today and the paper had been white and fresh" (ibid).

It turns out that his mother, whose "last coins of favor" were meant to "protect us / now and in other days," as one of his well-known poems puts it,[40] was able to give him the protection he felt he needed, reinforced symbolically by his father's religious heritage: "I asked my mother for some bags we could fill with sand and used for protection against a bombardment [...] She took the bag that held my father's prayer shawl, filled it with sand and sewed old clothes together into other bags." When he gets home, he avoids waking his wife, "the clerk of the company comes to call him back to duty. "I dressed silently. The clerk had already gone ahead [...]. This time I said my goodbyes to her [his wife's] forehead [...] Behind the hard forehead soft thoughts dwell, and beyond where thoughts harden, soft hair."[41]

Amichai survived the war, and the Jerusalem Brigade, apart from its commando unit, remained stationed far from the battle zones. His unit made preparations which he describes as fairly grotesque to capture a hill, an operation which was part of the deceptive plans for war with Jordan (15-16). The unit was also busy building a wire fence and telephone cables. The main burden placed on the easy-going company sergeant major Amichai was to deal with the childish requests of his soldiers for leaves; in other words, to be released from reserve duty: "I had to give every man an answer, and no man was dispensable" (32).

However, his life in the coming years would be a struggle. Although there were some months of true love, he would be forced to go back to his wife, tail between his legs, to father his oldest child.

CLARICE – LOVE AT FULL STRENGTH; THE TRAGEDY OF THEIR BREAKUP

"Out of a final effort to set things in order, and dimly, he divided his life into two periods: until now and from now on. Words were added. Conversations for two."[42] This is how Amichai tried to define the rift in his life, in the spring or summer of 1958, when his relationship with Clarice Kestenbaum, a medical student and an American Jew grew stronger. Clarice was a divorcee or in the process of separation from her husband Dr. Morton (Mordechai) Kaufman, who was a trainee Reform rabbi and future psychoanalyst at the Israel Psychoanalytic Society in Jerusalem. Love for this woman sweeps the protagonist of the story "Love in Reverse" off his feet,[43] and eats up Joel the archaeologist, the stand-in for Amichai, in the Jerusalem part of the novel *Not of This Time, Not of This Place* (1963).

Clarice, born in 1929, a pianist with literary talent, outgoing and attractive, decided to study medicine in Jerusalem to become a psychiatrist. Her father, a successful doctor in Los Angeles, had hoped for a boy, and perhaps there was something masculine about her determined pursuit of a career, her athletic prowess and strong shoulders.[44] Since her marriage to Morton Kaufman in 1951, she had gone with him on his search to find the right Ph.D. advisor and this had brought them finally to Israel.[45] While she was studying hard at medical school using her minimal Hebrew, and running between three campuses, her husband felt abandoned and went on a romantic adventure in Italy with a beautiful, wealthy Israeli woman. On his return Clarice decided to divorce him, despite his claim that he had remained "faithful to her from the hips up;" that is, in spirit.

For Amichai, his relationship with her meant "feeling alive": in the story "Love in Reverse," the narrator describes his joy at entering the house of his beloved, knowing that "the world is still alive. The tiny feather of his loneliness, which for many years had covered the mouth of the world, stirred." He parts company with the gravitational pull of reality and lives in the absolutist sphere of wish fulfillment: "More and more his entire body became involved in the precise and heavy activities of a dream." Similarly, in another passage: "A miracle had befallen him. Life had befallen him. Every night he would sink down into this woman" (150, 151). In a number of places in the story, as his intimate bonds with Clarice (in the novel Patricia, also Patrice) grow stronger, he defines his attitude through the rather surprising and very Israeli notion of "I deserve it!" "One night, when he heard her strange moaning as he climaxed, he suddenly thought again in a moment of inner anguish: I deserve it! I deserve it! I deserve it! And in the calm of afterward he said: 'Until now I have carried life; now my life has become independent and mature and it will carry me'" (155).

Amichai and Clarice first got to know each other thanks to a somewhat strange role he had taken on: his friend Murray – Meir Mindlin, depicted in *Not of This Time* as a restless journalist by the name of Klein,[46] had left the country and rented out his apartment in Gaza Street to Clarice. Mindlin asked Amichai to collect the rent, and it was in this comic role that he appeared at the apartment she had recently rented. He found her in the shower – could it have been otherwise? – which did not stop her from apologizing, as she emerged from the bathroom, for the hospital smell which still clung to her.[47] As she remembers it, Amichai invited her to a party where the future Prof. Elihu Katz and his brother Karl of the Israel Museum and later the Head of Bezalel, were invited. In the novel, he makes his move on a walk with friends in the Judean Hills. But Itzhak the doctor, a friend of Joel the archeologist (the protagonist of the novel), Yoske-Yosel the musician and Zeiger the photographer fail to show up at the bus stop where they are all supposed to catch a bus together into the hills. Each has his own excuse, and Joel-Amichai and Patricia-Clarice are left to their own devices.[48]

During their walk in the hills, Clarice caught sight of the poet in him, on those frequent occasions when he pulled out his tiny notebook to jot down lines that came to him, or to record passing impressions. In the novel, on the walk, they both felt rising desire;[49] they embrace and after an amorous tussle during which she "began to choke him," she declares: "You must be patient with me." Amichai played practical jokes to speed up the relationship: he would go to the department at Hadassah Hospital where Clarice was doing her internship, faking an imaginary illness, or broken bones and other injuries. When she was working in the orthopedic unit, he turned up complaining of a broken leg; when she moved to another department, he adopted a similar ruse. It was clear to her that he would persist courting her.

He described their common languages as "broken English and stammering Hebrew." Clarice's Hebrew was sketchy even by her own account; his English was much better. Her foreignness, which he accentuates by presenting her as not Jewish,[50] is seen in her naïve questions about the Hebrew expressions she hears and her queries about his Zionist frame of reference (she laughs when he uses a buzzword of the time "enemies of the land"), but this only makes her more charming in his eyes. "For some reason he sensed obscurely that only a strange woman could redeem him, as in ancient days when nations chose a king from a foreign land to rule over them."[51]

In conversation, Clarice at 83 remembered Amichai as having already separated from Tamar. This was perhaps a wishful recollection, to avoid the unpleasant thought of having been involved with a married man. Amichai indeed had misgivings about his married life even before meeting Clarice, but his breakup with Tamar – at this stage just temporary – only materialized when she felt his growing absence, physically and mentally, as he came home later and later, or so it seems in the novel.

Amichai-Joel's relationship with Clarice-Patrice took on a cosmic aspect; at least this is how he saw it in retrospect: "In the woman's room the floor was the ground, the earth. The earth of all life. Even when it was covered with smooth, colored tiles."[52] Their terms of endearment reflected the tension of their all-engrossing love – intense sexuality on his part and no less intense passion on hers, mixed with motherly affection and many worries about the future of their relationship: "She would suddenly say 'I'll tell your mother,' as children say while playing.[53] What would she tell his mother? She would tell his mother that he is sweet, that she has a sweet son. He called her big conch-shell, pink witch, mouth of the earth. And she called him my defeated army."[54] However, his guilty feelings towards Tamar persisted, despite his tumultuous affair with Clarice, and it was no easy decision to leave Tamar. In "Love in Reverse," the Hamlet-like indecision between the two women is evident in the narrator's constant play with the two apartment keys in his pocket. He needed a kind of dream-action to help him decide: "The key of the woman's [the lover's] house always won and was taken out first."[55] Only later does he realize that he has no other home.

The partial fiction depicting Amichai and Tamar in the character of Joel and his wife Ruth in *Not of this Time* is a way for the narrator to express his guilt about abandoning her. Tamar, transposed in the novel as Ruth, was an important part of Amichai's experience of the war, a foundation stone for him. Amichai described his first meeting with Tamar as having happened after a key battle in the War of Independence, and this may be the truth. Similarly, he describes Ruth, Joel's wife in the novel, as "the daughter of his beloved commander," probably referring to his brigade commander, Nachum Sarig, a kibbutznik from Beit Hashita, the only one of his commanders at that time who could have had a daughter close to adulthood. Amichai illustrates his intense wavering between Tamar and Pat/Clarice in a humorous scene where Joel goes late at night to see a young rabbi to ask for help getting a divorce. The rabbi is astonished that Joel wants to divorce in the middle of the night, while "Joel could not explain that only at night, when he was under Patricia's power, could he take such a step." To a certain extent he even turns his hesitation into a badge of identity, and does not try to decide. When Joel's friend Itzhak asks him what he will do now that Ruth has left town and has gone to her parents' kibbutz, he replies: "'I will let things roll.' – 'Like a billiard ball?'– 'Like hide-and-seek.'"

Clarice-Patrice, the third side of the triangle, perceived Yehuda-Joel's hesitation and his inability to shrug off responsibility to his wife. She in fact was no less ambivalent about continuing their relationship. At times she could be possessive, talking about squeezing him into a tube, so she could keep him forever.[56] When in the end she decided to stay with him and announced her intention to remain in Israel and learn Hebrew properly, his response was: "You have to go back." Although she suffered from his indecision over "either me or Ruth," she also encouraged him to go back to his wife, whom she felt he continued to love,[57] so that he could "make her a child."

The ping-pong of emotions and attitudes lasted throughout their relationship. Amichai urged her to tether her destiny to his, while she, despite her love and desire, may well have understood that they were not meant for life together.[58] It was also a question of where her life was centered. She understood that Amichai was connected to Israel and would not ever leave, not least of all because of the language in which he wrote his poems. He had come to the country in his youth, and cherished the language perhaps more than those born in Israel. She, by contrast, despite her strong feelings for Israel and her enthusiastic Zionism, did not see her future there; psychiatry, her chosen field was at an "extremely low level," as she put it (using the Hebrew expression *namukh beyoter* in a conversation otherwise in English). In her heart she knew that Israel would not welcome her or her aspirations which were indeed to be fully realized in the US.[59]

Clarice may have read Amichai's poems, using his translations or those of others, to understand his writing; but in any case, she deeply intuited the kind of life he was building and what he really needed. He was a poet, a master of images, who saw in her much more than was there. She sensed he needed a very different woman. "I am not like that. You attribute qualities to me that I don't have. I am domestic. I want a lot of pink babies," says Patrice in the novel, echoing Clarice's letter to Yehuda a few weeks after she left the country.[60] There was nevertheless a stage, after much pleading on his part, when she acquiesced and agreed to marry him. That very day or the next, while she was walking in the city center, in Ben Yehuda Street, she saw Yehuda sitting with Tamar in Café Atara, talking passionately. She took this to be a sign from both him and fate: she had to pursue her own path to happiness, pursue her career and finish her degree. This took her two years, even though in Israel the coursework could be accomplished in one. She was some years older than the other students at the School of Medicine, but this did not get in the way of her meeting the challenging demands of her studies with the force of her personality, vast intellectual talents and great sensitivity.

NOTES

1. Birnberg interview [in Hebrew], 78.
2. Wendy Zieler, "Dr. Wendy Zieler Explores How Yehuda Amichai's Poem resonates in Our Time," website of Hebrew Union College, January 21, 2021. http://www.huc.edu/news/2021/01/21/dr-wendy-zierler-explores-how-yehuda-amichais-poem-resonates-in-our-time
3. This concept gained traction in the discourse of the Jewish national renaissance after the publication of Ivan Turgenev's novel *Fathers and Sons* in 1861.
4. Matti Meged, "Between the Fire and the Dream", *Lamerchav – Masa*, May20, 1955. *Masa was* the literary supplement of *Lamerhav*, the journal of the *Achdut Ha'Avodah* (Unity of Labor) party, which broke with Mapam in 1954. At that time Masa was the stronghold of the writers of 1948 – the Palmach generation.
5. The old guard was quick to attack Meged's positive evaluation. Benjamin Yitzhak Michali, "With No Sense of Propriety" [in Hebrew], *Davar*, June 3, 1955.
6. Dan Miron, "The Present Tense Scrutiny of Other Days" [in Hebrew], *Zmanim*, June 17, 1955.

7. Shraga Avneri as well, in his article "The Poems of Yehuda Amichai" [in Hebrew], insisted that the poet had a decadent bent, but was not "morbid or pessimistic." *Mevo'ot* 11, July 1, 1955: 23.

8. Natan Zach, "The Poems of Yehuda Amichai" [in Hebrew], *Al Hamishmar*, July 29, 1955.

9. Cf. Sandbank, "Landscapes of the Soul" [in Hebrew], discussing "the human inanimate."

10. David Eren, "Directions in the Poetry of Yehuda Amichai" [in Hebrew], *Al Hamishmar*, July 10, 1956. At that time the new Israeli state was moving away from being a primarily agricultural society and was in the process of becoming industrialized.

11. The students' question and the poet's response were published in *Lamerchav-Masa*, March 8, 1957. The quatrains referred to by the students were later collected in the section "The Right Angle" in *Two Hopes Away* (quatrains 32, 33, 41, 42, 43, 44, 47), and again in *Poems, 1948-1962. Poems* [in Hebrew] 1; *Life of Poetry*, 41-44; *Selected Poetry*, 27-29; Poetry, 50.

12. The educator Benjamin Halevy attempted to mediate Amichai's response to the students. "Another Answer to the Students" [in Hebrew], *Lamerchav - Masa*, April 5, 1957.

13. Amichai was one of the poets to read his poems at the first award ceremony, when the prize went to Lea Goldberg, according to a report in *Al Hamishmar*, May 20, 1956.

14. *Al Hamishmar*, June 6, 1955.

15. Primarily Bialik and Tchernichovsky.

16. Imagist poetry is perception-based (rather than conceptual), leaning toward the concrete and objective in its ways of describing things.

17. "Tree-trunk and leaf-fall," *Warp and Woof* [in Hebrew], 223-224.

18. Lea Goldberg, "Unto Iron" [in Hebrew], *Al Hamishmar*, July 26, 1957. The title is borrowed from a poem of Amichai's.

19. Born in 1904 in Grodno, then tsarist Russia, he went to the US at age 12 and grew up there, before moving to Israel in 1951.

20. Shlomo Grodzenski, "The Poems of Yehuda Amichai" [in Hebrew], *Davar*, August 2, 1957.

21. *Poetry*, 4, 23; *Selected Poetry*, 8; *Life of Poetry*, 4, 23; *Poems* [in Hebrew] 1, 13, 78. See also his account of his relationship with Tamar in a letter to Ruth Hermann, in Chapter 5.

22. Interview with Omer, "In this Burning Country" [in Hebrew], 6: "I wrote poems for her birthday, and illustrated them. They were gift poems."

23. There is also here a reference to Johanan ben Torta's words to Hillel that "grass will grow from your cheeks" before the messiah comes, in the sense of something impossible, that would never happen. Jerusalem Talmud 65:4. "Grass grew on my cheeks" thus means "the impossible happened to me."

24. In Ida Zoritte, "Writers Tell" [in Hebrew].

25. *Life of Poetry*, 12; *Poetry*, 12-13 (Stephen Mitchell's translation).

26. First published in *Lamerchav-Masa*, September 9, 1957. *In This Terrible Wind* [in Hebrew], 246-238.

27. This may refer to the moon longing for what is beyond materiality and the everyday, evoked in the popular novel by Somerset Maugham, *The Moon and Sixpence* (1919), about the painter Gauguin.

28. "Terrible Spring," *The World Is a Room*, 71-85. Citation is from 72. Ta'amon Café is located on the corner of King George Street and Hillel Street in Jerusalem. In the story it is lightly disguised as "Ta'am Katan."

29. *Not of This Time* [in Hebrew], 229.

30. 54 Documents in the archive of the Hebrew Gymnasium of Rechavia.

31. Conversations with Dr. Bilha Kaplan-Noy, September 28, 2017, and with Ram Banin, October 5, 2017.

32. The same form, in the Hebrew University archive, lists the year he began teaching at Greenberg.

33. Conversations with Joseph Kaplan, and Susana Huler, Amichai's students in the 1962-63 school year, were sources for these insights into students' relationships with him at Greenberg College. There are similarly affectionate letters from ex-students preserved in his archive.

34. Some, however, see the Sinai Campaign, or Operation Kadesh, as having wider goals: the end of Nasser's rule, a peace treaty with Egypt, and the opening of the Suez Canal to Israeli shipping.

35. See Sachar, *A History of Israel*, 482-514; Morris, *Righteous Victims*, 288-301.

36. The story's surrealism is evident in its persistent interruptions of the linear narrative, giving it the quality of a dream bordering on nightmare.

37. Conversation with Yossi Langotsky, who was a commando in the Jerusalem Brigade, and later its commander, October 15, 2017.

38. According to legend, the mother of the future biblical and Talmudic exegete Rashi was walking in her hometown of Worms one day while pregnant, when a gang of Crusader horsemen hurtled towards her. The wall beside her opened miraculously and she escaped being trampled.

39. "I knew that I would never see my wife again. It was a winter day, but her face was as dry as if it had been parched by a sirocco. She didn't want to cry but the tears came. Her whole body shared them" (26).

40. "God Takes Pity on Kindergarten Children," *Poetry*, 6.

41. Cf. Robert Alter's analytical notes to the story in his "Introduction," *Israeli Stories* (New York, 1962), 18-19.

42. "Love in Reverse," *The World Is a Room*, 153-154. The whole story, 143-170.

43. The story was written in the late 1950s. In choosing to situate his affair with Clarice during the celebrations of the State's first decade, Amichai emphasized a form of alienation from national festivity by being primarily interested in his personal love and celebration.

44. In the novel *Not of This Time*, there are mentions of "her powerful legs" and her body as a whole which did not correspond to the feminine norm of being thin and elegant (e.g. 108-109).

45. Conversations with Clarice Kestenbaum, February 18, 2015, and September 1, 2015.

46. *Not of This Time*, 17.

47. In our conversation, she recalled the problem of the persistent smell, particularly after autopsies. She did not feel attractive then and was surprised by Amichai's amorous advances.

48. *Not of This Time*, 53-54.

49. "A great and unfamiliar passion arose within them, a passion [...] springing from remote depths within them [...] they would forget all boundaries; they would not remember their countries and their languages" (Ibid, 58, 64).

50. In the novel Klein presents her to his friend as a Christian doctor sent by an international health organization to do research (Ibid, 38).

51. Ibid, 152.

52. Ibid., 159.

53. Cf., "The Travels of the Last Benjamin of Tudela," *Poetry*, 110-111; *Poems* [in Hebrew], 2, 121.

54. "Love in Reverse," 154.

55. Ibid., 150.

56. *Not of This Time* [in Hebrew], 118-119.

57. When he went back to Clarice after a short, and in her mind suspicious, absence, he told her: "'I love you.' – 'You love your wife Ruth, I know.' – 'No, you.' – 'Darling, it's good to be deceived by you.'" Ibid., 504.

58. Conversations with Clarice Kestenbaum.

59. She became a professor of psychiatry at Columbia University in New York, was president of the American Academy of Child and Adolescent Psychiatry, and president of the American Academy of Psychoanalysis and Dynamic Psychiatry, according to her website.

60. Letter dated September 26, 1958. Heksherim Archive, Ben-Gurion University.

Chapter 8

1957–1959

Two More Volumes of Poetry; Clarice Leaves Israel

TWO HOPES AWAY: AN OVERVIEW

Between the autumn of 1955 and spring 1958, Amichai published a number of poems in newspapers and a literary journal, all of which were associated with the Labor Movement aligned with the *Mapai* or more left-wing. These included three poems based on photographs from different periods of his life, one of which was about his uncle who had frozen to death while doing his military service in the German army during the WWI. This group of poems appeared under the title "Three Photographs" in the final issue of the *Orlogin* annual collection edited by Avraham Shlonsky. By sending the poems to *Orlogin* Amichai was perhaps angling to have his next book, *Two Hopes Away*, published by Sifriat Poalim.[1] In general, the poems Amichai chose for publication at that time had a more controversial theological-metaphysical dimension, and seemed to suggest a new attitude towards life. The secular message was clear enough in *Now and in Other Times*: "Near my bed, the rustle of newspaper wings. / There are no other angels" ('Six Poems for Tamar', 1); the beloved is called on to give the gift of her body to the lover in a world which has no other sources of comfort ("The Two of Us Together and Each of Us Alone"). In the poem "God Has Pity on Kindergarten Children," the divinity is shown to have limited powers that need to be supplemented by "the last rare coins of compassion / that mother handed down to us."

Nevertheless, the theological discourse in *Two Hopes Away*, Amichai's second book, is much more focused and consistent. "Poem for Friday Night" responds indirectly to the Indo-China War of 1946-1954,[2] in which the State of Israel, still uncertain about its relationship to the major powers, was involved, albeit on a small scale: "War, which can never get enough, is somewhere else now."[3] However, the focus of the poem is the influence of religious faith and the experience of leaving its orbit: in a world of boundaries and restrictions typical of religious life, the father's prayer on Sabbath eve brings about the erosion or destruction of the land, in other words the contraction and subjugation of earthly, physical elements in the human soul.[4] When "the host of Earth," the worldly parallel to the host of heavenly bodies, darkens and extinguishes the light, all that remains is lovers' joy, who are obligated to finish what "heaven began," through a partnership in creation or by tearing apart Heaven and Earth (Genesis 1:6-7), a process which must now be brought to an end and made decisive.[5]

Whereas "Poem for Friday Night" only hints at a parody of Sabbath songs, it was followed by clear caricatures of traditional texts. These are among the best-known poems of Amichai of this period: "And That Is Your Glory"[6] and "Sort of an Apocalypse,"[7] the apparently lighter of the two. "And That Is Your Glory" comes out full force against the human image, even before it attacks the divine one. Amichai did not negate God's existence in his poems or interviews; rather he described God as weak, lacking the attribute of omnipotence, or indifferent to what goes on in the world. Sometimes Amichai claimed that the concept of God can be replaced by history or fate; in other words, concepts he considered to express arbitrary and blind processes, without meaning or purpose, in which the individual and the collective are leading their lives.

"Sort of an Apocalypse" is more humorous than "And That Is Your Glory," and contains a message that Amichai would later develop when issues of war and peace and the reconciliation between Israel and its neighbors were in the balance and hotly debated. Rather than the messianic option of "eternal peace," found in the vision of Isaiah or Immanuel Kant, Amichai develops a more modest thesis of "preventing war for as long as possible," and partial and certainly not perfect peace, which does not require any great love between the two opposing sides or the partners of the appeasement process.[8] The orders to prepare for war given by the "man under his fig tree" to "the man under his vine," much more so than what the fear-stricken lamb whispers to the wolf, are not resonant with an atmosphere of true peace; what remains to believe in is the hope that "they'll beat swords into plowshares and plowshares into swords [...] / Perhaps from being beaten thinner and thinner, / the iron of hatred will vanish, forever."[9] At best, one can only aspire to extending the periods of time between "swords" and thus make the world more bearable for humanity by enabling a partial or temporary remission from killing and bloodshed.[10]

Two very well-known poems – the mordant "God's Hand in the World," a condensation of secular pain, and "God Full of Mercy," a reverse hymn, a poem of non-thanks declaiming the absence of divinity in a world devoid of redemptive possibility – were published within four months of each other.[11]

"God Full of Mercy" is often read at funerals and is one of the reasons that Amichai, at least for a time, was unofficially crowned Israel's national poet.[12] God exists in both poems, but indifferently, gazing at the world through a sealed window, paying no heed to the horrors he has caused, or those committed in his name ("God's hand is in the world / like my mother's hand in the guts of the slaughtered chicken.") In "God Full of Mercy," the narrator cites allegedly biographical evidence, and his accumulation of experience, leading him to realize that "the world is empty of mercy." The speaker fought in wars and saw friends killed, took part in futile military operations, but felt irresolute and hesitant given painful alternatives (standing "indecisive at my window"), and would perhaps have been ready to live with ready-made answers were it not for the nagging doubt that forced him to search for answers to the world's enigmas, which in fact have no solution ("I, who must solve riddles despite myself"). Amichai justifies the relative sparseness of his poetic language which only employs "a small part / of the words in the dictionary," on the grounds of the limits of the perceivable world and the invalidity of all-embracing concepts and fine-sounding notions, which have no application or relevance for human existence. Words without ontological grounding are expunged from his dictionary.[13]

Apart from these poems and others such as "Out of Three or Four in a Room," "Not Like a Cypress" (perhaps the best expression of Amichai's philosophy of life and poetics),[14] and "Through Two Points Only One Straight Line Can Pass," all secured him an enduring presence in Hebrew poetry, there are three significant innovations in genre, which are placed strategically at the end of the first section and at the very end of the book. For the first time in Amichai's poetry, there is an elegy, "The Clouds Are the First to Die," which would have important extensions in *Poems 1948-1962*,[15] and there is a long poem, spectacular in its imagery, full of eroticism and replete with humor entitled "The Visit of the Queen of Sheba."[16] The volume *Two Hopes Away* also includes a series of 47 quatrains, apparently based on his reading of this form in Shmuel Hanagid. He would add a further series of quatrains in *Poems 1948-1962*.

In "Elegy" (aka "The Clouds Are the First to Die"), the forerunner to a series of poems in this genre, the influence of the German poet Rainer Maria Rilke (1875-1926) is evident. Amichai was impressed by his poetry and identified with his prose, as was apparent on several occasions in Amichai's letters to Ruth Hermann. He also made an attempt at translating some of Rilke's well-known poems (which appear in his letters and in a literary journal).[17]

Amichai said that the prime inspiration for "The Visit of the Queen of Sheba" was Sir Edward Poynter's 1890 painting, *The Visit of the Queen of Sheba to King Solomon* at the National Gallery in London, which he toured with Tamar in 1955.[18] In an interview with the journalist Edna Evron, he indicated that this long poem was written in 1958, just before he submitted the manuscript to the publisher and at the same time as his encounter with Clarice. There are parallels between the long poem and the description of the character of Patrice in *Not of This Time* in terms of the intense sexuality and the determination to fulfill this desire through stratagems of postponement and play. There are also parallels with the story "Love in Reverse," in particular in the sense of fatality about the death of love after the flowering of sexual abandon.

On February 22, 1957, Amichai published "Seven Quatrains" in *Masa*,[19] and nine months later, on November 22, another "Six Quatrains" appeared in *Davar*,[20] this time with the addition of a subtitle, in parentheses, "From the Cycle of Quatrains." When the "Quatrains" were published, and especially when they were included in *Two Hopes Away*, critics underscored the clumsy artifice of four-line verses strung together.[21] The constraint of finding a single rhyme for four lines appears to have forced Amichai to make concessions by distorting syntax or adding inessential fillers. However, this artifice – along with its density and apt message – may have drawn Amichai to the quatrain,[22] which he discovered in the Hebrew poetry of Spain, in Shmuel Hanagid. Although this particular pattern of rhyming quatrains is rare in Hanagid's *Son of Ecclesiastes* and other diwans, Amichai was impressed by the decisiveness of the message and atmosphere of the poems in *Son of Ecclesiastes*, and fashioned a strict and inflexible version of the quatrains to convey his vision of the world.[23]

PUBLICATION OF *TWO HOPES AWAY* AND ITS CRITICAL RECEPTION

In 1958, some of Amichai's poems appeared in a historically important anthology, *A Generation in the Land*, nearly all from *Now and in Other Times*. For the most part the anthology covered the prose and poetry of the Palmach generation, "a generation in our literary history whose hour and maturation overlap with those of the State of Israel," as the editors put it. Amichai straddled this generation; he later defined his status in a famous speech delivered to the Hebrew Writers' Association in 1968 as "a double agent."[24] In terms of age he belonged without question to the generation included in the anthology. However, in terms of poetic temperament, style, influences and educational background, he was from a later generation. Nevertheless, including his poetry in this anthology was no accident. Like a number of the contributors to the anthology, he had taken part in the wars of the previous two decades, and like them, his craft was significantly marked by those experiences and he shared the secular and socialist outlook of most of the contributors.[25]

It was natural for Amichai's second book, *Two Hopes Away*, to be published by a major arm of the Labor movement, *Hakibbutz Hameuchad,* in the spring of 1958. Among the publishers with a clear political orientation at that time, almost all of whom were Socialist-Zionist (*Sifriat Poalim*, established in 1939, *Hakibbutz Hameuchad*, 1940, and *Am Oved* 1943, which emerged out of *Davar*), *Hakibbutz Hameuchad* was the most suitable venue for a poet who was by now recognized as a representative of the sensibilities and leanings of a new generation.[26] All three publishers saw it as their cultural and educational responsibility to bring out books of poetry, despite the fact that they were generally unprofitable. This time Amichai's book came out with an illustrated cover and had a more elaborate layout.

The reactions to the volume suggested that the "Amichai shock" was over, and that the critics were better able to capture the nature of the poetic phenomenon that was Amichai. The critics had also mostly overcome the need to defend the nation dwelling in Zion against the moral assault of nihilism and the subversion of values which Amichai and his colleagues at *Likrat* seemed to be perpetrating. Abraham Huss, born like Amichai in Germany, who was about his age and a poet trained as a meteorologist, declared: "This is an original poet [...] responding to what happens around him with a genuinely open heart and soul [...] on a path unique to him, in expressive forms that have received the seal of approval from most of the young guard of Hebrew poetry".[27]

On the more conservative end of the spectrum, Gideon Katznelson, a prominent critic at that time, published two reviews of the book.[28] What enabled Katznelson – and perhaps others – to quell their unease at Amichai's poetry was that they now saw him as an authentic representative of a new generation: "Amichai's poetry is likely to pave the way to a new era in our poetry, to which, for personal reasons, we may feel averse."[29] "A nihilistic pessimism" characterized Amichai's generation "born of powerlessness [...] this generation which [...] does not rebel," which does not protest the decline of values. Katznelson was among the first to acknowledge the conversational qualities of Amichai's poetry by comparing two major works which he felt were emblematic of two generations: Amichai's *Two Hopes Away*, and Alterman's *Joy of the Poor*, a long poem published 15 years before Amichai's second book and which Katznelson felt was the embodiment of "faith in national and human fraternity alike [...] the poor could also expect days of joy." Nevertheless, Katznelson and his generation's tendency to cling to certain forms of literature as a source of comfort and strength may have prevented them from seeing how Alterman's poems, rather than being a vehicle of national optimism, were interwoven with a Gothic love of death.

Those already of like mind and sympathetic to Amichai celebrated the publication with supportive and sometimes valuable insights. In his review,

Gabriel Moked saw Amichai as both "picking up a thread of inner continuity from his early work," and "creating a poetic reality" which was "different, new for us, and even for himself."[30] Moked compared poems from both books and stated that "if one didn't already know which was earlier and which was later, one couldn't easily tell" which volume they came from.

Masa published a detailed review by Shaul Shaked, who had been a neighbor of Zach's in his student days, a member of the *Likrat* circle and later a professor of Indian and Iranian studies at the Hebrew University.[31] Shaked insisted on the naturalness and "taken for granted" approach in Amichai in terms of central themes and poetic language. "Amichai has succeeded for the first time in Hebrew poetry in presenting a natural and convincing synthesis of literary language, which includes a great many traditional sources […], and the spoken language," but this broadening of the language of poetry "is not undertaken under the banner of revolution, but in passing […]. In this respect, Hebrew poetry, with the appearance of the young guard, is taking another step towards freedom from language complexes."

The writer Shulamit Hareven published a particularly significant review.[32] She expressed considerable enthusiasm for Amichai's gift, "the writer's completely unmediated contact with the magic hidden in all of us," by which she meant the unconscious: "He has some lines […] touching directly on this territory, to which there is no access other than through dreams, in a moment of grace […]." She argued that this constitutes a key element in Amichai. The other is "an element I would call journalistic; a word-based outlook, as opposed to experience-based […] the two elements are almost unrelated, to the extent that if there is a connection, it is conscious, intellectual." Hareven considered that Amichai's weakness lay in that the "excellent images of essentially real things, […] can only be grasped through free associations in the reader's mind but the association is always verbal, restricted to what is known, idiomatic, useful, and this is not a reliable bridge."

Hareven's astute comments bring to light two aspects of Amichai's abilities, and to some extent his themes. The rational, or as Hareven calls it, "journalistic," foundation, preserves Amichai's ability to communicate with the human environment. It is a bulwark against the excessive intrusion of unconscious material, and protects him against the madness which tends to come with the gift of communicating with unconscious depths. The obsessive return to the same characters, such as Little Ruth, his childhood love in Würzburg, and Dicky, his commanding officer in Battalion 7 in the Negev, represent the two parts or poles of his personality. In interviews, Amichai often emphasized that what captivated him in remembering Ruth was precisely the fact that it had been a love between children, without a shred of sexuality.[33] However, there is no doubt that in adulthood, he imagined the intimate relations that could have existed if she had lived and gone to Palestine (when he talked about it to his interviewers he suggested they would have married). Ruth emerged again and again in his works; he revived her in the imaginative ruminations of the protagonist of the novel *Not of This Time,* when he returns to his childhood hometown. She represented the abundantly good and concerned mother, for whom Amichai, the child-youth, was the apple of her eye. Dicky was the father and like Yehuda's father, he was fatherly and devoted to his soldiers. He had a firm worldview, was demanding and capable of being punitive, but out of love and responsibility.[34] What is special in Amichai's poetry is not the existence of these two dimensions but their frequent proximity and parallelism. The father appears as an image of love for a woman, as a way of talking about these two opposing but complementary parts of the whole.[35]

The First Issue of *Achshav*: Zach and Amichai versus the Poets of the Previous Generation

After the Likrat group disbanded and their literary journal of the same name ceased to appear, there was a need for a new home for the many lively forces and antiestablishment vigor then current among younger writers.[36] Gabriel Moked, born in 1934, was enrolled in Hebrew literature and philosophy at the Hebrew University, and started editing a student literary journal called *Ogdan* in 1957. According to Moked, one alcohol-soaked dawn, he and Natan Zach decided to set up a publishing house for the new journal they called *Achshav* ('Now'), to replace *Ogdan,* perhaps echoing the title of Amichai's book, *Now and In Other Days*.[37] Zach insisted on having Amichai on the editorial board, whether out of friendship or because he believed that putting be on his name on the masthead would endow some prestige to the venture. The first issue came out in 1959.[38]

In the spirit of the times, the combative *Achshav* declared that it intended to adopt a clear and committed stance. It would be selective and take a stand in literary, cultural and ideological wars. The first issue published Amichai's "Poems to a Girl on the Seashore,"[39] whose automatic rhyming brings to mind the long poem "In the Public Garden." However, the literary material that established the journal's name and turned it into a sought-after venue was Zach's militant and argumentative challenge to Alterman and his generation in "Thoughts on the Poetry of Alterman."[40] This was the first in a number of sallies against the preceding generation of poets, in particular Alterman and Shlonsky, whose poetry Zach characterized as impersonal, lacking sensitivity to one-time occurrences, rhythmically mechanical and overly general in its outlook.[41]

Amichai produced little theory, and the public saw relatively little of his views on the nature of poetry, or about other poets past or present. In interviews he liked to emphasize that his poetry did not emerge from any conscious protest against earlier poetry but rather flowed from his heart and from a need to express feelings and sensations that the previous generation could not express.[42] However, he adhered to Zach's view of Alterman and Shlonsky, central figures in the previous generation of poets, and shared his likes and dislikes of the poets of earlier generations, and non-Hebrew poets. But although he shied away from the dominant figures of the previous generations of poets, he still saw himself as to some extent continuing what had been begun by these generations, though not the most prominent or most highly cherished by critics. When asked about the newness attributed to his use of the "I", replacing the pathos of the national "we" of the Palmach generation, or that of Alterman and Shlonsky, he would point out that poetry in the first person could already be found in David Vogel and even in the ultra-nationalist Uri Zvi Greenberg, certainly in his early poems.[43]

By contrast, he did express reservations about the poetry of Alterman and Shlonsky, albeit in simpler and less academic language than that of Zach, but just as decisively.[44] However, as fate would have it, when Amichai was in Buenos Aires at the beginning of April 1970 to give lectures at the Jewish Community Center (JCC), he heard the news that Alterman had died on March 31. The leadership of the JCC, who were enthusiastic Zionists, were not interested in the wars of succession in Hebrew poetry and most likely knew nothing about them. It seemed natural to them to ask their visiting poet to write an obituary for Alterman for the monthly *Raíçes* (Roots), put out by the Zionist Federation. Amichai acquitted himself honorably, without altogether concealing that Alterman's poetry was problematic for him:[45] "Like every Romantic poet, his poetry and in much of his work Alterman was concerned with death. He was a virtuoso of rhyme and a magician of metaphor," but his view of life was like a "radiant garment, which sometimes choked the object of his poetry, muting the vivacity of the image, event or object he wrote about, because his literary outlook was absolute and hermetic. [...] We can only hope that he will find the proximity to death and love he sang about in his poetry in the 'world of truth'",[46] knowing from personal experience how close these two poles can be.

THE PUBLICATION OF *IN THE PUBLIC GARDEN*; AN EARLY VERSION A DECADE PREVIOUSLY

Amichai had already laid the foundations for the long poem or series of poems entitled "In the Public Garden" at the end of 1947 and beginning of 1948, when he was anguished and consumed with longing for Ruth Hermann, whom he still expected to be his wife. On December 7, 1947 he wrote to her:

"Yesterday I finished a public reading of 'In the Public Garden.' It is difficult for me to tell you what it is. Picture after picture in free association." The abundant pictoriality tends to draw the reader into a kaleidoscopic view of reality.[47]

The actual length of the first version of this poem written in 1948 is not precisely known. It was the fruit of experimentation, a stage Amichai went through while trying out different stylistic directions. In passages he sent to Ruth Hermann, the influence of the younger Rilke in *The Book of Poverty and Death,* part of *The Book of Hours*, is striking.[48] At this time, while in Haifa, Amichai was naive and serious enough to absorb the tone of Rilke's religiosity, although he transposed it into more everyday realms with a hint of easy rhyme absent in Rilke: "Put the rustling in your pocket / God / Close the trees and the faucets. // Quieten the souls / Branching on the trunk, / Calm the running / On the feet of death." And in the second part: "Fold the tables / And the umbrellas / And the longings in girls' hearts."[49] After copying out the five passages in his letter to Ruth, the last two of which perhaps record the night they separated in Haifa,[50] he concludes excitedly: "This long poem is finished. In my opinion, it is one of my most successful pieces. It sings. What do you think?" He felt that he had found a path to a poetry that was freer than he had ever written previously, one that "sings." A basis had been laid to his later uniqueness: the daring syllogisms that allow him to make an analogy between verbs related to distant domains: "Close the trees and the faucets," "Put out [extinguish] her hands / And the fire";[51] and remote comparisons such as between lovers and a stew: "Prepare them for the next day, / Serve them / As a meal / In the morning: / So they will be/ So take care to keep them hot and steamy."

In 1959 Amichai stated that "my new book [*In the Public Garden*] began in a small garden beside Ahuza hospital in Haifa [in 1947-1948]. It was a time of a young man's pleasant loneliness. The little garden provided the frame for the poem, but I did not finish it. Ten years later, though, I was in a state of mind identical to the one back then, and started reworking the poem from scratch. After a few weeks all that was left of the original poem was the name."[52] Thus, at a certain period in his life, in 1958 and perhaps somewhat before, when he separated from Tamar and began seeing Clarice Kestenbaum, which also ended in a painful and unresolved separation, he felt he was in the same type of situation as when Ruth left Israel. The lovers' garden was beside the King David Hotel.[53]

Amichai exaggerated when he claimed in the same interview that "all that was left of the original poem was the name," since quite a few passages he sent to Ruth in January 1948 are still there in the complete version that appeared in 1959, but there is no doubt that the spirit of the poem changed dramatically as a result of the extensive editing. The kind of naive and gentle religiosity, the sense of potential wholeness, close and within reach, which infuses the passages sent to Ruth, were replaced by a cynical, macabre atmosphere, and alienated plays on words.

To conservative critics who had strong doubts about Amichai, the publication in book form of "In the Public Garden" confirmed their rejection of his poetry with its anti-conventional moral message. By contrast, the young Adir Cohen, then a rising critic, sought to justify *In the Public Garden* as manifesting a core characteristic of that generation by linking the individual with a divided society: "It is the poetry of public individuals, living, walking, imagining, loving, hating and sleeping in the public garden of our world." Cohen argued that Amichai's attention "to the chorus of inner and outer voices of our world" was commendable, since it documented diversity and multiplicity, the metonymy blending into the wholeness of the atmosphere.[54]

Gabriel Moked, the book's publisher, made efforts to promote it, but his review displayed poorly-concealed embarrassment: "There are many beings here [...] growing alongside one another, and one cannot connect one yearning with another [...] or classify individual events according to their importance." Moked was particularly concerned that "the loyal and attentive readers" of Amichai's poetry would be disappointed, after the enthusiastic reception of the first two books, and argued that *In the Public Garden* needed to be compared to the "Quatrains" or "The Visit of the Queen of Sheba."[55]

The most accurate analysis was penned, unsurprisingly, by Amichai's friend Natan Zach, who was not afraid of pointing out the many problematic features of the poem, the chaos of many sparks that did not coalesce into fire: The most recent book of poems by Yehuda Amichai, *In the Public Garden*, departs from the model of the short lyrical poem [...] and fails to achieve a richer and more complex unity. While there are intimations of a story within the poem, human characters relating and acting, these are largely "mechanisms for his talent for improvisation and verbal play." Devastatingly but accurately he wrote that despite isolated lines in the book recalling "the familiar Amichai [...], a poem needs meaning. It has to say something, it needs a center of gravity."[56]

The damning criticism of *In the Public Garden* seems to have made an impression on Amichai, who perhaps felt that he had overindulged in obscurantist play. An abridged version of the poem appeared in *Poems 1948-1962*. Whole passages, especially from the central part, were dropped, and other passages were shortened or moved. When the second edition of *In the Public Garden* came out in its complete form in 1970,[57] Amichai noted in his notebooks that "With the reprinting of *Public Garden* – [marginal] footnotes to my book of life, [are] dead. Not in existence. That's it, disappeared, dead."[58] This telegraphic style does not fully indicate whether he was talking about the long poem itself or the relationship memorialized in it.

THE HEIGHT OF LOVE FROM AFAR: CLARICE'S LETTERS FROM LOS ANGELES AND NEW YORK

Clarice was troubled by Amichai's ambivalence towards her: though he loved her, he was afraid to love "too much," as she put it, and was unable to sever his psychological ties with Tamar, and perhaps also his responsibilities towards her. Clarice packed her belongings and moved to Los Angeles, which meant additional time in medical school.[59] The poem beginning "Farewell, O Face of You, Already Face of Memory" was written about their separation.[60] Amichai's letters to her have not survived, but her letters to him, written in poetic English embedded artlessly here and there with Hebrew words, reveal a great deal about her experiences with him and what their relationship in Jerusalem continued to mean for her, his work at that time, his efforts to woo her and see her again, as well as his return to Tamar and the birth of their first son Roni in August 1961.[61]

On September 22 – almost certainly 1958 – she responded to the letters she received daily (reminiscent of the way he inundated Ruth Hermann with letters): "My dearest one, your letters are so full of love and pain I cannot bear it – Please accept the fate we made for ourselves [...] for this is what must be, and what you, and probably I, really wanted." She tells him that she is not miserable, that her day is packed with ordinary practical medical matters, as well as seeing psychiatric patients. She has been asked out on a few dates, but her heart is not really in it. She wonders whether he tells his students about "lonely poets and lonelier poets' loves," and implores him "please be again happy" without her. In the next letter, a little while later, she claims that she has not answered his apparently very frequent letters, "mostly because I think of you and feel near you." In concerned and loving empathy, mixed with an awareness of cruel reality, she writes that she does not see a solution: "I [...] know how you suffer – but I can see no way out. Our lives are not to be shared." Their respective needs for self-realization are not consistent. She wants to become a good doctor; and "I want to find a husband and have some small, sweet, pink children." "I shall see you again in my life – but I do not want to suffer or wait or have yearnings unfulfilled and hopeless love." She ends with a declaration of eternal love along with the decision to separate forever: "You are the most beautiful creature I ever met, anywhere – and I love you – but do not pursue me further. I must go on, for a while, alone."

Her letter dated October 3 is addressed to Amichai at Robert Friend's, almost certainly so as not to draw fire from Tamar, with whom Amichai had returned to live. She describes various younger suitors, medical students where she was finishing her degree. With her attention almost exclusively on work and studies, she imagines looking "over the hills, into the grey hill-horizon beyond many seas," to see Amichai's students listening to the "tapestries" he weaves with his words. His words "fly over the earth […] to more than one […] Amichai, you are not meant for one […] Is that bad, to be destined […] for love? I now have this great gift of your love, and I do not know what to do with it […] It's too big for a house", while in another letter, she "want[s] the *yom-yomi* [everyday] sort of love […] not mirror images but real live faces."

In subsequent letters she responds to works he has sent her, and encourages him to find comfort in his renewed togetherness with Tamar, urging him to become a father: "I don't see why Tamar should be sad now. I would prefer you not to love me so in spirit, but love her more in flesh, I think […] your poems are enough spirit." She tells him about her deep identification with her new work as a child psychiatrist: "My little ones […] frightened little ones of seven and eight who see demons and dragons and cry in their sleep." Despite her efforts to 'cure' them," she expresses insecurity about her ability, given her own mental state: "How can I make them not afraid, when my own heart is so weakly [..] mended?" She earns the praises of the children's mothers, and her teachers, "but all I do is play with them."

Her letter dated May 7, 1959 is concerned with life and death, as might be expected of an intern who sees people plucked from life daily before her eyes, and she compares their respective feelings. She notes accurately that "You will not be hurt by things like wars and wrecks – only big loves." Conversely, she wonders about the will to live of people who are literally on their last legs. She says she is planning to go to Europe and Jerusalem in the summer, which is why she writes just two weeks later on May 23 that she will not meet him "unless Tamar is there." He had been about to leave for Europe, almost certainly intending to spend time (perhaps longer than before) in the town of his birth, to write his long novel. It was important for her to make it clear that "I am very happy with your beautiful poems and I understand your feelings," but that their relationship was decisively over. "If you cannot do this, I cannot even see you like a friend."

Six months later, on November 2, 1959, she wrote to him saying that she had read, whether in the original or in translation, *In the Public Garden*. This long poem was clearly very dear to her: Amichai's relationship with Ruth Hermann had been the original springboard for the poem, but the entanglements of love with her had impelled the expanded rewrite. She knew that the garden "never was a garden," that is, a paradise. She tells him she went through a frightening and for a while dangerous experience: she had an operation to remove a small amniotic tumor "that I have been terrified about for two months." She describes her breast: "Now I have a little half-moon scar […] over the right *pitma* [the word for nipple written in Hebrew]." She begs him not to allow "any part – of your heart" to die, because of the child-like questions he obstinately raises about the world. Despite her very real enthusiasm for her work as a doctor, she is sometimes depressed: "I am not unhappy but very restless – where is the real life?"

In a letter dated February 14, 1960, she tells him about her pediatric residency in a community hospital near Los Angeles. Missing him was mixed with longings for other friends from her years in Israel including the poet and professor of literature Shimon Halkin, and Fanny (Professor Pines' wife), and Lea Goldberg. "I get pangs of memory which stab me, scattering visions like flowers spilled out of their basket, wildly and profusely on the ground." Two weeks later on February 29, her letter suggests that he is continuing to declare his love for her: "Shall I be for you forever that lovely thing, unreachable, to search for, never to grasp longer than an unbearably beautiful moment? [...] You know, I am real, too real, too touchable; isn't that what you ran away from, because you knew I was real after all?"

A month later, on March 30, she writes that she is an intern in the surgery department the last stage ("two months in hell") just before taking the board exam. She has found comfort in the poems he sent her, and hints that the poem "Jacob and the Angel" reminds her of "many such battles" between them: their lovers' tussles, about which the poem says "and both of them knew that a hold brings death."[62] One of her suitors, when compared with Amichai, is "like an empty egg shell with a face painted on it"; Amichai is in her eyes "like a golden egg which glistens and shines but cannot be eaten." She is as though "formed with no shell" and tries to build one for herself that will not get broken. In the summer of 1960, on August 7, she writes to him from New York, where she went for a series of job interviews with heads of psychiatry departments. Her letter two weeks later, on August 21, hints at some of the upheavals Amichai was going through at that time. Surprisingly, he had written her a number of letters in Hebrew, perhaps with the sense that in English he could not convey his enthusiasm about recent experiences, preferring to rely on her very slight knowledge of Hebrew. From what she managed to glean, it emerges that he had had "a fine summer *tiyul* [trip] to the sea," probably to Caesarea, perhaps the first of the times he spent on that coast with his future wife, Hana Sokolov, later to yield as a famous series of poems.

Her reading matter in the winter and spring of 1961, according to her letter of March 10, was Kafka's *The Trial*, Camus' *The Stranger*, and Lorca's poems. Amichai's book of stories, *In This Terrible Wind*, newly published, was sent to her, "but I must wait until I can have someone translate them for me. "I love you still," she confesses; "but one cannot live forever as in a dream, while the other continues to live and prosper [...] I'll never cut that special cord between us, but I must live, too." In her letter sent in the summer of 1961, on August 23, already from her new home in New York, she is "very excited about the psychiatric program" at Columbia where she had just been accepted. The letter focuses on Amichai's play *Journey to Nineveh,* just out in print, prior to the opening of Habima's (Israel's national theater) production. This was also just before the birth of his first son and Tamar's only child, Roni.

Little by little, and although their friendship was never broken off, the correspondence between Clarice Kestenbaum and Amichai seems to have lost its meaning. On May 25, 1962 she wrote telling him that she was happy in her work "for the first time in ten years," but that New York was "too unrestful" for her, and she did not plan to stay for more than two years. In time Clarice Kestenbaum became a professor at Columbia University in New York, and was appointed Chair of the American Academy of Child and Adolescent Psychiatry. She married twice and had two sons. She was convinced that Hana, Amichai's second wife, was an ideal match for him: "She looks after him, protects him," she told me when we spoke at her home.[63]

NOTES

1. The three poems were published under the same title in *Two Hopes Away*. See Amichai's letter to Shlonsky accompanying the manuscript, July 26, 1956. The letter implies that he had a preliminary agreement with Shlonsky that "material for a book of poems" would be published by Sifriat Poalim. Gnazim-55907.
2. Initially appearing under this title in the review *Mevo'ot. Poems* [in Hebrew] 1, 111.
3. Dan Miron reads this line differently: he sees Amichai as having broken with the Israeli public and poetic convention by viewing its wars as part of "the chaotic history of endless war in the twentieth century" rather than as specifically Jewish or Israeli. Amichai saw his participation in the War of Independence as part of his maturation rather than in the national perspective, which did not interest him. In "Revolutionist with Father," *More!* [in Hebrew] (Tel Aviv, 2013), 299.
4. In various interviews Amichai discussed the suppression of sexuality among the strictly religiously observant and the difficulty, his included, in escaping these taboos.
5. In the same journal, alongside "Poem for Friday Night," Amichai published the weak, overly blunt and mannerist "Two Autumn Poems," which he chose not to include in the book.
6. When first published, in *Mevo'ot* on October 25, 1955, it was called "Poem." It had an extra verse which Amichai deleted in the book version. *Life of Poetry*, 32.
7. *Poetry*, 27.
8. See, e.g., "Wildpeace": "Not the peace of a ceasefire, / not even the vision of the wolf and the lamb, / but rather / as in the heart when the excitement is over: / and you can talk only about a great weariness." The poem was first published in *Haaretz* newspaper on September 30, 1970. *Selected Poetry*, 88; *Poetry*, 184; *Life of Poetry*, 203. *Poems* [in Hebrew], 2, 287. Amichai himself placed the two poems together in a short

article, "Two Kinds of Vision," perhaps written in preparation for a talk, during debates over the Oslo Accords (15.711). A similar idea appears in a late poem, "An Addition to the Vision of Peace." For an English translation, see "Untitled" https://www.sefaria.org.il/sheets/119204.28?lang=bi&with=all&lang2=en; *Poems* [in Hebrew] 3, 294.

9. *Selected Poetry*, 10-11.

10. Zvi Luz writes that Amichai ridicules Isaiah's vision in "Sort of an Apocalypse". "The Ironic Allusion," in his *The Two-Way Flow of Hebrew* [in Hebrew] (Tel Aviv, 2011), 74-77. However, the derision in the poem is directed at humanity, which is unable to contain its violence and concretize the prophecy, not at Isaiah.

11. "God's Hand in the World", *Poetry*, 24; *Selected Poetry*, 10; another translation: *Life of Poetry*, 29; "God Full of Mercy," *Poetry*, 26; another translation, *Life of Poetry*, 31.

12. Although Ziva Shamir calls "God Full of Mercy" a "funeral poem," the fact that it is sometimes read at funerals does not, in terms of its content and essence, make it one. Shamir, "On Two Well-Known Funeral Poems – By W. H. Auden, and Yehuda Amichai," *Shvo* 12 (2004): 23-28. On the custom of reading this poem to mark tragic occurrences, see Mordechai Geldman, "Terrible Competitions," [in Hebrew] *Alpayim* 16 (1998): 121.

13. On "God Full of Mercy" see also the analysis in Naomi B. Sokoloff, "On Amichai's 'El Male Rahamim,'" *Prooftexts* 4:2 (1984): 127-140. Sokoloff's account is particularly interesting in that it reflects the characteristically American-Jewish difficulty not to view Amichai as religious.

14. See Rachel Tarass-Zukerman's analysis: "About One poem of Yehuda Amichai", in *From the World of Art* [in Hebrew] (Jerusalem, 1990), 79-83.

15. The poem was published in *Lamerhav-Masa* on March 21, 1958 as "Elegy." In the book *Two Hopes Away* the title is taken from the opening line, "The clouds are the first to die."

16. The sonnet cycle "We Loved Here" in the first book can be viewed as a long poem narrative sequence, but this cannot be compared to the explicit and tightly woven narrativity of "The Visit of the Queen of Sheba." Amichai also tried his hand at writing a long poem during the time he was teaching in Haifa, between September 1947 and April 1948, while working on the preliminary version of "In the Public Garden." The final version, which is thoroughly different, would only be published in 1959.

17. Letters to Ruth Hermann dated December 17, 1947, February 18, 1948 (a draft translation of "Love Poem" – "Liebeslied" by Rilke), February 28, 1948 (relating to Rilke's early book *The Story of the Love and Death of the Cornet Christoph Rilke*), March 7, 1948 (relating to *Letters to a Young Poet*), and October 12, 1949. His translations of some of Rilke's poems appeared in *Mevo'ot* 3 (27) (December 5, 1955).

18. In an interview with Edna Evron, "National Poet? That's All I Need!" he stated that "I stuck with the poem for four years, and now it seems to me that my whole life is in it."

19. These were later included in *Two Hopes Away*, in the cycle "In a Right Angle" (in a different order than published in the newspaper), as quatrains 33, 43, 41, 44, 42, and 47.

20. Later included in "In a Right Angle" as quatrains 13, 22, 3, 27, 39, and 46.

21. Shulamit Hareven, for example, in a generally positive review, wrote that the "Quatrains" were of very poor quality: "The poet set out to write a quatrain come what may; to stick empty flourishes together [...] helped along by intellectual acrobatics [...] but the distance between this and poetry can be very great." Hareven, "Fireworks," *Al Hamishmar*, September 5, 1958. However, G. M. (Gabriel Moked) thought that the "Quatrains" were the crowning achievement of Amichai's first period. Moked, "On Two Hopes Away by Yehuda Amichai," *Achshav* 3-4 (Spring 5719/1959).

22. On the anti-Romantic quality of the "Quatrains," see Reuven Tsur, "Two Quatrains by Amichai," *Romantic and Anti-Romantic Elements in Poems by Bialik, Tchernichowsky, Shlonsky and Amichai* [in Hebrew] (Tel Aviv, 1985), 29-31.

23. Tova Rosen, who has researched the influence of Hanagid's poetry on Amichai, conjectures that the actual source for his quatrains were the Persian poet Omar Khayyam's Rubaiyat (d.1131 in Nishapur, Iran). Tova Rosen, "Between Shmuel Hanagid and Yehuda Amichai," *Jerusalem Studies in Hebrew Literature* 15 (1995), 87-88. Katz-Benshalom's translation of Omar Khayyam into Hebrew first appeared in book form in 1937. Chana Kronfeld argued that Amichai's affinity with Spanish and Persian poetry was connected to what she perceived as his far-leftist political views. Kronfeld, *Full Severity*, 176-177.

24. "Generations in the Land," published in *Lamerhav-Masa*, May 3, 1968. See also the interview with Eyal Megged, "Towards the End You Become Simpler" [in Hebrew], *Yediot Acharanot*, November 8, 2011.

25. See Dan Miron's analysis in "Safeguarding the Vessels," *More!*, 276-78. For a contemporaneous review of recent literary generations in Hebrew letters, see Gad Issachar, "From the Palmach Generation to Neo-Judaism" [in Hebrew], *Maariv*, March 24, 1961.

26. Gideon Katznelson, "The Poet of a Generation whose Temple became Empty" [in Hebrew], *Haaretz*, July 18, 1958; David Eren, "Yehuda Amichai – In Poetry and Prose – An Attempt at Criticism," *Al Hamishmar*, June 16, 1961.

27. Abraham Huss, "On the Poems of Amichai and Galai" [in Hebrew], *Orot*, February 1959, 45-48.

28. Gideon Katzenelson, "Like a Stem of Flowers in a Vase" [in Hebrew], *Davar*, July 11, 1958; Idem, "Poet of a Generation."

29. Katznelson, "Poet of a Generation."

30. M. G., "Two Hopes Away" [in Hebrew], *Achshav* 3-4 (Spring 5719/1959): 169-171.

31. Sh. Shaul, "Yehuda Amichai's New Poems" [in Hebrew], *Lamerhav-Masa*, May 30, 1958.

32. Hareven, "Fireworks."

33. In the Liraz Punk interview, Amichai talked about Ruth as follows: "With her I felt the specialness of the girl. She played [the piano], and was very beautiful, but this didn't stop me being with the gang." In a similar tone, he spoke of the "purity" between them, in the Omer interview, "In This Burning Country."

34. Dicky in fact appears in a number of poems without being named. The figure of King Saul in "King Saul and I" is perhaps based on Amichai's view of Dicky.

The character of the devoted commander leading his troops always knowing what he is facing, and dying in the process ("Only the asses bare their yellow teeth / At the end"), is Dicky in his greatness, whereas "I" is the speaker of the poem, directionless but alive.

35. For example when he talks about a young woman, the beloved of the poem "The Smell of Gasoline in My Nose": "In my palm I held your soul that rose, / Like an *etrog* in a bowl of soft cotton – / My dead father did it every autumn." In his journal (file 439) he describes "the last evening at the hotel" – almost certainly when he separated from Clarice: "When I kiss her, it's like my father blessing me before going to synagogue on Yom Kippur." Similarly challenging is the positioning of the two father poems in the opening of the cycle "We Loved Here."

36. See Dan Eban's review, "The Crisis of the Literary Journals" [in Hebrew], *Yediot Acharonot*, April 30, 1959.

37. Gabriel Moked, "Memories of Achshav Publishing House" [in Hebrew], *Siman Kriah* 1 (September 1972): 297-282; Neiger, *Publishers*, 411-412.

38. Amichai gives an account along these lines in a letter to Zerubabel Gilad, poet and editor at Hakibbutz Hameuchad, June 15, 1959. Hakibbutz Hameuchad archives in Ramat Efal, 15-48/26/10.

39. *Life of Poetry*, 64-69.

40. In "Memories of Achshav Publishing House" Moked describes in detail how Zach was unhappy about the content of the first issue. After the publication of the journal in the expanded format, Zach resigned from the editorial board. *Siman Kriah* 2 (May 1973), 330-336 [in Hebrew].

41. Zach's most systematic and comprehensive statement can be found in his book *Time and Rhythm in Bergson and Modern Poetry* [in Hebrew] (Tel Aviv, 1966). Shlonsky, who was less important in his eyes, is attacked less aggressively.

42. Amichai told Edna Evron that "the transition to 'I' was something that had to happen. It wasn't that I wanted to break from the tradition of Alterman. It was natural for me to write 'I', just as writing itself is natural." Evron, "National Poet? That's All I Need!"

43. In the Evron interview Amichai argued that "they were already writing personal poetry before, Uri Zvi Greenberg for example, and others." In an interview with Aviva Barzel he names two others, "[David] Vogel and [Ya'acov] Lerner, who wrote in simple language, and didn't exaggerate themselves or their experiences within their historical contexts."

44. In an interview with Megged, when he and his interviewer talked about the presence of family life in Dalia Ravikovitch's poetry after her son's birth, Amichai observed that family factors are not always significant: "With Shlonsky you never feel that there's a daughter, or two. Neither in Alterman. He wrote about his daughter, but this was a generalized daughter, just as the mother was a generalized mother."

45. "On the Fresh Grave of Nathan Alterman" [in Spanish], *Raiçes* III, 17 (Buenos Aires, 1970). Spanish translation by Simja Sneh. The Hebrew original has not survived, and the translation here is based on the Spanish.

46. The young David Avidan transitioned from imitation of Alterman's poetry to parodying his style, denouncing what Zach and Amichai also sought to distance

themselves from. Like them he aimed for a real world in poetry, through blunt and direct expression, free of game-playing. See Chaya Shacham, *Echoes of Melody* [in Hebrew] (Tel Aviv and Haifa, 1997), 228-234.

47. This was part of his response to the high-school students who sent questions about his work: *Lamerhav-Masa,* March 8, 1957. See Chapter 7.

48. *Das Stunden-Buch von der Armut und vom Tode*, in R. M. Rilke, *Ausgewählte Gedicht* (Den Haag, 1948).

49. See the passages in the complete version of "In the Public Garden," towards the end, 144-194. Most of them were removed from the long poem as it appears in *Poems 1948-1962*, 133-147.

50. Scharf Gold's conjecture in *National Poet,* 253.

51. Cf. Reuven Tsur, "Two Quatrains," 32-34.

52. Eda Zoritte, "Writers Tell."

53. Conversation with Clarice Kestenbaum, July 15, 2015.

54. C. Adir (Adir Cohen), "Modernity and Conservatism in Our Poetry" [in Hebrew], *Haboker*, August 14, 1959.

55. Gabriel Moked, "Exposing the Experience of the Individual and the Collective" [in Hebrew], *Yediot Acharonot*, September 18, 1959.

56. Natan Zach, "The Nimble Muse" [in Hebrew], *Davar*, August 28, 1959; collected in *The Poetry Beyond Words* [in Hebrew], 337-341.

57. On February 11, 1994, a frustrated Amichai wrote to Moked asking him to "send me the rest of the books in Achshav's store and the list of everything you owe me from all the years you have been selling the book in shops and at different fairs." Archive of Achshav, National Library.

58. 30.1114.

59. Conversation with Clarice Kestenbaum. Before coming to Israel she studied English literature and musicology in Los Angeles.

60. First published in *Haaretz*, February 20, 1959. *Poems* [in Hebrew], 1, 219. Dan Miron wrote about this poem and another poem on parting, "Such as Sorrow," in "A Reading of Two Love Poems of Yehuda Amichai," *Anaf [A Branch]- for Young Literature* [in Hebrew] (Jerusalem and Tel Aviv, 5723/1962-1963). See next chapter.

61. Usually Amichai wrote to her in English, but at a certain point he tried writing in Hebrew, thinking that he would be able to convey his experiences better.

62. *Selected Poetry,* 40; another translation in *Poetry,* 76.

63. Conversation with Clarice, New York, July 15, 2015.

Chapter 9

1958–1963

Clarice in Amichai's Poetry, the Birth of Roni, Publication of Stories and a Novel

KEY POEMS RELATING TO CLARICE

Amichai's relationship with and separation from Clarice Kestenbaum yielded at least one story, entitled "Love in Reverse," as well as many passages in the Jerusalem part of his novel *Not of This Time, Not of This Place*. His relationship with Clarice was also the inspiration for some of his most beautiful and mysterious poems such as "Farewell," "Such as Sorrow," and "Jacob and the Angel." The latter came a little later and seems more playful and infused with a tone of acceptance of their breakup.[1] "Farewell," which is both stirring and somewhat obscure, was analyzed in a classic article by Dan Miron, "Reading Two Love Poems of Yehuda Amichai."[2] Miron knew about Amichai and Clarice's love affair, and made the association between "Farewell" and "Such as Sorrow" and the events of *Not of This Time*.[3] More can be learned about "Farewell" from drafts of the poem found in one of Amichai's many notebooks, along with notes he made about his relationship with Clarice.[4]

Some of these drafts, along with biographical information about Amichai's relationship with Clarice, contribute to clarifying the poem. Amichai wrote "For what you [unlike the "we" in the published version] didn't understand, we sang together". This is suggestive of the foreignness of the lover addressed in the poem, who lived for years in Israel without learning the language, and without really absorbing its ways.[5] By singing together they found points of convergence and commonality, while avoiding the linguistic and intellectual misunderstandings that could divide them. "Face of alternation" was originally "in alternation we will live" in the draft. By trying to console himself, the speaker may be promising himself that he can recover, and perhaps restore his relationship with his lover.[6] The last two verses of the poem may be the most interesting in terms of the couple's relationship and the worldview Amichai fashioned. "Forever sleepless" could reflect his admiration for Clarice's energy, as he watched her go from sleep to activity without self-indulgence.[7] "Forever sleepless" relates to "From now you weave / your own dreams" and suggests that the beloved's bustling activity and assertiveness prompted her to make the fateful decision to separate from the lover/speaker of the poem to pursue her dream of becoming a psychiatrist in the US. The use of the rare Hebrew biblical expression "dreaming [your own] dreams," in a seemingly celebratory tone, may hint at Amichai's disregard for Clarice's independent plans;[8] he would have preferred a woman with fewer aspirations for herself, and more devoted to his needs.

The line "for all came through our word, a profane word" [lit. "all is profane"], which places divine powers in the hands of the lovers, implies a sense of their ability to shape reality as they like while completely abolishing bothersome holiness and emphatically defying religious norms.[9] The description in *Not of This Time* of Joel and Pat's sexual relations on their first night together, and the narrator's subsequent reflections suggest that he sees his erection, which brings them such great satisfaction, as a kind of "rebellion."[10]

Another poem almost certainly relating to Clarice, which appears outwardly simple although actually disorienting and elusive, is "Jacob and the Angel."[11] Despite its plot seemingly being remote from Amichai's biographical experience, the one-night stand seems to be a way for Amichai to express the experience of transience and the severing of his relationship with the American medical student.[12] The title equates the couple to Jacob and the angel who struggled with Jacob as he was returning with his wives, family, sheep and cattle to the Land of Israel. Jacob was afraid of his brother Esau's murderous revenge.[13] A traditional commentary on Genesis 32-33 indicates that the angel wrestling with Jacob was indeed Esau, or Esau's guardian-angel.[14] In this reading, Jacob and the angel are not only kin but also bitter enemies to the point of endangering one another's existence, as was the case for the lovers. This may also hint at another problem that troubled Amichai in his love relationships: his awareness that "a hold / brings death" (something both lovers know in "Jacob and the Angel"). In other words, the dominance of one over the other means the latter's death, and in this case the death of spiritual aspirations, the goal the poet set for himself in this world.[15]

RETURN TO TAMAR, RONI'S BIRTH, AMICHAI'S LOVERS

In Clarice's letters to Amichai between 1958 and 1960, she repeatedly begs him to "make Tamar a baby" not only for her but for himself, to enrich his life and reunite them as a couple.[16] For close to 12 years he and Tamar refrained from having children, probably out of the fear that looking after a child would impede Amichai's creative work or interfere with their sexual relationship which was so important to him (perhaps the main factor). On August 21, 1961, Ron Meir was born. Meir, the name of Amichai's father, existed only on his identity card.[17] Roni's facial features were like Amichai's, and over the years, he also resembled him in character, linguistic ability and creativity. However, the birth of a child did not help mend the rift between the couple. From Clarice's letters to Amichai it is obvious that he had other lovers after their separation. She even tried to placate his conscience, saying "you are not meant for one [...] Is that bad, to be destined, as I know you are, for love [...]?"[18]

At a certain point, probably in 1963, Hana Sokolov, born in 1939 in Petah Tikva, began teaching literature at the school for working youth on HaRav Kook Street in Jerusalem. Friends and later Amichai called her "Rejah."[19] During her military service she was in *Garin Nahal*,[20] a group of high school graduates whose military service involved helping to build a new kibbutz or supporting one that was floundering. After earning her degrees in world history, literature and education, she became a university lecturer in education and was involved in the training of literature teachers.

Her close relations with her fellow teacher Amichai were initially secretive, and were made up of moments stolen during the day and night, with trips to Akhziv beach.[21] In 1964, when Roni was three, Amichai finally decided to leave home. This time he was not, or was less troubled by guilty feelings towards Tamar. He was clear that the separation was necessary. In a poem written years later he described the outbursts of anger preceding their separation: "I found a newspaper from ten years before. / From the week we separated [...] you [masc.] bury me. / You [fem.] bury me. / That's the kind of thing we said then / With crimson cheeks and far from death. // [...] I am burned. [fem.] / I am burned. [masc.] / That's the kind of thing we said then". The poem expresses something akin to a death-wish at the end: "It was enough that one of us was burned / To light the other with his fire."[22]

It was less easy for him to leave Roni. He was aware of the effect his leaving home could have on his son,[23] and when he traveled to the US with Hana in the summer of 1966, one of the things that prompted him to return to Israel after nine months – and perhaps the most important reason, according to his notebooks – was the need to be with his son.[24]

THE STORIES OF *NOW IN THIS TERRIBLE WIND* TAKE SHAPE

The late 1950s and early 1960s, a time of crisis for Amichai and Tamar, were extremely fruitful in terms of his work:[25] he published fiction including a novel, and wrote stage and radio plays, (in particular the novel *Not of This Time*), his plays were performed (mainly *Journey to Nineveh*, at Habima), and his radio plays (primarily *Bells and Trains*) broadcast. All elicited great interest, and the originality of his work with respect to canonical Israeli literature and drama was acknowledged.[26]

Amichai's first attempts at prose were a form of journalistic writing that consisted of reportage-memoirs written with great talent, such as "Auden Reads His Poems," whose title was modified when the piece was published in the book as "A Poetry Reading," and "A Visit to the Landscape of Dylan Thomas," which similarly became "A Poet's Landscape." Other stories from the period when he began writing prose which unintentionally rose to the level of poetic storytelling, were "The London Ballet in Jerusalem," which in the book became "Ballet in Jerusalem," "Hammarskjöld in Jerusalem" and "The Jewish Studies Congress." The latter two were never published in book form. Another story, "Dicky", which in the book became "Dicky's Death", was first published in *Mibifnim,* the literary organ of Hakibbutz Hameuchad which included Kibbutz Givat Brenner, where Dicky was a member and raised a family. Here as well, certain passages are suggestive of a eulogy which would develop into a rich story. "On Haggadot and the Departure from Egypt," which became simply "The Departure from Egypt," seems to have been based on an answer to a questionnaire of the kind submitted to writers and cultural agents by literary supplements, on "what does the Passover holiday mean to you?"[27] It contains a series of journalistic statements which, thanks to the talent of the poet perhaps not at first intentionally, became a sequence of stories full of metaphors and daring, and sometimes extravagant, analogies.

Clearly, the first stories were written in the same way as his poems: some event in the flow of everyday life that had an emotional charge for Amichai is chronicled; he grasps its symbolic potential and wonders about its meaning for him, and its impact on him. A case in point was the visit to Israel of UN Secretary-General, Dag Hammarskjöld (1905-1961), against the backdrop of tensions between Israel and Egypt, which resulted in the Sinai Campaign. His visit led Amichai to write the story "Hammarskjöld in Jerusalem," in which the narrator and his wife cross paths with Hammarskjöld heading to a meeting with Prime Minister David Ben Gurion while Yehuda and Tamar are on their way to a Sabbath dinner at his mother's. "My mother was already standing on the balcony waiting for me and my wife, like Sisera's mother who waited for her son. My mother never asked me to bring a spoil of embroidered cloths [Judges 5:30]. When I came back [from the war] she was happy just that I had brought myself and my eyes." While Hammarskjöld failed to create world harmony ("trying to be like a needle, he sometimes had no thread, continuing to make connections without it"), the narrator and his wife went hand in hand, "the only buckle holding the world together."[28]

The two obituaries which became stories – "Dicky's Death" and "The Times My Father Died" – are much more developed, given that they were written about key figures in Amichai's life. In these stories he found a formal alternative to the causal-chronological narrative of the realistic story so popular then in Hebrew literature.[29] "The Times My Father Died" is organized around the metaphor of death in life as a returning occurrence until the actual death of his father. In the eyes of his young son, he had not only died when he prostrated himself in the synagogue during the *Aleinu* prayer on Yom Kippur, but even earlier in WWI, since from a statistical point of view there was a strong probability that he would have been one of the millions of soldiers who fell in that war. He then died again when Germany turned against him, the faithful soldier and citizen: Nazi troops broke into their home when his son was suspected of having desecrated a Nazi symbol. Thanks to its clear structure and the absence of complicated metaphors and arbitrary plays on words, this story is often chosen to represent Amichai the prose writer in anthologies, in Hebrew and in translation.[30]

"Dicky's Death" follows the main events in the short life of Amichai's beloved company commander, Dicky – Haim Laksberger – who was indeed like a father to the lonely Amichai. The story focuses on the final dramatic days before his death in battle, and what happened after it: his burial by the Egyptians in a mass grave, along with others in his unit, the exhumation and the narrator's visit to his widow, who made a forced attempt to overcome her grief by immersing herself in the life of the kibbutz and her educational responsibilities there.[31]

PUBLICATION OF THE COLLECTION OF STORIES

Sifriat Poalim, the publishing house established by *Hakibbutz Ha'arzi (Mapam)*, had been in crisis since 1955; the momentum of gathering the best young writers into its fold had slowed, and *Hotza'at Hakibbutz Hameuchad*, established by another, less left-wing stream of the kibbutz movement, had taken its place.[32] Amichai, whose book of poems *Two Hopes Away* was due to come out at *Hakibbutz Hameuchad*, had asked them as early as 1958 to accept his volume of short stories for publication.[33] However, Amichai's innovative style, rich in metaphor, plays on words and sophisticated digressions disrupting the storyline may have been too much for the serious-minded Marxists in charge of the publishing house. At *Sifriat Poalim*, as well, where Amichai turned as a second choice, zealots stood guard;[34] but Azriel Uchmani (Schwartz), one of the senior editors, who was steeped in European culture and attentive to the winds of modernism, was apparently willing to take a chance with publishing this strange collection of stories, which nevertheless had clear echoes of Israel's social problems and historical upheavals such as "Dicky's Death," a laudatory and loving tribute to the kibbutz member and revered commander who fell in battle, "The World Is a Room" and "The Aswan Dam," with their resonances of WWII and the War of Independence, "Eat and Drink," which reflects to some extent a world of deprivation in the characters of the narrator's students, and "Nina of Ashkelon," which describes the entry of Mediterranean culture into young Israel.[35]

In This Terrible Wind came out in December 1960, with new editions in 1973 and 1985 published by Schocken, where by that time Amichai had become its house writer.[36] Two stories which had meanwhile been written were added in 1973: "The Orgy" (its title changed from the original, which was seen as off-putting to potential audiences, "The Orgy That Never Was"), and "Venice – Three Times."

In an interview in the weekly *Dvar Hashavua*, Amichai described the poetics of the story which was very similar to that of the poem he had already presented to a group of curious high school students some years earlier. Amichai spoke of his stories as "a mosaic," and "as with mosaics […] it makes sense to stand back a little so you can see the whole picture […] Each story is a unit, and each unit is divided into a number of parts, that you need to come back to over and over again." In his view, because of his Romantic-pessimistic worldview, his stories feature characters whose plans or aspirations repeatedly come to nothing, and who perhaps even lack the desire from the outset to bring them to fruition.[37]

Asher Nahor, in a critical piece in *Yediot Acharonot,* considered the stories to be the work of a poet, "laboring under the weight of poetic images […] reveries and dreams."[38] In the rival newspaper *Maariv*, Moshe Dor, Amichai's colleague in the Likrat circle, defended the book by arguing that blurring the lines between prose and poetry was already an accepted practice throughout the world.[39] His main argument was that the stories expressed the doubts endemic to Amichai's generation, the fighters of the Palmach generation, who were disoriented by the direction taken by the new state. He was nevertheless conscious of the problematic nature of imagistic prose of the sort written by Amichai"[40]

It remains unclear whether critics writing about the book realized that even the stories with a more regular narrative outer appearance, that adhered to reasoned causal lines, were surrealist in construction, and apparently influenced by Kafka: there is a repeated, obsessive attempt of main figures to escape loneliness and emotional emptiness, which ends in failure and deepening despair, for example, in recurring flights to the woman-mother, or penetration by the woman-mother in the life of the narrator of "Battle for the Hill," or Nina's hopeless flights from her husband preoccupied with his dealings in "Nina of Ashkelon." This structure is found in most of Amichai's stories, other than his documentary reports.

Later editions, in 1970s and 1980s, were met by a different cultural reality in Israel. Critical responses to the book's re-publication showed that Amichai's prose style had not only been assimilated by readers but also elicited enthusiasm about its path-breaking potential for future Israeli fiction. Menachem Ben wrote about how the beauty of the stories "was insufficiently understood when they first came out. [...] Israeli fiction being written today in the country seems to me to be very much in need of a kind of mental shift of the sort that Amichai's stories have the power to induce."[41] The poet Dalia Hertz went even further: "Amichai is still connected to the concrete image, to the real story, to the wisdom of life and of the heart [...]." Nevertheless, she saw his limitations as a storyteller, particularly an inability to break away from the "I" towards "minor characters," which despite "beautiful moments of observation," remain merely factors in the writer's world.[42]

STORIES WRITTEN AFTER THE FIRST PUBLICATION OF *IN THIS TERRIBLE WIND*

In the early 1960s two more stories by Amichai came out: "Football," which was never anthologized, and "Venice – Three Times," which was incorporated in the next edition of *In This Terrible Wind*, published by Schocken in 1973. A third story, also in the 1973 edition, "The Orgy That Never Was" ("The Orgy"), was published in *Moznaim* at about the same time as the publication of the new edition of the book.[43] The stories from the beginning of the 1960s continue the momentum of prolific prose writing that originated in the years of crisis with Tamar that led to the stories in the first edition of *In This Terrible Wind*, along with the novel *Not of This Time*. Unlike these texts, however, "The Orgy" experiments with a new type of prose which gave rise to the failed novel *Hotel in the Wilderness*. It reflects techniques and experiences similar to those of the novel, and its plot, like that of the novel, takes place in New York.

The story "Venice – Three Times" is based on a spiral principle similar to that followed in "The Times My Father Died" (and other stories such as "Battle for the Hill") that involves an obsession-tinged return to a person or place at different points in time. Here it focused on the narrator's visits to Venice: the first when he was a child of 12 and passed through Venice on the way to pre-state Palestine with his family.[44] It was a confusing experience for him: the pigeons in Piazza San Marco seemed "madly gluttonous," and he was fascinated by the fascist youth he saw marching in "their beautiful black uniforms." His second and third visits to Venice took place a year before the publication of the novel in 1963 or in close proximity. Between the two visits he spent five hectic months in Europe, almost certainly in Germany: "Many nights of insomnia, when I was afraid of others, and others were afraid of me. Journeys [...] that served as background to fates inappropriate for me to discuss here."[45] This is likely to have been during the last stages of consolidating the novel *Not of This Time*, and perhaps the writing of its German part.

Tamar, who met him in Venice in the summer (she is identified here explicitly as his wife of 14 years), is described as "a redeeming angel" who comes to calm his fears, among them the fear of flying. In other words, a year before he finally separated from her he still needed and depended on her, at least in the story. This points to the complexity of Amichai's relationship with Tamar, and how difficult the decision was to leave her, all of which is also reflected in the play that dates to that period, *Journey to Nineveh* (*Jonah*, in the first version).

POETS OF THE STATE GENERATION BECOME MORE POPULAR; DISCOURSE ON THE COMPREHENSIBILITY OF POETRY

From the 1960s onward the poets of the State generation – Amichai, Zach, Avidan, and Ravikovitch – began to be seen as the pillars of contemporary Israeli poetry, in a country in which poetry was still a relatively popular form. On the threshold of the 1960s this was no longer an insolent group of iconoclast youngsters who had to be taught the laws of poetry and morality but rather the tone-setters and arbiters of taste, whose poetry commanded an attentive audience.

This can be seen in literary surveys that asked Amichai and other prominent poets of his generation to expound on the creative process, and the deference of literary journalism to their essays and theorizing. Amichai wrote few essays, given his penchant for anti-intellectualism. It thus came as a surprise in March 1959 when he published an article entitled "The Poet in Modern Society." It dealt primarily with the public perception of the poet – a topic which would be central to his lectures and responses in his many interviews. In it he suggested that the position of the poet is complex since he or she is expected to be wretched, marginal, and wild, while in reality s/he could be quite normal in his external appearance and life conditions. Amichai maintained that a poet was not necessarily exceptional in character and behavior, or in fact even in talent. He or she simply packages the words of ordinary people: "the words are theirs [...] and the poet just arranges them a little, in an attractive way."[46]

Early in the Hebrew year 5723 (the autumn of 1962) he was again asked to contribute to a survey entitled "Poets on Our Young Poetry." On this occasion he was the only representative of his generation, alongside Lea Goldberg, Shin Shalom (Shalom Shapira) and Yehoshua Rabinov. Similar to his stance in his article on "flattening" the writing of a poem and the refusal to justify its uniqueness as Romanticism sees it, Amichai stated that "the written work of art in the Hebrew language is part of Hebrew literary heritage," and that there is no need to emphasize unique feature as concerns new poetry. There is no "new" and "old," only what is better and what is less good. The only relevant distinction, in his opinion, was between the canonical and non-canonical in religious texts, and between secular and religious poetry; in other words, distinctions that stem from the history of Hebrew culture.[47]

Another indication of the growing popularity of the State generation and its symbolic clout was an evening held in the second week of January 1962 at Beit Lessin in Tel Aviv. The event marked ten years since the publication of the first issue of *Likrat* (and took place a little before the actual anniversary date in the summer, in the month of Sivan 5722).[48] For the first and last time in their lives Amichai, Zach and Avidan, the great triumvirate of "the young poetry," appeared together on the podium. According to newspaper reports, the average age of the audience packed into the hall was twenty. Perhaps the most interesting aspect of what Amichai said was the sense of farewell to his youth and the beginning of a new period in his poetry and in his personal life. Amichai the poet was indeed different after 1962, and there is some justification to the dissatisfaction expressed by many people over the years who criticized his later poetry. The intense authenticity of the first three poetry collections (with the exception of *In the Public Garden*), which conquered the Israeli public, in fact seemed to dissipate and take on another quality.

THE POLITICAL AMICHAI

Along with becoming a major poet of his generation and the growing acknowledgment of his poetic direction, Amichai became an authority to be reckoned with both poetically and for his unconventional political opinions. Identifying his political stance, particularly in his poems, is a subtle and complicated task, because he was never a party man, though he did have firm views.[49]

Early in 1960 and in 1961 he published two poems, whose political interpretation is ambiguous, although contemporaries sensed that an opinion was being expressed about painful current events. In the first issue of a short-lived left-wing journal called *Ma'arach* edited by Baruch Hefetz, Gabriel Moked and Maxim Ghilan, he published a poem called "In the Full Severity of Compassion."[50] Chana Kronfeld, in an important book but extreme in its politicization of Amichai's poetry, identifies the lonely people in the poem "On the corner and in the street" who "[see] the sky through ruined houses [...] and they walk around outside and their hopes, unbandaged, / are gaping, and they will die of them" as the Palestinians who fled or were evicted from their lands and villages during the War of Independence. She reads a comparison between the Jews, who found no relief for their suffering in the Diaspora, and the Palestinians, who were forbidden to return to their villages even after "they / have already used up all the blood and there's still not enough."[51] More explicitly she argues that Amichai wrote a "lament" on the villages the Palestinians left behind in "Elegy on an Abandoned Village."[52]

Are the refugees from 1948 the "tenor" or the "vehicle" of the poem? Or is it Amichai the poet-refugee, the poet-child on the threshold of maturity (a second one) as he destroys the citadel of his marriage? Kronfeld's political reading, along with that of another critic, Hagai Rogni, is possible, but tends to disregard the complexity in Amichai's position on Israel's wars, including the War of Independence. As a citizen of the State, and as someone who saw its creation as necessary for the Jews, he identified with its defensive wars, but also agonized about the human reality that forced young lives to be sacrificed to the Moloch of war.[53]

THE NOVEL *NOT OF THIS TIME, NOT OF THIS PLACE*; PLANS FOR A NEW COLLECTION OF POEMS

With *Two Hopes Away* at the publisher, Amichai characteristically had plenty of new poems, and by the end of 1960, after the publication of his short stories at Sifriat Poalim, he wrote to Avraham Shlonsky, the editor of the publishing house's poetry and translation department: "For some reason it now seems to me, with the publication of my first book of stories with Sifriat Poalim, that I have found a home where I can publish my books."[54] He tried to set up a meeting with Shlonsky, and a further letter written a week later suggests that a date was set.[55] In a letter to David Hanegbi, coordinator of the editorial board of the publishing house, Amichai argued a month later that Shlonsky had "approved" his book of poems and asked "that it be brought up at your next board meeting, so that a date could be finalized;"[56] but it is clear that the publishers was stalling. In the same letter he reminded them that he also wanted them to publish his novel, which he intended to complete by the end of 1961.[57]

While in Germany and then back in Jerusalem in 1959, Amichai had already begun writing the novel *Not of This Time, Not of This Place*, which was revolutionary in structure, in terms of Hebrew literature, and perhaps beyond.[58] Its main protagonist is a German-born Israeli archeologist who has two existences, separate in space and time, in Germany and in Jerusalem. In the summer of 1957 Amichai wrote to the administration of the Beit Hakerem teachers' college, where he had studied ten years earlier, saying that he needed a graduation certificate to present as part of a request for reparation payments from Germany which he had not mentioned in any of the interviews bearing on his relationship with Germany.[59]

In the summer of 1959, according to his own notes, he began gathering material for a novel which took three years to write. He went to the city of his birth, Würzburg, on a breakneck single day visit during an extended stay in Switzerland.[60] The city had been almost completely destroyed during the last days of the war, because of the refusal of the Gauleiter, the Nazi district governor, to surrender to the American army, but had been rebuilt essentially as it was. "I didn't know I would return to Würzburg, [but] that summer evening, as I came back to the lake at Zurich, my desire to go back for a day or two grew stronger."

On his return to the city, he looked for lodging in "a hotel next to the station," signifying his lack of belonging to the city. His first stop was the square adjacent to the railway station, with its "large statue of the patron saint of the city, Saint K." Then he went on a hasty trip, "as if on a deep run of memory," discovering that it had been "dwarfed": "I placed the map of the memory of my childhood on the town and saw that I had grown. I had become a grown man and rather sad." He walked down Theater Street, which under the Nazis was called Adolf Hitler Street. "I ran past all this in crazy and unseeing haste; only my legs remembered." Where his parents' apartment had been there is now a "kitschy decorated building," the "international students' house," and he was flooded with memories from his childhood of both holidays and ordinary times. Ruth's parents' house "was the only one still standing amid its ruins, and within it was an oak spreading its limbs, as if to greet me for the last time."

Before leaving the city, "the same night," he visited the courtyard where the Jewish school and the synagogue had stood. "Other than the yard, no trace remained, neither of the school building nor the synagogue building [...] one of the workers told me that an enormous department store was to be built here in the American style. The German economic miracle had reached here too." He says that from the moment he got on the tram to go back to his hotel, "I knew that I wouldn't ever return to the town of my birth."

Nevertheless, there is almost no doubt that Amichai did indeed visit Germany again, and perhaps even Würzburg, and for much longer, while writing the novel. This return is hinted at by the narrator of "Venice – Three Times," when referring to a five-month period of nightmares, a terrifying time in his life which occurred between his second and third visits to Venice.[61]

ISRAELI SOCIETY IN THE EARLY 1960S AND ITS REFLECTION IN THE NOVEL

Let's for a short while situate *Not of This Time* in the literary, political and social context of the early 1960s, a context which clearly impacted its critical and public reception.

Amichai came up the idea for the novel and began writing it in 1959, a year before Adolf Eichmann was caught in Argentina and tried in Israel in 1961. The novel contains no direct reference to the trial or its reverberations in society,[62] but it is clear that by the time it was published it met with a different Israel in terms of its relationship to the Holocaust, Holocaust refugees in Israel, and Israelis who emigrated to live in Germany. The trial was the culmination of a decade of a complicated and painful relationship between the State of Israel and Germany. The postwar governments of Germany made attempts to atone for the Nazi atrocities with generous reparations to those harmed by what the Nazis had unleashed, but did little to bring criminals to justice whether in Germany or elsewhere. Nevertheless, in the late 1950s Germany engaged in arms sales to Israel.

The protagonist of the novel, Joel, is an archeologist, but importantly takes his distance from his profession. At a Hebrew University departmental meeting, Joel makes an accusation: "Archeology is a science fed by war and by the dead."[63] Falling in love with Patricia draws Joel seemingly forever away from archeology.[64] Joel accuses his advisor, Prof. Oren, of misrepresenting his findings, thus echoing a heated debate that was engaging the Israeli public. Archeologists were blamed for the role they took on themselves, either on their own initiative or at the request of politicians such as Ben Gurion, to base the claims of the Jewish people to the Land of Israel on the biblical past revealed through excavations.[65] As Joel saw it, and certainly similarly to how Amichai saw it, intensive engagement in archeology expressed the confused identity then prevalent in Israeli society – the attempt to use archeology to demonstrate ancient roots in the Land of Israel, and enhance a weak sense of belonging with "postcards of rabbis and Palmach commanders and photos of archeological findings."[66]

The novel's lukewarm reception was related to expectations of what a "total" novel should be. In the atmosphere at the beginning of the 1960s in Israel, serious literature was presumed to deal with the "questions of the generation;" that is, issues of general public concern. The novel does this to some extent by describing an Israeli scientist who fought in the War of Independence (Joel), and then confronts life in Germany after the Holocaust, the country he fled as a child because of Nazi persecution (the "I" of the novel).

These ideological expectations may have prevented critics from identifying the innovativeness of the novel's metaphorical parallelism between worlds, which Amichai brought daringly close as he revealed similarities between apparently different phenomena: stormy sexual love for a young woman and love for an old woman (Pat and Henrietta), childhood attraction for a boy and a love for a woman (Heinz and Pat),[67] the masculine and the feminine (suggestive of Pat's masculinity and Joel's femininity). Thus, with a somewhat pre-postmodern sensibility,[68] Amichai undercut the markers of gender and generational identities, and the boundaries of sexual desire. His postmodern approach also emerges in his refusal of the illusion of mimesis the novel is supposed to maintain, the illusion of verisimilitude which requires the reader to suspend disbelief. For example, the novel includes several variants on Joel's parting with Yosel, who is about to emigrate to Germany.[69] The novel also takes a deliberate meta-narrative stance in passages where the narrator ironically signals his commitment to narrative convention, saying that because he has read a great deal of prose he knows that when in distress, the character should hold his head in his hands.[70] The narrator tests several plotlines but suggests that each recollection is the product of different reasons and contexts that color the recollection.[71]

BETWEEN JERUSALEM AND WEINBURG: LOVE OVERCOMES REVENGE

The novel takes place alternately in Jerusalem and Würzburg, here called Weinburg ("the city of wine," rather than "the city of wheat"), and is set in the late 1950s, during the time it was written. The textual transitions between the two cities generally take place in alternating chapters, but not always. At times several consecutive chapters are set in Jerusalem or in Würzburg, particularly towards the end. The central character in the Jerusalem chapters is Joel,[72] who is unsure about his identity and direction in life. He is in the midst of a marital crisis and confronts the deterioration of the State he helped to found. The chapters in Weinburg are narrated in the first person by someone not identified by name (called "I") who is Joel, but not entirely. For example, at the end of the novel, Joel, after ardent lovemaking with the American Christian medical student (Patrice/Patricia-Pat), goes to the Hebrew University campus on Mount Scopus, steps on a mine and is killed.

The "I", on the other hand, returns to Jerusalem from the town of his birth, strengthened and purified by having reconnected with his roots, particularly the mother he finds in Henrietta, who survived the Theresienstadt concentration camp. Henrietta spoiled him when he was a boy and gave him a sense of the freedom he lacked at home. Now he goes back to close her eyes and stroke her old dry face one last time.[73] Thus, Joel who remains in Jerusalem is condemned to death, while the part of him that decides to return temporarily to the town of his birth survives.[74]

Joel the archeologist is surrounded by a circle of friends much like him in terms of background, aspirations and disappointments: Yosel the violinist, Zeiger the photographer, Mintzer the painter, Amron the poet, Itzhak the doctor, and Golgolus the lawyer, once a teacher. They represent a disappointed elite that tends to be critical of Israeli state and society in its first years. Despite a certain similarity of features, each character has a discernible identity.[75]

On the advice of Mina, Itzhak's mentally ill wife, Joel, who is hesitating between "here" and "there," between the town of his birth and the town where he has lived since his adolescence, decides on both. Part of him finds comfort in his ongoing fierce love affair with the American doctor who has left her husband, while the "other" Joel, who speaks in the first person singular, travels to Weinburg-Würzburg purportedly to avenge the community largely destroyed in the Holocaust, and in particular Ruth, his childhood love.[76] A further impetus is given him by Dr. Manheim, the city's rabbi between the wars and Little Ruth's father, who immigrates to Israel in his old age. Dr. Manheim wants him to collect the printed versions of his sermons that were scattered throughout the city, including the one he prepared for Joel for his bar mitzvah in Weinburg, but has remained in draft form since he went to Palestine with his parents before the event could be celebrated.

The plan for revenge is initially very sketchy and is only partially implemented in a grotesque way.[77] The rationale for vengeance evolves during his (the "I"'s) stay in Weinburg. The general aim shifts to his determination to avenge Ruth's death, and when he revives her in his imagination, he finds a new reason: to get back at the young Nazi supporters for abusing him and the handicapped Ruth when they were children.[78] Who should be the target of his revenge?[79] The whole city, in which many were born after the war, or who were children? The individuals who took part in the destruction? People who were opposed but carried on with their lives while the Jews were sent to the death camps, like the shopkeeper who remembered him, the "I", from his childhood and who opened his arms wide to greet him? Those who obediently took part in the destruction, who adapted to it, protecting their incomes and perhaps their lives, like the station master?[80]

Returning to Germany in the late 1950s, the "I" also encounters a new social reality: the young Germans he meets are different in temperament and ways of thinking from those he knew in his German childhood, and from what he expected of the children of the generation who took part in the war. He encounters the teenage children of wartime soldiers, who refuse to "forget the past," which adult society in Germany is trying to bury. These youth are interested in going to a kibbutz in Israel – then a favored destination – on a journey of atonement.[81] At the psychoanalytic institute, built on the site of his parents' home, he meets the daughter of a Nazi psychiatrist who conducted horrific experiments on Jews in the death camp. She is disgusted by her father's actions, and has disavowed him, telling the "I" that her parents and those of her friends "are angry with us for being sensitive."[82]

The crushing blow to his vengeful impulse is the thought that seeking revenge makes him no better than the murderers. To some extent he envies the Nazis, who were aggressively masculine enough to murder Jews, whereas he belongs to a confused and defeated generation. His desire for revenge wanes because he does not feel pure enough. This is manifested in his persistent feelings of paranoia, to the extent that he believes his dead father has sent people to spy on him.[83] "My vengeance was like a wax sword. A great sadness descended upon me because I was empty of vengeance."[84]

Joel, the "I", would have preferred to withdraw into a never-ending erotic union of the sort described in Amichai's poem "A Pity. We were Such a Good Invention,"[85] thus overcoming all his vengeful impulses and anger. On his last night of lovemaking with Patrice-Clarice, just before his death, "they attained perfection in their love. There was no postponement by resorting to violence as on the other nights. Life was no longer either vengeance or compensation, but great reconciliation and great peace."[86]

NOTES

1. In a conversation in New York Clarice hinted she was the person in the poem. "Farewell," *Poetry*, 57 (other translations: *Selected Poetry*, 31, *Life of Poetry*, 50); *Poems* [in Hebrew] 1, 219; "Such as Sorrow," *Selected Poetry*, 32); *Poems* [in Hebrew] 1, 227; "Jacob and the Angel," *Selected Poetry*, 40 (another translation: *Poetry*, 76); *Poems* [in Hebrew] 1, 307. Amichai's thoughts about his experiences with Clarice may also be reflected in "In the Middle of This Century," *Selected Poetry*, 30; (other translations: *Life of Poetry*, 49; *Poetry*, 55-56); *Poems* [in Hebrew] 1, 216-217.

2. Miron, "Reading of Two Love Poems."

3. For example, he sees a connection between "not ours to say: yes now, yes now" in "Farewell" and the description of lovemaking with Pat in *Not of This Time* [in Hebrew], 360, 543-544.

4. Drafts of "Farewell" – journal, October-November 1958, file 431.

5. Her astonished laughter at a favorite expression of his, the "enemies of the land" (*Not of This Time*, 56), suggests her unfamiliarity with the Israeli ethos of the time. The narrator identifies to such an extent with the spirit of the time in Israel that the thought briefly crosses his mind that perhaps she is also an "enemy of the land."

6. An attempt to revive the relationship with Clarice during her journey to Israel or Europe appears indirectly in her responses to his letters. However, this

interpretation is likely to mask the tragic clarity expressed in the poem of his acceptance of what had happened.

7. *Not of This Time* [in Hebrew], 173.

8. "Let not the prophets and diviners in your midst deceive you, and pay no heed to the dreams they dream." Jer. 29:8. The verb Amichai uses here, *mechalemet*, does not exist in modern Hebrew. More recent translators has emphasized the independence of the beloved interlocutor. Bloch-Mitchell have: "From this day forth, you turn into the dreamer of everything". *Selected Poetry*, 3. Robert Alter has: "From now you weave your own dreams." *Poetry*, 57. Neither caught the tone of dismissal.

9. "For all came through our word" echoes but subverts the traditional blessing over food and drink acknowledging God's beneficent kindness: "by whose word all things exist."

10. "And they raised the banner of revolt.' That's what the history books often say. Why did Joel suddenly recall raising the banner of revolt?" *Not of This Time* [in Hebrew], 285.

11. There is a similar description when Patrice returns to the room from taking a shower: "He saw her suntanned body and the places covered by the swimsuit which had stayed white" (*Not of This Time* [in Hebrew], 361). When Amichai sent the poem to Clarice in March 1960, she wrote in response: "'The Angel and Jacob' reminded me of many such battles between us" (March 30, 1960). When Joel leaves Patrice's apartment at night after having sex for the first time with her: "A shirt button had been torn off in their wild struggle at the beginning of the night (ibid., 261). By contrast, years later he was more interested in the memory of her playing a musical piece than their wild sex life. In a journal entry in 1990 he wrote: "Tradition: I was at a rehearsal of Emanuela's ballet: girls were dancing to Schubert's Impromptu; little did they know that Clarice had played this in 1958, that it was our love song."

12. In *Not of This Time* the narrator talks about Pat and Joel's relationship in terms of "one night" (ibid., 260-261). When Joel goes to Pat's on another night, she defines his visit as "part of that night. One long night" (English translation, 232). "One night" is interpreted in the novel as nights that were as fully experienced as the first (in Hebrew, 570).

13. Gen. 36:8.

14. Babylonian Talmud, Sota 41b; Genesis Rabbah, 77, 3 (Theodor-Albeck edition, 912).

15. Cf. *Not of This Time* (English translation), 66. Pat tells Joel, as things are heating up between them on their hike: "Careful, now, I am strong and I know many holds"; when they wrestle she indeed proves strong and difficult to overcome.

16. For example, "How is Tamar? Give her a baby. They are like flowers, so fragile, so new, so us" (November 30, 1959). And "How is Tamar – lucky woman after all, isn't she, but she should have a baby" (February 14, 1960).

17. The middle name of Emanuela, Amichai's daughter from his second marriage, is Meira, in memory of his father.

18. https://www.zemereshet.co.il/song.asp?id=3589October 3, 1958. A year later she wrote to him: "You probably write poems to Penina's eyes now, and after her, another pair" (November 30, 1959). It isn't clear whether "Penina" was the name of

an actual lover or just a symbolic name, as in Bialik's popular song, "New Custom": "Today Hana, tomorrow Penina."

19. In Amichai's notebooks her name is always written with the letter *raysh*, R. The name is hinted at in the poem "Return from Ein Gedi," where it is given a midrashic-style explanation as though it were derived from "the Arab name of the wadi [*ha'arugot*] / And after the Hebrew word for yearning [*erga*]," *Poetry*, 286; *Poems* [in Hebrew] 3, 309.

20. Conversation with Ehud Ben-Ezer, June 13, 2016.

21. The journalist Eilat Negev described the beginning of their affair in an interview with Amichai as follows: "In 1963, when Amichai was 39 years old, and was teaching at night school, he fell in love with Hana Sokolov, a 24-year-old student and substitute teacher." "Some months later he left Tamar and his toddler son and went to live with her." Amichai stated: "It was difficult, particularly since I had a little boy, but I didn't regret the decision to leave for a moment. I left everything to my wife." "Poems of Akhsiv" documents the beginning of the love affair between Yehuda and Hana: "Akhsiv was our place. We would travel there, to the village of Eli Avivi, to be alone." From the Negev interview, "I Am a Happy Man."

22. "I Found a Newspaper," *Poems* [in Hebrew] 3, 298. The poem mentions "twenty years," but this is likely due to Amichai's tendency to round up numbers, as he did in the poem "Sixty Kilograms of Pure Love" (*Life of Poetry*, 414; *Poems* [in Hebrew] 5, 28.

23. After he had already left Tamar, in a draft of a poem dated 1965 he expresses his strong ties to his son, and describes the need to protect and nourish him: "Thunder. My child needs me. / He is afraid of thunder. / I, no longer. // Until I manage to explain to him and until he understands / that he doesn't need to be afraid / I will begin again / to be afraid of thunder."

24. In his notebooks during his trip to the US: "My boy Roni is [the biblical] Job. / He's a great historian. / I come and go, go / And come. Repeating myself. / He knows" (November 7, 1966). "I dreamed – About the joining of two hearts, even a third. My love for R [Rejah - Hana], my love for Roni, my love for my mother, and all these loves are connected. [In the dream] I was in the bath in dim and pleasant colors [...] I had Roni's experience of being loved by me, and my own experience as his loving father. My mother knocked gently on the door and I felt her love for me in childhood, and her love for Roni, the same love she had for me." March 7, 1967.

25. In an article in *Haaretz*, September 21, 1960, "Writers on Their Projects and Vocation" [in Hebrew], Amichai said: "Currently I am finalizing my first book of stories that will be published by Sifriat Hapoalim. I am also working [...] on a book of poems that will come out next year, and am writing a novel. I initially entered the world of prose through the back door, with short stories, then longer stories, and am now trying to write a novel [...] it gives me a sense of release. I have had to struggle with the poetic impulse to prevent it from swallowing up the protagonists [...] I also wrote a play, Jonah [*Journey to Nineveh*]."

26. See chapter 10.

27. "Haggadot and the Departure from Egypt" [in Hebrew], *Lamerhav-Masa*, April 4, 1958; Sifriat Poalim, 253-262; Schocken, 247-255. On writers' surveys in

literary supplements, see Motti Neiger, *Literary Supplements and the Shaping of Israeli Culture* [in Hebrew] (Jerusalem 2000), 141-149.

28. "Hammarskjöld in Jerusalem."

29. For more on the literature of the 1948 generation see Gershon Shaked, *Modern Hebrew Fiction* (Bloomington, 2000), 139-156.

30. Yehuda Haezrachi (ed.), *The New Selected Israeli Story* [in Hebrew] (Jerusalem 5730/1969-1970), (along with "Ballet in Jerusalem"); Hillel Barzel (ed.), *Six Narrators – 16 Stories* [in Hebrew] (Tel Aviv 1972), (along with "Dicky's Death" and "A Poetry Reading"); Zisi Stavi (ed.), *30 Years, 30 Stories* [in Hebrew], (Tel Aviv 1993). In English, "The Times My Father Died," Shmuel Yosef Penuely and Azriel Uchmani (eds.), *Hebrew Short Stories*, vol. 2 (Tel Aviv 1965); Ezra Spicehandler (ed.), *Modern Hebrew Stories*, (New York 1971) [bilingual]; Gila Ramraz-Rauch and Joseph Michman-Melkman, *Facing the Holocaust: Selected Israeli Fiction* (Philadelphia 1985); and in other languages (French, Chinese, Czech).

31. The story about Dicky, and poems Amichai wrote about him throughout his life, turned him, and a few others, into mythic figures in Israeli collective memory. Cf. Dan Miron, "Changing Faces in the Mirror of the Platter" [the 'silver platter' (Alterman) on which the State of Israel was delivered, by the heroism and sacrifice of the young generation], *Facing the Silent Brother* [in Hebrew] (Tel Aviv 1992), 61-120.

32. Shaham, *Sifriat Poalim* [in Hebrew]; Neiger, Publishers, 397-401.

33. "Terrible Spring," published in *Haaretz* April 30, 1959, and "The Bar Mitzvah Party," published in *Al Hamishmar* September 21, 1960, had probably not yet been written. Zrubavel Gilad wrote to Menachem Dorman (both senior editors) about Amichai's proposal that Hakibbutz Hameuchad publish the stories: "The manuscript of Amichai's stories [emphasis in original] [...] I am in favor of our bringing it out, after some pruning ". June 23, 1958, Hakibbutz Hameuchad archive.

34. Amichai himself was far from being convinced that his book would be published by Sifriat Poalim. This can be gleaned from an interview with writer Israel Eliraz. Eliraz stated ironically at the beginning of the interview that "through the publication of the stories *of In This Terrible Wind*, Sifriat Poalim has given a 'reactionary' hand to original literature" not in the style of socialist realism. Amichai's response was that this was "the exception that proves the rule", *Yediot Acharonot*, February 17, 1961.

35. See Amichai's letter to Azriel Uchmani, January 4, 1961, where he expresses his appreciation for "what you did to ensure the publication of these stories." January 4, 1961. Gnazim 100147/1.

36. The Schocken edition differed from Sifriat Poalim in design and layout, but the texts are identical.

37. "Story Without Plot" [interview with Amichai, in Hebrew], *Dvar Hashavua*, January 31, 1961. The interviewer was probably Michael Ohad.

38. Asher Nahor, "The Poetic Prose of a Poet" [in Hebrew], *Yediot Acharonot*, February 3, 1961.

39. Dor supports his claim by referring to an anthology of modern poetry published at the time in the US, edited by Selden Rodman, which included prose passages by Franz Kafka and Norman Mailer, among others.

40. Moshe Dor, "Prose Which Is Poetry" [in Hebrew], *Maariv*, February 24, 1961.

41. Menachem Ben, "The World in a Room" [in Hebrew], *Yediot Acharonot*, July 30, 1971.

42. Dalia Hertz, "The Stories of Yehuda Amichai" [in Hebrew], *Yediot Acharonot*, August 3, 1973.

43. "The Orgy," *The World Is a Room*, 121-141. In late 1962, Amichai sent a story called "At the Painter's" to the editor of *Moznaim*, Yeshurun Keshet. From the description of the story in the accompanying letter (December 2, 1962), the story appears to be a section of *Not of This Time*, which was then being written (Mintzer the painter in the novel more or less embodies Yaakov Pines). Keshet was dissuaded from publishing the story partly out of fear that the painter depicted in it was too easy to identify. Gnazim 39514/1.

44. According to Amichai's later calculations, he was 11 and the journey to Israel via Venice took place in 1935. This would mean that the two last visits to Venice took place in 1962, assuming the autobiographical mentions are correct.

45. "Venice – Three Times" [in Hebrew], *In This Terrible Wind*, 294-295.

46. Amichai, "The Poet in Modern Society" [in Hebrew], *Yediot Acharonot – 7 Yamim*, March 13, 1959.

47. Razili, "Our Young Poetry."

48. The description of the evening is based on contemporaneous newspaper articles: Michael Ohad, "An Evening of Young Poets" [in Hebrew], *Davar*, January 12, 1962; Shulamit Lapid, "Modern Poetry Packs Beit Liessin," *Jerusalem Post*, 12.1.1962. See my article "An Evening That Won't Come Back," *Haaretz* [in Hebrew], September 20, 2017.

49. There is somewhat of a contradiction between his image as a spokesperson for the individualism of the generation of the 1950s and his support of *Mapam* with its aspiration to socialist revolution. This support is likely to have lessened after the publication of Khrushchev's speech, in February 1956 on Stalin's crimes, but not entirely abandoned, as he states in a letter to Azriel Uchmani, a *Mapam* activist, in response to the latter's request that he sign a party manifesto. Against the backdrop of the upcoming elections to the Knesset, Amichai wrote to him: "I think that a writer and a poet, most of whose writing has to do with humanity, war, love and so on, expresses his opinion in almost every line." As regards his view of history, he was apparently a Marxist, "but that is my business." Undated, though according to the date on the stamp it was Av 5621 (Summer 1961), Gnazim, 100148/1.

50. *Selected Poetry*, 38; Poems [in Hebrew] 1, 297.

51. Chana Kronfeld, *The Full Severity of Compassion* (Stanford, Ca., 2016), 135-144.

52. "Elegy on an Abandoned Village," *Selected Poetry*, 42-43; *Poems* [in Hebrew] 1, 363-365. Interpretation of the poem: Kronfeld, *The Full Severity*, 33-35. In a similar spirit, Hagai Rogni, *Facing the Destroyed Village* [in Hebrew] (Haifa 2006), 184-206.

53. In response to a high school student who asked about his apparent alienation from Israel's wars on a TV program, he clarified the difference between his stance as an Israeli and a Jew who accepted the necessity of defense, and his stance as a

man and a creative artist unable to accept the terrible waste of human life in every war. "Every poem" [in Hebrew], hosted by the poet Natan Yonatan, Educational Television, 1975.

54. Amichai to Shlonsky, December 16, 1960. Shlonsky archive at the Kipp Center, Tel Aviv University, 3: 10-3216. There was a plan to bring out a new book of poems as early as the end of 1959, according to an interview with Noa Nimrod, "A Hebrew Poet Abroad," *Jewish Chronicle*, August 21, 1959.

55. Amichai to Shlonsky, December 25, 1960. Shlonsky archive, 3: 10-3217. There was an ongoing argument between Shlonsky and David Hanegbi, another important figure in the publishing house, over authority and areas of influence. For more on this, see Hagit Halperin, *The Maestro* [in Hebrew], (Tel Aviv, 2011), 483-486, 496-499.

56. Amichai to David Hanegbi, January 18, 1961. Yad Yaari archive, Givat Haviva, files of Sifriat Poalim.

57. Amichai to David Hanegbi, August 21, 1961. Ibid.

58. Few plots were situated intermittently in both time and place before *Not of This Time*. Baruch Kurzweil was the only one to argue that a similar structure could be found in German Romantic literature. He may have been referring to *The Life and Opinions of the Tomcat Murr* by E. T. A. Hoffman, which is composed of two alternating narratives by a musician and his cat, that has a similar but not identical structure to Amichai's novel. I am grateful to Dr. Benny Perl for locating this source.

59. In *Not of This Time*, 13, the reparations his mother received from Germany are mentioned.

60. Yehuda Amichai, "Return to the City of Childhood," *Bamachane*, June 5, 1962. However, he may have visited other places in Germany, including Munich, according to his journal, July 1959. File 446.

61. "Venice – Three Times," *In This Terrible Wind* [in Hebrew], 294-295. His long stay in Germany while writing the book – in Würzburg or elsewhere – is also hinted at in an interview Amichai gave to a student journal: "When I visited Germany, while writing the book, I was completely detached from politics and history. [...] I was isolated, I didn't talk to anyone." "Germany and Judaism: Really Not of This Time, Not of This Place?" Interview by the editors of Egoz and Arieh Shor, *Egoz* 2, 5729 [1968-9], 141.

62. A vague allusion to the Eichmann trial appears in *Not of This Time* [in Hebrew], 368-369 (the description of the cabin of a bulldozer involved in the leveling of old Jewish sites as a "glass box"; during the Eichmann trial, he was seated in a glass box).

63. *Not of This Time* [in Hebrew], 594. In this context, William Briefly deals with Amichai's poems from the 1970s where he writes about archeology with a sense of revulsion and distance: Poem 53 in *Time* (*Poems* [in Hebrew] 3, 236), in which he talks about the meaning of the soil sieved from archeological findings rather than the findings themselves, and the well-known poem "Tourists" in his book *A Great Tranquility: Questions and Answers* (*Selected Poetry*, 137-138; *Poems* [in Hebrew] 3, 348), which considers that redemption has come when the fact of a man bringing vegetables home is seen as more important than the archeological spectacle of a Roman

arch. William D. Briefly, *A Christian Theological Exploration of the Memory of the Holocaust in the Work of Four Jewish Novelists* (Boston 1993), 202-251.

64. *Not of This Time* [in Hebrew], 545.

65. Joel tells him that he wants to save him from deception, on the assumption that intellectuals have the function of defending rationality (485ff [in Hebrew]). On archeology on the eve of the establishment of the State and in its first decade, see Michael Feige, Introduction, in Michael Feige, Zvi Shiloni (eds.), *An Axe to Dig with: Archeology and Nationalism in Eretz Israel* [in Hebrew] (Beersheva 2008), 1-17; Yael Zerubavel, *Recovered Roots* (Chicago and London, 1995), 57-59, 129-33.

66. *Not of This Time* [in Hebrew], 500, 507.

67. Heinz, the son of a widow, was "a handsome child [...] who, Joel recalled with happy surprise, resembled Patricia." *Not of This Time*, 212. Ludwig-Yehuda played sexually suggestive games with him in his childhood (see Chapter 1). Heinz was perhaps particularly vulnerable, since he grew up without a father.

68. Lyotard's book *Postmodernism* came out in 1979.

69. Alternative versions of the parting – *Not of This Time* [in Hebrew], 264, 284, 287.

70. Ibid. [in Hebrew], 354.

71. Ibid. [in Hebrew], 565-566 and others. Elsewhere he points to the possibility of creating an alternative narrative for Joel's "autobiography," when after Pat caresses his scarred leg, Joel "knew that in his heart he would have to rewrite his biography in the light of his love for Patricia," in other words, to revise his history as he had seen it up to that point. *Not of This Time*, 212.

72. Hillel Barzel and others attribute importance the fact that the protagonist is called Joel. The prophecies of the biblical Joel, one of the twelve minor prophets, shift between two axes: the disaster of the locusts, and the day of "vengeance and recompense" (Deut 32:35). However, Joel the character in the novel is ultimately not interested in a vendetta. Hillel Barzel, "Not of This Time."

73. When he looks at the dead Henrietta, he feels that "my whole childhood was concentrated in her tranquil face" (*Not of This Time* [in Hebrew], 564, 566). Henrietta was a kind of hyper-mother for him, more permissive and more prone to touching than his mother (ibid, 523-524). He even goes so far as to compare his love for Pat to his love for Henrietta (ibid., 289-290).

74. On a more superficial level, Amichai told a journalist in London, when he first came back from Germany, that he needed a peaceful "European" connection with the "Middle Eastern" and Israeli ferment in the life of the creative artist. Nimrod, "Israeli Poet."

75. Despite what scholars and critics have suggested (Shaked, *New Wave* [in Hebrew], 107; Blumerzon, "Transition of Writers from Poetry to Prose Writing" [PhD in Hebrew], 163), the minor characters in the novel are not just projections of the protagonist. Amichai stated in a survey by the writer Rachel Eytan that prose in Israel was adversely influenced by the smallness of the country. "Every novel automatically becomes a roman à clef." "Between Pen and Paper" [in Hebrew], January 1, 1965.

76. In the novel, leaving Jerusalem is described as stemming from wanting to escape "my waning life [...] so as to take get my due revenge and come back to Jerusalem, my city, strengthened and resolved, like solving a difficult puzzle" (*Not of This Time* [in Hebrew], 588-589), hence primarily from a need for personal closure.

77. He spits into the grocer's salt barrel, whom he remembered fondly from childhood (*Not of This Time* [in Hebrew], 288-289); and attempts to grab a fat German's testicle in the shower of the yoga classroom, apparently to reveal a swastika tattoo (ibid., 278-279).

78. Though he convinces himself that Ruth is somehow alive and that further vengeance is superfluous (ibid., 489), he nevertheless continues to want to justify the vendetta: "Since Ruth is alive [...] I will seek out the one who did the kicking" and the other thugs who roughed her up in the presence of young Ludwig, "and there will be no end to my search" (490). However, he understands that revenge is illusory: either these youths were killed as soldiers in the war, or he will not be able to identify them as adults (85-86).

79. The old nun, Elizabeth, who took care of the wounded Ruth, tells him that essentially everyone took part in the crime (*Not of This Time* [in Hebrew], 432). This reduces his thirst for revenge even further since he cannot single out particular individuals.

80. In the novel he mentions that in his childhood he dreamed of being a station master, and being in charge of the signal box (ibid., 211, 245).

81. 81 The young woman at the "Symposium on Forgetting the Past" he chances on, says: "We must not [...] forget what our parents did" (*Not of This Time*, 270). The audience hears a lecture about the kibbutz and decides to go to Israel on a "pilgrimage of friendship and atonement" (270-271). Even the daughters of the farmers in his grandparents' village, Bachfeld, seem sensitive, gentle lovers of American pop music, and taking revenge on them seems inappropriate (*Not of This Time* [in Hebrew], 585-586).

82. Ibid., 293. See also 392-393, 436. This was also Amichai's impression on his first visit to Würzburg, in 1959: he heard the older generation express sympathy for the Nazis, but had a good impression of people under 30 who spoke at a conference in Munich he attended. Amichai, "Return to the City of Childhood," *Bamachane*, June 5, 1962

83. *Not of This Time* [in Hebrew], 412.

84. *Not of This Time*, 106.

85. *Selected Poetry*, 57. *Poems* [in Hebrew] 2, 69.

86. *Not of This Time*, 323.

Chapter 10

1962–1964

Plays and Radio Scripts, Publication of Poems 1948-1962

PREPARATIONS FOR THE PUBLICATION OF THE NOVEL *NOT OF THIS TIME, NOT OF THIS PLACE*

During the years of Amichai's marital crisis with Tamar, when he left her and then returned, his output was more diverse than in any period before or after. Along with writing a novel and stories, he forayed into writing scripts for theater and radio.

Amichai began writing the novel *Not of This Time, Not of This Place* in 1959 (apparently right after he finished writing the play *Journey to Nineveh* in February-March of that year), and completed it in 1961. He told journalists that he was excited about writing a novel, and what the writing process had been like. In response to a survey of a number of authors conducted by Rachel Eytan, he said that "I wrote my book when I wanted to feel that I was doing something real, actually working [...] The novel was written over two and a half years [...] I knew that I would finish it, and everything was planned from the beginning."[1] Either out of pride or in jest, he told interviewer Bina Barzel that the novel was being taught in the "psychiatric ward" (probably at the School of Medicine), and that the students were told that if the author had not written the novel, he would have gone mad.[2] Did the split personality in *Not of This Time* weigh so heavily on him that for years it prevented him from writing the other novel he had planned?

Fortunately for Amichai, Dan Miron, a young lecturer at Tel Aviv University who was already making a name for himself as a critic, had just been appointed editor in chief at Schocken publishing house. Miron was married to Yael Schocken. His vision was to publish new voices, including the leading poets from the State generation, who started to write poetry in the early years of the State and whose first books appeared in the 1950s. Thus, the obvious choice for Miron was Amichai. In 1960 Amichai had made attempts to publish his early poetry along with new poems, in a single volume. In addition to the poems, he also brought the newly ensconced editor "thousands of pages" of a novel, penned in his clumsy, sprawling script.[3] The proof sheets in the archives indeed show that the novel needed "quite thorough editing," both for its awkward prose and unpolished Hebrew.[4] His imperfect Hebrew prose style reflected his immigration as a teen, and would do so until the end of his life. The editor found working with Amichai to be friendly and easy. At times, Miron even had to encourage the poet to stand firm and defend his own way of expressing his ideas.[5]

Not of This Time was the point of departure for Amichai's drama and radio plays of the late 1950s and early 1960s. The radio play *Bells and Trains* (Israel Broadcasting Authority, March 3, 1962), which depicts Hans-Jochanan's visit to a home for elderly Holocaust survivors in his hometown of Singburg which he had left as a child before the war, derives from the German part of the novel, while various aspects of the Israeli sections of the book were transformed into the commissioned one-act play *No Man's Land* which premiered at the Zavit Theater in November 1962, about governmental corruption and decay in the early days of the State; the radio play *The Class Reunion* (*Kenes ha-Kitah*),[6] first broadcast in 1963, a skillful adaptation of a short story with a similar title: "The Class Meeting" (*Pegishat ha-Kitah*); and *Journey to Nineveh* premiered at the Habima theater, July 1964. This play was Amichai's contribution to Israeli theater going beyond realistic "theater reportage." His short play *No Man's Land* was not the first he wrote, but was the first to be performed.

FIRST STAGE PLAY

In the first years of the State of Israel, audiences eagerly awaited original Israeli plays. Several outstanding 1948 writers of the Palmach generation, including Moshe Shamir, Aharon Megged, Nathan Shaham, and Yigal Mossinsohn,[7] wrote plays during this time that had enormous resonance. Mossinsohn's *In the Negev Plains* was performed at the height of the War of Independence. The play revolved around a fateful and painful dilemma: was it legitimate in wartime, morally and strategically, to evacuate settlements in danger of destruction if their inhabitants were likely to be killed or taken captive, or should they be held at any cost? The performance elicited a sense of genuine reverence among the audience and even the fiercest theater critics.[8] The play itself, however, was vulgar and declamatory in its presentation of the issues. Other plays written by the 1948 generation were hardly more nuanced.

At that time, major theaters such as Habima, the Cameri, and the Ohel (the Haifa Theater was founded in 1961) tended to stagnate, unlike small theaters that did not pay their personnel monthly salaries, since profits were shared by the cast. This made possible theatrical experimentation by bringing to the stage modern plays, that were considered at the time innovative, daring and even extravagant (Theater of the Absurd, Surrealism). These companies were also highly mobile and could travel anywhere, mainly to the kibbutzim and moshavim, no matter how remote. One of these small troupes, the Zavit Theater, planned to perform *The Typists* by the young playwright Murray Schisgal. The play won an award at the Edinburgh Festival,[9] and a year later had played off-Broadway. In order to round out the evening, Gideon Shemer, the manager of the Zavit, called Amichai and suggested that he write a play on a related topic.[10] At that time, a full-length play by Amichai was already scheduled at Habima, and his radio play, *Bells and Trains*, had won first prize in an Israel Radio competition.[11]

Shemer's gamble seemed to be a sure thing. Amichai's first reaction, however, was alarm: "How can something be written to order?" Afterwards, he reminded himself that works by his favorite medieval poets, and composers such as Mozart, Bach, and others had frequently been commissioned.[12] He considered that current day reality in Israel, which angered him as well as the intellectuals of his generation, could only be presented "satirically"[13]; in any case, not in a realistic style. Amichai apparently seized on the regular rumors of preparations for the funeral of Chaim Weizmann, the President of Israel, at the time alive and well. He turned the subject of the moribund living-dead into a metaphor for the country's leadership, by suggesting that its great past was already behind it.[14] The short play centers around two senior officials in a government institution. The more cynical of the two is a retired army officer. The two are related to the dying president through his young secretary, Shulamit. Amichai originally made her into "a simple typist, vulgar, beautiful, and cheap," but the writing process gave rise to "dreamlike conversations between the dying old man and the young woman. Meetings beyond the real were added to the satirical reality of the institution [...] for this was the task [of the young woman]: to be a bridge between cold, devilish reality and dreamlike humanity."[15]

Extensive newspaper coverage reflected public anticipation for the premiere of *No Man's Land* on November 17, 1962. Amichai was not yet considered the de facto national poet, but he was already seen as innovative and influential.[16] These high hopes, however, were soon dashed. Haim Gamzu, a prominent and sharp-tongued critic at the time, quoted Amichai as having retorted "I've got nothing!" when asked in a newspaper interview what he had said when asked to write the play. This enabled the witty theater critic to comment: "And so the prophecy was fulfilled." According to Gamzu, the play was "graphomanic verbiage," making Schisgal's positively Shakespearean in comparison.[17] Other critics were a little more balanced. The *Haboker* theater critic (most probably Ben-Ami Feingold) wrote that "despite its important ideas and excellent language [...] *No Man's Land* is closer to a dramatic sketch," and that the "sudden and speedy" end undermines the integrity of the play.[18] Nachman Ben-Ami, in *Maariv*, found that the play "lacked dramatic drive," but "is full of atmosphere, and has a wealth of symbols and allusions [...] that people can interpret as they like." By contrast, the author Yoram Kaniuk thought the main failing lay with the director. "There is much beauty in the play, both poetic and dramatic. He has an excellent idea," but the play needs editing, and the director did not work in a way that "would actually create the play, in cooperation with the playwright." A director-interpreter could have eliminated the play's choppiness and vague allusions.[19] The two short plays were not successful, and they were quickly taken off the stage.[20]

JOURNEY TO NINEVEH RUNS AGROUND

There are similarities between the commissioned play *No Man's Land* and *Jonah* or, as it was later called, *Journey to Nineveh*, which Amichai finished writing by the beginning of 1959, though *Journey to Nineveh* is broader in scope and aimed higher. *No Man's Land* contrasts the world of manipulative and cynical officials (who represent to some extent the Mapai-Histadrut leadership or the socialist hegemony in Israel at the time) with the lost world of dreams coming to life in the fragments of conversations between the dying old leader and his young secretary. In *Journey to Nineveh* Amichai attempted a forced comparison between the dilemmas of his personal life – whether to detach himself from his familiar home and dive into "an adventure" whose end was hard to predict – with his attitude toward Israeli society of the time.[21] Was it incumbent upon him, as an artist and intellectual, to seek to change Israeli society, which had disappointed him and many of his contemporaries who were raised in the pre-state Jewish community? As he himself explained, Jonah is a petit bourgeois who is afraid of leaving his warm safe home, even though it has lost its power to stimulate.[22] The personal and the public realms are united by the search for inner truth, authenticity, and sincerity, which are more important than conventional morality.[23]

Portions of the play were first published in April 1960. While theaters hesitated about staging it, the full libretto of *Journey to Nineveh* was published by the Achshav publishing house in 1962, in a thin paper binding with poor print quality.[24] This gave critics free rein before the play was even performed. The first to direct barbs was the poet Dahlia Ravikovitch, whose appreciation of his poetry did not stop her from criticizing him when she felt it appropriate:

"It is not clear to anyone what Jonah wanted from Nineveh, and hence unclear what the people wanted of him. I can hardly imagine a person less suitable for this mission than Amichai's Jonah."[25]

Ben-Ami Feingold, the levelheaded and knowledgeable theater critic of *Haboker*, more appropriately situated the play in the context of Amichai's poetry and the 1948 poets. He suggested that they all shared a longing for an ideal reality for the new country. This explains their vague sense of mission to repair the world. The worst thing about *Nineveh*, in Amichai's interpretation of the Bible story, is pretense; its inhabitants are willing to go through the motions of repentance, while in fact not changing at all. The play has a plethora of theatrical possibilities,[26] wrote the critic; this would guide the director a year and a half later.

THE TRIBULATIONS OF PRESENTING *JOURNEY TO NINEVEH*

Amichai initially wanted the play to be performed at the Cameri Theater, and asked the actor and poet Abraham Halfi to intercede on his behalf.[27] When the Cameri refused, the play made its way to Habima. An early commitment was made there to stage it, but a period of prolonged hesitation preceded the final decision as to how and when it would open. Initially the idea was to perform it on Habima's small stage, but "its seriousness and heaviness" dissuaded the Habima management.[28] The idea to take *Journey to Nineveh* on tour in the United States in the winter of 1964, along with *The Dybbuk*, was similarly rejected.[29] Amichai later told the journalist Rachel Eytan that Julius Gellner (1899-1983), a well-known Jewish director who was the artistic director of Habima at that time, began to take an interest in the play. "Gellner wanted to adapt the play and perform it in New York," because he believed that its universality would speak to a non-Israeli audience.[30] The Habima cooperative management, however, doubted that audiences in either Israel or abroad could enjoy a play replete with symbolism and linguistic gymnastics.

Julius Gellner, a native of Moravia and already a rising star in the German theater in Munich in the 1920s, took a special liking to Amichai. The German language was not the sole bond between them; for Gellner, Amichai epitomized all that was good in the new Israel: a cultured creative artist and an idealist who did not think the work of a primary school teacher was below him.[31] Gellner declared that he was "in love with the play, and only rarely have enjoyed the work of directing as much."[32] However it remains unclear how well Gellner really understood the play. Did Amichai translate parts into German for him? Habima probably sent him a literal translation, since as the writer and critic Yehoshua Kenaz noted in his review, *Journey to Nineveh* is untranslatable.[33]

After numerous postponements, intensive rehearsals were held for *Journey to Nineveh* which included live music and dance. The score was written by Gary Bertini and the stage set was painted by Shmuel Beck. The choreography was entrusted to the dancer and choreographer Ahuva Inbari.[34] The lead role of Jonah was given to Nahum Buchman, who said at the time that he found the play to contain great richness: "If one delves deeply into Amichai's play, we find that there still is hope for the world."[35] Eva Li-On (Kerbler), an Austrian convert in her thirties, played three characters: the foreign woman, the prostitute in the harbor, and a woman in Nineveh. At that time, she was Gellner's mistress, whose intense attachment to her was fueled by the despair of an elderly divorcé. The actors were among the best that Habima could offer. However, the premiere was a flop. Several critics found the first part of the play interesting, polished, and had enormous expectations, but the later scenes disappointed.[36]

The performance elicited numerous scathing comments. Feingold, who was receptive to Amichai's work, remarked that "The directing lacks style."[37] Like him, most of the critics felt that the actors and others involved in the production (the director, the set decorator, the composer) were unable to combine the spiritual-symbolic with the worldly realms of the play. Throughout almost the entire play, Eva Li-On played a sensual seductive woman while Buchman only accentuated the emotional, thus leaving no room for Jonah's intellectual side. The sets, which are crucial in this type of performance, missed their mark.[38] The music, which the composer and conductor Gary Bertini defined in a press conference on the eve of the premiere as "modern," and "not biblical," sounded "overblown" to the critics,[39] and the choreography seemed inappropriate.

Two months after the premiere the performances were cancelled, allegedly due to Eva Li-On's prior commitments in a Viennese theater. However, "the play itself was not a serious box office success," and Habima made no attempt to find a replacement for Li-On.[40]

The play has occasionally attracted the interest of researchers, students, and directors who view it as a chapter in the history of the Israeli stage or the history of Bible-themed drama.[41] The theater workshop of the Beit Hillel student group in Jerusalem attempted to revive *Journey to Nineveh* in 1989, under the direction of Shai Bar Yaacov, with students as the actors and a minimalistic set decor. Amichai at the time was in the USSR, which was then on the verge of collapse. The journalist who interviewed him intuitively linked his "longing" for the USSR with the 40 year old play. "In the 1950s I thought, like all my generation, that salvation would come from Soviet Russia, despite Stalin's actions." Amichai considered Jonah to be a type of revolutionary who knew in advance that his revolution would fail, but nevertheless never stopped fighting for it. "This was about human pride," he explained to the interviewer: Judaism does not abandon Yom Kippur (the Day of Atonement), despite knowing that sin and evil cannot be eradicated.[42]

THE FIRST RADIO PLAYS

Journey to Nineveh was developed from the Israeli part of *Not of This Time* that involves longing for another woman (Clarice in Amichai's case), and for the "other Israel," that would ideally embody lofty justice and exemplary individual qualities. This was the Israel the intellectuals of his generation had hoped for. *Bells and Trains*,[43] the first full-length radio script written by Amichai, which is still considered a masterpiece, emerged from the part of *Not of This Time* set in Germany.

The writing of radio scripts, unlike stage plays, came much more naturally to Amichai. He had already tried his hand at writing radio plays which are preserved in his class yearbooks.[44] In her study of Amichai's radio scripts Ruth Levitsky suggested that a radio play is a "genre for poets," and considered that Amichai's qualities as a creative artist came the fore to produce the best radio scripts ever written in Israel.[45] These qualities included his experience as the author of short stories, novels, plays, and poetry, all of which are important for the "mixed genre" of a radio play, his modernity combining times and places, a nonlinear plot and bold images, the everyday content that "he selects to represent his world", his use of the spoken language, and his love of live contact with the audience.

Radio plays were immensely popular in Israel at the time and Amichai and others devoted intense efforts to writing scripts in the 1960s (and the two next decades). Even though they were broadcast on the state channels, radio plays were often daring and innovative. They conveyed messages derived from modern European and American theater, and did not recoil from political criticism of painful subjects.[46] The announcement by Kol Yisrael (Israel Broadcasting Authority) in 1962 of a competition for original radio scripts only enhanced the standing of the genre. Amichai won first prize in the first competition.

In *Bells and Trains* Amichai exhibited masterful control in constructing a chamber work, circumscribed in time and place, oppressive in its tangibility, and soul-piercing in its symbolism, as befits the topic.[47] The more extensive visit of the novel's doubt-ridden "I" to his hometown in *Not of This Time* becomes a trip by Jochanan (formerly Hans) to a nursing home in the city of Singburg (literally "song-city"), and the script cuts the number of characters and plots in the corresponding parts of the novel down to a minimum.

As in the novel, the main character, a German who fled the Nazis to Palestine, goes back to Germany, ostensibly to sue for reparations. However, the real reason for his visit is to see his "Auntie," the beloved Henrietta who spoiled him in his childhood like a mother, and who survived the Holocaust together with a handful of other Jews. He tries, to no avail, to extricate Henrietta from Germany and the shadow of the past, but she is completely involved in helping the residents of the old age home where she lives, and trainspotting the nearby station through her window, while still waiting for the husband she married in Theresienstadt who was murdered three days later to come home.

Hans-Jochanan encounters three other characters who are a condensed version of Amichai's Würzburg experiences: Mr. and Mrs. Rosenberg, a couple who do not talk to each other and who had already lost their only daughter Laura when the Allies liberated them from the camp. The character of Mr. Rosenberg combines the figure of the city rabbi, Ruth's father, with the intimidating principal of the Jewish school, Mr. Hillman, who is mentioned a number of times in *Not of This Time*, and who would star in another radio script, *Lechah Dodi* (Come, my beloved), first aired in 1974.[48] The absent character of Laura brings together Little Ruth and another girl from his class, Laura, a stable-owner's daughter; the circumstances of her murder are depicted in a poetic and horrifying manner in *Not of This Time*.[49]

There is no music in the radio play, but symbolic sounds are incessant: the ringing of the church bells every fifteen minutes – perhaps a symbol of the Christian world's indifference to the fate of the Jews in the Holocaust, the blasts of train horns, the trains that bring Jochanan to his beloved childhood world, and also reminiscent of the trains that took the city's Jews to the concentration camps and their deaths,[50] the barking of the dogs fed by the teacher Rosenberg and which echo the terror elicited by the Nazi dogs, and the sounds of the voices in the nursing home dining room, the sole source of entertainment and activity for these elderly people waiting to die.

The aged survivors fluctuate between madness and sanity. Auntie, the elderly Henrietta, is very sane while she continues to be understanding and motherly to Hans-Jochanan, and acts as a mediator between the Rosenbergs who are not talking to each other. However, she is also confused: she is not willing to leave Singburg, because she sees herself as an expert on railroad sounds, and because she is waiting for her husband, whom she in fact knows was murdered. Mrs. Rosenberg also exhibits a mixture of sanity and dementia, although somewhat differently: she constantly gives an unexpected twist to well-known proverbs ("Judge a book by its cover, don't look inside. It's dark there"). As Amichai explained in a radio interview, she fills the role of the madwoman (like the fool or jester in Shakespeare) who exposes the hollow shell of normalcy and the emptiness of an education that seeks to create "decent people " by inculcating them with proverbs.[51]

Numerous literary critics at the time failed to separate their professional criticism from their ideological objections. The prime one was that Amichai did not deal properly with the sensitive question of Jews remaining in Germany. Notwithstanding this reservation, Shlomo Bin-Nun declared in *Davar* that "most of the achievement [the success of *Bells and Trains*] is to be credited to Amichai, who united many allusions and a whole set of motifs in a single poetic play" that presents Singburg – and with it, all of Germany – as Sodom.[52] In contrast to its mitigated reception overall in Israel, *Bells and Trains* was highly popular abroad. It was broadcast in translation in a number of languages including English, German, French, Hungarian, and others.[53] However, attempts to adapt the script to theater, television, and even cinema were only partially successful or failed to materialize.

Two years later Amichai once again entered the Kol Yisrael radio script competition. This time he chose to adapt one of his best-known and most interesting stories, "The Class Meeting."[54] He reeduced the number of characters to six. The basic theme of the story and the script were similar: The "I" ("Aryeh" in the script), someone for whom preserving the past is important, wants the members of his high school class to meet again, but his invitation is met with apathy and opposition from his classmates, who are now adults and apprehensive about anyone delving into matters that do not serve immediate, practical needs.

Although the adaptation was successful and produced a clear and consistent script, it was awarded third prize by the same panel of judges that had given him first prize for *Bells and Trains*.[55] Despite the script's integrity and clarity, the judges may have found its structure to be relatively conventional and its use of vocal effects to be less impressive than its predecessor. Like Amichai's prose, it tends to be wordy and there are not enough the silences and pauses between actions to preserve the sense of mystery this genre requires.

THE PUBLICATION OF *POEMS 1948-1962*

At the same time that Amichai was writing a novel, plays and radio scripts, he was also involved in the publication of a book that would include most of his earlier poems, with the substantial addition of new ones. *Poems 1948-1962,* totaling almost 290 pages in the first edition, was published in the spring of 1963, and contains the majority of the poems that established Amichai's dominance in Hebrew poetry, and made him such a popular and beloved poet.

The editor, Dan Miron, decided not replicate the division into sections in *Two Hopes Away*, and in several places changed the order of the poems. He made drastic cuts to the long poem "In the Public Garden." Whole sections of the poem were omitted, mainly from the mother's strange and rather repellent monologue, and the unconvincing soft porn. In addition, parts of the poem were moved, sometimes in abbreviated form. The editing, which eliminated roughly half of the original, reinforced the poem's musicality by concentrating the "prayer" sections toward the end in a way that intensifies and then relieves the tension in the lovers' exchanges, who become calmer as they are more receptive to each other's feelings. However, when the eighth edition of the book was reprinted in 1970, Amichai restored most of what had been omitted and edited. "In the Public Garden" was later reprinted in its entirety as a separate volume.[56]

The second part of *Poems 1948-1962*, which included poems previously unpublished in book format, is divided into roughly thematic sections. The poems in "The Place Where I Never Was" deal with locations that were imagined, aspired to or lost (as in the poems "In the Middle of This Century," "A Man by a Window," "My Parent's Migration," "Instructions to a Waitress," "Instructions for Her Journey," and "You Need to Return"). "City Poems" is mainly about life in Jerusalem ("Street," "The New Roads," "The Housing of Clerks," "Mayor," "In the Public Garden," the arguably political "The Place Where We Are Right," and others). "Summer, or Its End" is a series of love poems, some of which are among Amichai's best ("If with a Bitter Mouth," "During Our Love Houses Were Finished"). The section "In the Full Severity of Compassion" is a poetic meditation of an individual who is attempting to come to terms with life, and is willing to assess the painful distance between the possible and the ideal, near-success and near-failure. This is followed by a number of sections arranged according to genre: a narrative poem ("Poems to a Girl on the Seashore"); "Twenty New Quatrains," which the author and the editor preferred to separate from the older quatrains, possibly because they included a new narrative thread. The book ends with four elegies, the last two of which constitute some of Amichai's finest works.

The poems from the late 1950s, written after *Two Hopes Away* went to press, seem to reflect efforts to overcome a feeling of death and annihilation in the wake of the end of love, and perhaps also the soul-searching of someone who had covered "half of our life's path," as Dante writes in the beginning of *Inferno*. Defiance in the face of death, which closes in on the speaker of the poems like a chokehold, and the attempt to conjure death away are expressed in the poem "We Shall Live Forever." The latter had been written years before its appearance in a book, but Amichai waited for the appearance of *Now in the Storm* (*Poems* 1963–1968) to publish it.[57] In this homiletic poem, the poet provides different interpretations in the form of guidelines, both panic-stricken and confident, on how to deal with finitude. He can sing, though his mouth is twisted: "My heart rests / on my drying-up body, like a gasping fish, singing / with a crooked mouth. It must sing, lest it choke on land." He can also "build," by transforming a window meant for contemplation into a door that invites others in. On the door is a mezuzah of a new type, "one that is full / of a spirit that both holds and releases;" this is the spirit of "the little words of questioning," which "sail us towards the black ships," forever ready for a journey without a destination.[58]

Only the love embodied in sex can ward off death, not only physical death, but that which is much more threatening, death in life; namely, the hardening and desensitizing of the soul. For example the woman who "waged war on [lit: eradicated, murdered] bacteria" nevertheless gives herself to him: "In the bed, us / Without any of these / And each for the other" ("You washed the fruit").[59] The sexual experience reshapes the experience of time; it nullifies the surrounding events and lasts forever: "Wonderful was the dream / on the table. / The fruits we left / forever till tomorrow [...] // After midnight, when our words began / to influence the world." The sense of eternity in intercourse is so vivid that in its aftermath upon waking it seems that monumental steps, which usually take years, had been completed in the meantime: "During our love houses were finished / and someone who didn't know how / learned to play the flute."[60]

From within the confusion and disorientation of his personal life (his inability to decide whether to continue living with Tamar), he gives himself personal dictates: "Let the coin decide. Kings / Did so. Do not make up your mind [...] // Let the streets be your leaders."[61] He has reached the conclusion that he cannot decide based on any rational or moral principle, and a solution will come from a spontaneous impulse, from intuition ("Build a hut at the corner of Justice. / Let the judge judge his own game"). In the meantime, all that is left is to "adorn the chance," to relate to his dilemma as though he had devised it intentionally ("adorn the chance in words and flowers, / make a bracelet for your wife from the instructions"). Another 'didactic' poem from this period is "Do Not Accept." The essence of the advice – to himself here – is to temporarily look inwards and engage in submission, which can lead to renewal and perhaps turn back the clock without conscious and intentional effort on his part.[62]

A spirit of resignation, taking on the role of a mediator or agent rather than creating fundamental values, infuses the poem "And Let Us Not Get Excited." This poem also gives advice in the first-person plural, in some way addressing the public of which he is a part, possibly the community of creative artists or poets:[63] "And let us not get excited, for a translator / must not get excited. Quietly, let us pass down / words from one to another [...] // unawares, the way a father passes down / the features of his dead father's face to his son / [...] he's just a go-between." Nurturing words and "educating" them, as Amichai puts it in the poem, means to develop what exists and to prune what is unnecessary. Silence, the voice of love and morality that has no need of many words ("And let us no longer say unto other sayers / what has been said unto us. To be silent is to concede"),[64] is transmitted from one generation to the next.[65]

REVIEWS AND RESPONSES TO THE BOOK

Reviews published in newspapers and periodicals acknowledged the importance of the volume, but in a reserved, less enthusiastic way than might have been expected. The reviewers' attitude was somewhat ambivalent, and anticipated in great measure the kind of reviews Amichai would receive in the coming years. On the one hand, critics wondered why there should be a book of collected poems by someone who had only published for fourteen years;[66] on the other, Amichai was already depicted as an established poet, emulated by others. In this regard he was criticized for imitating himself, primarily the innovations of his early collections.[67]

In the journal *Ammot*, Shimon Sandbank suggested what constituted Amichai's innovativeness and greatness. He indirectly situates the Amichai revolution in the context of the decades-old battle in Hebrew poetry involving resistance to the domination of poetic language by ancient biblical verses and phrases: "He discovered the advantages of forced syntax, halting rhyme, and irregular meter." For Sandbank, Amichai decomposed the Hebrew sentence into its components, thereby imparting renewed force and semantic extensions to words and phrases taken from the sources.[68]

Baruch Kurzweil, a towering critic of the era who had challenged the attitude of the poets of the new generation to Jewish sources and traditions, was now more willing to admit that "Yehuda Amichai is the outstanding (albeit relatively moderate) representative of the mood of our young literature." He noted the features of Amichai's use of the language from ancient sources, especially the daily and holiday prayer books, but rejected his "destructive modernism." In his opinion, Amichai was frequently tempted to engage in an "artistic game" that resulted in banality.[69]

The younger critics were more sympathetic. Rina Litvin, who was already a well-known translator, wrote that "Amichai's style is extraordinary in its preference for witty imagery taken from prosaic reality [...] but his strength does not lie in any special wit [...] something else here touches us [...] this seems to be the special silence in his poetry, expressed in great simplicity," or, in Amichai's own language, the mouth "that reads the declaration of reality."[70] The poet and journalist Moshe Dor, a member of Amichai's school of poetry, credited him with "the flowering of a new school of poetry which [...] brought into our world the echoes of modern Western poetry." Dor wrote about the paradox in Amichai's poetic identity: a secular heretic who longs for a helpless God ("And That Is Your Glory"), a patriot and fighter who declares that his greatest aim is, as he puts it, "to die in my own bed." Dor, like Litvin, was more favorably inclined towards Amichai's early poetry, but was apprehensive of what he saw as mannerism in his later work.[71]

Amichai's friend, the poet and lecturer in English literature Aryeh Sachs, published an article that summarized Amichai's poetry for English-language readers who were only familiar with Amichai from translations.[72] Sachs showed that Amichai's poems were connected to the language of the ancient sources, as is all Hebrew poetry; "the Hebrewness of this poetry is still its core," wrote Sachs, and this association might have complicated its translation. But a feature of Amichai's poetry facilitates its translation and makes it international: "His poems are perceptual rather than conceptual. Where concepts appear they are treated purely as perceptions."[73]

NOTES

1. Rachel Eytan interview, "Between Pen and Paper" [in Hebrew], *Haaretz*, January 1, 1965, 10.
2. Bina Barzel interview, "Writing is a Necessity – Like Loving and Eating" [in Hebrew], *Yediot Acharonot*, June 1, 1973, 3.
3. Dan Miron [in Hebrew], February 16, 2017, email. In another email dated December 8, 2017, he stated that he knew Amichai well when they studied together at the Hebrew University in Jerusalem; he also met Yehuda and Tamar in London (in 1957).
4. Email from Miron, November 4, 2016.
5. Email from Miron, September 16, 2015.
6. *Bells and Trains* [in Hebrew], expanded ed. (Tel Aviv: Schocken, 1992), 221-49.
7. A total of 74 original plays opened in the first 15 years of the State, many more than in the three decades of the British Mandate (Yona Bahur, "Israeli Theater" [in Hebrew], *Haaretz*, July 3, 1964, 13).
8. Emanuel Levy, *Habima - National Theater* [in Hebrew] (Tel Aviv: Eked, 1981), 237-39. In English: idem, *The Halima, Israel's National Theater, 1917-1977* (Columbia, 1979), 194-96.
9. "The Small against the Great" [in Hebrew], *Hatzofeh*, November 8, 1962.
10. Yehuda Amichai, "How I Wrote No Man's Land" [in Hebrew], *Haaretz*, November 2, 1962.
11. "Amichai's Play at Zavit," *Davar* [in Hebrew], October, 3, 1962, 2; B. H., "Bells and Trains – The Radio Script that Won First Prize in the Kol Yisrael Competition" [in Hebrew], *Maariv*, June 22, 1962.
12. See a comment by Amos Aricha, a writer and playwright: "The Problem of Commissioned Plays" [in Hebrew], Literary Section, *Davar*, February 8, 1962, 5. Aricha thought that the writing of commissioned plays in particular could promote

the quality of theater in Hebrew, since such writing promoted – the sorely lacking – cooperation between playwright and director.

13. Amichai, "How I Wrote No Man's Land" [in Hebrew].

14. Another interpretation connects the character of the president with Ben-Gurion, who was still prime minister at a time when many felt that he was ill.

15. Amichai, "How I Wrote No Man's Land" [in Hebrew].

16. Nathan Dunevich, "Another Israeli Play" [in Hebrew] *Haaretz*, November 9, 1962; Sylvie Keshet, "An Israeli Satiric-Tragic No Man's Land" [in Hebrew], *Yediot Acharonot*, October 10, 1962.

17. Hag (Haim Gamzu), "No Man's Land at the Zavit" [in Hebrew], *Haaretz*, December 18, 1962. A review in a similar spirit in *Haolam Hazeh* stated that this was "nonsense [...] faded clichés, instead of living people [...] coarse symbols, instead of ideas" ("Without a Meeting Point" [in Hebrew], November 21, 1962, 15).

18. "No Man's Land at the Zavit Theater" [in Hebrew], *Haboker*, November 18, 1962.

19. Yoram Kaniuk, "No Man's Land at the Zavit" [in Hebrew], *Lamerchav*, November 23, 1962.

20. Two months after the premiere, the play was still running, although less frequently (according to the "In the Theaters" column in *Cherut*, January 27, 1963, 4 [in Hebrew]). It was broadcast on the radio, under Manor's direction, on December 24, 1962 (according to the listing in *Maariv*, December 21, 1962, 6 [in Hebrew]).

21. Amichai told Rachel Oren frankly that "In the first act Jonah leaves his wife, because their married life had lost all content" (Rachel Oren, "The Playwright in the Belly of the Whale," *Dvar ha-Shavua*, August 7, 1964, 23 [Hebrew]).

22. While still in high school Amichai wrote an essay on the character of the biblical Jonah as a petit bourgeois who shirks his obligations to society of the time, namely, defense and settlement. According to Amichai, he was almost expelled from his religious school for this daring interpretation of the biblical allegory. Amichai's part of the playwrights' conversation "Where the Bible Falls Short" [in Hebrew], *Teatron* 3 (June-July 1962): 23-32, at 26. A little differently he told one of his interviewers that in his youth he viewed Jonah as "a petit bourgeois type, who is primarily interested in his own well-being. Now I portray him as a small, confused person." Oren, "Playwright in the Belly," 23.

23. This apparently was what Glenda Abramson meant when she wrote that "Jonah's intrinsic mission is to bring the truth [...] to the attention of the masses [...] to acquaint 'them' with the fact [...] that independent judgment and the pursuit of inner wisdom and inner knowledge are worth everything in the world." Glenda Abramson, "Jonah in Modern Dress," *Jewish Affairs* (September 1971), 53-55, at 55.

24. *Journey to Nineveh* [in Hebrew] (Jerusalem: Achshav, 1962).

25. Dahlia Ravikovitch, "A Little Fish between Two Whales" [in Hebrew], *Yediot Acharonot*, November 2, 1962. Aviv Ekroni, in "Jonah in Modern Garb" [in Hebrew], *Al Hamishmar*, January 4, 1963, wrote in a similar spirit: "The reader finds it difficult to identify the values the hero is seeking."

26. Ben-Ami Feingold, "Yehuda Amichai and His Journey to Nineveh" [in Hebrew], *Haboker*, November 23, 1962. See also his lengthy article, written prior

to the premiere, "A Study of Journey to Nineveh by Yehuda Amichai" [in Hebrew], *Mibifnim*, April 1964, 43-48.

27. Gnazim, 3968/4.

28. Amichai heard this from the famous Habima actor Shimon Finkel. Raphael Bashan, "Monologue of Yehuda Amichai - 'I Don't Remember When I Fled and from what God'" [in Hebrew], *Maariv - Yamim ve-Leilot magazine*, August 29, 1964, 2.

29. "From Nineveh to New York" [in Hebrew], *Haaretz*, November 11, 1963. Gellner wanted to encourage original Israeli plays, as he stated when appointed artistic director ("In the Gates of Habima" [in Hebrew], *Bamah* 15, no. 68 (Autumn 1962), 9.

30. Oren, "Playwright in the Belly", 23. He was also invited to stage it in the US, according to Amichai's letter responding to Benjamin Zemah. Aza Zvi archive, Arc. 4* 2009 01 103 [in Hebrew], Archives Department, National Library of Israel.

31. Oren, "Playwright in the Belly," 3, 15.

32. Michael Ohad, "The Prophet in the Fish and the Failed Revolution" [in Hebrew], supplement, *Haaretz*, July 17, 1964, 12-13.

33. Yehoshua Kenaz, "Journey to Nineveh at Habima" [in Hebrew], *Lamerchav - Masa*, August 7, 1964.

34. On the performance as a musical, see Tehila Ofer, "Nahum as Jonah" [in Hebrew], *Haboker*, July 27, 1964. The *Davar* journalist Hava Novak, who attended a dress rehearsal on the "Small Stage", had the impression that they were "full of movement [...] they are learning dances and songs, because the play includes many songs." *Davar*, July 2, 1964, 11 [in Hebrew].

35. Oren, "Playwright in the Belly," 15. Buchman voiced similar sentiments to Emanuel Bar-Kadma, in a very favorable portrait of the actor. Emanuel Bar-Kadma, "The Voice of God Issues forth from the Throat of the Actor" [in Hebrew], *Yediot Acharonot*, July 24, 1964. Later, when Buchman wrote his memoirs – after the failure of the play with both audiences and critics – he claimed that he had not liked this role, "since Gellner did not understand the essential nature of the performance; nor was the stage setting appropriate." Nahum Buchman, *My Habima* [in Hebrew] (Tel Aviv, 1998), 47.

36. The high quality of the "first half" (probably the first two acts) was noted by various critics, including Avraham Oz, "Myth in Drama and Its Adaptation to Israeli Theater" [in Hebrew], *Haaretz - Literary Section,* January 13, 1967.

37. Ben-Ami Feingold, "Journey to Nineveh at Habima" [in Hebrew], *Haboker*, July 28, 1964.

38. Taken from a more detailed review by Ben-Ami Feingold, "Journey to Nineveh at Habima" [in Hebrew], *Haboker*, July 31, 1974. Almost all the reviewers criticized the clumsy and uninspired stage design.

39. Bertini was quoted in *Haaretz* [in Hebrew], July 15, 1964. Journey to Nineveh was first performed at the end of July.

40. "Journey to Nineveh Will Be Taken off the Stage in Mid-September" [in Hebrew], *Maariv*, August 25, 1964, 4.

41. Gideon Ofrat, "Biblical Allegory," in his *Israeli Drama [*in Hebrew] (Tel Aviv: Cherikover, 1975), 131-43; Hila Levi, "Journey to Nineveh by Yehuda Amichai" [in

Hebrew] (seminar paper, Haifa University, 1988); Matityahu Shafriri, "Journey to Nineveh and Its Production in Habima, 1964" [in Hebrew], in his "Biblical Drama on the Hebrew Stage" [in Hebrew] (Ph.D., Tel Aviv University, 1999), 161-186.

42. Rachel Ross, "Journey to Nineveh by Yehuda Amichai" [in Hebrew], *Yerushalayim*, May 12, 1989, 20. In his notebook entry for May 15, 1989, Amichai commented bitterly after attending the performance of Nineveh at the university: "[The actors were] young and full of enthusiasm, and I came home with heartache."

43. First full publication in *Teatron* 4 (September-October 1962), 12-17 [in Hebrew].

44. See Chapter 2.

45. Ruth Levitsky, *The Radio Plays by Yehuda Amichai: Six Aspects of the Radio Art* [in Hebrew], (MA thesis, Tel Aviv University, 1997), 7. In her Ph.D, she places radio scripts in the "lyrical genre," and regrets that this gold mine for poets has not been better exploited in Israel. Levitsky, *The Hebrew Radio Play: socithematics and Radio Art*, [in Hebrew] Ph.D, Tel Aviv University, 2007, 7, 9-10. See also Amichai in his own words: in this genre, "there is no difference between external and inner dialogue. Unlike in a play, a radio script fully utilizes the magical power of the word." B. H., "Bells and Trains – A Radio Script that Won First Prize in the Kol Yisrael Competition" [in Hebrew], *Maariv*, June 22, 1962.

46. One example is the broadcast of Amichai's *No Man's Land* in 1963, despite what was seen as implied criticism of Ben-Gurion. Levitsky ("Hebrew Radio Play" [in Hebrew], 52-53) gives examples of political criticism in other authors' radio plays.

47. Shimon Levy considered that radio scripts were particularly well-suited to tackling the subject of the Holocaust: *Israeli Theater* [in Hebrew] (Tel Aviv, 2016], 226-30.

48. "Come, My Beloved" is based on the first verse of a hymn chanted during the Sabbath eve service. First published in *Yerushalayim* 9-10 (1975), 175-87 [in Hebrew]; included in *Bells and Trains* [in Hebrew] (1992), 171-90.

49. *Not of This Time* [in Hebrew], 147-48, 151-52. *Bells and Trains* was directed by the head of the drama department, Hanna Ben-Ari, like Amichai a native of Germany who fled before the Holocaust.

50. In an interview for an Israel Radio literary program with Shmuel Huppert (probably in the 1980s), Amichai defined the use of the sound of train whistles in the script as an act of "double exposure." For him, the trains were comforting sights from his childhood, later overlaid with the threatening sound of the death convoys.

51. See Amichai's poem "Instruction for Voyage," composed entirely of counter-normative instructions: "Bend your head outside the window [...] Confuse the schedule." *Life of Poetry*, 53.

52. Shlomo Ben-Nun, "The Performance of a Radio Script and Scandinavia" [in Hebrew], *Davar*, September 7, 1962, 6.

53. "Original Israeli Radio Script on French Radio" [in Hebrew], *Davar*, November 21, 1966, 2.

54. The story was published in the collection *In This Terrible Wind* (first edition: Tel Aviv, Sifriat Hapoalim, 1961 7-42; later edition: Tel Aviv, Schocken, 1973), 7-48

[in Hebrew]. It was probably written in 1957, or a little later, during Amichai's unsuccessful attempt to arrange a class meeting (alternatively it might have been written in 1954 – see *In this Terrible Wind*, 48).

55. An article in *Davar* [in Hebrew], May 20, 1963. The panel of judges was composed of two authors - Lea Goldberg and Shlomo Tanni, and two representatives of Kol Yisrael - director Yeshayahu Shapira and the head of the drama department, Hanna Ben-Ari.

56. See Chapter 8, "The Publication of In the Public Garden."

57. "We Shall Live Forever," *Poems* [in Hebrew] 2, 83-84.

58. Mezuzah - a set of ritually prescribed texts written on parchment, rolled up and inserted into a decorative casing, affixed to the doorposts of Jewish homes.

59. From the cycle "Summer or Its End,'" *Selected Poetry*, 36; *Poems* [in Hebrew] 1, 274-275.

60. "During Our Love Houses Were Finished," *Poetry*, 72; *Poems* [in Hebrew] 1, 287-288.

61. "Let the Coin Decide," *Life of Poetry*, 62; Poems [in Hebrew] 1, 329.

62. "Do Not Accept," *Life of Poetry*, 59; Poems [in Hebrew] 1, 302.

63. *Poetry*, 77; *Poems* [in Hebrew] 1, 313.

64. Based on a saying by the Talmudic sages: "Silence is consent."

65. For a similar interpretation, see Chana Kronfeld, *Full Severity*, 180-85.

66. Maksim Gilan, "Selection of Amichai's Poetry" [in Hebrew], *Yokhani* 4 (July 1963), 104-5.

67. Ben-Ami Feingold, "Amichai 1948-1962" [in Hebrew], *Haboker*, May 24, 1963.

68. Shimon Sandbank, "The Collected Poems of Yehuda Amichai" [in Hebrew], *Ammot* 1, 5 (April-May 1963), 93-95.

69. First published as "Notes to Poems of Yehuda Amichai" [in Hebrew], *Haaretz*, June 28, 1963. It was published with an additional article two weeks later, entitled "Autobiographical Poetry in the Great Desert," in Baruch Kurzweil, *In Search of Israeli Literature* [in Hebrew], (Ramat Gan: Bar-Ilan University, 1982), 231-46.

70. Rina Litvin, "The Poetry of Yehuda Amichai" [in Hebrew], *Lamerchav - Masa*, May 10, 1963. "Declaration of reality" (*megilat ha-metziut*) is Amichai's wordplay on *megilat ha-atzmaut*, the Israeli Declaration of Independence.

71. Moshe Dor, "The Grace of Poetry" [in Hebrew], *Maariv*, May 31, 1963.

72. Arieh Sachs, "The Poetry of Yehuda Amichai," *Judaism* 14, 4 (1965), 407-13. At that period Amichai's poems appeared in English translation in the first issue of a journal specializing in the translation of poetry, edited by Ted Hughes and Daniel Weissbort: *Modern Poetry in Translation* (1965). His poetry was already included in the French anthology: Nicola Moshe Lazar (trans.), *Poètes israéliens d'aujourd'hui* (Paris: A. Michel, 1960). Several poems appeared in *Poetry* 92, 4 (July 1958), and in the anthology: Ruth Finer Mintz (ed. and trans.) *Modern Hebrew Poetry: A Bilingual Anthology* (Berkeley and Los Angeles: University of California, 1966).

73. Sachs, "Poetry of Yehuda Amichai," 413.

Chapter 11

1964–1968

A Year in New York, Friendship with Ted Hughes, Return to Israel after the Six Day War

THE "FAMILY" – A GREAT FRIENDSHIP THAT WENT SOUR

In his autobiography, the distinguished poet Natan Zach describes the Abu Tor neighborhood of Jerusalem in the 1950s as a pastoral corner of the city.[1] The poet Arieh Sachs, who was also a lecturer in English literature at the Hebrew University, and a theater director, lived in an old Arab house in that isolated neighborhood. Dennis Silk, an English poet and puppeteer who had come to Abu Tor in 1955 or 1956, lived in a one-and-a-half-room shack not far away. In England he had been a member of the *Habonim* youth movement. When he first came to Israel he had tried for a while to live on a kibbutz.[2]

In the first half of the 1960s, two new members came to make up what would become a literary quartet of friends. Amichai moved first with Hana to the neighborhood, where they rented an apartment next to what would become the Mount Zion Hotel. Then came the American poet Harold Schimmel who wrote primarily in Hebrew. Amichai and Sachs knew each other from Sachs' time as a student at John Hopkins University in Baltimore, Maryland.[3] A friend of Schimmel's, who had rented him her apartment in Abu Tor, told him about "an English poet living nearby," and both got to know Sachs and Amichai. Thus, on the fringes of a no-man's land, a Jerusalem school of poets of sorts came into being, intentionally or not, as an alternative to the dominant Tel Aviv school. Schimmel, the most naïve of the company, and perhaps the one most vehemently attacked as a poet, called it "an island of beauty and purity."[4]

The four regularly met at Sachs' house, on the Sabbath as well as on weekdays, when he invited prestigious foreign guests, including John Berryman,

Saul Bellow and Jorge Luis Borges. "Arieh knew how to host both distinguished people and students, especially female ones," Gabi, a former student who married him in 1946, noted.[5] They would drink a lot, have lunch together, dance, and read poetry and translations. Sometimes they danced with inanimate objects, perhaps inspired by Silk, who was a proponent of "object theater." Sachs was a great DJ, according to Gabi, and Amichai an excellent dancer. Schimmel thought that Amichai had inherited a tendency for showmanship from his father since his dancing was also a performance. For example, he would play the broken violin hanging on the wall in Sachs' home. Amichai did not drink alcohol out of fear of a heart attack and a premature death like his father. He was not enthusiastic about reading his poems to the group. Nevertheless, his obsession with writing was clear: he could drop everything if a line of a poem came to mind, and would write it down in a notebook or on a cigarette package.

Though love of poetry was what held the four together, they were not all cut from the same cloth. Their poetic ideal was embodied in the reclusive Silk, ensconced in his shack along with his mechanical puppets and props for his performances ("He's like our bank / Where we deposited what we had in our hearts').[6] Sachs, by contrast, was a libertine, and their insatiable attraction to women drew Amichai and Sachs together. When Sachs discovered Gabi, Amichai wooed her friend, the literature student Abigail Agranat, who is immortalized in the poem "The Sweet Breakdowns of Abigail."[7] Sachs and Amichai were intellectually close as well: in their worldview, the holy was imbricated in the secular, and religious ritual amounted to a variety show.[8] They also shared a keen awareness of death.

Sachs made an original contribution to artistic life in Israel. As an academic and an artist, he was particularly interested in the puppet and shadow theater of the Far East as well as medieval theater.[9] He considered that late medieval theater, and mystery and morality plays in particular, were "an all embracing theater, where we see good and bad, serious and funny, appearing as polarities, but with pronounced theatricality."[10] He got Amichai, Silk and Schimmel involved in his theater productions. In 1966, he staged *The Flood* for the English Department at the Hebrew University. Amichai personified the sin of gluttony by pouring a glass of buttermilk over his head.[11] While Amichai was in New York in 1976 he considered working with Sachs on writing a film script, or on developing his radio drama "The Day Martin Buber was Buried," which was by then already near completion.[12]

The poems Amichai wrote about or dedicated to the other three group members show his love for them, along with a special fondness and concern for the lonely Silk, who was in poor mental health and was interned in a psychiatric hospital in the last years of his life.[13] Amichai wrote a "Poem of Friendship" to Sachs in which he calls them both "wretched lovers of the same sleep."[14] Thanks to Schimmel, Amichai and Hana discovered the northern Achziv beach which became their place of predilection for wild lovemaking, and an unfailing inspiration for Amichai's poems. When Schimmel and Varda got married, Amichai wrote a "Hymn to the Lovely Couple Varda and Schimmel" and even insisted on reading it, though it bordered on the lewd, under the *huppah*, to the embarrassment and amusement of the guests: "Jerusalem still drunk, / Tourist foam on her lips. // [...] 100 degrees of happiness / In the aperture of the golden ring [literally 'anus']."[15] Sachs, Schimmel and Silk translated Amichai's poems into English,[16] and Amichai translated Silk's poems and one of his puppet shows into Hebrew.[17]

The English mother tongue connected the lonely Silk to the stable and faithful Schimmel, who wanted to love his companions and Israel idealistically, like the first pioneers in Palestine. There was nevertheless a true intellectual symbiosis between Schimmel and Amichai. They had both been religiously observant in their youth (Schimmel had studied at a yeshiva in New York).[18] He took the credit, with evident justification, for Amichai's turn from British literary sources of influence (in his early poetry such as Auden and Thomas) to American poets such as William Carlos Williams and Robert Lowell. In "Seven Poems of Yehuda Amichai," an analysis presenting translations of poems from *Now in the Storm*, Schimmel emphasized "the international style" of the poems and a "kinship with the persona of [John] Berryman, Allen Ginsberg, or [Eugenio] Montale."[19]

However, this firm friendship floundered and in time came to an end. The other three experienced Amichai's global success and phenomenal popularity in Israel as degrading.[20] When Amichai's book *From Man You Are and to Man You Shall Return* came out, Sachs published a review which began with a description of himself as belonging to "the large camp of Amichai-lovers" and among "his veteran recruits," but ended with the crushing conclusion that Amichai's pain was "a synthetic product." "Amichai's 'difficulty' with this poem ['Inside the Apple'] (and with many others) is to have produced an unconscious parody of the very real difficulty of human pain."[21] Sachs' jealousy may have caused him to see Amichai as superficial and kitschy;[22] whereas for Silk, who as a poet and puppeteer remained esoteric and anonymous to the general public, Amichai had betrayed the ideal of the poet striving for purity and wholeness by riding the waves of acclaim.[23]

Silk died in 1998, a few years after Sachs in 1992. When Amichai was asked to deliver a eulogy for the latter, he did so reluctantly, after many entreaties.[24] Schimmel, Amichai's most trustworthy and faithful friend, continues to mourn his death to this day.

POEMS IN MPT, – ON THE SPRINGBOARD

At the end of 1965 an unexpected event in Amichai's life had far-reaching consequences. The British poet Ted Hughes, one of the major poets in English of the second half of the twentieth century, together with his friend Daniel Weissbort, began publishing a journal of English translations of modern poetry called *Modern Poetry in Translation* (MPT). Weissbort indicates that when Hughes was in America in the 1950s together with his wife Sylvia Plath, he became interested in the poets of Eastern Europe he met at poetry festivals. He realized that their difficult living conditions and the political repression they had experienced had led to "a new thing" in poetry.[25] The Hughes and Weissbort editorial in the first issue conveys the sense that poetry in English was in trouble, and that it needed to be more permeable to poetry with different sensitivities and mentalities. The first issue of the journal was dedicated to poets of the Eastern Bloc, but there were also several poems by Amichai, including sections of the long poem "The Visit of the Queen of Sheba" in Abraham Birman's translation,[26] and part of the cycle "King Saul and I," translated by Rachel Sauer, Amichai's sister.[27]

Including Amichai's poems in an issue devoted to poetry from the Communist Bloc shows the editors' acknowledgement of Amichai, in particular on the part of Hughes, an Anglican who was charmed by what he saw as the miracle of the revival of the language of the Bible, and Amichai was for him a unique representative of this phenomenon.[28]

SPOLETO – FIRST TIME AT AN INTERNATIONAL FESTIVAL

With typical humor Amichai described how his home "exploded" with "telephone calls and messengers summoning me immediately to the department of cultural affairs in the Foreign Ministry" in June 1966. His poems in MPT prompted the famous composer Giancarlo Menotti (1911-2008), who founded the Festival dei Due Mondi (The Festival of the Two Worlds), to invite Amichai to read his poems in the ancient Umbrian town of Spoleto, Italy. The Italian postal workers were on strike, and Ehud Avriel, the Israeli ambassador to Italy, was asked to help quickly make arrangements for Amichai to travel. It was the first time an Israeli poet had been invited to the festival.[29]

Amichai began his newspaper report on "A Festival in Spoleto" by saying that the year since his visit to the festival in the summer of 1966 was like "a bomb destroying what would otherwise take centuries to destroy." This was the year that he and Hana spent in New York, and being poet on an international stage was indeed a "revolution." He may have only realized a year later that the Spoleto festival was the springboard for his international fame, when Hughes invited him to a festival he was organizing.

Amichai's description of the festival more than a year later shows just how intoxicating he found the myriad of encounters with both better and lesser known poets, as well as with the beautiful women who hosted the poets or attended the festival as poetry enthusiasts. Sometimes there was no common language, for example with the Hungarians; sometimes communication was partial, as with the poet-doctor Takis Sinopoulos (1917-1981), where he struggled to communicate in his limited French. This did not dispel his wonder and excitement, or his desire to stay in touch.[30] Another poet he met, the beatnik Gregory Corso (1930-2001), exemplified the extrovert poet, who "looks like a poet," a favorite subject in Amichai's lectures over the years.

Twenty-five years later he told a journalist that "when they invited me to a huge festival in Spoleto, Italy, in 1966, I read alongside Ezra Pound and Pablo Neruda and many others. I was the youngest there, a wunderkind. It was beautiful. And it is always so [the magic accompanying every such gathering]."[31] In an account of the festival at the time, however, he devotes a modest, somewhat embarrassed passage to Pound, who had played a significant role in the evolution of his poetry: "The eighty-year-old Ezra Pound, perhaps the father of modern poetry in English, also appeared, his face stony and voice rather broken, but steadfast [...] I avoided talking to him. It was difficult to be in his presence." The reasons were clear: Pound's cooperation with Mussolini's fascist government during the war and, in fact, with the Nazis.

MIDDLE PERIOD (1964-1966), THE RIPENING OF *NOW IN THE STORM*

Amichai was never an official political activist, and made do with occasional participation in demonstrations and signing manifestos,[32] but he was not averse to the activities of non-political, professional organizations. In this context "professional" meant being both a teacher and a writer.[33] This may have been a German, middle-class cultural view in which the political realm was considered to be an issue of individual conscience,[34] while the professional domain could nevertheless be a legitimate locus for committing oneself to a societal struggle. In the 1960s Amichai was active in the Writers' Association, particularly their push to secure better royalties for authors.[35] This is perhaps why he was asked to join the editorial board of *Moznaim*, the Writers' Union monthly, as the representative of the "younger generation"; the senior generation was not prepared to concede more, entrenched as they were in their beliefs and imaginary hold on power.[36]

When Amichai came back from the US, and Israel was roiling in the fateful questions arising from the Six Day War, the elders had no choice but to give him a speaker's slot at their council meeting in May 1968, alongside balding lions such as the critic and editor Dov Sadan and the writer Haim Hazaz. With his "I do not believe" speech he rang the death knell of the obsolete flowery phrases and petrified ideologies characteristic of the previous generation.

In previous years, Amichai had laid the foundations for his next book of poems, *Now in the Storm* (Poems from 1963-1968). This book differed from its predecessors in orientation. From that time on, Amichai employed fewer metaphors, his graphic images were less daring, and he became more of a rationalist, and more wittily discursive.[37] The unequivocal veracity which imparted a dangerously high voltage to his early poetry ("God Full of Mercy," "Out of Three or Four in a Room") was transformed to make room for a more contemplative style of thought that was more aware and indulgent of the vicissitudes and brevity of human lives. He now seemed more relaxed, and allowed himself to enjoy the privileges and possibilities afforded an established and widely known poet. Something of this resonates in his poem "I Am a Living Man."[38] When the book was published in the late 1960s, and even more so in the 1970s, Amichai would become a frequent target of professional criticism in Israel, even while his circle of admirers and imitators continued to expand.

The transition to a sober maturity that took advantage of things as they were and from chance occurrence was also evident in his waning interest in predicting the end of the world that had been so prevalent among young intellectuals and artists in Israel and the Western world in the 1950s and 1960s. Perhaps changes in the world's political climate had an impact as well: after Stalin's death came the Khrushchev era, and the terror of an end-of-days nuclear exchange between the ideological blocs receded. Amichai expressed this explicitly in in the poem "They Fooled Us": "They fooled us. / They told us: We'll die, we'll be wiped out / in one of the wars. / […] We ate and we drank and on the morrow / we didn't die. / We wasted whatever we saved."[39]

Chana Kronfeld connects the title of the book of poems that came out at the end of 1968 to the Six Day War, whose signature and fallout are indeed recognizable in these poems.[40] However, "Now in the Storm" was the title of a poem published in March 1964. Did this storm reflect the turbulence of Amichai's personal life: the transition to an openly shared life with Hana after a period of secrecy?[41] Amichai is aware of the fall that comes after ultimate pleasure: "And now too soon for archeology / and too late to correct what has been done"; he is not altogether comfortable with himself and his decisions "in becoming intertwined / arms and a shin, words, hips […] // and I am already entangled with everything: / in a comb not mine / in my handkerchief the sweat of a strange and rival woman [*tzarah*] / and I won't know what is truly mine."[42]

AMICHAI AND HANA IN NEW YORK (SEPTEMBER 1966-MAY 1967)

At the end of summer 1966, after two years of living together, Amichai and Hana left for New York. There he laid the foundations for his future as a popular poet on a global scale that few at that time could equal.

What led the couple to leave Israel? Amichai hoped that in the US it would be easier to arrange his divorce with Tamar, who was refusing to accept a *get* (divorce agreement).[43] Hana wanted to complete a master's degree in education at Yeshiva University.[44] During this time she was the main and more stable breadwinner: she taught Hebrew to children at a Jewish school, although she did not enjoy it.[45] Amichai worked part time in a Jewish college in Philadelphia, where he would travel once a week during the first two quarters.[46] In addition he gave occasional lectures to Jewish and Israeli students in New York and university towns in the Eastern US (Boston, Princeton, Pittsburgh, Cleveland), paid by the Jewish Agency, the Zionist Organization of America and the Hebrew Histadrut.[47]

One of the key factors prompting his escape to New York for a time will sound familiar to Israeli ears: the feeling of pressure involved in constantly coping with shortages, difficulties and conflict. From his perspective, "Israel is so difficult, and only in childhood is there any grace and refinement in young girls. Not in the adult world" (November 7, 1966), implying that womanliness could not blossom in an Israel that was constantly under security threat and economic deprivation. The same applied to creativity: "If Mozart had grown up in today's Israel, he'd have written a *debka* (Arab music for dance) instead of a minuet" (ibid.); in other words, he would not have achieved the musical summits of the famed Mozart. There are also more personal overtones to his difficult decision to leave his country: New York is "a city of refuge / wherein to find shelter from the one and only city / Jerusalem"; in other words, he fled the intensity of Jerusalem.

Amichai drew on New York's vast cultural reservoirs. He had not entirely given up on the dream to write for the theater, despite the bitter experience of seeing the curtain come swiftly down on both productions of his plays. Soon after his arrival he saw a play by Edward Albee which he considered a fulfillment of his artistic ideal: "a surrealist atmosphere which is nevertheless realistic" (September 13, 1966). He visited New York's best on and off Broadway theaters such as La Mama, Bread and Puppet, Hirondelle, saw a "cynical theater of homosexuals" at the Cino Café (March 10, 1967, April 14,

1967), and met with the director Peter Fry and the actor Philip Diskin. He was not enthusiastic about the experimental performances he saw, but took away ideas for plays based on ancient texts (prayer) or traditional genres (*maqam*). He toured the museums (the Whitney, Metropolitan, Guggenheim, MOMA, the Museum of Natural History, and the Jewish Museum on September 9 and 30, and November 7 and 19, 1966, and January 4, 1967),[48] but was apparently more interested in the people looking at the pictures than the artworks themselves ("Art interests me / for how it / reminds me of familiar / things [...] this one has a mouth / like yours.") He was present at poetry readings by the greatest American poets of the time: Robert Lowell, John Berryman, Allen Ginsberg (end of March; end of April, 1967) and Auden – this time without a sense of disappointment (November 6). He met Berryman and Ginsberg; with the latter he was reserved. In his notebooks he described him as "an ageing Jew with a fracture [in the groin]." In a late interview he claimed that Ginsberg had turned his "perversion" and oddness into a public-relations stunt.[49]

Amichai earned some of his income by giving lectures, and attracted an interested public.[50] He often discussed the event that was exciting everyone in Israel: S. Y. Agnon's winning of the Nobel Prize for Literature in 1966.[51] Amichai was cognizant of his debt to Agnon, as well as that of his generation as a whole, and wrote about him with esteem and warmth, diluted by slight derision of the great writer's studied conservatism.[52] However, the Agnon he wrote about was mainly Amichai himself, or who he wanted to be. He emphasized how Agnon was loved by students, despite his stories being taught – a problem that bothered him at the time with regard to his own work, once his poetry had been integrated into school curricula. Another commonality between the two was Agnon's avoidance of all political-party involvement and his consistent focus on the past, rather than the immediate and the present.[53]

Social life was important to Amichai no less and perhaps more than taking advantage of New York's cultural events. He mostly frequented Israelis who were staying in New York to study or do research, or who had lived there for a long time. He relates meeting the Hebrew poet Gabriel Preil, whom he calls "an old wunderkind," with affection and a certain modicum of pity (January 18, 1967). He began what would be a longstanding friendship with the Hebrew-speaking literary researcher Robert (Uri) Alter (November 11, 1966) which also had repercussions on his popularity in the US. He also met with Shlomo Katz, the editor of *Midstream*, who was then busy translating *Not of This Time*. Amichai had to give his approval for the many cuts Katz made to the novel that removed the unevenness and peculiarities to the point that it became a novel for all, as was the norm at the time.[54]

A significant figure in his social circle was the philosopher Fred Sommers, who taught during the early 1960s at Columbia University in New York

City, before going on to lecture at Brandeis University in Boston.[55] Amichai associated Sommers with a recurring theme in his poetry of the period, as well as in the later "American Notes" and the story "The Orgy": his well-rooted atheism, and that of Israelis in his circle, by contrast to American religiosity. Like Amichai, Fred had an observant background (he had in fact been to a yeshiva), and shared a certain exuberance about sex, ostensibly as a counterweight to religion and its prohibitions (October 14, 1966). In the story under its original title of "The Orgy that Never Was," Sommers appears as "Steve" and as "an ex-orthodox rabbi," taking part in arguments "about everything connected to the death of God."[56] When sparring with a Protestant theologian who captured the narrator's heart with his naiveté, Steve provides logical-mathematical proof that God "lives and exists," that he is "dead," and that there is no contradiction between these claims and the despair of the astounded theologian, who wonders how sophisticated atheists of this ilk could have emerged from the people that brought monotheism to the world.[57]

Amichai and Hana were on the face of it a married couple, apart from official rabbinic recognition, and were perceived as such by those around them.[58] "Now I am in the city, / where people fear to go, / with a woman who is not afraid / to be with me," he announced soon after their arrival, in a poem published in a New York Hebrew-language journal.[59] However his notebooks reveal that although Yehuda and Hana resembled a loving couple who were passionate and eager for one another, they were also threatened by the possibility of unfaithfulness, as the blinkers of their initial idealization fell away.[60] Amichai pursued women, but respected Hana and was afraid of losing her (March 7, 1967). His love for her was always combined with his love for his son Roni (March 26). At a certain point in February, she urged him to return to Israel without her, but when he made serious preparations to do so, she was alarmed, and he felt confused. This was at the end of March. Finally, the tense days before the Six Day War hastened their decision to go back to Israel.[61] On May 30 he flew alone to London as a stopover.

Amichai acquired cultural baggage in the US, met with exciting individuals, and towards the end of his stay went on fascinating trips. However, the main benefit of nine months on the Eastern seaboard of the new world was recuperation, as he saw it: "Carefully and slowly / I begin to enjoy life / as if acclimatizing to danger." A clear expression of this was the pause in his need to write poetry; writing poetry at his age even seemed to him ridiculous (Spoleto notebooks, July 1967);[62] he was not sure however that he would be willing to give up writing.

IN LONDON: TED HUGHES AND ASSIA, FIRST BOOK OF POEMS IN ENGLISH TRANSLATION

London Festival

Amichai was surrounded by his acquaintances in London, including the editor Meir Mindlin, who was a good friend from the 1950s, and the Jewish poet-physician Dannie Abse. A flight directly back to Israel was nearly impossible. On June 15, he understood that "the war and everything is over," but was alarmed at the size of the territories conquered by Israel and unified Jerusalem. Contradicting his claim that he never reacted hurriedly as a poet to stirring events, he wrote a draft that very day of "We Have No Unknown Soldiers," just as Haim Gouri, in far-off Vienna, had written "Here Lie Our Bodies" when he heard about fallen comrades – the convoy of 35 – in Gush Etzion in January 1948. Amichai dedicated the poem "We Have No Unknown Soldiers" to the memory of a young man who had briefly been his student, Yonatan Yahil, whose mother and father were a well-known historian and diplomat, respectively.[63] There is an enormous difference between this poem and "Here Lie Our Bodies" (both are read frequently at Independence Day ceremonies). In Amichai's poem there is no "we will return to meet [...] / [...] Then we will blossom," no life after death, only a desperate plea to remember a fallen soldier. Now slain, his name calls out to be remembered.[64]

Before Amichai left for the US a year before, the poet Ted Hughes invited him to take part in Poetry International, a festival of spoken poetry in London.[65] Despite the formal address to "Mr. Amichai" and the typed letter on letterhead paper, it is immediately obvious that Hughes had a special relationship with the addressee. At the beginning of May 1967, Hughes responded saying he was delighted that Amichai would read his poems at the festival, and told him the sensational news that a woman, whom he presented as "my wife, who grew up in Israel," had already translated a number of Amichai's poems together with Hughes. The initial motivation was perhaps to encourage Amichai to read his poems at the festival, but the translator hoped to translate more poems for a whole book.[66]

From this moment on, Amichai became a passive witness to a Shakespearian romance that traversed the bounds of life and death. The translator was Assia-Anastasia – née Guttman – Wevill from her previous marriage to a Canadian poet. Assia immigrated at age 7 in 1934 to Tel Aviv with her Jewish father, her Catholic mother, and her younger sister. Her father was alienated from Judaism, and the family's move to Palestine was forced by Nazi persecution and Nazi laws prohibiting Jews from exercising numerous professions.[67] Assia attended a Hebrew elementary school in Tel Aviv, and a Christian Arab high school in Jaffa, where the language of instruction was

English. She was thought of as a rare beauty, with many untapped talents. She lacked a firm identity as a result of her circumstances and upbringing, and tended to cling to the identity of an English lady inculcated by the elitist high school she attended.

She left Tel Aviv in 1946, and when she rented a flat in London in the spring of 1962 from the famous poet couple Ted Hughes and Sylvia Plath, she was already on her third marriage. That year Hughes' and Plath's second child, Nicholas was born, and the tall and very sexual Hughes was in crisis. Plath and Hughes invited Assia and her husband, their tenants, to their rural home of Court Green, in North Tawton in Devon. From here things began to deteriorate – whether initiated by Assia or Ted.[68] By the summer of 1962 they were already lovers. Plath, an important poet with a history of mental health problems, was aware of her husband's infidelity. In February 1963 she committed suicide. She left a manuscript of a book of poems entitled *Ariel*, and other works which have not survived, including a denunciation of her rival and the latter's relationship with her husband.[69]

Ted and Assia were perhaps victims of their imagination, of mutual projections of desires and dreams that shaped their inner worlds. Assia wanted a poet like Wevill or Hughes as a lover, perhaps to compensate for her own only very partially realized creative aspirations (she could paint and had also made attempts at film). Perhaps the impulse to take the place of a path-breaking poet like Plath propelled her into Hughes' arms. For his part he earmarked her for a role in bringing him closer to the people of the Bible, to a Hebraicity and a Jewishness that were at times so meaningful in Anglican history as the foundation of religious spirit.[70]

In 1965 their daughter Alexandra-Shura was born. In the beginning Assia brought her up in partnership with Wevill, her official husband, but before the toddler was a year old, Assia and Hughes were living together again, first in Ireland, far from the hostility of Ted's aging and unwell parents. When they came back to Court Green a year later, it was to the hell of a shared life with Ted's parents and his betrayals with his longtime female acquaintances.[71]

When Amichai got to London, Hughes rapidly set up a meeting with him on June 2, 1967. The enthusiasm was apparently mutual: Amichai wrote a draft in his notebooks of a "Poem to Ted Hughes": "There's a heavenly Jerusalem / and an earthly one. / There's England and there's Ted Hughes / who is of heaven and earth [...] He is like an elevator always between them. / He is the elevator" (June 15, 1967).[72] Two weeks later Hughes wrote to Amichai to give him details of the London festival on July 14. The language of the letter is more informal with Hughes addressing him as "Yehuda," and his interest in having Amichai take part is evident.

Amichai had time to attend the Spoleto Festival a second time, in the first week of July.[73] As expected, his presence was affected by the Six Day War and the rapid and decisive victory of the IDF. "I came for them to praise me for my poems / and they praised me for my comrades' war." He was less enthusiastic about the festival than the previous year, and his notebooks contain disparaging remarks about the poets, whom he felt resembled "children who every year / see another candle / on the birthday cake […] to blow out / another year gone by" (file 473). He frequently made fun of 40- and 50-year-old poets who were still writing. On the other hand, he enjoyed getting to know South American poets who later would be important to him: Mexican Homero Aridjis ("so friendly") and the future Nobel prize laureate Octavio Paz ("he and his wife are pleasant").

He flew directly from Italy to London. The *Jewish Chronicle* reporter who greeted Amichai on his arrival wanted to know how to interpret Israel's lightning victory in the war. Amichai pointed out that he came from an observant background, but he was certain that if there was somewhere where God was absent, it was in war.[74] On July 11 he met other participants in the London poetry festival, including from the Spoleto festival like Ungaretti. Amichai showed interest in Ingeborg Bachmann, an Austrian-born poet living then in Italy; he had already published translations of several of her poems,[75] but she was shy and he found it difficult to connect with her (July 11, 1967). He and Hana, who had arrived in London, stayed with Olwyn Hughes.

The *Times Literary Supplement* (*TLS*) report on the festival claimed that Ungaretti was applauded because of his age more than on account of his poems. The critic considered that the Austrian Bachmann, the Polish Zbigniew Herbert and Amichai to be the most successful, in part because of the excellent translations of their work.[76] The first letter Hughes sent after the festival was to Amichai, some weeks after it had ended. The letter shows the extent to which Hughes was interested in Amichai's experiences when exploring the Old City of Jerusalem for the first time (The Old City was part of the Kingdom of Jordan until June 1967, and Israelis were forbidden to enter). Hughes was enthusiastic about Assia's translations of his friend's poems, and the plans for a first limited edition published by Cape Goliard followed by a full Penguin version.[77] In the end, alongside the British publication of an attractively designed *Selected Poems* (1968), a more extensive *Poems* was published in the US by Harper and Row, which would also publish the American editions of most of Amichai's books in English translation.[78]

The British edition, this time by Penguin, had an introduction by Michael Hamburger, a poet and translator of German-Jewish extraction.[79] Hamburger had met Amichai and Hana in London, and based the introduction on what he knew of Amichai from English translations in anthologies that had come out in the preceding years, and from the novel *Not of This Time,* which was already out in translation. He found a similarity between "the alternating chapters of first and third person narrative" and the metaphoric nature of

Amichai's poems. He considered that both prose and poetry presented a "multiple awareness" of layers of personal experience and biblical and Jewish history.[80]

By the summer of 1967 Ted and Assia's relationship was floundering.[81] Their apparently joint translation of Amichai's poems was aimed to some extent at averting their break up. Assia's Hebrew was superficial and not up to date. Amichai sent a draft translation of most of the poems, and Ted was supposed to make the formal arrangements but he could not know whether he was being accurate in terms of the meaning of the original. Assia did not know how to use rhyme or meter, which characterize much of Amichai's early work. When she wrote to him about "my incredibly impoverished qualifications [...] to translate you," she was perhaps not simply being modest.[82] She was more successful with poems in free verse, but also failed to capture key elements, as in "Rain on the Battlefield."[83] Beyond her complete lack of knowledge of the religious texts channeled in Amichai's poetry, she had only an awkward grasp of the range of the spoken language.[84] Nevertheless, the book was well received in the English and American press. Reviews of the book claimed that translation was no impediment, because of the freshness and originality of Amichai's style, which were manifested despite the difficult transition to English.[85] Amichai himself would respond to inquiries about translations of his poems by saying that a poem needed to be sufficiently robust to move a reader even after something had been lost in its transition between languages.

Assia maintained warm ties with Yehuda and Hana, but her deteriorating mental health emerged from her letters, against the backdrop of her unstable relationship with Hughes and financial difficulties (January 11, 1968). In one of her letters she reports that various newspapers and journals, including the venerable *Encounter*, were about to publish poems of Amichai's in her translation, but that she herself was exhausted by her office job and had problems devoting herself to creative tasks. She suggested that Dennis Silk translate the expanded edition of Amichai's poems, then in the planning stage with Penguin Books. Two months later, on March 6, encouraged by her release from the hospital, she told Yehuda and Hana that she was ready to dive into translating the recent poems Amichai had sent her. She found them to be "infinitely more varied" than the earlier poems, "with their fine steel backbones." On June 5, 1968 she told him that the British edition had now been sent to him with her apologies for places Amichai had found wanting. She argued that the rewordings she and Ted had suggested were the best possible solutions.

On March 26, 1969 Yehuda and Hana received a short message from Olwyn, which unusually was handwritten: "I have terrible news. Assia and Shura died on Sunday evening." Assia had taken a large dose of sleeping pills, and as she hugged her sleeping daughter, they inhaled gas in a room she had sealed tightly.

THE RETURN TO A "UNIFIED JERUSALEM," JERUSALEM POEMS

Amichai came back to a suddenly enlarged country; Israel had gone from being "a place" to "a super-place," or as others had it, the country had acquired its true, messianic significance, having fought and won a larger part of the land of the biblical ancestors. In the aftermath of the 1967 war, Amichai was in no doubt as to where he stood in the argument that broke out between supporters of the "whole land of Israel" (who took up the slogan *af sha'al*, meaning "not one foot" of the land conquered in war should be relinquished) and the peace camp, which upheld universal justice and human life as ultimate values. The victory and memorialization literature which flourished after the war sickened Amichai,[86] but he contributed to books to remember the fallen, when he thought they were written simply and in an appropriately restrained tone, as with Yonatan Yahil, where he had "no desire to present Yonatan as a genius or a hero."[87] He saw "a satchel of letters from another soldier, Hubi [Ya'acov] Eilam, a captain in the paratroopers" that Eilam's widow had brought him in a similar light. "For some days I read them with great admiration and excitement." Amichai added a short introduction to the book that came out in Eilam's memory.[88]

He was clearly intoxicated by the new possibilities of wandering around and getting to know Jerusalem's Old City, which had been an integral part of his adolescence before the establishment of the State. A trip to the Old City helped Amichai get over his personal troubles (August 4, 1967). His beloved Roni was causing him concern, and he felt that his son's behavior, which was defiant at times, was the symptom of an absent father; seeing his mother again, now aged 72,[89] was less heartwarming than expected. His dead father was perhaps more present in his life than his living mother. As he put it, the struggle between his father and himself over the right path in life had reached an equilibrium out of exhaustion: "And on sabbaths my bitter father holds / demonstrations against me, repeating / the positive and negative commandments [...] / and we are both sad, because he has no / more anger, but still he must / demonstrate."[90]

From a political point of view, Amichai's heart was with unifying the city of Jerusalem. In his eyes, the breaching of the wall created an organic connection between the parts of Jerusalem, and in light of the significant neglect of its eastern part, he expected the progress associated with Jewish rule to be welcomed.[91] He was excited about acquaintances and friendships with Arabs, both well-known and anonymous. He hoped these connections would be the start of a true thawing of relationships. His notebooks list meetings in the Old City, by chance and planned, especially in the Christian Quarter. These meetings took on a symbolic cast, as is evident in their evolution from notebooks entries to the more fully realized "Postcards from Jerusalem," which appeared in *Midstream*, and from there to his poems. "In the Old City. [...] A young man [...] opposite me in an empty alley, with a coffin on his head".[92]

Regardless of Amichai's views on Jerusalem there was a difference between his political stance and the existential notions expressed in his poetry which was always humanistic and deeply egalitarian. The early poem "Jerusalem 1962" was written in response to a public argument about the need for an IDF march in Jerusalem on Independence Day. In this poem he presents the humanity of the enemy, who seen from this perspective cannot be an enemy ("the white sheet of a woman who is my enemy / the towel of a man who is my enemy / to wipe off the sweat of his brow"), and associates the human weaknesses of the two sides, so barely covered up: "We have put up many flags, / they have put up many flags. / To make us think that they're happy. / To make them think that we're happy."[93]

In a later poem, "On Yom Kippur in 1967," the speaker stands in "my dark holiday clothes," opposite "an Arab's hole-in-the-wall shop," which reminds him of his father's haberdashery in Würzburg before the calamity.[94] The speaker talks in his heart with the shop owner to explain "the causes and the events, why I am now here / and my father's shop was burned there and he is buried here."[95] It is not an apology but rather an explanation of historical necessity, in a soul to soul communication, taking place only in the poet's imagination.

The closing poem in the cycle "Jerusalem 1967" compares Jerusalem to Sodom, but one that was not destroyed: "Many births gaping below, / A womb with boundless teeth, / Woman of many mouths double edged and holy beasts."[96] For Amichai this was the city whose womb, teeming with toxic faith and spirituality, knows no limits in its desire to assimilate whoever penetrated it. The choked cry of Jerusalem, and "all the victories [that] are clenched inside her" (poem 10 of the cycle)[97] require that "a slight warning remains in everything" (poem 2);[98] caution and reserve in face of the danger of becoming inebriated with victory and messianic delusions.

NOTES

1. Natan Zach, *From Year to Year, it* [in Hebrew] (Tel Aviv, 2009), 25-26.

2. The biographical information on Dennis Silk comes from the introduction by Gabriel Levin to Silk's collected poems which were published posthumously: *A*

Cloud Inhaled Me: Collected Poems (New York, 2014). *Habonim* ("the builders") was a socialist-Zionist youth movement.

3. Conversation with Harold Schimmel, September 23, 2014. On Amichai and Tamar's landing in Maryland on their way to New York, see Chapter 6.

4. See the article by Nissim Calderon "This Whole Sweet Jerusalem Thing" [in Hebrew], *Siman Kriah* 5 (February 1976): 465-462.

5. Conversation with Gabi Aldor, November 11, 2015.

6. "Dennis Was Very Sick," *Life of Poetry*, 257; *Poems* [in Hebrew] 3, 167.

7. *Selected Poetry*, 99; *Poems* [in Hebrew] 3, 159. A section of a poem in his notebooks displays his "intimate" interest in her: "Lazy Abigail hangs / her underwear out to dry on a barbed wire fence / and she doesn't care" (30.1114). Their friendship lasted for many years.

8. See, for example, Arieh Sachs, "A Purely Righteous Person: Introduction to the Medieval Mystery: *The Flood* at the Khan Theater in Jerusalem" [in Hebrew], *Yediot Acharonot*, January 2, 1976, and his book *The Jester's Downfall* [in Hebrew] (Tel Aviv, 1978), part 2.

9. See his lecture series *The Essence of Theater* [in Hebrew] (Tel Aviv, 1989), chapters 5-8.

10. Sachs, *Essence of Theater* [in Hebrew], 57. He was similarly drawn to Silk's "theater of objects," with its clean lines and schematic presentation, as he explains elsewhere in a lecture series.

11. Perhaps a need for publicity was behind his decision to involve his famous friends in the performance. A decade later the play was performed at the Khan Theatre, directed by Sachs, with professional actors. See Yaacov Bar-On, "*Flood* as an Outcome of … Sickness" [in Hebrew], *Davar*, January 8, 1976.

12. Journal, March 12, 1967. In his brief, printed journal, Amichai heaped praise on the performance of *Everyman*, directed by Sachs at the Khan: "This is how a play should be: a hint of childish naiveté, beautiful movements […] Arieh gave us the play with great love and wonderfully skillful realization." "Pages of a Journal" [in Hebrew], *Moznaim* 29: 1 (June 1969), 23.

13. Poems about Silk: "Dennis Was Very Sick," *Life of Poetry*, 257; *Poems* [in Hebrew] 3, 159; "Dennis Travels to Bury His Father," *Poems* [in Hebrew] 3, 324. Conversation with Hadass Ophrat, Silk's theatrical coworker, who described Silk's hospitalization.

14. *Poems* [in Hebrew] 3, 154-155. The poem "The Death of a Citrus Grower" was a sort of eulogy for Mendes, Arieh's father. *Poems* [in Hebrew] 4, 192.

15. *Life of Poetry*, 206-207; *Poems* [in Hebrew] 2, 293-294. According to Schimmel and his wife, the poem's recitation under the ḥuppah made them quite uncomfortable, and the officiating rabbi interrupted the enthused poet.

16. Their translations were published in various journals and books. Of particular significance for the launch of Amichai's international career were Sachs' and Silk's translations in the first issue of *Modern Poetry in Translation*, in 1966, edited by Ted Hughes and Daniel Weissbort (see below). Other translations of Amichai's poems by Silk appeared in an anthology he edited, *Retrievements: A Jerusalem Anthology* (Jerusalem, 1968).

17. The play Amichai translated, *Mr. Charles' Chair*, exists as a handwritten manuscript. Courtesy of Hadass Ophrat.

18. *Yeshiva ketana* ("small yeshiva") – An intermediate stage of traditional Jewish studies between the elementary Heder and the Yeshiva (usually for boys aged 13-17).

19. Harold Schimmel, "On Seven Poems of Yehuda Amichai," *Orot* 9, 5730 [1969-1970] [in Hebrew and English]: 86-97. Schimmel also wrote about Amichai and the figure of the latter's father, as described by Amichai, in a long poem entitled *Lowell* (1986).

20. The poet Aharon Shabtai, a friend of Amichai's, noted that Amichai's worldwide success in the 1970s and 1980s, which was unprecedented for an Israeli writer, perhaps made him embarrassed about the group, which was hurtful to them. Shabtai, conversation, July 8, 2015.

21. Arieh Sachs, "A Poet of Hollow Wonder" [in Hebrew], *Haaretz*, November 29, 1985. In an interview dated September 1993 with Shirli Yuval, she asked Amichai: "Do you have friends who go all the way with you?" He replied: "Not all the way, because it is long. And there are those who broke with me out of envy." Shirli Yuval, "Words Absorb the Pain of my Life" [in Hebrew], *Olam Ha'isha,* 119, September, 84-88, 266 (at 87).

22. In a book of personal impressions, in which he openly and sensitively describes artists he admires, he recounts a brief meeting with Amichai at Café Ta'amon, which left him bored. *Lightheadedness* [in Hebrew] (Tel Aviv, 1988), 37.

23. Conversation with Hadass Ophrat, June 2, 2016. Fay Tzu, who also directed a number of Silk's plays, thought that "he had difficulty with Amichai's success," June 12, 2018.

24. Interview with the lecturer and writer Zvi Jagendorf and Fay Tzu. Amichai wrote in his notebooks in June 1990 with barely concealed anger: "those who were my friends have passed on, even those who didn't die."

25. D. Weissbort, "Introduction" to Ted Hughes, *Selected Translations* (New York 2006), vii.

26. Birman was one of the first to publish a comprehensive anthology of new Hebrew poetry (including Amichai's) in English translation. See Abraham Birman, *An Anthology of Modern Hebrew Poetry*, London 1968.

27. As early as February 14, 1965, Amichai received a letter from Weissbort responding to poems of his that Dennis Silk sent to the editors. The letter expresses the interest of both editors in including this work into the planned first issue of the journal, and urges him to send more poems (12.589). His sister Rachel's translation was done earlier, before Amichai left Tamar. Amichai to Gabriel Moked, December 12, 1961, the Achshav archive, National Library. In July 1958 two of Amichai's poems, translated by Robert Friend, were published in an issue of the American journal *Poetry* dedicated to Hebrew poetry. They made little impression, however. See "On Israeli Poetry in Chicago" [in Hebrew], *Ma'ariv*, August 8, 1958.

28. Jonathan Bate, Ted Hughes: The Unauthorized Life (New York, 2015), 85-86; Yehuda Koren and Eilat Negev, *Lover of Unreason* (Cambridge, Mass., 2007), 165-6; according to Weissbort, a friend and colleague of the British poet, Hughes was more drawn to Amichai's poetry than to any other poet of the time; Amichai was "a kind

of guide for Hughes through the Biblical lands." Weissbort, Introduction, Hughes, *Selected Translations*, 50.

29. "The festival was patterned along the lines of the small town of Spoleto with its many squares and alleys [...] everything functioned without directions and written instructions." Amichai, "A Festival in Spoleto" [in Hebrew], *Lamerchav-Masa*, October 4, 1967. A nearly identical version of the article was published during Amichai's stay in the US, "Impressions of Spoleto" [in Hebrew], *Bitzaron* 28, 3 (Shvat-Adar 5727 [February-March 1967]: 170-177.

30. "Poets are like magicians: / each knows one trick, one stunt. / Each brings much loneliness from the fruits of his land," wrote Amichai, summarizing his experience at the festival, in "Spoleto – A Meeting of Poets," *Poems* [in Hebrew] 2 188. He met Sinopoulos in New York in 1966-1967. See the poem "Takis Sinopoulos, Greek Poet," *Poetry*, 140; *Poems* [in Hebrew] 2, 169. Sinopoulos sent him a moving letter of concern from Athens on June 20, 1967, a week after the end of the Six Day War. 4.144.

31. Dalia Karpel interview, "Hoping for the Nobel" [in Hebrew], *Ha'ir*, November 3, 1989.

32. In the period discussed here, Amichai took part in an artists' evening to protest the government's decision to continue enforcing military rule over Arab Israeli areas. Tamar Avidar, "Against the Government" [in Hebrew], *Maariv*, March 28, 1962.

33. A rare letter from Amichai to a newspaper editor praises Uri Oren for "his elevated, courageous and ethical stand as a journalist, in his notes on the government-teachers affair." *Yediot Acharonot - 7 Yamim* magazine [in Hebrew], January 8, 1971.

34. Amichai wrote to Azriel Uchmani, who was aligned with *Hashomer Hatzair* (associated with the *Mapam* party, radical socialists) and Sifriat Poalim, concerning this interpenetration of cultural, political and personal spheres, apparently in response to Uchmani's request that he sign a political manifesto: "A writer and a poet, a large part of whose writing bears on the human being, war, love etc., expresses his opinion in almost every line. If he doesn't succeed at this, his work is not really fully formed." While the party has the right, in his view, to change direction from time to time, when "there is a need, not so for someone who is a creator, who apart from keeping faith with himself, has nothing." Amichai to Uchmani, August 3, 1961. Gnazim 100148.1.

35. In his letter dated June 10, 1962 to the secretary of the Writers' Association, Avraham Broides, he commends him for "your honorable stand in the matter of Writers' Week". Broides was trying to get writers paid for their appearances during Writers' Week. *Gnazim* 10081-a. On June 26, 1963, *Haaretz* reported that a compromise had been reached in the "council of the Writers' Association": The *Moznaim* editorial board was made up of five people, three of whom were from the old guard, and two from the younger generation, namely the poets Haim Gouri and Amichai.

36. See Amichai's letter to the poet David Rokeach in which he asks him to send poems or translations, "as it is down to me to edit one issue," September 1, 1963. *Gnazim* 5/1585.

37. The poem "Forever We Live," which critic Menachem Braun-Ben praised for its metaphors (Ben, "Ripeness Is All" [in Hebrew], *Yediot Acharonot*, January 31, 1969), had been published in a newspaper some years earlier, but there was a delay for some reason in including it in a book.

38. *Poetry*, 100 (translation modified); *Poems* [in Hebrew] 2, 52.

39. *Poetry*, 148; *Poems* [in Hebrew] 2, 211.

40. Kronfeld, *Full Severity*, 43-44.

41. "Now in the storm before the calm / I can tell you what / in the calm before the storm I didn't say / because they would have heard us and discovered our hiding-place." *Selected Poetry*, 59-60; *Poems* [in Hebrew] 2, 209.

42. In biblical Hebrew the word *tzara* refers to a rival wife (I Samuel 1:6), whereas in modern Hebrew it signifies "trouble." The poem quoted here, "And afterwards," was not collected in Amichai's books. There is an open hint at the shared life with Hana in a poem published a year later, "Rest Your Head": "It was decreed / that your birth in the year war broke out / would predict / my end / And that my end will be yours." *Poems* [in Hebrew] 2, 196.

43. There is an oblique reference to the *get* in the poem "Days of Awe in New York" (first published in the American Hebrew journal *Bitzaron* 54, 7 [5726 (1965-1966)], 10; *Poems* [in Hebrew] 2, 187): "I came because I was told that New York is a good country for a man to obtain a *get*."

44. Indicated in Amichai's diaries, but there is no corroboration.

45. Conversation with Hana, October 12, 2014. Her discontent was reflected in Amichai's notebooks: "she comes back irritable. She's teaching small children" (September 13, 1966).

46. Gratz Teachers' College. See the letter from the Dean, Elazar Goelman, telling students about the MA literature class to be given by "the prominent Israeli poet" Yehuda Amichai, September 20, 1966. 5.206. Amichai to Elazar Goelman, New York, September 30, 1966. *Gnazim* 6855/11. The course was taught in Hebrew. 38.1307

47. For example, an invitation to "a welcome reception to be held in honor of the Israeli poet Yehuda Amichai" on October 23, 1966 provided by "the Hebrew Histadrut of Greater Boston." 10.450. On September 15 he gave a lecture in New York, in Hebrew, on "Literature in Israel Today." On April 2 he presented "some of his works" at an evening dedicated to him, and as part of a lecture series in New York. 52.1360. Amichai also tried to get teaching work in Jewish schools, but the administrators, after carefully verifying his level of observance, were not enthusiastic (notebooks, November 12, 1966).

48. Also according to "American Notes" [in Hebrew], 426.

49. Weber interview.

50. Conversation with Prof Benjamin Kedar, who heard Amichai give a lecture at the time to Israeli students at Yale University (February 13, 2015).

51. Part of the content of his lectures also emerge from two fairly similar articles he published in *Bitzaron*, and in *Midstream* which is associated with the Conservative movement. Amichai, "Thoughts in Seven Paragraphs about Agnon" [in Hebrew], *Bitzaron* 28, 2 (Kislev-Tevet 5727 [December-January 1967]): 91-93; Amichai, Notes

on Agnon, *Midstream*, XII: 2 (Feb. 1967): 12-15. The Hebrew version though is shorter and harsher than the English.

52. See Chapter 3 and "Words to Agnon," which Amichai wrote a short while after his return to Israel. *Haaretz* [in Hebrew], August 2, 1968. A hint of derision emerges in the description of Agnon's support of the previous mayor of Jerusalem, the more conservative Labor Party representative, Mordehai Ish-Shalom, in his electoral battle against the energetic and practical Teddy Kollek (Amichai, "Thoughts" [in Hebrew], 92-93; idem, "Notes," 15). Amichai, who felt a natural affinity with Kollek, met him in New York. He even presented him with a plan for cultural projects, some of which were eventually realized (May 10, 1967).

53. Amichai, "Thoughts" [in Hebrew], 93; idem, "Notes," 15.

54. Ruth Zinger reports on Amichai's joint work with Katz on translating the novel, in her article "The Poet Amichai – and New York" [in Hebrew], *Haynt*, Montivideo, May 23, 1967. Anthony West reacted positively to the American edition of the novel, finding that "one tastes to the full in his pages the experience of being lost, and of loss that comes of the realization that the world cannot be remade in the image of one's desires." *New Yorker*, May 3, 1969. But when the British edition came out in 1973, a critic in the *New Statesman* pointed to weaknesses in the structure; according to an article in *Maariv*, January 11, 1974. Amichai eventually regretted having agreed to the many cuts in the translation and hoped that Harper & Row, the publisher, would bring out a new complete translation. Zahavi interview, "Poetry as Consolation" [in Hebrew], *Davar - Masa,* May 7, 1976; Montenegro interview, 18.

55. The poem "First Days in New York" was dedicated, when first published (in *Bitzaron*, Nisan 5727 [March-April 1967], 218), "to F. Summers," certainly the philosopher who was also friends with Sachs and Gabi Aldor. Email from Aldor, February 24, 2018.

56. "The Orgy," *The World Is a Room*, 121-141. "The Orgy that Never Was" [in Hebrew], *Moznaim,* August-September 1972, 208-216; "The Orgy" [in Hebrew], *In This Terrible Wind* (Schocken edition), 270-286.

57. "The Orgy," *The World Is a Room*, 126-7; "The Orgy" [in Hebrew], 274. Cf. The poem "First Days In New York": "On the first days in New York / We spoke a lot about the death / of God. We didn't really say what we thought, / But only wondered at others discovering / Now what we had discovered / In the great desert / After bar mitzvah." *Poems* [in Hebrew] 2, 162-3. Regarding the public controversy, see also "American Notes" [in Hebrew], 429.

58. Conversation with Prof. Aharon Komem and his wife Ilana who were in New York that year, staying in the same residential hotel as Amichai and Hana. February 14, 2018.

59. "Autumn at Last," *Bitzaron*, Tishrei-Cheshvan 5727 [September-October 1966], 9. The poem does not appear in any of Amichai's books.

60. Cf. the description of the relationship between the narrator and Ora, whom he represents as coming from the "*moshava*" of Hadera (then an agricultural settlement, today a city), in the novel *Hotel in the Wilderness* (Tel Aviv, 1971).

61. He initially recoiled from the media's preoccupation with Israel, especially in times of war: "The journalists aren't coming / to my country / to see my flowers but /

to see those crushed among the dead. [...] The journalists aren't coming / To see the bright sand beside the sea," but to see his son filling sandbags. "The Journalists Aren't Coming," New York, May 1967. Manuscript, Gnazim, 19689-b.

62. When he got to London, he wrote in his notebooks: "My poems have become obsolete. Tension and fear. Now hope and happiness [-] I won't be able to go on writing."

63. As hinted at in the poem, they also met again in the army, almost certainly when Amichai gave a lecture and Yonatan accompanied him as commander of the hosting unit. https://www.eng.chagim.org.il/LITERATURE/We-have-no-unknown-soldiers; *Poems* [in Hebrew] 2, 28-9. See also Amichai on his participation in the memorial booklet for Yahil, "Pages of a Journal" [in Hebrew], 22-23. Dr. Leni Yahil, Yonatan's mother, wrote to the poet that "the symbolic nature of the love you brought to light, loving him after his death, is significant. It symbolizes the great love of all the mourners." 12.604

64. Amichai plays on the double meaning of the word *ḥalal* ("slain", "killed in war" and "space", "void").

65. Hughes to Amichai, September 11, 1966. All of Hughes' letters to Amichai (sometimes also addressed to Hana), as well as letters from Assia, Olwyn (Hughes' sister), and Carol Orchard his wife – to Amichai or to the couple – are housed in the Beinecke Library, Yale University, in folder 853, Box 50.

66. Hughes to Amichai, May 7, 1967.

67. The details here on the background to the story of Assia Guttman-Wevill were taken from the moving book by Koren and Negev, *Lover of Unreason*. Another source is the excellent biography by Jonathan Bate, *Ted Hughes*, especially chapters 12-16; ibid.

68. Koren and Negev, *A Lover of Unreason*, 90-94.

69. Ibid., Chapter 12.

70. Hughes told an English children's writer that he would rather have been Jewish than "a question-mark Anglican," and his admiration for the Jewish cultural self-confidence that made the Jews so prolific in religious thought. According to Koren and Negev [in Hebrew], 199. In a contract that he drew up with Assia in an attempt at a renewed union with her in 1968, he wanted her to identify more with her Jewish roots. Bate, *Ted Hughes*, 265-266. A poem he wrote on her death is titled "Shibboleth," (Ted Hughes, *New Selected Poems, 1957-1996* (London 2001), 307) hinting at Judges 12: 1-7, where the word is used as a test to see whether or not a man comes from a certain tribe. In the poem "Heptonstall Cemetery," Hughes calls Assia by her Hebrew name Esther.

71. The details about Assia and her relationship with Hughes are based on Koren and Negev, *Lover of Unreason*, chapters 10-11. However, Assia's character and abilities appear to be idealized in Koren and Negev's book.

72. Amichai's visit to Court Green at that time testifies to his increasing closeness with Ted, a visit recorded in his notebooks and "Pages of a Journal," (in the extracts published by *Moznaim*). The troubling details of the dead Sylvia's presence in Hughes' life come from the latter.

73. This time the Spoleto Festival paid for his return airfare from London, according to a letter dated October 6, 1967, from Amichai to the historian Randall Sanders. Central Archive of the New York Library.

74. "Six-Day War Inspires New Poet," *Jewish Chronicle*, September 1, 1967.

75. *Haaretz* [in Hebrew], February 28, 1964.

76. "Performing poets," *Times Literary Supplement*, July 20, 1967, by a special correspondent.

77. Hughes' sister Olwyn also told Amichai about these developments. She was a literary agent, negotiating with publishers on behalf of her brother, whom she revered, and his friends. Letters from Olwyn to Yehuda and Hana, August 8, 1967; September 22, 1967. Penguin publishers were initially very anxious about bringing out a book of Amichai's poems in translation, and according to letters from Olwyn and Assia to Amichai, they suggested publishing one volume combining Amichai's poems with those of another poet (January 31, 1969; January 12, 1970). Amichai refused and in the end a selection of his poems came out.

78. Amichai's popularity increased rapidly in the US with the publication of a collection of his poems in translation; this emerges from the 1969 atmospheric film, shot in Israel, *Nights to Come*, by the American Jewish director, Marvin Lichtner. In the film Haim Topol reads Amichai's poems in English translation against the backdrop of Israeli landscapes, highlighting the repercussions of wars past and present. Steven Spielberg Jewish Film Archive, Hebrew University, B00106 1, 2.

79. Born like Amichai in 1924, Hamburger left Berlin with his family for England in 1933.

80. Yehuda Amichai, *Poems*, Translated from the Hebrew by Assia Guttman, with an Introduction by Michael Hamburger (New York, 1968; 1969). The Penguin edition, *Selected Poems*, only came out after Assia's death, in 1971, with Guttman's and Harold Schimmel's translations.

81. They nevertheless visited Germany together that summer together, and on impulse even went briefly to Würzburg.

82. From Assia to Yehuda Amichai, August 19, 1967.

83. See Leon Israel Yudkin's harsh criticism, *Jewish Writing and Identity in the Twentieth Century* (London 1982), 150-151.

84. Amichai only let Assia know about the gross errors which went beyond issues of interpretation. From her letter to him dated October 31, 1967 it is clear she had translated *motz* (chaff, straw) as *botz* (mud) in "King Saul and I." Robert Alter has written about the mistaken translation of *ḥol* as sand by Assia and other translators, including Chana Bloch and Stephen Mitchell. Alter rightly translates it as "profane." See *Poetry*, xx.

85. The Hebrew poet Gabriel Preil, who lived in New York, thought Amichai's poems in this translation were "abundant in sophisticated poetic wisdom." Preil to Amichai, July 7, 1969. 9.444 a. A very short review in *TLS* considered that "Amichai's power is evident even in translation." October 24, 1968. The Anglo-Irish poet P. J. Kavanagh, who apparently befriended Amichai at the London festival, thought the book translations "so stunning, such good poems in English, it seems absurd to

treat them as translations at all." Patrick J. Kavanagh, "An Awkward Shyness," *The Guardian,* July 12, 1968.

86. Amichai, "Pages of a Journal."

87. Ibid., 23.

88. Hubi, *Letters to You* [in Hebrew] (Tel Aviv, 1970), and in an expanded edition put out by Yediot Acharonot publishers, 1997, 6-7. Amichai related to Eilam's bravery and death in poem 28 of the cycle "Songs of Zion and Jerusalem," (also translated as "Songs of the Land of Zion and Jerusalem,") collected in the book *Behind All This a Great Happiness Is Hiding, Poems* [in Hebrew] 3, 30-31. The poem conveys Amichai's thoughts that Hubi's humanity, the integrity manifested in his willingness to help his wounded comrades when it clearly endangered his life, made Jerusalem, which Hubi fell fighting for, worthy of his love.

89. Amichai's mother and sister did not speak to him after he left Tamar; his mother nevertheless agreed to see him on his return from the US, and later when she was nearing death.

90. "Yom Kippur" (The Day of Atonement). "Evening." "My Father," *Poems* [Hebrew], 2, 47.

91. "Postcards from Jerusalem," *Midstream*, January 1968, 28 [26-31].

92. The moment is described in greater detail in the "Postcards from Jerusalem."

93. *Selected Poetry*, 32, *Poetry*, 60; *Poems* [in Hebrew] 1, 230.

94. *Selected Poetry*, 49, *Poetry*, 83. Another translation: *Life of Poetry*, 81; *Poems* [in Hebrew] 2, 13-14. Chana Kronfeld rightly notes that "dark holiday clothes" are not customary on Yom Kippur (when people wear white), and are more reminiscent of mourning. However, she greatly exaggerates the significance of the scruples that she attributes to the poem's speaker. Kronfeld, *Full Severity*, 44-48.

95. Poem 5 in the cycle "Jerusalem 1967," *Poems* [in Hebrew] 2, 13-14.

96. *Life of Poetry*, 87. Another translation: *Selected Poetry*, 54, *Poetry*, 89; *Poems* [in Hebrew] 2, 21-22.

97. *Selected Poetry*, 50-51.

98. *Life of Poetry*, 80-81.

Chapter 12

1968–1971

Publication of Now in the Storm, *the Mashkof Group, Visits from Major Poets*

REACTIONS TO *NOW IN THE STORM*

Before the publication of *Now in the Storm*, Amichai sent some key poems to daily newspapers and *Moznaim*, the monthly bulletin of the Writers' Association. These poems, which were to become some of the most popular from the book, deal with his soul-searching in relation to religion, and what in his article on Agnon he called a sense of responsibility for the Jewish past. These poems help clarify what Amichai meant in his speech to the Writers' Association when he defined himself as a "double agent."[1] Amichai was consistently secular, while sensing the presence of God; he could not erase this mental presence since it was fundamental to his humanity. In this sense, Amichai differed considerably from other writers of his generation, and even more so from those of later generations, since the overwhelming majority were firm secularists. They did not grow up in a religious environment and found it difficult to understand his multilayered paradoxical and contradictory secularity, as in this poem: "God's fate now / is like the fate / of trees and stones, sun and moon, / when people stopped believing in them / and began to believe in Him. // But He has to stay with us: / at least like the trees [...]."[2] In a seemingly evolutionary process, when an abstract monotheistic god appeared, the trees and stones, sun and moon lost their sacred qualities and simply became material entities. Likewise, although faith in God is a thing of the past, God is still a psychological presence; "He has to stay with us" – just as the trees and stones continue to be part of our lives.

In the poems "National Thoughts," "My Child has the Fragrance of Peace," and "Because Now is the Time" he takes stock of his relationship to a people descended from a great and continuing tradition, born of catastrophes and continually threatened by near-extinction.[3] Establishing a new life in Israel and beginning history from square one are evidently the outcome of a powerful force which amounted to open denunciation of the forefathers' death wish, and their predilection for the mourning and sorrow characteristic of Jewish Diaspora life. The beloved woman in "National Thoughts" is "caught in a homeland-trap of the Chosen People," but wearing the "Cossack's fur hat on your head," in jest, despite being "the offspring of their pogroms." She is "naked on a rock," a kind of Andromeda expecting to be abducted and annihilated, while actually longing for sexual pleasure ("body open like hair".)[4]

Ancient Hebrew has been "torn from its sleep" and, dazzled by the strong light, like those awakened from slumber, must now utter words of technology and destruction ("car", "bomb"), and, again, "God" in a new form for a technological and violent generation, while the square letters of the aleph bet just "want to close in on themselves [...] and sleep [...] forever." The ancestors, the "fathers" of the people of Israel, were seekers of death, "stubborn and lonely in the Cave of the Patriarchs," sunk in a "childless silence." But what the God of the fathers "cannot promise us," "my child's mother's womb could" ("My Child has the Fragrance of Peace"). The poem "Because Now is the Time" (frequently titled "I Am Their Last") constitutes a spectacular association of the individual and collective. The speaker wants to enjoy the moments of relief denied the biblical Job between the last disaster and the next. Despite being "like ashes that have forgotten what came before", a Holocaust survivor who has erased his traditional past, "My heart's visage still shows on my face". In other words, the speaker is still in touch with his inner spiritual world, and longs for a place "at the end of the dark stairs" in the Cave of the Patriarchs ("the dead of Machpelah"), to merge, paradoxically, with a history he seeks to obliterate.

THE RECEPTION OF THE BOOK

Now in the Storm was published in late 1968, and consisted of 200 dense pages, a large book by poetry standards. "Jerusalem Gate" is the first section, which was appropriate to the historical moment in the life of the State after the Six Day War; the "Caesarea" and "Achsiv" sections, or "gates", named for the places Amichai and Hana delighted in visiting on vacation, are second and last respectively. The long autobiographical poem "Travels of the Last Benjamin of Tudela" is the third section, followed by the "Countries' Gate," which mainly includes Amichai's trips to the US and Italy (for literary festivals). Amichai considered "Travels of the Last Benjamin" to be the pinnacle of his poetic achievement,[5] perhaps because of the tendency of writers and readers to attribute special value to a work that communicates a sense of totality.

Most reviews were positive. Menachem Braun (later Ben), who was close to Amichai, described the book as an expression of the poet's psychological and poetic maturity.[6] In Ben's view, "only a poet who has reached full maturity can control and bring consistency to a sequence of this sort." Nissim Calderon, at the time a very young critic, tried his hand at defining what had changed in Amichai's poetry since his first books and suggested that he wanted to avoid having the situations framed in his poems become a "generalized symbolic picturesqueness." Of all the psychological journeys Amichai had taken in recent years, he suggested that "more than in all the previous books, behind these poems there is the threatening force of an impulse [...] toward self-exposure," which could lead to "a shocking banality." [7] Haim Be'er argued that Amichai critics tended to find that "after an excellent first line of the poem, comes a steady deterioration line by line," a weakness he considered to be true not only of Amichai but also other well-known contemporaries. [8] The literary critic of *The Jerusalem Post* wrote that she felt uncomfortable as a woman with Amichai's love poetry, which had previously been "so joyful and positive," but had become purely erotic; she considered that his love had shifted from the woman to the child. [9]

WINNING THE BRENNER PRIZE

Some months after the book came out, Amichai was awarded the prestigious Brenner Prize.[10] Biographical summaries of Amichai often point to his series of prizes, but not once was he bitter about them. The literary establishment, at least its older representatives, were deeply conflicted about Amichai. They recognized, or at least sensed his inventiveness and originality and also took notice of his widespread influence, but still had difficulty understanding his poetry.

The Brenner prize was then in its 25th year, and the Haft family, the benefactors of the prize, wanted to celebrate this milestone. It was decided that the prize would be awarded to three recipients: the novelist Yehuda Ya'ari, the poet Yehuda Amichai, and the critic Benjamin Yitzhak Michaly. However, elation soon turned sour when the check arrived: the prize money had been divided by three. Amichai and Ya'ari, who were friends, wrote a letter to the central committee of the Writers' Association, arguing that the small sum had "caused us anguish and put us in unpleasant social and family situations."[11] The Association's secretary, Dov Chomsky, suggested that the committee should simply return their letter: "We will only humiliate ourselves [...] and there'll be no rain" (quoting the biblical saying "Clouds, and wind but no rain").[12]

PUBLICATION OF *THINGS THAT HAPPENED TO RONI IN NEW YORK*

The first book to be published by Amichai on his return from the US was not *Now in the Storm*, but rather a children's book, *Things that Happened to Roni in New York*, put out by Am Oved. It appeared at the beginning of 1968, with Amichai's own illustrations.[13] Roni, his beloved son with Tamar, was raised by his mother. The Amichai archives contain a long draft of an introduction to the book explaining its background.[14] At age six Roni was obviously not with his father during the latter's year in New York, but with great charm the book creates an imaginary reality to replace a painful experience: "Every day Roni asks his mother, when is father coming back, and his mother says: in three months. How much is three months? Mother says: it isn't so long. Mother also says that sailors' children sometimes don't see their fathers for a long time […] every evening at bedtime there are conversations like that." Or elsewhere: "Roni knew that his father was in New York. His father would send him postcards with photos of tall buildings. But Roni really didn't want to ever go there. It was the city that had taken his father from him." Still, Roni thought of "dropping himself into the mail box," and a week before his father's return he could no longer stand his longing and went to the airport intending to fly alone to New York.

In the book, the content of the introduction is squeezed into the first two poems; "Roni Goes Out" – "A boy, already five, going on six. / A boy neither quiet nor noisy, / decided / to go to the USA"; and then "On the airplane": "the flight attendant / wakes the boy: shalom Mr. Roni / […] Below, the blue Mediterranean / and now it's time to eat." Roni's uncle only explains at the end of the book that all the pictures of New York are imaginary, the product of dreams; and yet "what transpires in a dream is no lie, it's true […] Because you long / for father, there, / you dreamed that you too were where/ he is."[15]

In a radio interview with father and son, some years after Amichai returned to Israel, he emphasized the extent to which the book was not only a product of his empathy for his faraway son pining for him, but also expressed the perceptions of the child he himself had been: "New York often seemed terrifying to me at that time […] ,in the book I tried to show the beautiful things in the jungle."[16] When Dalith Ormian, the radio host, asked Roni, then aged 12, if he thought that the boy in the book "was like you as you were then," he replied that he did not remnember "how I was then," and Amichai answered for him: "I think in some ways yes. He already had a simple approach to life. The joy of meeting new people and things […] perhaps I adopted his more communicative side: serenity in face of life, a sense of humor and curiosity." Amichai added: "I wrote this book as a personal gift," and then promptly theorized: “As a matter of fact, writing for adults is also a personal gift the author gives to somebody he loves”.

The reviews of the first edition were middling. M. Mashav (the poet and critic Moshe Dor) thought that “Amichai is an excellent poet for... adults,” but doubted whether the author understood the limitations of children’s thinking and acquaintance with the world by suggesting that the run-on phrases Amichai used were likely to confuse them (“He didn’t know how / it happened”), the similes were too adult, and some of the topics unfamiliar (for example, a mayoral reception). In their reviews Dor and others thought that Amichai had been wrong to illustrate the book himself.[17] However, after Amichai’s death, when the same publisher released a new edition, Yael Darr argued that “the disorganized lines, the free verse [...] the near-complete absence of an adult in the story all scraped the skies of children’s literature of the time almost like the tall buildings of New York.”[18] Even the opinions of Amichai as an illustrator had changed: “Amichai’s illustrations simply stay true to the text.”[19]

Was Amichai a pioneer of a free and courageous approach to writing for children that was only acknowledged many years later? Or did his status as a canonical and sanctified figure in the years after the book’s publication – not to mention after his death – cause critics to alter their evaluation of his writing for children?

HOTEL IN THE WILDERNESS: BELATED PUBLICATION OF HIS AMERICAN NOVEL

During Amichai’s stay in New York in 1966-67, he had already begun to think about writing a satirical novel about the experiences of Israelis in America, and especially the relentless drive on the part of the Israeli government envoys to convince émigré Israelis and Diaspora Jews to return to the land of their ancestors. Commercialized America, frittering away its intellectual resources on entertainment and consumerism, was no less an object of his ridicule. The novel only came out in 1971 at a little-known publishing house after it was rejected by his publisher, Racheli Edelman. Edelman saw it as the work of a man in his forties fearful of his waning sexual powers, an assessment similar to Moshe Dor’s opinion of his volume of poetry *Not for the Sake of Remembering*.

The title (which is more explicit in Hebrew) is reminiscent of the words of the prophet Jeremiah 9:1, “Oh that I were in the wilderness, in a lodging-place of wayfarers, that I might leave my people and go from them! For they are all adulterers, an assembly of treacherous men.” Amichai situated the assembly of “adulterers” and “treacherous men” in the hotel where he was staying part of the time in New York, at the corner of 86th Street and Park Avenue.[20] Many hotel residents were Israelis who had come to study or work for a while in New York, and had got stuck there. Like many Israelis, they were gripped by feelings of guilt, were preoccupied with comparing the two countries, and planning their honorable return to Israel. The narrator, a poet who had been a kind of emissary for the State to bring Israelis back to the country, fails in his attempts, which mostly consist of pursuing women. He is asked by the proprietor of the hotel, who also has a successful women's underwear factory, to write advertising copy for the factory: this would allow him to find the inspiration he lacks, while making good living to boot.[21]

The reception of the novel, which is replete with descriptions of sex unprecedented in Hebrew literature, was deadly. Apart from the weekly *Noar 71 – Iton shel Achshav* [Youth 71 – A journal of today],[22] all the critics were scandalized that the poet had descended so low despite the fact that he was universally admired among the reading public. Sara Rifin, in the woman's monthly *At,* thought that "the wretched protagonist of the novel, a poet, an aging good-for-nothing [...] is up to his neck in feminine intimate anatomy [...]."[23] Miriam Arad's opinion was that the author had borrowed an anti-Zionist and anti-establishment style derived from contemporary American literature such as Roth's *Portnoy's Complaint,* but unlike Roth had failed to entertain.[24] The prominent poet and critic Meir Wieseltier had the same opinion, attacking Amichai for his inflammatory use of images of blood and death, for imitating American style (Updike, Roth), his crude and repulsive humor, and disproportionate use of "chunks of erotica in humor sauce." Wieseltier did however point to a number of beautiful passages and even suggested that Amichai should use them as the basis for new stories.[25]

Amichai never came to terms with the critics' or readers' invalidation of the novel. When he sensed that interviewers avoided considering it as one of the high points of his literary career, he insisted on bringing it up and defending it: "It is just as I wanted it to be."[26] He called it "a grotesque Israeli comedy" and contrasted the difference between its irony and cynicism and the apparent romanticism of his poetry as similar to features found in the great works of the poet Heine and the composer Mahler.

THE MULTIDISCIPLINARY ARTS GROUP MASHKOF

When Amichai came back from the US after the Six Day War, he was by no means alone in his decision. At that time a number of artists returned to the country, and introduced new ideas and trends they had been exposed to abroad. These included Yossi Ofek, who was just starting out as a poet, and his wife the painter Tzivia Weinman; Tzvi Tolkovsky, already an acknowledged painter, whose search for new directions in Paris and the US had transformed his art; and the musician Yossi Mar-Haim, back from Juilliard.[27] Together, they brought back multidisciplinary art in the form of collective work in different media which also included audience participation (happenings).

The Jerusalem Mashkof group came together as a confluence of the search for new forms of art-making and a desire for Bohemian good times.[28] Amichai may have joined the group primarily for social reasons, to be with his friends Sachs, Schimmel and Silk, in addition to the draw of night-time pleasure-seeking at Café Ta'amon.[29] At that time in Tel Aviv the 10+ group led by Rafi Lavie was very active, and the Jerusalem group was perhaps an attempt to follow in their footsteps, while aspiring to undermine the Yekke establishment who ran the Jerusalem Artists' House by outspokenly challenging the status quo.

The basic principle guiding the group's artistic activities was cooperative work in twos and threes that brought artists from different fields together. The painters appeared to have benefitted the most from these encounters. The main medium enabling their joint work with poets was print craft (stone lithography and silk screening). Amichai worked with Avraham Ofek and later Yoram Rozov. Rozov, who did not ascribe much importance to printing ("it's on the fringes of reproduction"),[30] misplaced the work he did with Amichai. Avraham Ofek's prints made for Amichai's famous and much-quoted poem "A Pity. We Were Such a Good Invention," is not overly impressive.[31] Schimmel and Tolkovsky's joint work, however, was significant[32], due to Schimmels' natural feeling for working with found, ready-made objects and images, as did several of the conceptual artists. He wrote his first book in Hebrew, as he himself related, by combining passages from a pile of discarded *Haolam Hazeh* magazines.[33]

The group went its own different ways two to three years later in 1969-70. The painters tended to work on their own, while the poets got involved in holding evening poetry readings, accompanied by improvised music, "without harmony or clear rhythm."[34] The musician Yossi Mar-Haim wrote a score for Amichai's poem "A Pity. We Were Such a Good Invention." He would later set the poem to music in a film by a Russian immigrant director, whose first film in Israel dealt with a subject close to Amichai's heart: the coming to terms with the materialistic reality of the country after the War of Independence by members of the Palmach.[35]

PUBLICATION OF ELSE LASKER-SCHÜLLER'S POEMS IN AMICHAI'S TRANSLATION

The centenary of the birth of the Jewish poet Else Lasker-Schüller, a pioneer and prominent figure in the Expressionist movement, was celebrated in Germany in 1969. Lasker-Schüller went to Palestine twice in the 1930s, and on her third visit in 1939 she was forced to remain, after Switzerland, her country of refuge, refused to take her back, since she was elderly, mentally unstable and impoverished.

In her centenary year, Eked publishing house put out *Poems of Else Lasker-Schüller* in Amichai's translation, accompanied by illustrations by Lasker-Schüller, who was also an impressive artist.[36] While Amichai's prose translations (*Wanderung – Wandering* – by Herman Hesse), and translations of plays and radio scripts (Hochhuth's *Der Stellvertreter – The Deputy*, Joseph Chaikin's *The Dybbuk*, *Rip Van Winkle* by Max Frisch)[37] were done out of financial need and were generally sidelines that did not require profound engagement,[38] he displayed a deep and almost lifelong commitment to the work of Else Lasker-Schüller. This had much to do with her impact on him in his youth, in particular her poems with disjointed couplets (two-line stanzas) that frequently lacked a clear connection to each other. This influence was evident in his first two books (for example in "Six Poems for Tamar").[39] His encounter as a young poet with the work of such a daring and genre-breaking writer was likely to have had a liberating effect on him, for example by legitimizing esoteric metaphors, and the intentional use of logical contradiction.

He may also have been intrigued with this female poet who fluctuated between madness and sanity, and who was perhaps a beatnik before her time. Her sexual daring also fascinated him: her poems describe sexual positions, and violence to achieve orgasm;[40] in Jerusalem, the aged and unwell Lasker-Schüller uninhibitedly courted the handsome Ernst Simon (a future professor of education at the Hebrew University), thirty years her junior.

However, Amichai's consistent involvement in translating Else Lasker-Schüller's poems, from his time in the British army to his later years,[41] did not only stem from his sense of obligation to her as a poet. His admiration perhaps included some guilty feelings about his school days at the Ma'aleh school when he took part in making fun of the diminutive, stooped poet, adorned in heavy jewelry, as she paced the Jerusalem streets. They would watch her caring for the street cats, the calves being taken to slaughter, and suggesting ways to make peace between Jews and Arabs through rides at the amusement park.[42] In his article "The Blue Piano" Amichai describes how he and his classmates would read "passages from her fiction which made us laugh uproariously. She talks there about wild desert Jews with camel's eyes flying on tallitot, which was almost certainly from her book *Das Hebrärland* (*The Land of the Hebrews*) that came out in Switzerland after one of her visits to Palestine.[43]

Over the years Amichai reworked his translations of her poems and added new ones, both on his own initiative and in response to requests.[44] He worked with the playwright Motti Lerner to adapt his translations to the stage, when

Lerner put *Else* on at Habima theater.[45] In the 1990s Amichai joined the Else Lasker-Schüller Society which met every two years in her birthplace, Elberfeld-Wuppertal, to read and discuss her work.[46]

LIFE IN YEMIN MOSHE

In 1969 Yehuda and Hana bought a home in the Yemin Moshe neighborhood, since they were thoroughly tired of moving from apartment to apartment. Yemin Moshe was one of the first Jerusalem neighborhoods to be built outside the walls of the old city in the 1860s, through the initiative of an aristocratic English Jew, Moses Montefiore.[47] In the years between the establishment of the State and the Six Day War it was a slum on the border with Jordan, whose impoverished residents, mainly immigrants from the first years of the State from Turkey, Iran, Romania and other countries were almost constantly exposed to gunfire from snipers just beyond the nearby wall.[48] In 1965, after Teddy Kollek was elected mayor of Jerusalem, some residents of Yemin Moshe were evicted. In June 1967 there was a dramatic turnabout in the status of Yemin Moshe and the little neighborhood adjacent to it, Mishkenot Sha'ananim. The wonderful views on every side and its historical legacy (including the windmill which had not moved since Montefiore's time)[49] made it and Mishkenot a coveted location full of cultural, economic and tourist potential.

After the Six Day War, efforts by the Jerusalem municipality to turn Yemin Moshe into a neighborhood of artists, writers and academics intensified. The plan was to attract people by offering preferential conditions and loans on easy terms.[50] With time, doctors, economists, and a large number of foreign residents considered to be "benefactors of Jerusalem," bought apartments there, thus sidelining the vision of a neighborhood of galleries and artists' workshops.

The government's efforts at expropriation of the vast majority of the previous Jewish residents were viewed as a stain on its history, and certainly was seen as reprehensible by Amichai with his socialist background. To interviewers he liked to say that when he and his wife came to the neighborhood in 1969, it was still very far from being wealthy.[51] In fact, his house there was initially relatively small. In the summer of 1972, when he returned from half a year in California, and the couple hoped to have a child, a basement was dug out from under the house so that the poet could have a study. In 1985, when he was economically more comfortable as a result of his rising worldwide popularity, the house was substantially extended.[52]

He hosted well-known poets and writers in Yemin Moshe, who found it an attractive place to visit. He left it to go on trips, sometimes for several months and sometimes for a whole year with his family, during which he gave readings of his poems, held writing workshops and taught courses in creative writing at universities, various institutions and community centers. In the 1970s, this was mainly in the US, Latin America, and then Spain. In the 1980s, Germany, the country of his birth, discovered him with all the force of guilty feelings about the Holocaust. In the early 1990s, his popularity with writers, intellectuals and students in the Far East (South-East Asia) encouraged a wave of translations into the languages of this region. Italy was the last to discover his poetry and translate it.

A FIG INSTEAD OF AN ALMOND: THE VISIT OF A TRAGIC POET

Israel on the eve of the Six Day War gave cause for great concern to those who loved it everywhere in the world, including those who previously were not aware of their sense of obligation and deep connectedness to it. This was also true for Paul Celan, a poet living in Paris who wrote in German, and was born in 1920 in Czernowitz, Bukovina, then part of Romania.[53] Celan – originally Antschel (Ancel in Romanian) – was the only child of an assimilated Jewish family, in an area once part of the Austro-Hungarian Empire. The language of his education and culture was German. His parents were murdered during the Holocaust, and he survived in a labor camp. After some years in Romania under the Communist dictatorship he fled to Vienna and from there went to Paris.

As an adolescent, Paul Celan was ambivalent about his Jewish identity, but later, after the Holocaust, became deeply involved in his Jewishness, and with time even sympathetic to Israel and Zionism. The basic Hebrew he learned in an elementary Hebrew school in Romania his father forced him to attend left scars,[54] but also strengthened his awareness of his complex connection with "the murdered Jewish people," the people who "is not."[55] This was characteristic of the writer of *No-One's-Rose* (1963), essentially the rose of no-God.[56] In October 1969, in coordination with the Hebrew Writers' Association, Celan visited Israel. Haunted by neurosis and a deepening sense of loneliness (his wife left him, and his 14-year-old son refused to come to Israel with him), he impressed those crowding to meet him as distant, trepidatious, but also full of observations and brilliant insights. Amichai translated a number of Celan's poems for a radio interview and his public appearances. When Amichai and Shmuel Huppert, the head of the Israel radio literature program, spoke with him about the translations, Celan surprised them both, coming across as a Hebrew speaker with suggestions for corrections. In particular he remembered the Hebrew roots, which he thought made Hebrew better suited than other languages for rendering his poetry, which is both delicately sensual and violent.[57]

Celan was very excited about Amichai's poetry, which he knew only in English translation. The actual face to face meeting with Amichai confirmed his positive response to the poems. In a letter to Amichai after his visit to Israel he commented: "The poem you write is... you yourself,"[58] hinting at the vitality and authenticity which makes Amichai's poetry so impressive.

The encounter between these two poets brought opposites together. The divide between them was not only in the implicit decisions they had made about the direction of Jewish destiny: on the one hand a national existence in the land of the ancestors, and its life pursued in the old-new language, and on the other, remaining in exile, living a tragic life of foreignness and alienation, though in a mother tongue rooted in a rich and well-established culture. Their different personalities, and perhaps their different fates, led them to different poetics: the paradoxes of nothingness, the wrangling about the emptiness of divinity in Celan ("Black milk of daybreak we drink it at sundown, / we drink it at noon in the morning we drink it at night / [...] we dig a grave in the breezes there one lies unconfined"),[59] as opposed to the love of existence for its own sake and a kindness-infused closeness to humanity in Amichai. However, there was also a common ground in their spiritual, "pneumatic" approach to Judaism, as Celan termed it. During his tour of Israel he expressed reservations about visiting the holy sites or places of heroic national significance. Thus he avoided the Western Wall, and got out of the climb to Masada, but was moved by a braying donkey beside Absalom's tomb.[60] He saw himself as a Jew, not in terms of observance or because he used Jewish themes in his poetry, but in terms of his spiritual stance toward the world, and by relating to language in a "midrashic" way.[61]

In April 1970, some months after his visit to Israel, Celan committed suicide by jumping into the Seine. His attempt at closer ties with Israel may have deepened his despair: the salvation he longed for from afar emerged as insurmountable given his personality and unique spiritual needs. Amichai heard of his death while in London: "I heard about it in London. / They said he killed himself. / The same rope / was tugging lightly at my neck."[62]

TED HUGHES AND OTHER POETS FROM ENGLAND VISIT ISRAEL

For years Amichai and Hana had hoped to host Hughes in their new home. On December 16, 1970, Amichai told Hughes that the British Council was planning to invite a number of British writers to Israel .[63] The writer Aharon Megged, then the cultural advisor to the Israeli embassy in London, had taken note of the success of poetry evenings in the British capital starring Israeli poets (T. [Tcharni] Carmi, Amichai, Dan Pagis, Abba Kovner, Amir Gilboa), reading in English translation. This prompted the initiative by the Israel Ministry of Foreign Affairs and the British Council in Israel to invite prominent British poets to go on reading tours with their Israeli colleagues.[64] Five poets were chosen to represent British poetry, most prominently Ted Hughes, then considered the country's leading poet, in particular after the publication of his book *Crow*. The others were the relatively elderly D. J. Enright, a poet, storyteller, and translator, and assistant editor of the important literary journal *Encounter*; Peter Porter, professor of literature and writer of critical-satirical poetry; and two Jews, Dannie Abse, a poet and playwright, who worked as a physician, and Jeremy Robson, a young poet and performer, and the editor in chief of the Valentine-Mitchell publishing house, which specialized in publishing books about Israel.[65] In the poetry evenings in Israel at which the British poets read, Amichai was one of those chosen to read their poems in Hebrew along with Haim Gouri, T. Carmi, Abba Kovner, Dan Pagis and Amir Gilboa (two or three of the group read on each occasion).

The British provided a number of amusing and somewhat embarrassed accounts of their visit, particularly Jeremy Robson.[66] The Israeli public filled the halls to capacity for these events. The British poets were surprised by the interest in poetry and impressed by the unruffled approach to the English language. They were curious about the differences in reading styles of the Israeli poets such as the melodramatic Kovner compared to the gentle hushed voice of Pagis. The British also differed in delivery which Robson characterized as Enright's "dry wit," Porter's "educated irony," Abse's "incisive insights," and Hughes' "intensity."

Seeing the holy sites in Jerusalem and the Galilee stirred the visitors, which they tried to offset with British humor. For example, they explained that Jesus walked on the waters of the Kinneret (the Sea of Galilee) because the water was so cold it made actual immersion out of the question. Hughes was perhaps more powerfully affected than the others by the holy sites. During a visit with Abse and Amichai to the Umar Mosque in the Old City of Jerusalem, Hughes suddenly prostrated himself on the ground, his face against the grille of a pit, mumbling, "black, black," as though summoning darkness from the pit. When he stood up he saw that his palms bore the imprint of the grille and triumphantly showed them to his friends, as though they were the stigmata of Jesus.[67]

NOTES

1. He returned to this metaphor on a number of occasions, including in the introduction to his poems for the first issue of *MPT*.

2. "God's Fate," *Poetry*, 98; *Poems* [in Hebrew] 2, 42.

3. "National Thoughts," *Selected Poetry*, 57; *Poems* [in Hebrew] 2, 45; "My Child Has the Fragrance of Peace," *Poetry*, 90; another translation, *Life of Poetry*, 88; *Poems* [in Hebrew] 2, 23; "Because Now is the Time," collected as "I am Their Last," *Poetry*, 103; *Poems* [in Hebrew] 2, 59.

4. Perhaps a play on words: in Hebrew *se'ar* – hair – is spelled like *sh'ar* – gate.

5. In the Montenegro interview, 18, Amichai said that this was his longest poem, and that it had taken several weeks to write. He stated that the poem was written in 1967, when extreme events (the Six Day War, occupation of the West Bank) clashed or came together with a personal crisis and a "breakthrough," which he did not specify. In the Weber interview, 14, he indicated several times that this was his longest poem, and that he considered it to be one of his best.

6. Menachem Braun, "Ripeness Is All" [in Hebrew], *Yediot Acharonot*, January 31, 1969.

7. Nissim Calderon, "A Sure Step" [in Hebrew], *Masa-Lamerchav*, February 14, 1969.

8. Haim Be'er, "Now in the Storm – by Yehuda Amichai" [in Hebrew], *Haaretz*, March 21, 1969.

9. Miriam Arad, "Amichai's Poetry Begins to Mellow," *Jerusalem Post Magazine Weekly*, May 12, 1969.

10. This award is considered second in importance to the Bialik Prize, and in Amichai's case, it was a step towards it. For more on the prestige associated with these literary awards, see Nurit Govrin and Rachel Stepak, introduction, *Crown of Thorns* [in Hebrew], 15-17. For more on the judges' deliberations before awarding the Brenner Prize to Ya'ari, Michali and Amichai, see *Davar*, December 21, 1969.

11. November 21, 1969. Gnazim 96954.

12. Implying that the effort would be useless. Letter from Dov Chomsky to Yehuda Amichai, November 30, 1969. Amichai's letter to Kalman Aharon Bertini, the editor of *Moznaim,* which published Amichai's "American Notes," is indicative of his financial difficulties when he returned from the US: "I have something to ask of you: that I could receive payment of royalties as soon as possible, because I am in financial straits just now." Gnazim 65316.

13. Six years later, on Dalit Ormian's radio program "Not on the Soul Alone," Roni said his father would read him the poems when he was 6 when they met at a café. Dalit Ormian (moderator), "Daddy Wrote a Book on me" [in Hebrew], Voice of Israel, June 10, 1973. The book was announced in *Davar,* January 19, 1968. A review by M. Mashav [Moshe Dor], "Amichai Speaks to Small Children in Adult Language" [in Hebrew], appeared in *Maariv*, March 6, 1968.

14. 15.714. The translation into English is in prose, not rhymed as in the original.

15. *Things that Happened* [in Hebrew], (Tel Aviv: Am Oved, 1968). No page numbers.

16. In her 2002 review of the revised edition of the book Yael Darr noted that "This unique blend of the imagined viewpoint of the child Roni with that of his father is particularly striking in the context of the wonderful observations of the great city."

Darr, "When the Tops of Buildings Scrape the Sky and You Are So Very Small" [in Hebrew], *Haaretz-Sefarim*, May 29, 2002.

17. Menachem Regev, "Poems on New York" [in Hebrew], *Yediot Acharonot,* June 7, 1968; he also found the book to contain "not a few routine verses." Miriam Arad, who loved the "cheerful book," was appalled by the illustrations. Miriam Arad, "Happiness Made to Order," *Jerusalem Post*, July 7, 1968.

18. Yael Darr, "When the Tops of Buildings".

19. Yael Israel, "When There Was a Hole at the ATM" [in Hebrew], *Maariv-Tarbut*, August 23, 2002.

20. According to Amichai, "All the genuine materials I gathered for the novel [*Hotel in the Wilderness*] were gleaned from the nine months I stayed there [...] I turned it over in my mind until I knew more or less what I wanted." Interview with Nurit Unger, "Poems in a Great Outburst" [in Hebrew], *Bamachane*, July 13, 1971, 72-74.

21. Chapter 21 in the novel.

22. "Amichai's Complaint," *Noar 71*, 1 (June 1, 1971). The title is a direct reference to Philip Roth's novel *Portnoy's Complaint*, which at the time had caused an enormous scandal.

23. Sara Rifin, "Yehuda Amichai's *Hotel in the Wilderness*" [in Hebrew], *At*, August 1971.

24. Miriam Arad, "Amichai Pulls a Bloomer," *Jerusalem Post*, July 16, 1971.

25. Meir Wieseltier, "Questions to Yehuda Amichai" [in Hebrew], 445-448.

26. Unger interview, *Bamachane*. Amichai's enthusiasm about the novel can be seen in the Zahavi interview, "Poetry as Revenge" [in Hebrew]. In an interview with Naomi Gutkind, he said that the novel was before its time and "will still find its place." Gutkind, "The Poet, Criticism, and the Readership" [in Hebrew], *Hatzofeh*, November 20, 1981.

27. For sources for this paragraph see: on the group as a whole – Gideon Ofrat, "'Mashkof' – Bohemia in Red and Blue – The Rise and Fall of Environmental Art Jerusalem Style" [in Hebrew], *Kol Yerushalayim*, March 23, 1984, 39-40; Noa Avron-Barak, *The Mashkof Group, 1968-1970* [in Hebrew], (MA thesis, Tel Aviv University, 2015); Noa Avron Barak, "Revisiting Israeli Art Canon: The Story of the Mashkof Group," *International Journal of Art and Art History* 4:2 (December 2016): 27-44; Information based on conversations with Harold Schimmel, Yossi Ofek, Tzivia Weinman, Yoram Rozov, Arieh Shor, Malachi Beit-Arié, and Yossi Mar Haim.

28. *Mashkof* – literally "a lintel," while other senses are hinted at: "point of view," "perspective," "to observe," "to reflect."

29. Arieh Shor, one of the poets of the group and a future news editor of the Voice of Israel radio station, remembered Amichai as "very involved," particularly in the performance-exhibition at the Engel Gallery on October 21, 1968. Conversation with Shor, April 8, 2015. Mar-Haim sheds light on Amichai's position in the group: "Everyone respected him highly. And of course there was a distance between him and the young poets." December 24, 2016.

30. Conversation with Rozov, December 5, 2016.

31. *Avraham Ofek: The Prints* [in Hebrew] (Jerusalem, 1989), 110.

32. Noa Avron interview with Schimmel and Tolkovsky, May 23, 2014. Schimmel's book *Katzida* was published in 2009 with drawings by Tolkowsky (Jerusalem, 2009).

33. Avron interview. Around that time, Amichai was asked to write poems to be published with the work of the artist Yitzhak Pugacz (1919-2017), who had been appointed Head of the Painting department at Bezalel. Amichai wrote a quite interesting series of poems, which he composed in response to Pugacz's semi-abstract paintings ("Picture and Poem" [in Hebrew] [Jerusalem, 1970]). As the artist and critic Leah Majaro-Mintz observed, the link between the poet and the painter was not organic and was only successful for a few pictures: "For the painter gold is a warm and radiant color [...] while the poet feels choked under the veil of gold." Leah Majaro-Mintz, "What Is the Artist Angry About?" [in Hebrew], *Davar*, May 18, 1970.

34. Avron-Barak, "Mashkof" [in Hebrew], 86. In early 1971 Amichai took part in a series of "chamber evenings" at the Jerusalem Artists' House, but as Majaro-Mintz noted, "there was no attempt to integrate the different arts into one creative unit; the aim was simply to enable the visitor to experience different art forms under one roof." Leah Majaro-Mintz, "Combining the Arts at the Jerusalem Artists' House" [in Hebrew], *Davar*, February 19, 1971.

35. Conversation with Mar-Haim, 24.12.2016: "Yehuda Amichai took part in an evening at my home, where I recorded him reading his poems in different forms. For example, the poem 'They Amputated' [the first line of "A Pity. We Were a Good Invention."]. Four years later I set the poem 'Bankruptcy' to music for a film called *Three and One*, and the poem 'They Amputated' for a film by the Russian director Kalik."

36. Her paintings were exhibited twice in Israel, at the Anna Ticho House in Jerusalem: "I and I," 1997, curated by Irit Shalmon, and at the Hecht Museum, at the University of Haifa, in the spring of 2006, also under Shalmon's curatorship. The catalogue from the Haifa exhibition: *Else Lasker-Schüller – Poet-Painter* [in Hebrew] (Haifa, 2006), includes an article by Gabriel Zoran, "Else Lasker-Schüller en Route to Hebrew" [in Hebrew], which analyzes Hebrew translations of her poems by Uri Zvi Greenberg, Amichai and Natan Zach. Ibid., 21-31.

37. Frisch's radio play was broadcast as part of "The Curtain Rises" program, Voice of Israel, on September 20, 1965 according to listings in *Maariv*, September 17, 1965.

38. Even though he owed so much to Rilke who was clearly an influence on his early work, he only published a few of his translations: "Day in Autumn," "Lullaby," and "Piano Exercise," in *Mevo'ot*, 3, December 12, 1955, 8.

39. Convincingly analyzed by Shimon Sandbank, "The Couplet and Modularity: Amichai and Else Lasker-Schüller," in *The Voice Is the Other* [in Hebrew] (Jerusalem, 2001), 72-89. Sandbank argues that this seemingly disintegrated structure returns in the late Amichai in *Behind All This*. Amichai himself deals with this structure and its hidden inner unity in an article on the publication of a new edition of Lasker-Schüller's last book *The Blue Piano* [in Hebrew], *Lamerchav-Masa*, January 1, 1958.

40. "At night I lie on your face" – quoted in Sandbank, "The Couplet," 72. Lerner, the playwright, captured her approach to love in old age: "Innocent love has remained. Without cynicism but also without inhibitions." Ricky Rivlin, "Coocoo, God, Where Are You" [in Hebrew], *Maariv,* January 26, 1990.

41. He discusses his attempts to recite translations of her poetry to members of his unit in Egypt during WWII, which he had perhaps learned by heart and delivered half-jokingly, with journalist Rivlin (note above). Amichai contributed a translation of what is considered the best Lasker-Schüller poem, "An Old Tibetan Rug", to the Ticho House exhibit. Handwritten manuscript of the poem – 29.1063; Irit Shalmon, to Amichai, February 23, 1995. 9.399.

42. In his article "The Blue Piano," Amichai wrote about his and his classmates' youthful pranks when they saw this unusual woman. See also newspaper articles on Amichai's Lasker-Schüler translations: David Lazar, "Dear Spotted Leopard" [in Hebrew], *Maariv*, April 25, 1969; Shraga Har-Gil, "The Poet Who Wrote Poems of Jerusalem in German" [in Hebrew], *Maariv*, February 28, 1969.

43. "The Blue Piano" [on Else Lasker-Schüler, in Hebrew], *Lamerchav – Masa*, January 1, 1958.

44. When Ricky Rivlin interviewed him about Motti Lerner's play *Else*, Amichai told him that within a year, a book of his translations of her poetry would come out, including new and old work. Rivlin, "Coocoo, God".

45. Lerner to Amichai, November 23, 1989. 7.344.

46. Hajo Jahn, chair of the society, to Amichai, November 14, 1992; December 11, 1994; Amichai's name appears on the membership list – 4.152.

47. Yehuda Haezrachi, *Jerusalem I Have Chosen* [in Hebrew], (Jerusalem 5731 [1970-71]), 219-225.

48. The older Jewish residents of the neighborhood left during the War of Independence. Eliezer Jaffe, *Yemin Moshe: The Story of a Jerusalem Neighborhood* [in Hebrew], (Jerusalem, 1985), 67-69; Yaron Sahish, "Alas, We Were Nonchalant" [in Hebrew], *Yerushalayim* weekly, August 16, 1993.

49. See Amichai, "The Windmill at Yemin Moshe" [in Hebrew], first published in *Maariv*, May 31, 1979. *Poems* [in Hebrew] 3, 349. On Kolleck's consultation with him about how to develop Jerusalem's cultural life – Journal, May 10, 1967.

50. Jaffe, *A Jerusalem Neighborhood* [in Hebrew], 77-89; Reuven Gafni, *Winds of Hope* (Jerusalem, 2015), 98-105.

51. Naomi Gutkind, who interviewed him when he won the Israel Prize, described his house before it was expanded as "modest among the gorgeous villas, simple and not pretentious, like its owners." Gutkind, "The Poet, Criticism, and the Readership" [in Hebrew], *Hatzofeh*, November 20, 1981.

52. On the building of the basement – a letter from Amichai to Ted Hughes, August 30, 1972. On the extension – interview with the architect Prof. David Guggenheim who, with Alex Bloch, designed it, April 15, 2016; also Yotam Reuveni interview, "This is the Place".

53. One of the beautiful poems he wrote to his Czernowitz-born Israeli friend, Ilana Shmueli, after his visit to Israel, begins "Your lip held / a sliver of fig." Celan may have believed for a time that the fig in Israel, the land of milk and honey, could

replace the bitter almond, a prominent motif in his poetry. Felstiner, "Translating Paul Celan's 'Jerusalem' Poems, *Religion & Literature* 16 (1) (Winter, 1984): 37-47.

54. Sandbank, epilogue to Paul Celan, *Speech-grille* [in Hebrew], trans. Sandbank (Tel Aviv, 1994), 173-177. Celan told Yehoshua Tira (Tan-Paï) that he discovered Bialik and Tchernichovsky in his youth, and had read them in the original. Tira, "Conversation with Paul Celan" [in Hebrew], *Haaretz*, October 17, 1969. In his poetry, especially pieces related to his visit to Israel, Hebrew words appear, and even the word *hachnisini* ("let me in") – addressed to a woman – which he remembered from Bialik, and which he uses in its full erotic sense.

55. The phrase is taken from the title of a poem by Yitzhak Katzenelson.

56. "No-One's Rose" in the poem "Psalm" is capitalized, as is "Blessed art thou, No One" in the same poem. *Selected Poems and Prose of Paul Celan*, trans. John Felstiner (New York and London, 2001), 157. Also at the Poetry Foundation https://www.poetryfoundation.org/poems/57173/psalm-56d23a67be159.

57. Amichai, Notes on my Meeting with Celan, handwritten manuscript, 34.1171. Shmuel Huppert, "Meetings in Jerusalem, 1969" [in Hebrew], *Yediot Acharonot*, May 27, 1983.

58. Letter from Celan to Amichai (in German), November 7, 1969. Translation into English, and an analysis by a Celan scholar, John Felstiner, "Paul Celan and Yehuda Amichai: An Exchange between Two Great Poets," *Midstream,* Jan-Feb. 2007, 28-30. For an analysis of the correspondence and relationship between the two poets, see also Naama Rokem, "German-Hebrew Encounters in the Poetry and Correspondence of Yehuda Amichai and Paul Celan," *Prooftexts*, 30, 2010, 97-127.

59. Death Fugue, *Poems of Paul Celan*, trans. Michael Hamburger, Carcanet, 1997.

60. Perhaps a passing allusion to the messiah's donkey? See Ilana Shmueli, *'Say That Jerusalem Is': Notes on Paul Celan October 1969 – April 1970* [in Hebrew] (Jerusalem, 1999), 18-19.

61. See John Felstiner, *Paul Celan: Poet, Survivor, Jew* (New Haven, 1995), 269-271; Lydia Koelle, *Paul Celans pneumatisches Judentum* (Mainz, 1995), 113-124.

62. "The Death of Celan," Amichai, *Songs of Jerusalem and Myself*, trans. Harold Schimmel (Jerusalem, 1973), 66; *Poems* [in Hebrew] 2, 342. In his last book, *Open Closed Open,* he dedicated a poem to Celan's death, the paradoxes of a suicide that perhaps revealed "the frothy concentrate / of the heaviness of your life." *Poetry*, 497; *Poems* [in Hebrew] 5, 270.

63. Letter from Yehuda and Hana to Hughes, Hughes archive at Emory University.

64. Nissim Kivity, "The Proximity of Literary Hearts" [in Hebrew], *Yediot Acharonot- Leilot Hashavua,* January 28, 1971, 4.

65. Kivity, ibid; Zehava Mendelssohn, "Five Poets from England Come to Read Their Works in Israel" [in Hebrew], *Maariv*, February 12, 1971.

66. Jeremy Robson, "Copy for Mr. Feinstein." Unidentified newspaper article. [possibly *London Magazine*, 1971].

67. Joseph Cohen, "Conversations with Dannie Abse," in *The Poetry of Dannie Abse*, ed. Joseph Cohen (London, 1985), 163.

Chapter 13

1970–1990

Volumes of Poetry in Hebrew and in Translation, Major Prizes at Home and Abroad, becoming the Middle-Aged Father of Young Children

FRUITFUL YEARS: BOOKS OF POEMS, CHILDREN'S BOOKS, RADIO PLAYS, INTERNATIONAL RECOGNITION

This chapter takes a relatively brief look at Amichai's life and works in the 1970s and 1980s, on the eve of the last decade of his life. It was a very fruitful period for his poetry, since seven fairly hefty volumes were published: *Not for the Sake of Remembering* (1971), *Behind All This a Great Happiness Is Hiding* (1974), *Time* (1977), *A Great Tranquility: Questions and Answers* (1980), *The Hour of Grace* (1982), *From Man You Are and to Man You Shall Return* (1985), and *The Fist, Too, Was Once the Palm of an Open Hand, and Fingers* (1989). He also published two children's books describing the worlds of the two children he had with Hana that follow the days of the week: *Numa's Fat Tail* (1978),[1] dedicated to his son Dadi, and *Book of the Great Night*, dedicated to his daughter Emanuela. He also wrote radio plays, which are less well-known: *To Love in Jerusalem*, *Come, My Beloved* and *To Kill Him*.

These 20 years of Amichai's life saw his poetry (and to a much lesser extent, his prose) achieve worldwide publication and fame. This recognition was unprecedented for a poet writing in Hebrew. His poems appeared in close to 40 languages, including whole volumes of poetry in translation in English, French, German, Polish, Chinese, Japanese, and others and bilingual editions (Hebrew-English, Hebrew-Russian, etc.). Appreciation of his poetry, which encompassed nearly every social stratum in Israel, was reflected in the prestigious awards he received (the Bialik Prize, the Israel Prize). His worldwide popularity, which began in English speaking countries before spreading to Europe, Southeast Asia, and the Arabic-speaking Middle East, can be seen in his frequent invitations to events abroad where he was asked to lecture on his poetry, give poetry workshops, take part in poetry festivals (where he was often the star attraction), give interviews to newspapers, as well as radio and TV stations, and receive numerous honors and prizes in a range of countries, thus making him unique among Israeli poets.

Because Amichai was such a popular and cherished figure in Israel, he could make his voice heard on current affairs – mainly political matters which moved him to the core – in interviews, articles, and both indirectly and directly in his poems. Amichai's position on this issue was complicated: on the one hand he strongly disagreed that the poet or writer's vocation was to be a *shofar*, or a clarion call, for any particular ideology, or that he or she should represent a political party or tendency. On the other hand, he recognized that in life in general, and particularly in Israel with its complex tensions surrounding issues of identity and national direction, "everything is political," in one way or another.

THE AMICHAI SCHOOL

When writer Shammai Golan was appointed director of the Writers' House in Jerusalem in 1970, one of his first initiatives was to set up a writers' workshop which was then a new phenomenon in Israel. He wanted the best possible instructors, and in his view, for poetry this meant Amichai.

Amichai had already given a writers' workshop at Hillel House, in which Agi Mishol, a Hebrew University student, who later became a well-known Israeli poet, took part. At the first session at the Writers' House, Ronny Someck, a young soldier and youth leader from the development town of Beit Shemesh (near Jerusalem), a no less popular poet in Israel in the years to come, got involved. Ronny would go with Amichai to the Writers' House in the Old City, attend his workshop, "pouring water on his hands", the Hebrew expression for a devoted student.[2] This was the start of the "Amichai school," not of imitators – though there was no lack of these – as much as those who developed Amichai's poetics in their own ways.

CONQUEST IN BUENOS AIRES

Amichai was considered an ambassador of Israeli culture in the 1970s. In the late 1960s the book of poems translated by Assia Gutmann, and his participation in the Spoleto and London festivals introduced him to Europe. The early 1970s brought him to the US. The ensuing decades would take him there repeatedly on reading tours, and to give poetry writing courses and workshops that garnered him enormous popularity in the US, most of all in the Jewish community. The latter, conflicted about identity and struggling for belonging, was eager to hear an Israeli figure who was seen as a poet-warrior, a soldier-poet, a combatant in the wars of the Jewish State from its inception but at the same time a cultured intellectual, softly spoken and modest poet.

Amichai was invited to read at the International Poetry Festival at the Library of Congress in Washington on April 15 and 16, 1970.[3] The New York Hebrew newspaper *Hadoar* announced that "Mr. Amichai will tour a number of campuses in America and will lecture on Hebrew literature in Israel."[4] His trip to the US involved two international stopovers: he lectured and read in London,[5] and then spent two weeks prior to going to New York in Buenos Aires, Argentina, as a guest of the Argentinian Writers' Association and the Jewish community, which asked him to give a series of lectures on literature in the bustling community center in the city. He was surprised by the giant city that spread out before him: rather than exotic, he found it to be "the sum of all the famous European cities [...] without the wars."[6]

Amichai was already famous enough to become the focus of attention in the mainstream media. At that dramatic moment after the Israeli victory in the Six Day War, he told journalists that he supported contact between Israeli and Arab intellectuals, and would himself take part in a meeting of that sort in another month. Yiddish newspapers published in the capital welcomed his visit, but also deliberated as to how to present an unorthodox poet. Amichai frequently wrote without meter or rhyme, and dealt with the world of the individual rather than with national themes as their readership was used to, but was nevertheless thought to be head and shoulders above the rest in Israel. *Raiçes* (Roots), the Zionist monthly, interviewed him at length.[7]

Those attending his Hebrew lectures were mainly students at the Hebrew Midrasha, a post-high school institution that trained teachers for the Jewish high schools run by the Buenos Aires Zionist community.[8] However, Amichai apparently paid the most attention to a Hebrew teacher at the Israel Embassy *ulpan* (Hebrew language class), who had been his student at Greenberg College nine years earlier. In 1961, Susana Huller had been sent to do her advanced year at the Shalom Aleichem Jewish school in Jerusalem and Amichai had been the Hebrew teacher.[9] Amichai had not at that time showed any particular interest in Susana, although he said that he had been impressed by her presence. During the nine intervening years she had lived through marriage and divorce, studied physics, and then after a psychoanalysis, decided to study psychology and become a psychoanalyst. To defray the costs of her sessions she taught at the *ulpan*. Amichai asked her to come to his lectures, and she made it to the second one. When the lecture was over, he disappeared, but when she came out of the elevator at the exit, he burst upon her breathlessly and told her that he had already come down and gone back up the staircase several times hoping to find her. She told him that she had been married and divorced, and he too presented himself initially as divorced. Formally, he was indeed not married at that point.

From that evening on, and for 12 days as she remembers it, they were inseparable, spending nights and every free day time hour together. "It only did me good," she noted. The very fact that he was 20 years older, an old man in her eyes, and lived in another country, allowed her to enjoy their uncommitted relationship. Even today she continues to consider the encounter as a peak experience in her life.[10] "I don't remember details of my past relationships the way I remember the details of my relationship with him," she confessed, "because he had a lot of presence [...] he didn't talk nonsense [...] he is not one given to small talk. Everything prompted him to interesting thought [...] he loved to think and get excited about words. His seriousness and banter went together." His fame as a poet did not impress her ("The city of Susana who had not heard about me"),[11] but she knew him to be a poet in the way he loved her: "He was very sensitive, always speaking from passion [...] He knew how to come close, to break through barriers." Nevertheless, she did not allow him to dominate her: she refused to change her name to the Hebrew Shoshana, as he suggested, and she did not express love for Israel, although he made attempts to convince her otherwise: during her first stay in Israel she had found it desolate and the landscapes monotonous.

"I think it was bliss for us both. [...] He needed some sort of adventure, and so did I", after the difficulties and instability of her love life. He told her about his partner, expressing wonder about the femininity of young women in Buenos Aires and their scanty clothing. In her opinion, he needed women most of all to write poems; "perhaps it would be more true to say – and more deeply so – that he had to write to recover from women." Rather surprisingly, he told her that "women are castrating." Half-seriously she once told him, while slicing bread, as he stood with his back to her: "Don't turn round, because I am cutting bread, and it might frighten you." However, Amichai did not value her profession and thought that the psychological counselling he had received about his son Roni had been damaging to his nine-year old son whom in his opinion understood him better than anyone else in the world.[12]

When she told him at a certain stage: "you're using me," he told her that to use one another was love by another name.[13] Although she told him she would not grieve at their impending separation, he felt her becoming increasingly tense as his departure approached, and he teased her: "You see, it's difficult for you to part. Why are you playing?" In fact, when he left, she felt as though someone had thrown her out of an airplane.

Further invitations awaited Amichai in the coming months, including a reading of his poems at the Library of Congress in Washington and giving a series of lectures.[14] His relationship with Susana continued in the coming years, initially when a year later she visited her brother who had immigrated to Israel and had become a father, and then when she herself settled in Israel in 1976, escaping the "Dirty War" by the last military junta in Argentina. Amichai claimed her for himself. She saw his continuing lust for her as an expression of the stability of his love.

Susana's recollections help us understand the "Poems of Buenos Aires" cycle, which would take pride of place in Amichai's next book, *Not for the Sake of Remembering* (1971). In the cycle, partly written in a rhythm taken from the work of the Spanish poet Federico García Lorca, Susana appears only slightly camouflaged. She is called Dolores, a Spanish name that is rare in Argentina (Susana's cleaning lady was called Dolores), but the name Susana recurs prominently (in the poem "Susana Mass" and others). Susana was indeed a psychology student, but she was not Christian, and her ancestors did not "eradicate Indian tribes."[15] One particular feature of Amichai's relationship to Buenos Aires was the importance he attached to experiencing the city as though it were Jerusalem, and he refused to acknowledge the sea – or more accurately the very broad Rio de la Plata river – that lay alongside it ("And I didn't want to hear, so that / Buenos Aires would be / like Jerusalem, without a sea").[16]

In the book, in lines combined with references to the Spanish world (though not necessarily to Argentina),[17] he sketches the development of this short and intense love affair between a man in his forties and a young woman in her twenties who has been through hard times and seen her limitations as a spouse. "Her body was shaped like the opening to my life"; she was the sexual opening through which Amichai's self could emerge from his "container." However, separation and the fear of alienation were already lying in wait: "There's an illusion of togetherness / at first, then later, of being apart", and towards the end: "The room. How lonely and abandoned was / the Spanish language in the room. Later Hebrew too. // The city that gave me tranquility and took it from me."[18] Nevertheless, he also cherished the tokens of intimacy between them: "And he won't be there when the soap and the cream are finished / And he won't be there when the clock is wound up again / […] And she will lock his wild letters in a quiet drawer / And lie down to sleep near the water in the wall."[19]

PUBLICATION OF THE BOOK OF POEMS *NOT FOR THE SAKE OF REMEMBERING*

The 12-day love affair with Susana Huller was so much on Amichai's mind that in the first edition of *Not for the Sake of Remembering*, which came out in the summer of 1971, the sections of the book are entitled "With poems of Buenos Aires," "Poems of Buenos Aires," and "After Poems of Buenos Aires," even though the first and third sections did not touch on the affair at all.[20] Apart from love poems about other women as well, the book has several poems on deaths and weddings that took place while he was writing the book : two were written when he learned of the suicides of Assia Gutmann and Paul Celan; the others are the moving and oft-quoted poem on the death of Lea Goldberg, and the mischievous poem for the wedding of Varda and Harold Schimmel.[21]

A number of critics and poets were lying in wait to dethrone the poetry king. The most heavy-handed of these detractors was Nissim Calderon, who noted the centrality of autobiography in Amichai's poetry, but argued that in this book it had become an unbearable, self-indulgent, "autobiographicality."[22] While *Not for the Sake of Remembering* is indeed not one of Amichai's best poetry collections, his easily won creative capital appeared to be a thorn in the side of many critics and writers who could not stifle their jealousy of his endlessly burning flame of inspiration and growing worldwide reputation, the invitations from universities and festivals throughout the world, and the unprecedented sales of his books in Israel and abroad: almost 50,000 copies of *Poems 1948-1962* in Israel. Even in the US, where poetry book sales are generally negligible, 5,000 copies of *Selected Poems* were sold.[23]

BEHIND ALL THIS A GREAT HAPPINESS IS HIDING: WHERE, AND BEHIND WHAT?

In the summer of 1974, Amichai published a large volume of poems entitled *Behind All This a Great Happiness Is Hiding*. Where was this great happiness? Behind what? When the volume came out, Israel had just emerged from a series of virtually continuous wars: The Six Day War, the War of Attrition, which residents on the home front perceived as a slow, everyday blood-letting, and the terrible Yom Kippur War. While Amichai's response to the shock of the Yom Kippur War appears in some of the new poems in the book, "Laments for the War Dead," a well-known cycle and important part of the volume, had already been published on Independence Day 5733 (1973) nearly six months before the war.[24]

The book contains large cycles of poems. It starts with "Songs of the Land of Zion and Jerusalem," followed by "Laments for the War Dead," and "Poems of Lies and Beauty" at the end. "Songs of the Land of Zion and Jerusalem," also translated as "Songs of Zion the Beautiful," are a continuation – brimming with anger and critique – of the "Jerusalem 1967" cycle, from *Now in the Storm*. The poem that starts the latter is suggestive of the first signs of Amichai's delight at the unification of the city, alongside fears formulated with restraint and elegance, about the explosive potential of historic Jerusalem: "And already the demons of the past are meeting / with the demons of the future and negotiating about me" (poem 2); "This summer of wide-open-eyed hatred / and blind love, I'm beginning to believe again / in all the little things" (poem 7); "Jerusalem. An operation that was left open. / The surgeon went to take a nap in faraway skies" (poem 27). The famous poem 5, "On Yom Kippur in 1967," consists of an imaginary dialogue between the poet and an Arab shopkeeper that comes to a provisional resolution leaving room for hope of mutual understanding.[25]

The "Songs of the Land of Zion and Jerusalem" cycle in *Behind All This* is different, starting with the weaning of his son David – Dadi – born in January 1973.[26] This "catastrophe" that befalls every baby, forced at some stage to be separated from the mother's breast and suffer from now on from insatiable hunger,[27] is here a reflection in miniature of apocalyptic Jerusalem, which out of sexual hunger for her many conqueror-lovers, perpetually gallops towards destruction. Having quenched his thirst for the undivided city as he knew it in his late childhood, Amichai now longed for the partitioned city, a humble city content with the human dimensions of his adolescence: "The undivided noisy matron has returned / with her gold and bronze and precious stones / to her fat legitimate life. / But I don't love her. / I sometimes remember the quiet one" (poem 24).[28]

He rebels against all rituals of remembrance and memorials to the past so typical of life in Jerusalem (poem 34). He wants to turn the city into a plain, by filling in the surrounding valleys with all the "dung and deliverance, bliss-and-balls, / dregs of nothingness, bomb and time" the city is full of (poem 37). Still, "in spite of all that, I must / Love Jerusalem and remember him / Who perished for her on the bridge of Gethsemane, / Whose death was a watershed / Between memory and memory, hope and hope" (poem 38) which refers to Captain Hubi, the multi-talented Ya'acov Eilam, who fell on this bridge in the Six Day War during a heroic mission to extricate the wounded. In his blood-soaked vest was a book of Amichai's poems. The poet saw this as expressing all the beauty and nobility of the people of Israel.[29]

The dimension of a prophecy of anger, and his drive to fracture the rites of memory and the burdensome historicality of the Israeli experience, are expressed vividly in "Songs of the Land of Zion and Jerusalem" in comparison to "Laments for the War Dead." In "Laments" there is a tone of amused compassion, for example in the portrait of Mr. Beringer, whose son was apparently killed in the War of Attrition: "He has grown very thin, has lost / the weight of his son" (poem 1). Even the description of the military cemetery is gentle and is suggestive of a possible restoration ("*tikkun*"), unlike the "Songs of the Land of Zion and Jerusalem," which suggests the levelling of the valley by cramming it with the ancient rubbish and impersonations in which Jerusalem flounders: "how long / can you go on building the homeland / and not fall behind in the terrible / three-sided race / between consolation and building and death? // Yes, all of this is sorrow. But leave / a little love burning always" (poem 6).

The reception of the book was highly ambivalent in terms of its ideological leanings, its humane stand, and its different sections, which are indeed not all cut from the same cloth. Amichai was sensitive to these comments. In his notebooks he attempts to take the critics' invalidation of his poetry with a pinch of salt: "critics are like fortune tellers. I only believe in those who say good things about me" (File 486. Approximately August 1972).

YOUNG CHILDREN IN MIDDLE AGE

While Amichai was writing the poems for the book *A Great Tranquility: Questions and Answers* (1980), Emanuela-Meira was born in June 1978. Amichai was already 54.[30] Emanuela, whose name Amichai insisted on pronouncing with all its five syllables, as written in the children's book dedicated to her,[31] would indeed illuminate his life with her clever remarks and endearing qualities (notebooks entries from March-May 1983, July 1984, and others).[32]

His son Dadi, born in 1973, made endless demands for attention, and to a great extent dictated his parents' routine. When Dadi was six, Amichai noted in his notebooks: "Trip to the US, January 23, 1979. I called from the airport [...] Dadi is my most problematic child. I love him a lot and fight with him a lot. He's really the apple of my eye. Roni is like me, so I am in him, in any case."[33] Later, when Dadi was an adolescent, Amichai took pride in his son's height, since he was so much taller than his parents. He surprised himself by learning to enjoy music incompatible with his refined classical sensitivity from Dadi.[34]

In his book of poems *The Hour of Grace* (1982), the family he had founded, as well as his son from his previous marriage, are present. Amichai was thrilled at being the father of a daughter who could have been his granddaughter. He liked to say in interviews that fatherhood of this sort kept him young; but in the poem "Daughter of My Old Age" from the book, he acknowledges that he is already exhausted by bringing up his older children: "All the games I played with your big brothers, / all the tales I've already told [...] // I am using your own ointment / so as to soothe my skin too / cracked all these years. // [...] But I make the blessing over the last fruit, / the biggest blessing of all."[35]

When Roni his son with his first wife Tamar, whom she brought up, was a soldier in the Nachal Brigade in the north (1980-1982),[36] Amichai worried about him, but expressed his feelings with characteristic humor: "But now again you worry me. / I'm always looking for you, / this time among the mists of the Upper Galilee. / I am a mist father".[37]

He dedicated a stirring Holocaust poem to Hana, perhaps influenced by the well-known poem by Dan Pagis, "Written in Pencil in the Sealed Freight Car," by giving it a similar staccato: "If my parents and your parents / Had not immigrated to Israel / In 1936, / We would have met in 1944 / On the ramp in Auschwitz. [. . . .] Where's mame [mommy]? / Where's tate [daddy]?"[38] After his endless peripatetic search for love (successful to some extent; see "In the Hotel," "Herbal Tea," and others), he returns to his wife: "her passionate screams are ordered / One after the other [...]: / Domestic dove, then wild dove, / Then a peacock, a wounded peacock" – but though representing routine, she is also the anchor and respite, and his shoes "on the rug by the bed [...] point toward her."[39]

HIS MOTHER'S DEATH, AND A LATE MARRIAGE

Amichai's book of poems *From Man You Are and to Man You Shall Return* was published in late 1985 and reflected both personal and national death. In 1983, Amichai's 87-year-old mother contracted cancer, and in the last months of her life his mother and sister were more inclined to take him back into the fold.[40] He took his daughter Emanuela to visit her grandmother whom he thought looked more like his mother than like him or his wife.[41]

It remains unclear how successful he was in communicating with his dying mother. The opening of the poem "Last Conversations": "To talk with my mother in the final days, / Was like entering an elevator / In an old wobbly house about to fall down," appears more like a confession that he came too late to talk cogently with her.[42] His attempt to reconstruct a monologue or parts of her conversation while she was still conscious is heart-rending: "You're so clean now, / [...] your eyes are full of light. Is Rabbi Hanover / Still alive? Open yourself a can of sardines";[43] but it is difficult to say what he reveals and what he occludes in how she had lived her life.[44] Her last request, "Take the flowers out of the room," recalls familiar advice, already incorporated in an earlier poem ("My mother once told me / Not to sleep with flowers in the room"). The message she was conveying was to abandon his rebellious nature, a wish that he failed to honor when he left Tamar and his young son and made a "wild" connection with Hana (something that his mother considered to be tantamount to his decision to become secular).[45] It is no coincidence that this poem ends with a childhood memory of a fight with his mother and grandmother, who dragged him out of the house to take him to kindergarten for the first time at age 4: "The wooden bannister I clutched / When they dragged me off to school / Was burned down long ago. / But my clutching hands remained / Clutching." He never abandoned his independent, undisciplined nature, despite his love and fond memories of the "hand that felt my forehead, in childhood."[46]

When he officialized his marriage to Hana in the presence of his children he was amused and a little afraid of being seen "in the waiting room with bridegrooms many years / Younger than me." This confusing situation led him to create a metaphor which has been much commented on: "The pressure of my life brings my date of birth closer / To the date of my death, as in history books [...] with only a hyphen between them // I hold onto that hyphen with all my might, / like a lifeline."[47]

REPERCUSSIONS OF THE LEBANON WAR

In addition to his mother's death, *From Man You Are* reflects the collective experience of death of Israeli soldiers killed in Lebanon, the many wounded and those experiencing post-traumatic symptoms, in a war that had begun as an operation but had dragged on in different forms for nearly two decades. The verses from the poem that constitutes the title of the book "From Man You Are and to Man You Shall Return," which is moving but also vague, are often quoted: "Death in war begins / with the going down the stairs / of a single man, a young man. // Death in war begins / with the silent closing of a door [...] // And in this spring / who will rise and say to the dust: / from man you are and to man you shall return." Amichai expands on a biblical text (Jeremiah 22:10), suggesting that it is appropriate to cry for the living who once were, not for the dead who are no more. In particular, crying and head shaking are the futile, perhaps not completely sincere efforts to preserve the memory of the dead: "Weep for the photo that remembers instead of us, / weep for the paper that remembers,/ weep for the tears that do not remember."[48]

A poem that is much more direct and uncharacteristic of Amichai is entitled "I Guard the Children": "I guard the children as they play [...] / I lift up my face to a hideous vision: / the honorable men [...] clerks of war, merchants of peace [...] I see them pass over us like death-angels / stalking the firstborn, / their wide-open groin dripping / a honeyed drool."[49]

He may have been more true to himself when he condensed his political-existentialist worldview in a short and sensitive poem: "Scribbled wishes stuck between the stones / of the Wailing Wall: / bits of crumpled, wadded paper. // And across the way, stuck in an old iron gate / half-hidden by jasmine: / 'Couldn't make it, / I hope you'll understand'."[50] Banal requests, addressed to nothingness, unlike a message conveying a human relationship marked by sincere pain.

THE POET AT THE CENTER OF JOURNALISTIC INTEREST

When *From Man You Are* was published, journalists jumped at opportunities to interview Amichai. They may have been drawn to what they saw as much more of an "autobiographical exposure". Amichai did not consider that the autobiographical nature of the poems was the result of changes in his life (the birth of children, for example). Instead he claimed that "facing the end you become simpler," as he told Eyal Megged, a writer himself and a journalist at the time. Adulthood and life experience, he thought, create the ability "to express yourself more easily, [and] being responsible for offspring produces lucidity," because of the need "to hold on to actual realities [...] children hold me to the earth [...] they don't let me look up and see the end."[51]

The critics and interviewers reveal the younger generation's appreciation of Amichai's poetry. Yig'al Sarna, a leading journalist on *Yediot Acharonot*, noted that "I have been reading Amichai for many years. Not poetry. Amichai [...] So I see the world a little Amichai-like. By means of images [...] He is the warmest, most fertile, and most well-rounded of the Hebrew poets."[52] The popular singer Shlomo Artzi, who at that time wrote a column in the weekly *Koteret Rashit*, recalled that "we would read Amichai in the army, and we read him together at night, after weddings. We always found a line to hold on to. He's the poet who takes the words out of your mouth." He would read a poem from the book to himself a number of times, feeling that "hidden in the poem is this melody, it's just that I wouldn't dare set it to paper."[53] The writer Meir Shalev, then a columnist for *Kol Ha'ir*, said in his review that he had all of Amichai's books in his library, and that he was "on another level" compared to other poets of the day.[54]

RECIPIENT OF MAJOR PRIZES IN ISRAEL

While Amichai was spending a semester teaching at the University of California at Berkeley, he received the announcement that he had won the Bialik prize for the Hebrew year 5736 (1976).[55] This time as well he shared the prize with someone much older: the poet, critic and translator Yeshurun Keshet (Kopelewitz) who was born in 1893. Making Amichai share the Brenner and Bialik prizes with writers more acceptable to the old guard but much less popular seems to have been an expression of the literary establishment's entrenched ambivalence towards him. This was evident when Amichai began to be recognized as a poet and at the peak of his fame. His greatness and originality were recognized, but his world of values was perceived as problematic and at times outrageous. When interviewed by Alex Zehavi after receiving the Bialik Prize, Amichai responded harshly to its being shared: he complained that the sum he received was paltry. As regards his duality towards the State and its wars, he explained the tension in his poems between skepticism and the undermining of values on one hand and commitment to the national cause on the other was typical of his generation. Eventually, he stated, "I suppose that my way outrages the ideologues of right and left, and this explains the intensity of their criticism."[56]

In early November 1981 the newspapers reported that Amichai and Amir Gilboa would be the recipients of the Israel Prize for poetry awarded on Independence Day 5742 (1982).[57] This time the jury, Professors Gerson Shaked, Israel Levin and Yehuda Friedlander, were closer in age and spirit to the recipients, and the combination of Gilboa, a representative of the Palmach generation, and Amichai, the central figure in the state generation, seemed ideal.[58] Gabriel Moked, a critic and a professor of philosophy and Hebrew literature, wrote that "this is a most wonderful juxtaposition"; the two combined the many layers of the Hebrew language with experimental poetry, and in both the turn to the personal was bound up with "overtones of social humanism."[59] Editor and translator Benny Ziffer acknowledged the enormous impact of Amichai's poetry. However, in his opinion "Amichai turned Hebrew into a language of war, a language of emergency." Amichai's much vaunted simplicity was the simplicity of a soldier shouting "into the radio under fire." This was why his poetry was so successful, in translation too.[60]

The sharing of the prize itself created a disturbing tension between the two great poets. Amichai may have considered sharing the prize with Gilboa as a way to diminish the honor bestowed on him. Gilboa planned to have a get together with Amichai and his wife after the ceremony, but was given the cold shoulder and had to shelve the plan.[61]

THE FIST, TOO, WAS ONCE THE PALM OF AN OPEN HAND, AND FINGERS: CONTENT AND CONTEXT

Towards the end of 1989 a large new book of Amichai's poems came out entitled *The Fist, Too, Was Once the Palm of an Open Hand, and Fingers*. At the time, the Lebanon War was dragging on, as was the First Intifada which began in late 1987. In the poem "Huleikat – The Third Poem about Dicky" Amichai returns to the message of ordinary life and the hopes of his youth before war and killing: "remember the fruit that fell and remind it / of the leaves and the branch [...] and don't forget that the fist, too, / was once the palm of an open hand, and fingers."[62] A hint and more of Amichai's mental state and his proclivities at that time can be gleaned from the poem "The Land Knows," which returns to the image of a lean, divided Jerusalem, compared to the fat and lustful Greater Jerusalem described in "Poems of the Land of Zion and Jerusalem" (24): "The Greater Land of Israel is like a fat and heavy woman,/ And the State of Israel [before becoming "greater"] like a young woman, / Supple and thin-waisted, / But in both of them / Jerusalem is always the nakedness of the land, / The unsated nakedness."[63]

The book has a sense of conclusiveness about it, of a man contemplating the end. He revisits sites meaningful for him from the War of Independence with his children, and relates his concealed emotional and guilt-laden experiences. In the previous book, there was "Itzhak's Last Rucksack"; in the current volume the opening poem is entitled, "Tel Gath": "I brought my children to the mound / Where once I fought battles, / So they would understand the things I did do / And forgive me for the things I didn't do."[64] The wars and in particular the War of Independence in which he was an active participant taught him "the wisdom of camouflage": not to stand out, and to keep avenues of escape and retreat open.[65]

There is an important self-portrait also conveying a sense of closure in the poem "I Am a Poor Prophet," where he returns to a self-description as a painter of his life "with only / Two colors: I paint my life in war / And in love." This may be the ultimate camouflage: he lives "inside the hope of others / As inside a beam of light not meant for me." His visions are those of "everyday people," and his uniqueness is simply to channel "Despair and hope, joy and sorrow, calm and rage [...] In a new cycle," thanks to his ability to empty words of their banal, overblown and rhetorical meanings, making them "narrow and tough"; in other words, loyal, fundamental, returning to their basic aridity, their authentic meanings, before being crushed and distorted by gross overlays.[66]

NOTES

1. *Numa* is also the literary imperative "go to sleep." Since this form appeared in earlier children's poetry ("*numa, numa*, my child"), parents and children had turned it, humorously, into a verbal noun meaning "going to sleep" ("and now – *numa, numa*").

2. Conversation with Agi Mishol, June 23, 2017; conversation with Ronny Someck, October 20, 2015. See also Someck, "And They Call Me Yuda from Love [in Hebrew], *Maariv*, September 29, 2000; idem, "The Words that Once Were Stuck in My Mouth", in Ruth Karton-Blum (ed.), *Writers and Poets on Sources of Inspiration* [in Hebrew], (Tel Aviv, 2002), 187-188.

3. Amichai's invitation from the librarian, July 23, 1969. 7.346. Rafael Rothstein, "Israeli Intellectuals Throng to the US" [in Hebrew], *Haaretz*, March 27, 1970; "The Poet Amichai Will Take Part in an International Poetry Festival" [in Hebrew], *Maariv*, April 12, 1970. More detailed reports about his appearances in New York can be found in *Hadoar*, February 2, April 3, and May 1, 1970. The festival program

which includes Amichai's presentation, with the works he read, are in his archive, 56.1716, 11.533.

4. "Poet Yehuda Amichai to Visit the US" [in Hebrew], *Hadoar*, April 3, 1970. Before going to the festival Amichai corresponded with the eminent poet Ann Sexton, whom he knew from previous festivals. She was happy that they would be meeting and sorry about Assia's death, saying that the loss must be "particularly dreadful for you." Sexton to Amichai, February 11, 1970. 10.488.

5. Gabriel Strassman, "English Imports and Israeli Exports" [in Hebrew], *Maariv*, March 11, 1970. Amichai lectured at Jewish Book Week on the theme of "Fathers and Sons in Jewish and Hebrew Literature," and read at the Poetry Society.

6. On the *She'at Ratzon* radio program. He told his lover Susana (see below) that he "melted" in this city because of its lack of tension.

7. Tzvi Braunstein, "The Visit of the Israeli Poet Yehuda Amichai" [in Yiddish], *Yiddishe Tzeitung*, March 26, 1970; [unattributed], "A Couple of Words About Yehuda Amichai and His Poetry" [in Yiddish], *Di Presse*, April 2, 1970. *Raiçes*, the monthly put out by the Argentinian Zionist Federation, published a wide-ranging interview with Amichai in April 1970. The interview revealed the pronounced differences between the interviewer's and Amichai's views of Zionism. The interviewer took a stand typical of Argentinian Zionism, which considered Yiddish and Hebrew as languages of equal status. Amichai thought that Yiddish could not be artificially revived, and that it lived on within Hebrew.

8. See the words of welcome and the excited response to his poetry: "Come in Peace, Our Hebrew Poet, Yehuda Amichai" [in Hebrew], unidentified local Hebrew newspaper.

9. The details of Amichai and Susana's relationship are based on a long conversation with her at her home on April 27, 2015. A psychologist and psychoanalyst, she has lived in Israel almost continuously since 1976.

10. The strength of her impressions of Amichai is in many ways reminiscent of Clarice Kestenbaum's perceptions of him (see Chapters 8 and 9).

11. The poem beginning "The city of Borges and of Tzivia," in the cycle "Poems of Buenos Aires," from the book *Not for the Sake of Remembering* (1971), *Poems* [in Hebrew] 2, 317.

12. He quoted comments that Roni, aged eight or nine, had made to him while watching a film: "I don't like the way they mix war and love," and added, "and I don't like that there is war in love" (a similar quote from Roni appears in his notebooks, file 481).

13. As in the version of the poem that begins "Of this time" from the cycle "Poems from Buenos Aires," in *Not for the Sake of Remembering*; *Poems* [in Hebrew] 2, 314. Susana said that she was not sure that there had really been such an exchange but that the spirit of the exchange seemed authentic.

14. See "Poetry as a Shared Homeland" [in Hebrew], *Haaretz*, April 26, 1970 (on his lecture at the Library of Congress festival); "Noted Israeli Poet Amichai to Speak at University of Judaism," *World Over*, New York, May 8, 1970 (on Amichai's planned visit to Los Angeles).

15. The poems beginning "A young woman in Santa Fe Avenue" and "She was born beside the sea." *Poems* [in Hebrew] 2, 304.

16. The poem starting the cycle: "In all the days that I was there," *Poems* [in Hebrew] 2, 297. "She was born beside the sea in Del Mar" refers to a city near Buenos Aires, on the coast of a fresh water sea formed by inflow from the enormous Rio de la Plata river.

17. This is a play on words on the Spanish city of Cordoba, which is important in Jewish history, and the similarly named major thoroughfare in Buenos Aires. In another poem, beginning "In deep passages," he mentions bullfighting.

18. The poem beginning "There is the smell of fresh paint here," *Poems* [in Hebrew] 2, 321. Another poem, beginning "The remains of a funeral," ends "And there's a man who has nothing / to bring to the grave / but the memory of one night." Ibid., 301.

19. "Ballad in the Streets of Buenos Aires," *Life of Poetry*, 211-212. The wall clock in Susana's house needed winding once every two weeks.

20. Interviewed by a student paper, Amichai expressed the opinion that the "Poems of Buenos Aires" section was the most successful in the book. *Pi Ha'aton* 24:11 [in Hebrew], May 26, 1971.

21. In the third cycle there are a number of passionate love poems, in one of which he thanks his lover who "let me live a few months / Without needing religion / Or a world view" ("Gifts of Love," *Life of Poetry*, 226; another translation *Songs of Jerusalem*, 40; *Poems* [in Hebrew] 2, 364), and then a poem of separation taking an amused stance, "Abigayil – Not the Biblical One" (*Songs of Jerusalem*, 43; *Poems* [in Hebrew] 2, 366). The first was perhaps written for his student in a workshop, who became a well-known poet. The poem "Order" (*Poems* [in Hebrew] 2, 370) is about Margot, the ex-lover of his friend Fred Sommers, who apparently visited Israel.

22. Nissim Calderon, "Wearing out" [in Hebrew], *Siman Kriah*, September 1972, 307-310.

23. Racheli Edelman interview, July 20, 2017; *Pi Ha'aton* interview, 71. Shimon Sandbank also discusses envy of Amichai's poetic success in a review of Amichai's *Behind All This*. Sandbank, "The Question of the Light Poem" [in Hebrew], *Siman Kriah* 12-13 (February 1981), 331-34.

24. As Amichai himself pointed out on the radio program *Galgal Hamazalot*: *A Literature and Culture Club* [in Hebrew], hosted by Dalia Amit and Shmuel Huppert (a live show with audience), October 2, 1975.

25. Mordechai Geldman's reading of "On Yom Kippur in 1967" is erroneous, in my opinion. He argues that the speaker sees the Arab shopkeeper as a kind of God, and compares the Jews who conquered East Jerusalem to the Nazis who brought about Amichai's father's flight from Germany (Geldman, "Keeping Far from the Western Wall" [in Hebrew], *Maariv*, January 31, 1997). Amichai was disgusted by the comparison of the Israeli army, with all its injustices, to the Nazis and the poem does not lend itself to this comparison. What does emerge directly from the poem is the attempt to get to know the shopkeeper by explaining the historical reasons that led to Jewish settlement (including that of the Pfeuffer family) in Palestine and the founding of the State of Israel. The poem thus advances a secular, Herzlian view of

Palestine as first and foremost a land of refuge, a shelter for persecuted Jewish communities, over and above claims of inherited rights to an ancestral land.

26. He wrote about this poem in his notebooks, after relating to the death in war of Lior, the poet Nathan Yonathan's son: "The function of a poem is to *destroy* reality with words and pictures. Not to react immediately but to establish important strongholds and outposts, from where one can gain control and return to the offensive: 'My child was weaned during the war' – both child and war (file 494)" (emphasis in original).

27. "Our baby was weaned during the first days / of the war [...] // And that's how, while he was still an infant, / his hopes closed and his complaints / opened – / never to close again."

28. In mentioning "the beautiful love letters" of "the quiet lover" which "burn," Amichai finds a way to unpack painful personal experiences unconnected to Jerusalem. A parallel image to the two "lovers" appears in poem 24 of the cycle.

29. See Chapter 11 on Amichai's relation to Hubi, who fell on this bridge. Despite the mention of Gethsemane (Gat Shemanim), the place where Judas Iscariot betrayed Jesus, the reference does not seem to be to the latter.

30. See the poem "On the Day My Daughter Was Born No One Died," *Selected Poetry*, 131; another translation, *Life of Poetry*, 324; *Poems* [in Hebrew] 3, 306. In an interview with *The Jerusalem Post,* September 28, 1981, he was asked if his daughter's name was testimony to what was left of his faith. His answer was decisive: "It's just a romantic name."

31. *Book of the Great Night* [in Hebrew] (Tel Aviv, 1988), 5. The name is pronounced with the stress on the last syllable [thus meaning "a Goddess is with us"]. Sarit Fuchs interview (with Emanuela), "Everything Is Still a Kind of Whirlwind" [in Hebrew], *Maariv-Sof Shavua*, January 26, 2001.

32. Meira – after his father's name "Meir." In Hebrew Meir-Meira means "He/She casts light."

33. Notebooks, file 505.

34. See the poem "How Do You Control a Wild Child?" *Poems* [in Hebrew] 3, 307, and passages in his notebooks (May 1975, September 27, 1975, January 1977, and elsewhere). Difficulties coping with Dadi also surface in the children's book he dedicated to him, which came out the same year, *Numa's Fat Tail,* 1978 (the fat tail refers to the drawn out process of the child's bedtime ritual). Amichai discussed his falling in love with rap music during a stay in the US with his whole family, and Dadi's connection to African-American teens in an interview with Shirli Yuval, "Words Absorb the Pain", *Olam Ha'iisha* 119 (September 1993): 84-88, 266.

35. "Daughter of My Old Age," *Poems* [in Hebrew] 4, 45.

36. Nahal, a program combining military service with founding or working in agricultural settlements (usually collective, like kibbutzim).

37. "And the Child Is No More," *Poetry*, 325; *Poems* [in Hebrew] 4, 61. Notes from Amichai's notebooks: "Now you [Roni] go up / again to Merom Hagalil [the name of a region, the upper Galilee]. / Again we speak / This clear language / (which doesn't) exist between / a father and his son." Unbound notebooks pages, 25.846.

38. "Almost a Love Poem," *Life of Poetry*, 356; *Poems* [in Hebrew] 4, 84.

39. "A Precise Woman," *Life of Poetry*, 363; other translations: *Selected Poetry*, 154 and *Poetry*, 333; *Poems* [in Hebrew] 4, 112. There is a certain ambiguity in the end of the poem. It's not entirely clear whether his shoes point to the bed or to his wife.

40. During their years of estrangement he would sometimes bump into her in his wanderings in the city, perhaps actively looking for her. According to notes in his notebooks from May 1975: "A stroll in my mother's neighborhood [...] My mother in the Old City, climbing steps." And from a later period: "Today I saw my mother at the Alba pharmacy. I doubt she saw me. She stayed there a while, not heading for the door but going further in, as if searching. I was with Dadi. I was afraid to approach her, in case something would happen to her; and for Dadi too, I was afraid." His mother died on the eve of the Shavuot holiday, on May 17, 1983. In the last months of her life Amichai would take his mother out for walks. Conversations with Aviva Sauer, widow of Amichai's nephew, Yigal, June 22, 2015, June 6, 2018; conversation with Dov Zahavi, widower of Hanna, Amichai's niece, July 2, 2016.

41. Poem 9 in the "My Son Was Drafted" cycle from *Open Closed Open*, *Poetry*, 518; *Poems* [in Hebrew] 5, 298. A note to this effect appears in his notebooks.

42. "My Mother's Death and the Lost Battles for the Future of the Children," *Life of Poetry*; *Poems* [in Hebrew] 4, 133.

43. "Last Conversations," *Poems* [in Hebrew] 4, 134.

44. "Oh, Ivy Growing," *Life of Poetry*, 367; *Poems* [in Hebrew] 4, 135.

45. "My Mother Once Told Me," from *Now in the Storm*, is in *Life of Poetry*, 107; *Poems* [in Hebrew] 2, 85. His mother's attitude to his leaving Tamar was gleaned from conversations with family members and acquaintances.

46. "My Mother on her Sickbed," *Life of Poetry*, 368, *Poetry*, 341; *Poems* [in Hebrew] 2, 85. After his mother's death Amichai fluctuated between "petty" calculations and anxieties nourished by magical thinking. Unbound notebooks entries, 30.1113.

47. Gerson Shaked was particularly impressed by Amichai's ability to blend "humor and poetry [...] Their conjunction borders on the impossible made possible, as it becomes clear that the metaphor has a poetic logic." Shaked, "A Journey of Stages" [in Hebrew], *Haaretz*, December 27, 1985. "Late Marriage," *Selected Poems*, 163-4, *Poetry*, 363; another translation, *A Life of Poetry*, 394; *Poems* [in Hebrew] 4, 202.

48. "From Man You Are and to Man You Shall Return," *Poetry*, 354, another translation, *Life of Poetry*, 384; *Poems* [in Hebrew] 4, 169.

49. "I Guard the Children," *Selected Poetry*, 165-166 [in Hebrew] 4, 176-177. Benny Ziffer in *Haaretz* was enthusiastic about the poem, and considered the end to depict "a dark political apocalypse." Ziffer, "From Man You Are and to Man You Shall Return, Poems" [in Hebrew], *Haaretz*, November 1, 1985.

50. "Jerusalem, 1985," *Selected Poetry*, 169; another translation, *Life of Poetry*, 385; *Poems* [in Hebrew] 4, 170. See article by Yaira Ginosar, "Couldn't Make it, I Hope You'll Understand" [in Hebrew], *Iton 77*, 72-73 (January-February, 1986): 28. The poem also caught the attention of Uri Sela in the weekly book review section of

Yediot Acharonot, "I Hope You'll Understand" [in Hebrew], November 15, 1985, and Haim Pesach, "Amichai at His Best" [in Hebrew], *Bamachane*, November 13, 1985.

51. Eyal Megged, "Yehuda Amichai: Facing the End You Become Simpler" [in Hebrew], *Yediot Acharonot*, November 8, 1985.

52. Yig'al Sarna, "He Got Tired of Jerusalem" [in Hebrew], *Chadashot*, November 8, 1985. Sarna found that Amichai had a quality popular among young people: a restrained, Yekke "lustiness." Amichai was indeed conscious in the interview that "my life is quite centered on sex. The relation of man and woman, attraction, love."

53. Shlomo Artzi, "Poems for All the Family" [in Hebrew], *Koteret Rashit*, November 27, 1985.

54. Meir Shalev, "Effort without Sweat" [in Hebrew], *Kol Ha'ir*, November 8, 1985.

55. Amichai sent a polite letter expressing his delight at having received the prize, but said that he could not attend the ceremony since he was in the US. From Amichai to Michali, November 3, 1975, Gnazim 53839/1. In fact, he took part in the ceremony which was held on April 29, 1976.

56. Zehavi interview, "Poetry as Revenge" [in Hebrew].

57. "Israel Prize for Hebrew Poetry" [in Hebrew], *Yediot Acharonot*, November 8, 1981.

58. The poet and journalist Moshe Ben-Shaul, in a note published on receiving news of the award, sought to emphasize that the *Likrat* group, which he and Amichai belonged to, had initially expressed a positive attitude towards Gilboa's early poetry. "Two Poetic Authorities" [in Hebrew], *Maariv*, November 13, 1981.

59. Gabriel Moked, "An Award for Great Poetry" [in Hebrew], *Yediot Acharonot*, November 13, 1981. Among those congratulating Amichai were Ruth and Azaria Rapaport (a well-known journalist at the time) who emphasized "the wonderful tension in which a unity of destiny [of the Jewish people] and continuity of heritage are expressed" in his poems. Jerusalem, November 8, 1981. 5.217.

60. Benny Ziffer, "Two Scales: Major and Minor" [in Hebrew], *Haaretz*, November 13, 1981. A similar preference for Gilboa was expressed in an article by a poet of the same age and generation as Gilboa, Avner Treinin. In his opinion, Gilboa had a rare ability to express identification with the collective "without it sounding like overblown rhetoric," while Amichai approached Zionist and national proclamations as a kind of "sad joke [. . .] preferring to skip repeatedly between weighty matters, to produce [technical] metaphors, to produce love." "Gilboa and Amichai – An Analysis of Elements" [in Hebrew], *Maariv*, April 30, 1982.

61. According to Dan Omer, a friend of Amichai's who reviewed the award ceremony, Gilboa had vetoed a plan to only have a poem by Amichai sung at the ceremony. Dan Omer, "On the Israel Prize Ceremony" [in Hebrew], *Kol Ha'ir*, April 30, 1982. Gabi (Gabriela), Gilboa's widow, claimed that Amichai blocked a plan for one of Gilboa's poems to be sung, and this may be more accurate. Conversation with Gabi Gilboa, November 26, 2017. In the Montenegro interview, 19, after Gilboa had died, Amichai avoided expressing an opinion about him.

62. "Huleikat – The Third Poem about Dicky," *Selected Poetry*, 179, *Poetry*, 372; another translation, *Life of Poetry*, 410; *Poems* [in Hebrew] 5, 14. Cf. "From Man

You Are," *Poetry*, 354, another translation, *Life of Poetry*, 384; *Poems* [in Hebrew] 4, 169.

63. "The Land Knows." Robert Alter translates as follows: "it's the nakedness of the land / it's the insatiable nakedness of the land" (*Poetry*, 405); another translation, *Life of Poetry*, 464; *Poems* [in Hebrew] 5, 134. The term *ervah* is indeed open to different readings, inflections and degrees of explicitness, and can be rendered as "female sexual organ," "a hidden place," or "a vulnerable part" (as when Joseph accused his brothers of coming to "see the land in its nakedness" in Genesis 42:12).

64. "Tel Gath," *Life of Poetry*, 409; *Poems* [in Hebrew] 5, 11.

65. The scholar Chana Kronfeld suggested that the critical Amichai, the one with strong reservations about the Zionist enterprise and the State of Israel, was in hiding, and that the camouflaged heretic hinted at in the poems needs to be released. Kronfeld, *Full Severity*, 103-108.

66. "I Am a Poor Prophet," *Life of Poetry*, 425; *Poems* [in Hebrew] 5, 61-62.

Chapter 14

Amichai's Last Volume of Poetry: the Eve of his Death and Posthumous Projects of Remembrance

LIFE'S CLOSED CORRIDOR, RELENTLESSLY LEADING

Reaching the age of 70 was doubtlessly a significant milestone in Amichai's journey, but his relationship with death was not new. He had always been in a romance with death, just as he was a great lover of life, in particular everything that had to do with the erotic, sex, and the female body[1]. In his frequently anthologized poem "A Pity. We Were a Good Invention," longing for a complete negation of life is associated with the ultimate and absolute erasure of pain, remorse and suffering in an eternal erotic union. In "The Body Is the Reason for Love," death is described as liberating the love imprisoned in the body, when finally, "like a broken slot machine," it "pours all at once, / with a roaring ring, all the coins / Of generations of luck."[2] The title of his last book, *Open Closed Open*, may provide some insights into the meaning of the spilling out of these coins: to live means being shut in, leading one's existence in a spiritual or psychological prison, while before and after this besieged and restricted life are infinite possibilities that are woven, disrupted and rewoven in the imagination.

Many years before he was diagnosed in the summer of 1998 with lymphoma, Amichai talked about himself in his poems as well as in conversations as someone who was close to death. Even in his autobiographical poem "Travels of the Last Benjamin of Tudela," which he wrote when he was 43, he was already anticipating the ultimate and decisive separation: "I've been patched together / from many things, I've been gathered in different times, / I've been assembled from spare parts [...] / And already now, / in the middle of my life, I'm beginning to return them, gradually." The poem ends: "I didn't kiss the ground / when they brought me as a little boy / to this land. But now that I've grown up on her, / she kisses me, / she holds me, / she clings to me with love, / with grass and thorns, with sand and stone, / with wars and with this springtime / until the final kiss."[3] In his book *From Man You Are*, his poems about his children are pervaded with a feeling that he does not have long to live with them. He writes metaphorically that "The pressure of my life brings my date of birth closer / to the date of my death, as in history books/ […] // I hold onto that hyphen with all my might, like a lifeline, I live on it".[4] He would remind his interviewers that he "live[s] with the dead": his father who continued to live inside him, so much so that his father would say the Yizkor memorial prayer for him while he was still alive;[5] Little Ruth, the heroine of his childhood who haunted his memories;[6] Dicky, his commander in the War of Independence; his student Yonatan Yahil, who fell in the Six Day War, and Ya'acov Buchman, "Hubi," in whose rucksack "they found a bloodstained book of my poems."[7] However, at the same time, he also proclaimed how fortified he was by happiness and a sense of wellbeing from being married to a woman fifteen years his junior, and being a father of young children.[8]

His trips with his wife and children to battle sites in the Negev desert, and to his parents' birthplaces in Germany in Bavaria and Hesse at the end of the 1980s and beginning of the 1990s, are commemorated in his two last volumes of poetry: "Tel Gat" and "My Child" in *A Fist, Too*, and "Jewish Travel," parts 8-12 of *Open Closed*. These were heritage trips of a sort. They were seen as his last, in the hope that the seeds scattered in the air of the battlefields of the Negev and the farmland of Bavaria would blossom in the hearts of the next generation.[9]

In the spring of 1998, when journalist and biographer Eilat Negev interviewed him, he was still smoking a pipe and joked that in the worst case scenario "he would only get cancer of the lips, and not the lungs."[10] This time as well he indulged in his self-image as "a happy man, one of those for whom life goes well," and presented himself as a model of "natural" and gradual aging: "it unfolds smoothly, without explosions." The Hebrew inscription "Amen," engraved on a stone on his desk, "a fragment of a gravestone, a remnant from the Jewish cemetery destroyed a thousand years ago in Würzburg," was an affirmation of his life "including the good and the bad."[11]

AMICHAI AT HIS PEAK IN ISRAEL AND THE WORLD

In the 1990s Amichai was at the height of his fame. Starting in the 1960s, high school students would typically try their hand at writing Amichai-type poetry and no small number of recognized poets followed in his footsteps[12]. Apart from Israeli composers and singers of light music (Moshe Wilensky, Moni Amarilio, Shlomo Artzi, Yehudit Ravitz, Shlomo Gronich, Hanan

Yovel and others), who wrote melodies to his poems, other composers also showed great interest. Tzvi Avni, who was initially charmed by Amichai's surrealism ("Collage – the Moon Hung from a Chain"), later composed music for his poem "Zedekiah's Cave," which was performed soon after the giant tunnel known as Solomon's Quarries was opened to the public.[13] Mark Kopytman, a modernist musician who immigrated to Israel from the Soviet Union in 1972, wrote one of his first works in Israel for Amichai's Yom Kippur War poems "October Sun" (based on poem 3 from "Songs of the Land of Zion and Jerusalem"/"Songs of Zion the Beautiful" cycle). For Koptyman, as for many other immigrants, Amichai's poems were the embodiment of Israeliness.[14] In 1983 the Israeli composer Shulamit Ran heard Amichai in Chicago reading his poems from a bilingual collection entitled *Love Poems*. She subsequently wrote a work based on them for Jan Degaetani, an American singer she admired, to the accompaniment of baroque instruments.[15]

In 1986, Boaz Arpali published *The Flowers and the Vase*, a comprehensive review of Amichai's poetry, followed by Glenda Abramson's study *The Writing of Yehuda Amichai: A Thematic Approach* in 1989.[16] Both books were based on doctoral dissertations, which reflect these authors' interest in elucidating the thematic, conceptual and stylistic aspects of Amichai's work. Amichai tended not to appreciate criticism or research on his work, and sometimes even ridiculed academics who looked for difficulties in poems which seemed straightforward to him.[17] Nevertheless, these books confirmed his status, which was rare among poets.

In 1994, Oxford University organized a conference on the initiative of his friend and colleague at the School for Overseas Students at the Hebrew University, Dr. Rivka Maoz, and Prof. Glenda Abramson, a lecturer in Hebrew literature at the University and a well-known researcher. The lectures dealt with a rich array of perspectives on his work, including the stylistic aspects of his poems and their translations, his dramas, prose and children's writings, and the impact of his work in the Arab world.[18] Israeli universities – and academic institutions in the US – flocked to confer honorary doctorates, as did the Hebrew University in 1990. When he received this honor from Tel Aviv University in 1995, he was asked to give the acceptance speech on behalf of all those awarded an honorary degree that year. This was his opportunity to settle the score with academia by combining inward self-deprecation and a sense of inferiority with the somewhat superior stance of an artist towards the perceived sterility of academia.[19]

In 1995, a 500-page comprehensive selection of his poetry entitled *Yehuda Amichai: A Life of Poetry, 1948-1994* was published in the United States and translated by his friend from the *Likrat* days, Prof. Benjamin Harshav, and his wife Barbara. Opinions as to the quality of the Harshavs' translations were mixed.[20] His poems, stories and novels have been translated into 37 languages, in most cases directly from Hebrew, but occasionally via English or French. The literary specialist Pu Hao wrote the first Chinese translation, based on English translations that was published to coincide with his visit to China in February 1993.[21] The prestigious Golden Wreath award which Amichai received in 1995 in Struga in Macedonia, was based on translations of his poems from French by well-known writers.[22] For years Amichai was a leading contender for the Nobel Prize for Literature. He wanted the prize, not least of all because of its monetary value, and many have argued that it was only the Swedish image of Israel as an occupier that prevented him from receiving the award.[23]

LAST BOOK OF POEMS: *OPEN CLOSED OPEN* AS A MIDRASHIC SUMMARY

Open Closed Open (1998) appeared nine years after Amichai's previous book. It contains more than 200 poems, arranged in 23 cycles. The title suggests that closure is a defining characteristic of life, since in life there is always an existential need to choose one path from among a plethora of others. Closure is perhaps also the result of the coerciveness of living by social norms, whereas everything before and after life can be seen as open and possible.[24]

According to a critic at the time, "readers did not wait for the critics' evaluation, and the book ranks seven on the *Haaretz* bestseller list."[25] Thus, there was still strong interest in Amichai's poetry.

Political crisis was at its peak at that time. The rollercoaster of the peace process had reached a high point, suggesting that an end to the Israeli-Palestinian conflict was in sight, and with it the Arab-Israeli conflict in general. Amichai and others were shocked by the assassination of Prime Minister Yitzhak Rabin in November 1995, and the wave of Palestinian suicide bombings in Israel.[26] However, there is almost nothing of this in the book, with the exception of a few indirect references in poem 13 of the cycle "In My Life, on My Life," where he asks former enemies to forge a relationship, without needing to love each other, to delay the outbreak of yet another war.[27] In another poem a tacit reference is made to the disastrous collision on February 4, 1997 of two IDF helicopters transporting 73 soldiers to the security zone in Lebanon.[28]

In keeping with his well-known stance, Amichai did not waste much time on fleeting political events. He apparently felt that he had written a scriptural work, a long midrashic story, in which he summarized his life by interpreting it, his thoughts, and all of his previous works anew. When writing these poems, Amichai had still not been diagnosed with his terminal illness, but in any case he was nearly always concerned with epilogues and preparations for the end. He may have been feeling the first twinges of cancer,[29] as in poem 10 of the "Israeli Travel" cycle he writes: "As for that math book: Now I've reached / the final pages [...] Now I check / where I was right and where I went wrong."[30]

Although superficially the volume could be misinterpreted as "a notebook full of drafts,"[31] it was planned to form a symphony, where each part restates one of the major themes Amichai dealt with throughout his life. It forcefully weaves recurring motifs from his poetry : "On my desk there is a stone with the word 'Amen' on it," and the suitcases on top of the wardrobe, ready for the final journey.[32] The volume starts with a theological section referencing a poem from a previous book about a humble message written out of love that contrast with pleas for help from Heaven pushed into the interstices of the Western Wall.[33] In various places he suggests how to create "a new religion"[34] that emerges in circumstances of great confusion, persistent searching, and conflicts between the major powers: "I go against the longings and the prayers [...] This could be the start of a new religion, / like striking a match to make fire" (poem 20 in the cycle "Jerusalem, Jerusalem, Why Jerusalem?"). "New religion" had positive connotations for him if only because of the attempt to resolve what is irresolvable in human experience.

The book is composed entirely of interpretive observations and reflections, based in part on reacquaintance with different sites encountered on walks, and rereadings of earlier poems (poems 1 and 2 in the cycle "Once I Wrote Now and in Other Days," poem 4 in the cycle "My Parents' Lodging Place," and poem 5 in the cycle "Evening Promenade on Valley of the Ghosts Street,"[35] in which he goes back to a poem in *A Fist, Too*), new reflections on earlier periods of his life such as his childhood in Germany (poem 5 of the "In My Life, on My Life" cycle, poems 14-15 of the "Names, Names" cycle), his childhood and adolescence in Palestine and then Israel, and the songs he absorbed at that time (poems 5-8 in the "Israeli Travel" cycle), the period of the War of Independence and the sites of battles where he fought (poems 4-9 in the cycle "What Has Always Been," poems 3-4 in the cycle "In My Life, On My Life," poems 15-16 in the cycle "Israeli Travel"), significant people in his life (in the "Names, Names" cycle), the development of his relationship with Hana (the cycle "Houses (Plural), Love (Singular)" while together violating sacrosanct norms by having sexual relations in "the Forest of Remembrance for the Shoah Dead" (poems 9-10 of the "Summer and the Far End of Prophecy").

The book was received much better in the US than in Israel. The literary specialists and translators Chana Kronfeld and Chana Bloch considered the book to be Amichai's magnum opus, written when he was "at the peak of his powers, and increasingly conscious of his role as a mediator of cultural memory."[36] In Israel, this book, like its predecessors since *Now in the Storm*, was rejected by some critics.[37]

Nevertheless, Amichai was a favorite with Israelis from all walks of life, including those for whom poetry was not generally part of their lives. He was considered the de facto national poet, and a go-to source for striking poetic lines recited at times of joy and sorrow. Almost every week his poems were read at Israeli weddings and funerals.[38] Secular Israelis saw him as a symbol of liberalism and normalcy,[39] while for the religious he was a poet of dialogue with Jewish spiritual worlds. Even his overt atheism did not seem to significantly transgress the legitimate limits of wonder at the ways of the Creator.

DIAGNOSIS OF CANCER AND THE LAST TWO YEARS

In the summer of 1998, Amichai was invited to be a guest lecturer at Baruch College in New York City. He also intended to work with Kronfeld and Bloch to translate *Open Closed Open*. Both were old friends: Kronfeld was a literary scholar who had long focused on his work, and Bloch had done an excellent translation with Stephen Mitchell of *The Selected Poetry of Yehuda Amichai* (1986, expanded edition 1996). However he was diagnosed with cancer in New York and remained there a whole year for treatment. On his return to Israel, though exhausted, the journalist Edna Evron noted after interviewing him that "his mental and emotional faculties and fine sense of humor were intact."[40] Despite his weakness, he conveyed optimism, at least in public, about his condition. "Now I feel better [...] the main thing is I got out of there," he told Evron.[41]

In more intimate contexts he could not conceal that his illness was terminal. At a certain point he was confined to a wheelchair, needed a caregiver, and eating was difficult.[42] Contrary to expectations of a man who thought that a true poet knows when to die,[43] he did not accept the approaching end stoically. David Ehrlich was with him on several occasions during his last year. Ehrlich had at one time been a journalist, and had published some biographical articles about Amichai, whom he revered. He later opened the literary restaurant Tmol Shilshom in Jerusalem. Amichai encouraged him and read there several times. Now, when close to death, he asked him to help proofread the manuscript of a collection of translations of his poetry Hughes had prepared before his death in 1998.[44] It was difficult for Amichai to read, and Ehrlich read the English text out loud. Amichai had no comments on the translations, perhaps because he considered translation to be an independent form of work, but he did tell Ehrlich stories about the background to a number of the poems, as he often did in his poetry workshops. Ehrlich remembered Amichai crying wholeheartedly on several occasions, but not out of self pity.[45]

When writers and researchers were asked what Amichai would be remembered for, and what made his poetic presence so significant to Israeli culture ("Amichai and Us"), the novelist Meir Shalev responded that "it was because of the Bible." He thought that Amichai interpreted the Bible in the full sense of the word, and found "amazing" perspectives, such as seeing the angel who struggled with Jacob as a woman, or giving Abraham another son, Yivke ("he will weep", in addition toYitzchak, "he will laugh"). Literary scholar Menachem Perry believed it was "the images," which were original and surprising. The writer David Grossman said that Amichai's poetry "accompanies me in almost all of life's circumstances," that lines of his poems "have become part of my inner speech," and that his poetry about Jerusalem enabled him "to love this insufferable and fanatical city." The writer A. B. Yehoshua recalled his trips with Amichai in Jerusalem on his motorbike in the early 1960s.[46] The writer Sami Michael mentioned the Arab woman and the residents of Haifa, the Arab protagonist of his novel *Trumpet in the Wadi,* who often quote Amichai as an expression of her Israeliness. He explained Amichai's magic as follows: "He was a humanist more than an ideologue." Likewise, literary scholar Gershon Shaked saw Amichai's greatest contribution as having "depatheticized" Hebrew poetry, "by virtue of his humor and understatement."[47]

Amichai's last wish was to revisit three places connected to his acculturation as an Israeli in his youth. He had close ties with Meir Shalev, whose father Yitzhak Shalev, a well-known poet and writer of his time, had awarded him his first prize as a young poet. His friendship with Meir began when Shalev was staying at Mishkenot Sha'ananim in 1987 to write *A Russian Novel*, which would be translated into many languages – in English as *The Blue Mountain* – and make him popular internationally.[48] When Meir spoke at an evening held in honor of the ailing Amichai, the poet was impressed that Meir "travels the country and knows its paths and places." He asked him to take him to "some landscapes that I want to say goodbye to [...]. One trip is to Michvar Observation Point (Mitzpeh Michvar) in the Judean Desert, where I once went on a mission with the Palmach."[49]

To prepare for the trip, Shalev loaded his truck with "a chair and a mat, in case my passenger wanted to sit down or lie down," and writer and journalist Leon Wieseltier, who had come from the US, went with them. When Amichai got out of the vehicle and Shalev supported him, "I felt his body, so light and with so little flesh." The second trip was to areas near the Gat and Galon kibbutzim with his wife Hana, where Amichai had taken part in battles during the War of Independence (see Chapter 5). When they returned to the neighborhood where Amichai lived, "Hana brought the wheelchair, and I carried Amichai in my arms to it [...] I sat him in the chair, and when I wanted to straighten my back, I felt his weak arms wrapped around my neck in a hug [...] our faces were very close to one another. He told me: "Meir, before today we were friends. Let's decide that from now on it's love." The third trip, to Moshav Sde Ya'akov, where family members on his father's side lived, and where he would sometimes go work in the fields on summer holidays when he was at school, never came to pass.[50]

Amichai left instructions for the preparation of his body in a well-known poem from *Open Closed* which were both humorous and entirely serious: "When I die, I want only women to handle me in the Chevra Kadisha / and to do with my body as they please: cleanse my ears of the last / words I heard [...] / and fold my arms across my chest like sleeves of a shirt after ironing. /[...] and arrange in my pelvic basin like in a fruit bowl / testes and penis, navel and frizzy hair / [...] / and then with a feather tickle my mouth-hole and asshole to check / if I'm still alive."[51] In Amichai's world, death and life are one; life after death is real, just as life before death is only apparent; in death, the poet sought to maintain sensual contact with women from whom he had derived so much pleasure during his life.

AFTER HIS DEATH

The funeral took place at a time when hopes for peace had not yet faded. Amichai died on the eve of the Sabbath, on Friday, September 22, 2000 at Hadassah hospital. His coffin, draped in the Israeli flag, lay in state for the next two days in Safra Square at the Jerusalem City Hall.[52] Echoes of misgivings about Arafat's unclear manouvers in negotiations over the peace process between Israel and the Palestinians were evident in the eulogies given by representatives of the government and the army. Prime Minister Ehud Barak repeated Shimon Peres' comment that Amichai's poetry had "trained hearts for the great reconciliation between the Israelis and the Palestinians." Barak related to Jerusalem in Amichai's poetry: "There is no city so fitting for Amichai as Jerusalem: the city of peace and the center of conflict [...] in which one can achieve the impossible."[53] Perhaps the best at describing the "Amichai impact" on Israeli society was columnist Doron Rosenblum in "Citizen Number One," published on the day of the funeral where he wrote that lines by Amichai naturally pop up in conversation, in articles, in many songs; Amichai had penetrated the "collective unconscious" of Israelis.[54]

From Safra Square his coffin was transported to the small Sanhedria cemetery where he was buried alongside his parents. More than a year after his death a headstone was erected, constructed of two joined stones, "in the form of a wave at sea without beginning and without end," designed by Moshe Safdie.[55] Lines from Amichai float on it: "Even death does not separate but brings us to a renewed encounter which has no end in the universe."

To honor Amichai, the Education Ministry and Jerusalem Municipality established the "Amichai Prize" for poetry in 2001. The prize money is 60,000 shekels (about $17,000), quite a large sum, similar to that of the Israel Prize, but is generally divided between two recipients. For the first time the prize was given to two women: Agi Mishol, Amichai's one-time student, who had maintained a close relationship with him, and the poet Shin Shifra.[56]

When Agi Mishol was taking Amichai's first poetry workshops, he recognized her talent and gave her his translations of Else Laske-Schüller, which she said influenced her poetic development, as did the poet-translator himself. Awarding the prize to her was in a sense closing the circle. In 2014 Erez Biton won the award. This prepared the groundwork for later awarding him the prestigious Bialik and Israel prizes.

IN LIEU OF AN EPILOGUE: AUTO-POETICS

Theory was not Amichai's strong point. On occasion he said he disliked dealing too much with poetics or the ideology of poetic practice in his poetry. Nevertheless, when still a young poet he published short articles on the subject. These, along with later talks and interviews, provide some insights into his perspective on the nature of his poetry.

Amichai liked to emphasize what he had learned in the Egyptian desert, when he came across the poetry of the new generation of British and American poets in the anthology he found on the ground beside an overturned mobile library abandoned in the sand. When reading Auden, Eliot, Pound, and other modernists, he discovered "what European languages had been through, two or three decades earlier, a process of disrobing themselves of their finery, of lofty expression, adopting everyday language as a legitimate poetic medium."[57] He said in the same interview that "I write simply, for me poems aren't verbal expressions of poetic theories but describe what's around me."

Amichai thought in democratic terms about poetry as well as society, politics and ontology. This egalitarian attitude may have been rooted in the rebellious nature of the son of a wandering peddler, the grandson of farmers, against a hierarchical class society of the sort he knew in the Jewish community of the German city of his birth. In interviews and lectures throughout his life he would state that "There is a poet in hiding in everyone, but not everyone takes the trouble to dig down and draw out the poetry hidden inside."[58] He thought that the poetry within people is manifested in what they write in their diaries, letters, and express in prayers. Poetry can be found everywhere, spilling out of children's pronouncements, in intimate and heartfelt phrases, in lovers' whispers.

In his own version of the approach already voiced by different modernist trends (Acmeism in Russia, Imagism in the US and Britain, New Objectivity – Neue Sachlichkeit – in Germany), he spoke in detail about the seemingly serendipitous objects populating his poetry, claiming that they bore witness to the truth, the truth of the soul, more than any more systematic description.[59]

It might seem paradoxical that he told his interviewer Doron Weber that "I'm crazy about exactitude," but exactitude was a shield against hackneyed and cloying expressions of emotionality, which he hated, and "tedious tracts of half-abstract philosophy." He considered Eliot's "Four Quartets," to be an example of great poetry and called it a "sermon." "Eliot uses a lot of real things," materials from external reality. He felt that the philosophy in this work was superficial, but "that's actually how it should be. Poetry should never be a kind of new way in thinking. It should be very old ways in thinking, but newly told."[60] When the interviewer reminded him of a line from one of his poems where he urges the lover to "remember some details" before his lover's face disappears, Amichai responded: "Yes [...] The details keep the memory and the ideas alive. And they keep the spirit alive." He recalled a lecture given by Vladimir Nabokov in the US on Russian literature. Nabakov asked those present what Anna Karenina wore. The listeners were disappointed; they wanted a talk full of ideas and attitudes. Amichai thought that Anna's dress was the repository of an idea and an atmosphere.

In his opinion, building poetry around concrete details was related to the way it emerged: the details help rememember lines of poetry as was done before the invention of writing. "You just think about a blue stocking or a green stocking and then you have a whole night of love in it": the green stocking was a secret code, in Amichai's playful terms that captured his penchant for far-fetched analogies that mixed humor with serious intention.[61] Amichai's autopoetics brings to mind similar stances in other modernist outlooks. Thus, beyond their differences in style, artistic movement and tendency, great poets echo one another in striving to reveal the eternal in the transient and the concrete.

NOTES

1. He still ascribed ultimate importance to love in his last interview, with Avirama Golan. https://www.youtube.com/watch?v=9BoF_nqh_WU

2. "A Pity. We Were a Good Invention," *Penguin Book of Hebrew Verse*, 568; other translations, *Selected Poetry*, 57, *Life of Poetry*, 101, *Poetry*, 104; *Poems* [in Hebrew], 2, 69. "The Body Is the Cause of Love," *Selected Poetry*, 162; another translation, *Life of Poetry*, 370; *Poems* [in Hebrew] 4, 141.

3. "Travels of the Last Benjamin of Tudela", *Selected Poetry*, 76, 86; other translations, *Life of Poetry*, 177, 188; *Poetry*, 127, 139; *Poems* [in Hebrew] 2, 142, 158.

4. "Late Marriage," *Poetry*, 363, *Selected Poetry*, 163; another translation, *Life of Poetry*, 394; *Poems* [in Hebrew] 4, 202; "My Little Girl Looks," *Poetry*, 349; *Poems* [in Hebrew] 4, 185. The headline for Amichai's interview with Eyal Meged for the launching of *From Man You Are* was: "Towards the End You Become Simpler," *Yediot Acharonot*, November 8, 1985.

5. "My Birthday," *Poems* [in Hebrew] 3, 129.

6. "Now and then, I remember you in times / Unbelievable. And in places not made for memory." "Little Ruth," *Life of Poetry*, 431; *Poems* [in Hebrew] 5, 69-70. See Chapters 1 and 2.

7. On Dicky, see Chapter 5; on Yonatan Yahil, Chapter 11; on Hubi see Chapter 13.

8. Interviews with Edna Evron and with Eilat Negev, see following notes.

9. On the trips, see interview with Edna Evron, "National Poet? That's All I Need"; "In Our Love," hosted by Tzipi Gon-Gross, with members of Amichai's family and others in his life [in Hebrew], Army Radio, April 19, 2011.

10. "Truth Guaranteed" [in Hebrew], *Yediot Acharonot – 7 Yamim*, March 23, 2001; based on the interview "The Secular Prophet" [in Hebrew], *Yediot Acharonot*, April 3, 1998.

11. On the origin of the twelfth-century stone in the Jewish cemetery in Würzburg, see note 32 below.

12. Naomi Gutkind noted that "it's difficult to find apprentice poets who escape the tendency to write about 'big things' in everyday terms, in the style of Amichai." When she put this to him, the poet responded modestly that: it is "quite understandable [...] that when a young person begins to write – he doesn't yet have his own style. He holds onto those with an identifiable style, and who are easy to imitate." The interviewer: "Why are they influenced by you and not, or less so, by other well-known poets of your generation?" Amichai: "I like to define myself by what is around me, by things close to me [...] and I write about these things without sophistry, word games, or complicated rhymes, without obscure or complicated images." Gutkind, "The Poet, Criticism and the Readership" [in Hebrew], *Hatzofeh*, November 20, 1981.

13. Avni interview, January 14 and 28, 2015. In his opinion, Amichai's poems have a graphic quality that kindles the imagination. In the music for "Zedekiah's Cave" Avni wanted to mimic the dripping sounds evoked in "In deepest Jerusalem, shafts and graves, caves and holes." The poem was published in *Maariv* on May 2, 1986 and is not in the collected works.

14. Assaf Shelleg, *Jewish Contiguities and the Soundtrack of Israeli History* (New York 2014, 196-198).

15. Conversation with Shulamit Ran, December 1, 2015.

16. Boaz Arpali, *The Flowers and the Vase* [in Hebrew] (Tel Aviv 1986); Glenda Abramson, *The Writing of Yehuda Amichai: A Thematic Approach* (New York 1989).

17. An offended letter addressed to him on January 9, 1987 (1.48) by Boaz Arpali testifies to this, as well as Glenda Abramson (September 1, 2016). Amichai satirized literary scholarship in his radio play *Killing Him* (first published in *Yerushalayim*

7-8, edited by Yehuda Haezrachi and Shulamit Hareven (Jerusalem 5733 [1972-3], 101-132). The play expresses his half serious belief that literary scholars wanted him dead, or anyway wished for the death of the writer they wrote about, so that they could finally summarize his oeuvre. See Gutkind interview, "The Poet, Criticism and the Readership."

18. Written versions of these lectures appear in *The Experienced Soul*, edited by Glenda Abramson (Boulder, 1997). Longer versions of some were published in Hebrew. Nili Scharf Gold reviewed the conference in "An International Conference in Honor of Yehuda Amichai at Oxford: Impressions" [in Hebrew], *Hadoar*, May 9, 1994, 19-21. Another source: conversation with Rivka Maoz, October 29, 2014.

19. "Poetry Is the Language of the Soul" [in Hebrew], *Haaretz*, June 2, 1995.

20. While the book sold 6,000 copies in less than a year some criticized the quality of the rhymes. A writer for the *Forward* found that some of the translations were poor, lacked elegance, and complained, as others did, that the book needed an index and an introduction. M. Tarnopolsky, "Visiting the Poet of Jerusalem," *Forward*, March 24, 1995.

21. See Ricky Rivlin, "Amichai in Chinese" [in Hebrew], *Maariv,* January 29, 1993; Irit Hameiri, "Reciting Amichai in Chinese and Japanese" [in Hebrew], *Yediot Acharonot*, March 10, 1992.

22. See Irit Hameiri, "Europe Embraces Amichai" [in Hebrew], *Yediot Acharonot*, September 15, 1995; conversation with Vivian Eden, who was with Amichai when he received the prize, June 10, 2017. Amichai consistently stated that translators' failure to hear the echoes of the Jewish sources in his poems did not bother him: "I think that my poems can be understood on an emotional level by people from diverse traditions." Interview with *Urim v'Tumim*, Winter 1991, 27.

23. Sa'ar Dayan, in an article published when Amichai died, quoted Gershon Shaked, who felt that "political considerations" prevented Amichai from receiving the award; Natan Zach pointed to "a series of poets far inferior to Amichai" who had received the prize in recent years. Gabriel Moked argued that "there is no better poet in the second half of the century." Dayan, "We Lost One of the Greats of World Poetry," *Maariv*, September 24, 2000. See also Karpel interview, "Hoping for the Nobel" [in Hebrew].

24. Other readings of the title were suggested by Zehavi, and Kronfeld and Bloch in the articles cited below.

25. Alex Zehavi, "Pondering the Presence of God" [in Hebrew], *Eretz Aheret,* June 1998, 56. Shulamit Gilboa, in an article published after Amichai's death, when the book had a revival, stated that it was on the bestseller lists "even while he was alive. Not in first place, and not for long, but nevertheless." Gilboa, "Love of Amichai" [in Hebrew], *Yediot Acharonot*, November 12, 2000.

26. Amichai's eulogy for Yitzhak Rabin on the *sheloshim* (30 days after death), "Living History" [in Hebrew], *Yediot Acharonot – 24 Sha'ot*, December 5, 1995. Collected in *Who You Love, Isaac* [in Hebrew], (Tel Aviv 20;05), 44.

27. In various interviews and articles, he advanced the idea of deferring war instead of cultivating a messianic hope for eternal peace. In a television interview with Ram Evron he said: "I believe in peace so much, in postponing the next war

[...] if we make of peace too many demonstrations and hallelujahs and hugs, then people will lose patience and begin a new war. If we postpone the next war – then sublime things will come as a matter of course." Ram Evron, "In the First Person" [in Hebrew], Israeli Television, May-June [?] 1998. He repeated this idea in his poems throughout his life. For example: "In My Life, On My Life" (poem 13) *Poetry*, 481, *Open Closed Open: Poems*, trans. Chana Bloch and Chana Kronfeld (New York: Harcourt, 2000), 112 [appearing as poem 12].

28. Poem 4 in the cycle "And Who Will Remember the Rememberers?" *Open Closed Open*, 170 [appearing as poem 5], *Poetry*, 524. Amichai read this poem on a TV program to mourn the lost soldiers and kindled "great emotion" in writer and publicist Meir Shalev. Meir Shalev, "Thought in Tatters" [in Hebrew], *Yediot Acharonot*, February 7, 1997.

29. Amichai told Irit Hameiri, writer of the "Third Ear" column, on the eve of the publication of the book: "The poems give no indication of my age. There were poems about death in my first books." Hameiri, "Yehuda Amichai, a New Book (and Surprises) After Nine Years" [in Hebrew], *Yediot Acharonot*, March 27, 1998. Thirteen years earlier, in interviews marking the publication of *From Man You Are*, he spoke about himself in terms of the approaching end. David Avidan, a famous poet and a scathing critic, was suspicious at the time that this was a gimmick. Avidan, "Just Don't Disappear on Us, Yehuda" [in Hebrew], *Yediot Acharonot,* October 27, 1985.

30. *Poetry*, 453, *Open Closed Open* (appearing as poem 6), 71. Similarly in poem 12 of "In My Life, on My Life" cycle in *Open Closed Open* [appearing as poem 11], and poem 5 of "I Wasn't One of the Six Million" cycle: "my [...] eyebrows black, like the charred lintels / above the windows in a house that burned down. / My life span is over." *Poetry*, 492, *Open Closed Open*, 6.

31. Yitzhak Laor, "And he Didn't Have Time" [in Hebrew], *Haaretz*, June 5, 1998.

32. The stone with the engraved "Amen" is a fragment from a 12th century Jewish cemetery uncovered in Würzburg in 1987, when a monastery was demolished in the town center to make room for a new building. Hundreds of Jews murdered during the Second Crusade were buried there. In the 14th century the Jewish community of Würzburg was destroyed (during the plague) after which the local Christian population would sometimes make use of the gravestones for building purposes. The stone was sent to Amichai by his friend, theology professor Karlheinz Müller, who dedicated many years of his life to deciphering the inscriptions on desecrated gravestones and preserving them. See Avraham Reiner, "Fragment Upon Fragment: Finds from the Jewish Cemetery of Würzburg" [in Hebrew], *Zmanim* 95 (2006): 52-57.

33. "Jerusalem, 1985," *Selected Poetry*, 169, another translation, *Life of Poetry*, 385; *Poems* [in Hebrew] 4, 170.

34. Cf. "A Great Tranquility," *Poetry*, 305, *Selected Poetry*, 142; another translation, *Life of Poetry*, 339; *Poems* [in Hebrew] 3, 274.

35. Emek Refaim, a commercial street in current day Jerusalem; the literal meaning of the name is "Valley of the Ghosts."

36. Chana Bloch and Chana Kronfeld, "Amichai's Counter-Theology: Opening *Open Closed Open*," *Judaism* 49, no. 2 (2000): 153.

37. Yitzhak Laor, "And He Didn't Have Time". Shimon Sandbank's review was somewhat reserved. Sandbank, "Longing for What Is Open" [in Hebrew], *Yediot Acharonot*, April 24, 1998.

38. Negev interview, "I am a Happy Man": "Every week I hear the same thing, [that my poems are recited] at funerals as at weddings". This is confirmed in many letters preserved in his archives. Some dedicated their own poems to him, others made him the hero of their poems, and still others in Israel and abroad sought his opinion of their work.

39. In Zionist thought, Jews in the Diaspora, who had suffering persecution and humiliation as a weak minority throughout history, were considered to have been turned into weaklings who could only recover and achieve normality by having a land and state of their own.

40. Edna Evron interview, "National Poet? That's All I Need".

41. He made the same comment to Yossi Langotsky when they met on his return at the Jerusalem Theater. Conversation with Yossi Langotsky, October 15, 2017.

42. Conversation with David Ehrlich, June 12, 2017; Meir Shalev, "Farewell" [in Hebrew], 229.

43. This view can be seen for example in his poem "Leah Goldberg Died": "The professor in her was / perhaps ready to live many years more. / But the poet did not want / to grow old, and won out." "Leah Goldberg Died," *Poetry*, 185; *Poems* [in Hebrew] 2, 290-291. See also a late poem where he compares the rewards of love with those of death, which is given to a man or woman in recompense for the work of his/her life. Poem 6 in the cycle "I Foretell the Days of Yore," *Open Closed Open* [poem 5 in this edition], 12; *Poetry*, 437; *Poems* [in Hebrew], 5, 186.

44. In the introduction to *Selected Poems*, Hughes expresses his esteem for Amichai and for the Zionist revival that permeated his life and work. Yehuda Amichai, *Selected Poems*, edited by Ted Hughes and Daniel Weissbort, (London 2000), xiii.

45. Conversation with David Ehrlich, June 12, 2017.

46. Conversation, November 24, 2015. Yehoshua ("Bulli") defined his relationship to Amichai in a letter to Amichai of December 6, 1989: "You are turning into a kind of Bialik for me. I pick up a book of your poems and say – this is it. This is familiar and right, poetry after my own heart."

47. Interview with Edna Evron, "National Poet? That's All I Need" [in Hebrew].

48. Conversation with Meir Shalev, July 10, 2017.

49. Amichai's strong connection to the Judean Desert, from his time in the Palmach and perhaps even when he was in high school, was almost certainly one of the reasons for initiating a joint endeavor with the Swiss immigrant Franz Wieler that led to a book of photos accompanied by poems, *Open Eyed Land* [in Hebrew-English-German] (Schocken, Jerusalem and Tel Aviv, 1992); see interview with Ronny Someck, "The Judean Desert is the Landscape of My Soul" [in Hebrew], *Yediot Acharonot*, February 7, 1992. His connection to the desert may have even deeper roots: the desert was a vast expanse that enabled concentration, contrary to the confusion and mystical obfuscation he hated. For his rejection of mysticism, see interview with Joseph Cohen, 31.

50. Meir Shalev, "Farewell" [in Hebrew].

51. Poem 14 of the "In My Life, on My Life" cycle, *Open Closed Open* [in this edition poem 13], 113; *Poetry*, 481-2; *Poems* [in Hebrew] 5, 249-250.

52. Apart from the coffins of fallen members of the IDF, only important leaders are draped in the flag of the State. Two thousand people took part in the funeral procession. *Haaretz* journalist Avi Katzman had the impression that there were just a few hundred: "A few people who came perhaps to say goodbye to him." Katzman, "Jerusalem Bids Farewell to its Innocence" [in Hebrew], *Haaretz*, September 29, 2000. Arik Bender in *Maariv* saw "a large crowd." "The Poet Is Dead, His Poems Live." *Maariv*, September 25, 2000.

53. Sagi Green, "In Amichai's Jerusalem One Can Resolve Conflict, Said Barak Beside the Coffin," *Haaretz*, September 25, 2000.

54. Doron Rosenblum, "Citizen Number One" [in Hebrew], *Haaretz*, September 24, 2000.

55. Moshe Safdie, "Headstone on Yehuda Amichai's Grave" [in Hebrew], *Haaretz*, January 4, 2001.

56. Conversation with Agi Mishol, June 23, 2017. Shiri Lev Ari, "The Yehuda Amichai Prize to Shin Shifra and to Agi Mishol" [in Hebrew], *Haaretz,* December 26, 2001. See also Agi Mishol, "The Soundtrack of Our Lives in This Country" [in Hebrew], *Yediot Acharonot,* August 30, 2002; Amira Lam, "The Successor" [in Hebrew], *Yediot Acharonot – 7 Yamim,* September 2, 2007.

57. Gutkind interview, "The Poet, Criticism and the Readership," after the announcement that Amichai was to be awarded the Israel Prize. The formulation here is Gutkind's, but expresses Amichai's intention.

58. Ibid.

59. Weber interview, 45-46.

60. Ibid., 47.

61. Amichai was so intent on his "theory of objects" that when audiences asked him if there was any essential difference between poems written in different historical periods, he replied that the difference was only in the materials provided by external reality that poetry represents. However, he baulked at committing to this rather superficial response, and hinted with humor at changes in stylistic convention: images appearing in the Song of Songs such as "Your nose is like the tower of Lebanon" would not today be considered compliments.

Bibliography

PRIMARY SOURCES

Collected Poetry in Hebrew

Amichai, Yehuda. *Shirei Yehuda Amichai [Poems of Yehuda Amichai]*. 5 volumes. Jerusalem and Tel Aviv: Schocken Publishing House, 2004.

Non-Canonic Poetry

Pugacz, Itzhak and Yehuda Amichai. *Picture and Poem*. Jerusalem: Bialik Institute, 1970. [in Hebrew]

Wieler, Franz and Yehuda Amichai. *Open Eyed Land, Poems: Yehuda Amichai, Photographs: Franz Wieler*. Jerusalem and Tel Aviv: Schocken Publishing House, 1991. [Hebrew/ English/ German]

Bilingual Editions

Amichai, Yehuda. *Shirei Ahava – Love Poems*. Various translators. Jerusalem and Tel Aviv: Schocken Publishing House, 1986.

Amichai, Yehuda. *Poems of Jerusalem*, Jerusalem and Tel Aviv: Schocken Publishing House, 1987.

Amichai, Yehuda. *Od Shirei Ahava – More Love Poems*. Various translators. Jerusalem and Tel Aviv: Schocken Publishing House, 1994.

Amichai, Yehuda. *Caesarea and One Love*. Translated by Barbara and Benjamin Harshav. Jerusalem and Tel Aviv: Schocken Publishing House, 1996.

Anthologies in English

Amichai, Yehuda. *Yehuda Amichai: A Life of Poetry, 1948-1994*. Translated by Benjamin and Barbara Harshav. New York: HarperCollins Publishers, 1994.

Alter, Robert, ed., *The Poetry of Yehuda Amichai*. New York: Farrar, Straus and Giroux, 2015.

Prose Works

Amichai, Yehuda. *Baruach Hanora'a Hazoth* [In This Terrible Wind], (first edition: Sifriyat Poalim, 1961; first Schocken edition, 1973). Selected English translation: *The World is a Room*, Translated by Elinor Grumet et al., Philadelphia, 1984.

Amichai, Yehuda. *Lo Meachshav, Lo Mikan [Not of This Time, Not of This Place]*. Translated by Shlomo Katz. New York: Harper & Row, 1963, 1968, 1973.

Amichai, Yehuda. *Mi Yitneni Malon [Hotel in the Wilderness]*, Tel Aviv: Bitan, 1971.

Collection of Plays

Amichai, Yehuda. *Paamonim ve-Rakavot [Bells and Train]*. Jerusalem and Tel Aviv: Schocken, 1968; Expanded edition: 1992.

Articles and Talks authored by Yehuda Amichai (in chronological order)

Foreword to Flowers of Perhaps, Selected Poems of Ra'hel, translated by Robert Friend. London, 1955.

"The Blue Piano." [on Else Lasker-Schüler]. *LaMerhav/Masa*, January 1, 1958. [in Hebrew]

"Writers on Their Projects and Vocation." *Haaretz*, September 21, 1960. [in Hebrew],

"Journey in the Map of the Past." *Bamachane*, January 2, 1962, 10-11. [in Hebrew]

"Return to the City of Childhood," *Bamachane*, June 5, 1962. [in Hebrew]

"How I Wrote No Man's Land." *Haaretz*, November 2, 1962. [in Hebrew],

"Thoughts in Seven Paragraphs about Agnon." *Bitzaron 28*, 2 (Kislev-Tevet 5727 [December 1966-January 1967]): 91-93. [in Hebrew],

"Notes on Agnon." *Midstream*, XII: 2, February 1967: 12-15.

"Impressions of Spoleto." *Bitzaron 28*, 3, Shvat-Adar 5727 [February-March 1967]: 170-177. [in Hebrew]

"A Festival in Spoleto." *LaMerhav/Masa*, October 4, 1967. [in Hebrew],

"Generations in the Land." Speech for the Writers' Union annual conference, published in LaMerhav/Masa, May 3, 1968.

"Postcards from Jerusalem." *Midstream*, January 1968, 26-31.

"Words to Agnon." *Haaretz*, August 2, 1968. [in Hebrew]

"Diary." *Moznaim* 1, 29, June 1969. [in Hebrew],

Acceptance speech for the Brenner Prize, 1969. In *Crown of Thorns: Writers' Words in the Brenner Prize Ceremonies*, edited by Nurit Govrin and Rachel Stepak, 108, Tel Aviv, 2017. [in Hebrew]

"Sobre la fresca tumba de Natán Alterman." Translated into Spanish by Simcha Sneh. *Raices*, Buenos Aires, April 17, 1970.

Introduction to Hubi [Yaakov Eilam], *Letters to You*. Tel Aviv, 1970, expanded edition published by *Yediot Acharonot*, 1997, 6-7. [in Hebrew]

"Living Reality." *Yediot Acharonot*, November 30, 1973. [in Hebrew],

Foreword to *Lea Goldberg: Selected Poems*. Translated by Robert Friend. London, 1976.

"Yehuda Amichai." In *Mein Judentum*, edited by Hans Jürgen Schultz, 20-35. Stuttgart-Berlin, 1978.

"Agnon and I." *Yediot Acharonot*, December 17, 1978. [in Hebrew],

"Memories from Israel." *Diversion*, May 1986.

"A Divided Soul." *Yediot Acharonot*, December 26, 1997. [in Hebrew]

"Every man is born a poet." Draft for a talk [1995? 1998?], archival origin unknown.

SECONDARY SOURCES

Biographical Background

Avidar, Tamar. "Against the Government." *Maariv*, March 28, 1962. [in Hebrew],

Amichai, Hana. "Little Ruth is my Private Anne Frank." *Haaretz*, August 8, 2010. [in Hebrew]

Avron-Barak, Noa. "The Mashkof Group, 1968-1970." MA diss., Tel Aviv University, 2015. [in Hebrew]

Avron-Barak, Noa, "Revisiting Israeli Art Canon: The Story of Mashkof Group," *International Journal of Art and Art History*, 4:2 (December 2016): 27-44.

Bahur, Yona. "Israeli Theater." *Haaretz*, July 3, 1964. [in Hebrew]

Bar-Kadma, Emanuel. "The Voice of God Issues forth from the Throat of the Actor." *Yediot Acharonot*, July 24, 1964, 11. [in Hebrew]

Bate, Jonathan. *Ted Hughes: The Unauthorized Life*. New York: HarperCollins Publisher, 2015.

Bin Nun, Sagil "The Muse: Emanuela Amichai's Relationship with Her Father is Complicated." *Maariv Weekend Edition*, February 5, 2012. [in Hebrew]

Birnberg, Yoav. "A Long Poem to a Father and Daughter." *Yediot Acharonot*, October 19, 2011.

Birman, Amnon "Yehuda Amichai." *Kol Ha'ir*, September 29, 2000. [in Hebrew]

Dor, Moshe. *Coals in the Mouth*. Tel Aviv, 1995. [in Hebrew].

Ehrlich, David. "The Class Meeting: Yehuda Amichai's Year." *Haaretz Supplement*, July 10, 1987. [in Hebrew]

Felstiner, John. "Paul Celan and Yehuda Amichai: An Exchange between Two Great Poets." *Midstream*, Jan-Feb, 2007, 28-30.

Har-Gil, Shraga. *Alte Liebe rostet nie [Old love does not rust]*. 2004. [in German]

Har-Gil, Shraga. "The Poet Who Wrote Poems of Jerusalem in German [on Else Lasker- Schüler]." *Maariv*, February 28, 1969. [in Hebrew]

Huppert, Shmuel. "Meetings in Jerusalem, 1969 [on Paul Celan]." *Yediot Acharonot*, May 27, 1983. [in Hebrew]

Kivity, Nissim. "The Proximity of Literary Hearts." *Yediot Acharonot- Leilot Hashavua*, January 28, 1971, 4. [in Hebrew]
Koren, Yehuda, and Eilat Negev. *Lover of Unreason*. Cambridge Mass: Da Capo Press, 2007.
Kramer, Rita. *Maria Montessori: A Biography*. Cambridge Mass: Da Copo Press, 1988.
Kressel, Getzel. *Encyclopedia of Modern Hebrew Literature*. Tel Aviv, 1965.
Kronzon, Yitzhak. "Like a Steel Wall." *Haaretz*, November 5, 2016. [in Hebrew]
ibid. "The First Day at the Geulah School [a story-memoir]." In *See the Land at a Distance*. Tel Aviv, 2010. [in Hebrew]
Lanski, Naama. "Protest Poem." *Yisrael Hayom Weekend Supplement*, March 8, 2011. [in Hebrew]
Lapid, Shulamit. "Modern Poetry Packs Beit Liessin." *Jerusalem Post*, December 1, 1962.
Lazar, David. "Dear Spotted Leopard [on Else Lasker-Schüler]." *Maariv*, April 25, 1969. [in Hebrew]
Leo, Christian. "Die deutsch-jüdischen Wurzeln Jehuda Amichais [German-Jewish Roots of Yehuda Amichai]." In *Zwischen Krieg und Liebe [Between War and Love]*. Edited by Renate Eichmeier and Edit RaimBerlin, 2010, 33-60. [in German]
Ibid. *Zwischen Erinnern und Vergessen [Between Remembering and Forgetting]*. Würzburg, 2004. [in German]
Levin, Gabriel. "Introduction." In *A Cloud Inhaled Me: Collected Poems*. By Dennis Silk, New York: Sheep Meadows Press, 2014.
Lipkin-Shachak, Tali, "The Lost Battle." *Maariv,* February 3, 2006: 13-17. [in Hebrew]
Lorch, Netanel. *The Day will be Passing: A Sort of Autobiography*. Tel Aviv, 1999. [in Hebrew]
Melamed, David. "The Story of the Hebrew Weekly called Hagalgal." *Haaretz*, August 26, 2016. [in Hebrew]
Mendelssohn, Zehava. "Five Poets from England Come to Read Their Works in Israel." *Maariv*, February 12, 1971. [in Hebrew]
Narkiss, Uzi. *Soldier of Jerusalem*. Elstree, UK: Vallentine Mitchell, 1998.
Negev, Eilat. "The Face of My Comrade." *Yediot Acharonot*, September 22, 2005. [in Hebrew]
Ofer, Tehila. "Nahum as Jonah." *Haboker*, July 27, 1964. [in Hebrew]
Ohad, Michael. "An Evening of Young Poets." *Davar*, January 12, 1962. [in Hebrew]
Oren, Rachel. "The Playwright in the Belly of the Whale." *Dvar ha-Shavua*, August 7, 1964, 23. [in Hebrew]
Raim, Edith. "Verfolgung und Exil der jüdischen Familie Hanover aus Würzburg [Persecution and Exile of the Hannover Family from Würzburg]." In *Zwischen Krieg und Liebe: Der Dichter Jehuda Amichai*. Edited by Renata Eichmeier and Edith Raim, Berlin, 2010.
Rothstein, Rafael. "Israeli Intellectuals Throng to the US." *Haaretz*, March 27, 1970. [in Hebrew]
Rottenbach, Bruno. *Zwischen Würzburg und Jerusalem*. Würzburg, 1981.

Sahish, Yaron. "Alas, We Were Nonchalant." *Yerushalayim* [a weekly], August 16, 1993. [in Hebrew]

Sokolov-Amichai, Hana. "Jehuda Amichai - Die Jugendjahre in Palestina/Eretz Israel [Yehuda Amichai – Adolescence in Palestine]." In *Zwischen Krieg und Liebe: Der Dichter Jehuda Amichai,* Edited by Renata Eichmeier and Edith Raim, Berlin, 2010), 101-142.

ibid. "For the Sake of Remembrance." *Achshav* 73-74, Autumn-Winter 2013-2014, 32-33. [in Hebrew]

Someck, Ronny. "And They Call Me Yuda from Love." *Maariv*, September 29, 2000. [in Hebrew]

Stepak, Rahel. "What Do Amichai's Poems Have to Do with the Censorship File of the Davar Newspaper?" *Haaretz*, September 24, 2014. [in Hebrew],

Strassman, Gabriel. "English Imports and Israeli Exports." *Maariv*, March 11, 1970. [in Hebrew]

Strätz, Reiner, ed. *Biographisches Handbuch: Würzburger Juden 1900-1945 [Biographical Handbook: Jews of Würzburg, 1900-1945)].* 2 Teilen, Würzburg, 1989. [in German]

Strauss, Herbert A. *In the Eye of the Storm: Growing Up Jewish in Germany, 1918-43, A Memoir.* New York: Fordham University Press, 1999.

Tikotzsky, Gideon. "'At Desolate Moments of My Life, I Read It, and It Was Good for Me': The Young Yehuda Amichai Writes to Lea Goldberg." *Ot* 1 (Autumn 2010), 215-26. [in Hebrew]

Tira, Yehoshua. "Conversation with Paul Celan." *Haaretz*, October 17, 1969. [in Hebrew]

Weissbort, Daniel. "Introduction." In *Ted Hughes, Selected Translations.* Edited by Daniel Weissbort, New York: Faber and Faber, 2006, VII-XI.

Yitzhaki, Moshe. "You Don't Know Me and I Don't Know You, But We Are the Jewish People." *Haaretz*, March 29, 2013. [in Hebrew]

Zach, Natan. *From Year to Year, it [Autobiography].* Tel Aviv, 2009. [in Hebrew]

Zeret, Elad. "Between Amichai and Goldberg." *24 Sha'ot - Yediot Acharonot*, December 21, 014, 10-11. [in Hebrew]

Zinger, Ruth. "The Poet Amichai – and New York." *Haynt*, May 23, 1967. [in Hebrew]

Articles Dealing with Yehuda Amichai's Works

Arad, Miriam. "Amichai Pulls a Bloomer." *Jerusalem Post*, July 16, 1971.

ibid. "Amichai's Poetry Begins to Mellow." *Jerusalem Post Magazine*, May 12, 1969.

ibid. "Happiness Made to Order." *Jerusalem Post*, July 7, 1968.

Aricha, Amos. "The Problem of Commissioned Plays." *Davar*, February 8, 1962. [in Hebrew]

Arpali, Boaz. "Words 'Not of This Time, Not of This Place.'" *Hasifrut* 29 (December 1979): 44-57. [in Hebrew]

Artzi, Shlomo. "Poems for All the Family." *Koteret Rashit*, November 27, 1985. [in Hebrew]

Avneri, Shraga. "The Poems of Yehuda Amichai." *Mevo'ot* 11, July 1, 1955. [in Hebrew]

B. H. (unknown, pseud). "Bells and Trains - A Radio Script that Won First Prize in the Kol Yisrael Competition." *Maariv*, June 22, 1962. [in Hebrew]

Bar-On, Yaacov, "Flood as an Outcome of … Sickness." *Davar*, January 8, 1976. [in Hebrew]

Barzel, Hillel, ed. *Six Narrators – 16 Stories*. Tel Aviv: Israel Ministry of Education 1972. [in Hebrew]

Bassok, Ido. "An Evening That Won't Come Back." *Haaretz*, September 20, 2017. [in Hebrew]

Be'er, Haim. "Now in the Storm – by Yehuda Amichai." *Haaretz*, March 21, 1969. [in Hebrew]

Ben (Braun), Menachem. "Ripeness Is All." *Yediot Acharonot*, January 31, 1969. [in Hebrew]

ibid. "The World is a Room." *Yediot Acharonot*, July 30, 1971. [in Hebrew]

Ben Meir, A. "Journey to Nineveh at Habima." *Cherut*, July 31, 1964. [in Hebrew]

Ben-Nun, Shlomo. "The Performance of a Radio Script and Scandinavia." *Davar*, September 7, 1962. [in Hebrew]

Ben-Shaul, Moshe. "Two Poetic Authorities." *Maariv*, November 13, 1981. [in Hebrew]

Braunstein, Tzvi. "The Visit of the Israeli Poet Yehuda Amichai." *Yiddishe Tzeitung*, March 26, 1970. [in Yiddish]

Briefly, William D. A Christian Theological Exploration of the Memory of the Holocaust in the Work of Four Jewish Novelists (Boston 1993), 202-251 [microfilm].

Calderon, Nissim. "A Sure Step." *LaMerhav/Masa*, February 14, 1969. [in Hebrew]

ibid. "This Whole Sweet Jerusalem Thing." *Siman Kriah* 5 (February 1976): 462-65. [in Hebrew]

ibid. "Wearing out." *Siman Kriah* 1 (September 1972): 307-10. [in Hebrew]

Cohen, Adir. "Modernity and Conservatism in Our Poetry." *Haboker*, August 14, 1959. [in Hebrew]

Darr, Yael. "When the Tops of Buildings Scrape the Sky and You Are So Very Small." *Haaretz-Sefarim*, May 29, 2002. [in Hebrew]

Dor, Moshe. "The Grace of Poetry." *Maariv*, May 31, 1963. [in Hebrew]

ibid. "Prose which Is Poetry." *Maariv*, February 24, 1961. [in Hebrew]

ibid. "Amichai Speaks to Small Children in Adult Language" *Maariv*, March 6, 1968. [in Hebrew]

Dudman, Helga. "Disembodied Voices." *Jerusalem Post*, October 4, 1974.

Dunevich, Nathan. "Another Israeli Play." *Haaretz*, November 9, 1962. [in Hebrew]

Ekroni Aviv, "Jonah in Modern Garb" [in Hebrew], Al Hamishmar, January 4, 1963.

Eliezer, N. "Poetry Intelligible and Unintelligible." *Al Hamishmar*, July 8, 1955. [in Hebrew]

Eren, David. "Directions in the Poetry of Yehuda Amichai." *Al Hamishmar*, July 10, 1956. [in Hebrew]

Eren, David. "Yehuda Amichai. In Poetry and Prose. An Attempt at Criticism." *Al Hamishmar*, June 16, 1961. [in Hebrew]

Feingold, Ben-Ami. "A Study of Journey to Nineveh by Yehuda Amichai." *Mibifnim*, April 1964, 43-48. [in Hebrew]

ibid. "Amichai 1948-1962." *Haboker*, May 24, 1963. [in Hebrew]

ibid. "Journey to Nineveh at Habima." *Haboker*, July 28, 1964. [in Hebrew]

ibid. "Journey to Nineveh at Habima" *Haboker*, July 31, 1964. [in Hebrew]

ibid. "Yehuda Amichai and His Journey to Nineveh." *Haboker*, November 23, 1962. [in Hebrew]

Geldman, Mordechai. "Keeping Far from the Western Wall." *Maariv*, January 31, 1997. [in Hebrew]

ibid. "Terrible Competitions." *Alpayim* 16 (1998): 121. [in Hebrew]

Gilan, Maksim. "Selection of Amichai's Poetry." *Yokhani* 4 (July 1963): 104-5. [in Hebrew]

Ginosar, Yaira. "Couldn't Make it, I Hope You'll Understand." *Iton 77*, 28 (January-February, 1986): 72-73. [in Hebrew]

Gluzman, Michael. "Dicky's Death: Amichai's Traumatic Text." *Jerusalem Studies in Hebrew Literature*, XXXI (2020): 453-88.

Goldberg, Lea. "Unto Iron." *Al Hamishmar*, July 26, 1957. [in Hebrew]

Gouri, Haim. "The Reverse Fridge Method: On Yehuda Amichai." *Maariv*, April 5, 1985 [in Hebrew]

Grodzenski, Shlomo. "The Poems of Yehuda Amichai." *Davar*, August 2, 1957. [in Hebrew]

Halevi-Zwick, Yehudit. Introduction to *Yehuda Amichai – Selected Articles on His Work*. Edited by Yehudit Halevi-Zwick, 7-60. Tel Aviv: Am Oved, 1988. [in Hebrew]

Halevy, Benjamin. "Another Answer to the Students." *LaMerhav/Masa*, April 5, 1957. [in Hebrew]

Harel, Ma'ayan. "Her Little Book Was Always in My Kit Bag." *Mikan,* 10 (September 2010): 99-133. [in Hebrew]

Hareven, Shulamit. "Fireworks." *Al Hamishmar*. September 5, 1958. [in Hebrew]

Harshav, Benjamin. "Personal Reflections on Amichai – Poetry and the State." *Alpayim*, 33 (2008): 121-139. [in Hebrew]

ibid. "On the Beginning of Israeli Poetry and Yehuda Amichai's Quatrains." In *The Polyphony of Jewish Culture*. 175-182. Stanford CA: Stanford University Press, 2004.

Hertz, Dalia. "The Stories of Yehuda Amichai." *Yediot Acharonot*, August 3, 1973. [in Hebrew]

Holztman, Avner. "The Fiction of the 'Generation in His Country.'" In *The First Decade: 5708-5718* [1948-1958], edited by Tzvi Tzameret and Hanna Yablonbka, 263-280. Jerusalem: Yad Yitzhak Ben Zvi. [in Hebrew]

Huss, Abraham. "On the Poems of Amichai and Galai" *Orot* (February 1959): 45-48. [in Hebrew]

Israel, Yael. "When There Was a Hole at the ATM." *Maariv-Tarbut*, August 23, 2002. [in Hebrew],

Kaniuk, Yoram. "No Man's Land at the Zavit." *LaMerhav*, November 23, 1962. [in Hebrew],

Katzenelson, Gideon. "Like a Stem of Flowers in a Vase." *Davar*, July 11, 1958. [in Hebrew]

ibid. "The Poet of a Generation Whose Temple Became Empty." *Haaretz*, July 18, 1958. [in Hebrew],

Kavanagh, Patrick J. "An Awkward Shyness." *The Guardian*, July 12, 1968.

Kenaz, Yehoshua. "Journey to Nineveh at Habima." *LaMerhav/Masa*, August 7, 1964. [in Hebrew],

Keshet, Sylvie. "An Israeli Satiric-Tragic No Man's Land." *Yediot Acharonot*, October 10, 1962. [in Hebrew],

Kronfeld, Chana. *The Full Severity of Compassion.* Stanford CA: Stanford University Press. 2016.

Kurzweil, Baruch. "Stories - In This Terrible Wind." and "Autobiographical Poetry in the Great Desert." In *Search of Israeli Literature.* Ramat Gan, 1982, 221-230 and 231-246. [in Hebrew]

ibid. "Notes to Poems of Yehuda Amichai." *Haaretz*, June 28, 1963. [in Hebrew]

Lee, Rina. "On One of Yehuda Amichai's Sonnets." *Bitzaron*, Shvat-Adar 5733 [February 1973]. [in Hebrew]

Levi, Hila. *"Journey to Nineveh" by Yehuda Amichai.* Seminar paper submitted at Haifa University, 1988. [in Hebrew]

Levin, Amos. *No Line* [on the "Likrat" group, in Hebrew]. Tel Aviv, 5744 [1983/84]).

Levitsky, Ruth. "The Hebrew Radio Play." PhD diss., Tel Aviv University, 2007. [in Hebrew]

ibid. "The Radio Plays by Yehuda Amichai: Six Aspects of the Radio Art." MA diss., Tel Aviv University, 1997. [in Hebrew],

Levy, Emanuel. *The National Theater Habima.* Tel Aviv, 1981, 237-39. [in Hebrew]. In English: idem, *The Habima, Israel's National Theater*, 1917-1977. Columbia, 1979.

Levy, Shimon. *Israeli Theater.* Tel Aviv, 2016, 226-30. [in Hebrew]

Litvin, Rina. "The Poetry of Yehuda Amichai." *LaMerhav/Masa*, May 10, 1963. [in Hebrew]

Luz, Zvi. *The Two-Way Flow of Hebrew*. Bnei Brak, 2011, 74-77. [in Hebrew]

Majaro-Mintz, Leah. "What Is the Artist Angry About?" *Davar*, May 18, 1970. [in Hebrew]

ibid. "Combining the Arts at the Jerusalem Artists' House." *Davar*, February 19, 1971. [in Hebrew]

Meged, Matti. "Between the Fire and the Dream." *LaMerhav/Masa*, May 20, 1955. [in Hebrew]

Michali, Benjamin Yitzhak. "With No Sense of Propriety." *Davar*, June 3, 1955. [in Hebrew]

Mindlin, Meir. "An Ill-Ground Axe." *Jerusalem Post*, July 12, 1957.

ibid. "Major Poetic Event." *Jerusalem Post*, May 9, 1958.

Miron, Dan. "The Present Tense Scrutiny of Other Days." *Zmanim*, June 17, 1955. [in Hebrew] ibid. "A Reading of Two Love Poems of Yehuda Amichai." *Anaf [=A Branch] for Young Literature*. Jerusalem and Tel Aviv, 5723 [1962-1963]. [in Hebrew]

ibid. "Safeguarding the Vessels and their Repair: A Discussion of Now and in Other Days." In *Facing the Silent Brother*, Tel Aviv, 1992, 271-313. [in Hebrew]

ibid. "Open – Closed – Open"; "Revolutionist with Father," In *More!* Tel Aviv, 2013, 259-79, 280-303. [in Hebrew]

Moked, Gabriel. "Exposing the Experience of the Individual and the Collective." *Yediot Acharonot*, September 18, 1959. [in Hebrew]

ibid. "Now and in Other Days." *Haaretz*, March 17, 1961. [in Hebrew],

ibid. "Memories of Achshav Publishing House." *Siman Kriah*, 1 (September 1972): 297-282. [in Hebrew],

ibid. "An Award for Great Poetry." *Yediot Acharonot*, November 13, 1981. [in Hebrew],

ibid. "On Two Hopes Away by Yehuda Amichai." *Achshav*, 3-4, Spring 5719 [1959].

Nahor, Asher. "The 'Mission' that Cannot be Shirked." *Yediot Acharonot*, July 29, 1964. [in Hebrew],

Nahor, Asher. "The Poetic Prose of a Poet." *Yediot Acharonot*, February 3, 1961. [in Hebrew],

Ofrat, Gideon. "Biblical Allegory." In *The Israeli Drama*, Tel Aviv, 1975, 131-43. [in Hebrew]

ibid. "'Mashkof' – Bohemia in Red and Blue – The Rise and Fall of Environmental Art Jerusalem Style." *Kol Yerushalayim*, March 23, 1984, 39-40. [in Hebrew]

Ohad, Michael. "The Prophet in the Fish and the Failed Revolution" *Haaretz Supplement*, July 17, 1964, 12-13. [in Hebrew]

Oz, Avraham. "Myth in Drama and Its Adaptation to Israeli Theater." *Haaretz Literary Section*, January 13, 1967. [in Hebrew]

Perry, Menachem. "In the face of the Dead: The New Poetics of the Young Yehuda Amichai." In *Pastor Fido*, edited by Ziva Shamir and Menachem Perry. Tel Aviv, 2016, 193-231.

Pesach, Haim. "Amichai at His Best." *Bamachane*, November 13, 1985. [in Hebrew]

Pnueli, Shmuel Yosef. "Three on One Subject." *Al Hamishmar*, September 20, 1957. [in Hebrew]

Ravikovitch, Dahlia. "A Little Fish between Two Whales." *Yedioth Acharonot*, November 2, 1962. [in Hebrew]

Rav-Nof, Ze'ev. "Journey to Nineveh at Habima." *Hapo'el Hatzair*, August 4, 1964, 26. [in Hebrew]

Regev, Menachem. "Poems on New York." *Yediot Acharonot*, June 7, 1968. [in Hebrew]

Rifin, Sara. "Yehuda Amichai's Hotel in the Wilderness." *At [=You]*, August 1971. [in Hebrew]

Rogni, Hagai, *Facing the Destroyed Village*. Haifa, 2006, 184-206. [in Hebrew]

Rokem, Naama. "German-Hebrew Encounters in the Poetry and Correspondence of Yehuda Amichai and Paul Celan." *Prooftexts*, 30, 2010, 97-127.

Ron, Yitzhak. "Journey to Nineveh." *Cherut*, January 11, 1963. [in Hebrew],

Rosen, Tova. "'As in a Poem by Shmuel Hanagid' – Between Shmuel Hanagid and Yehuda Amichai." *Jerusalem Research in Hebrew Literature* 15 (5755 [1995]), 83-106. [in Hebrew]

Ross, Rachel. "Journey to Nineveh by Yehuda Amichai." *Yerushalayim*, May 12, 1989, 20. [in Hebrew]

Sachs, Arieh. "The Poetry of Yehuda Amichai." *Judaism* 14:4, 1965.

ibid. "A Poet of Hollow Wonder." *Haaretz*, November 29, 1985. [in Hebrew],

Sandbank, Shimon. "The Collected Poems of Yehuda Amichai." *Ammot* 1:5 (April-May 1963), 93-95. [in Hebrew],

ibid. "Landscape of the Soul: Rilke, Auden, Amichai." In *Two Pools in the Forest.* Tel Aviv, 5736 [1975-6]), 197-214. [in Hebrew]

ibid. "The Couplet and Modularity: Amichai and Else Lasker-Schüler;" "'Turn, Stand, Tarry': Rilke, Amichai and Looking Back," In *The Voice is the Other.* Jerusalem, 2001, 72-89;90-98. [in Hebrew]

ibid. "The Question of the Light Poem." *Siman Kriah*, 12-13, February 1981, 331-34. [in Hebrew],

Scharf-Gold, Nili. *Yehuda Amichai: The Making of a National Poet.* Boston, 2008.

Schimmel, Harold. "On Seven Poems of Yehuda Amichai," *Orot* 9, 5730 [1969-1970], 86-97. [in Hebrew and English],

Sela, Uri. "I Hope You'll Understand." *Yediot Acharonot*, November 15, 1985. [in Hebrew],

Shafriri, Matityahu. "Journey to Nineveh and Its Production in Habima, 1964." In *Biblical Drama on the Hebrew Stage.* PhD diss., Tel Aviv University, 1999, 161-186. [in Hebrew]

Shaked, Gershon. "A Journey of Stages." *Haaretz*, December 27, 1985. [in Hebrew],

ibid. "The Early Amichai and His Literary Reference Group." In *The New Tradition,* Cincinnati, 2006, 144-172.

Shaked, Shaul. "Yehuda Amichai's New Poems." *LaMerhav/Masa*, May 30, 1958. [in Hebrew]

Shalev. Meir. "Effort without Sweat." *Kol Ha'ir*, November 8, 1985. [in Hebrew]

Shamir, Ziva. "On Two Well-Known Funeral Poems – By W. H. Auden, and Yehuda Amichai." *Shvo,* 12, 2004, 23-28.

Shavit, Uzi. "Outlines of the Prosody of Yehuda Amichai." In *A Cloak for Benjamin: A Jubilee Book for Benjamin Harshav.* Edited by Ziva Ben-Porat, 36-49. [in Hebrew]

Soffer, M. "A New Voice in Hebrew Poetry." *Here and Now*, June 16, 1955.

Sokoloff Naomi, B. "On Amichai's 'El Male Rahamim.'" *Prooftexts*, 4:2, 1984, 127-140.

Tarass-Zukerman, Rachel. "About One Poem of Amichai." In *From the World of Art.* Jerusalem, 1990, 79-83. [in Hebrew]

Treinin, Avner "Gilboa and Amichai – An Analysis of Elements." *Maariv*, April 30, 1982. [in Hebrew]

Tsur, Reuven. "Two Quatrains by Amichai." In *Romantic and Anti-Romantic Elements in Poems.* Edited by Hayim Nachman Bialik, Shaul Tchernichowsky, Avraham Shlonsky and Yehuda Amichai. Tel Aviv, 1985, 28-38. [in Hebrew]

Yudkin, Leon Israel. *Jewish Writing and Identity in the Twentieth Century*. London: Rutledge, 1982, 142-158.

Zach, Natan. "The Nimble Muse." *Davar*, August 28, 1959. [in Hebrew]

ibid. "The Poems of Yehuda Amichai." *Al Hamishmar*, July 29, 1955. [in Hebrew],

ibid. "Yehuda Amichai's Poetic Stories." *Yochani*, August 1961. [in Hebrew]

ibid. *Time and Rhythm in Bergson and Modern Poetry*. Tel Aviv, 1966. [in Hebrew]

Zieler, Wendy. "Dr. Wendy Zieler Explores How Yehuda Amichai's Poem resonates in Our Time," January 21, 2021. http://www.huc.edu/news/2021/01/21/dr-wendy-zierler-explores-how-yehuda-amichais-poem-resonates-in-our-time.

Ziffer, Benny. "From Man You Are and to Man You Shall Return, Poems." *Haaretz*, November 1, 1985. [in Hebrew]

ibid. "Two Scales: Major and Minor." *Haaretz*, November 13, 1981. [in Hebrew]

Zussman, Ezra. "No Man's Land at the Zavit." *Davar*, November 23, 1962. [in Hebrew]

Historical and Literary Background Material

Abrams, M. H., ed. *The Norton Anthology of English Literature, Vol. 2, Fifth Edition*. New York: W. W. Norton & Co., 1986.

Bar-On, Mordechai. *Challenge and Struggle*. Jerusalem and Beersheva, 1991. [in Hebrew]

Bar-On, Mordechai and Hazan Meir, eds. *Citizens at War*. Jerusalem and Tel Aviv 2010. [in Hebrew]

Birnbaum, Max P. "The Union of Communities of the Bavarian Galilee." In *History of the Holocaust - Germany,* Edited by Avraham Margaliot and Yehoyachim Kochavi, Jerusalem 5758 [1998], 421-9. [in Hebrew]

Borut, Yaacov. "Religious Life among the Jews of the Towns and Villages of Western Germany in the Weimar Period." In *Weimar Jewry*. Edited by Oded Heilbruner, Jerusalem, 1994, 90-107. [in Hebrew]

Brezner, Amiad. *The Negev in Settlement and War: The Battle for the Negev*. Tel Aviv, 1994. [in Hebrew]

Cohen, Ardon, Michael Cohen, and Amos Mendelsson. *The Negev Brigade in the War of Independence*. Tel Aviv, 2011. [in Hebrew],

Dexelmüller, Christian. *Jüdische Kultur in Franken, [Jewish Culture in Franconia]*. (Würzburg, 1988). [in German]

ibid. "Tausend Jahre Juden in Würzburg – eine wechselvolle und tragische Geschichte [A thousand years of the Jews of Würzburg – a tragic history with many upheavals]." In *Ruth hat auf einer Schwarzen Flöte gespielt [Ruth played a black flute]*. Edited by Christian Dexelmüller and Roland Flade, Würzburg, 2005, 7-42. [in German]

Eban, Dan. "The Crisis of the Literary Journals." *Yediot Acharonot,* April 30, 1959. [in Hebrew]

Elam, Yigal. *The Haganah*. Tel Aviv, 1979. [in Hebrew]

Encyclopedia of Jewish Communities. Germany, Vol. i: The Jews of Bavaria. Jerusalem, 5733 [1973]. [in Hebrew]

Encyclopedia of Jewish Communities. Germany, Vol. iii: The Jews of Hessen, Hesse-Nassau, Frankfurt. Jerusalem, 1992. [in Hebrew]

Feige, Michael. "Introduction." In *An Axe to Dig with: Archeology and Nationalism in Eretz Israel.* Edited by Michael Feige and Zvi Shiloni, Beersheva 2008, 1-17. [in Hebrew]

Flade, Roland. *Würzburger Jüden [The Jews of Würzburg].* Würzburg, 1987. [in German]

Fuller, John. *A Reader's Guide to W. H. Auden.* London: Thames and Hudson, 1970, 218-222.

Gafni, Reuven. *Winds of Hope.* Jerusalem: Yad Itzhak Ben Zvi, 2015, 98-105.

Gavish, Dov. *Land and Map.* Jerusalem, 1991. [in Hebrew]

Gelber, Yoav. *A Nucleus of a Hebrew Regular Army.* Jerusalem, 1986. [in Hebrew]

ibid. *"Masada" – The Defense of the Land of Israel in the Second World War.* Ramat Gan, 1990. [in Hebrew]

ibid. *New Homeland.* Jerusalem: Yad Itzhak Ben-Zvi and Leo Baeck Institute, 1990. [in Hebrew]

Gilbert, Martin. *Israel: A History.* New York: William Narrow and Company, INC., 1998.

Givati, Moshe. *On the Road of Desert and Fire.* Tel Aviv, 1994. [in Hebrew]

Gluzman, Michael. "Sovereignty and Melancholia: Israeli Poetry after 1948." *Jewish Social Studies* 18, 3 (Spring-Summer 2012): 166-169.

Gouri, Haim. "Until the Break of Dawn [1950]." In *The Imprint of Memory, Vol. I.* Jerusalem and Tel Aviv: Hakibbutz Hameuchad - Sifriat Poalim Publishing House, 5775 [2014/5]. [in Hebrew]

Haas, Lotte. "The Method of Freedom in the Montessori Educational Method." *Würzburger General Anzeiger*, January 3, 1931. [in German]

Halperin, Hagit. *The Maestro [biography of Abraham Shlonsky].* Tel Aviv, 2011. [in Hebrew]

Heilbruner, Oded, ed. *Weimar Jewry and the Crisis of Modernization, 1918-1933.* Jerusalem, 5754 [1994]. [in Hebrew]

Heller, Joseph. *The United States, the Soviet Union and the Arab-Israeli Conflict: 1948-67.* Manchester: Manchester University Press, 2010, chapters 1-5.

Horowitz, Dan and Moshe Lissak. *Trouble in Utopia.* Albany, N.Y.: State University of New York Press, 1989.

Issachar, Gad. "From the Palmach Generation to Neo-Judaism." *Maariv*, March 24, 1961. [in Hebrew]

Jaffe, Eliezer. *Yemin Moshe: The Story of a Jerusalem Neighborhood.* Jerusalem, 1985, 67-69. [in Hebrew]

Kaufmann, Walter. "A History of the Jewish Teachers' Seminary." In *ILBA: Israelitische Lehrbildungsanstalt Würzburg 1864-1938.* Edited by Max Ottensoser and Alex Roberg, Detroit, Michigan, 1982.]

Kimchi, Ruth. *Zionism in the Shadow of the Pyramids: The Zionist Movement in Egypt 1918-1948.* Tel Aviv, 2009. [in Hebrew]

Mindel, Meir. *They're Ours*. Sha'ar Hanegev, 2009. [in Hebrew]

Miron, Guy. "Zionism and Jewish Nationalism in Germany." In *World Regional Zionism: Geo-Cultural Dimensions, Vol. 1*. Edited by Alon Gal. Jerusalem and Beersheva, 5770 [2009/10]. [in Hebrew]

Morris, Benny. *Righteous Victims: A History of the Zionist-Arab Conflict, 1881-2001*. New York: Vintage, 1999.

Mosse, George. *German Jews beyond Judaism*. Bloomington: Indiana University Press, 1985.

Neiger, Motti. *Literary Supplements and the Shaping of Israeli Culture*. Jerusalem, 2000. [in Hebrew]

ibid. *Publishers as Cultural Mediators: The Cultural History of Hebrew Publishing in Israel*. Jerusalem, 2017, 379-396. [in Hebrew]

Niederland, Doron. "From Frankfurt to Jerusalem: The Unique Path of the Horeb School in Religious Education in the Land of Israel." *Dor le-Dor 25*, 2005, 81-121. [in Hebrew]

ibid. *German Jews: Immigrants or Refugees?* Jerusalem,1996. [in Hebrew]

Oren, Baruch, ed. *The Netzach Israel School at Eighty - 1909/10-1989/90*. Petah Tikva, 1991. [in Hebrew]

Pa'il, Meir and Avraham Zohar. *Palmach*. Tel Aviv, 2008. [in Hebrew]

Patishi, Hanoch. *Underground in Uniforms*. Tel Aviv and Haifa, 2006. [in Hebrew]

Rilke, Rainer Maria. *Ausgewählte Gedicht [Selected Poetry]*. Den Haag, 1948.

ibid. *The Poetry of Rilke, Bilingual Edition*. Translated and edited by Edward Snow, introduced by Adam Zagaiewski. New York: Farrar, Straus and Giroux, 2014.

Sachar, Howard. *A History of Israel from the Rise of Zionism to our Time. 2nd ed.* New York: Alfred A. Knopf, 2000.

Sachs, Arieh. "A Purely Righteous Person: Introduction to the Medieval Mystery 'The Flood' at the Han Theater in Jerusalem." *Yediot Acharonot*, January 2, 1976. [in Hebrew]

Sandbank, Shimon. "Epilogue." In *Paul Celan, Speech-grille*. Translated by Shimon Sandbank (Tel Aviv, 1994), 173-7. [in Hebrew]

ibid. "Afterward." In *Desire and the Object: An Anthology of Expressionist and Imagistic Poetry*. Tel Aviv, 2014, 223-57. [in Hebrew]

Schmidt, D. "Some Historical Notes," In *Soldiers' Stories of the Hebrew Mapping Company 524*. Edited by Paz-Ner, 1990, 17-29. [in Hebrew]

Shacham, Chaya. *Echoes of a Nigun*. Tel Aviv and Haifa, 1997, 228-34. [in Hebrew]

Shaked, Gershon. *Modern Hebrew Fiction*. Bloomington: Indiana University Press, 2000, Chapters 10-11.

Shapira, Anita. *Yigal Alon, Native Son: A Biography*. Philadelphia: Pennsylvania University Press, 2008, chapter 10.

ibid. *Israel: A History*. Massachusetts: Brandeis University Press, 2012.

Sorkin, David. *The Transformation of German Jewry, 1780-1840*. Detroit: Wayne State University, 1987.

Sprock-Pfitzer, J. *Die ehemaligen jüdischen Gemeinden im Landkreis Würzburg*. Würzburg, 1988.

Tevet, Shabtai. *Moshe Dayan: A Biography*. London: Quartet Books, 1972, chapter 5.

Tikotzsky, Gideon, *Light Along the Edge of a Cloud: Introduction to Lea Goldberg's Oeuvre.* Tel Aviv, 2011. [in Hebrew]

Tsur, Eli. *Landscapes of Illusion: Mapam 1948-1954.* Beersheva, 1998. [in Hebrew]

Walk, Joseph. *The Education of the Jewish Child in Nazi Germany.* Jerusalem, 1976. [in Hebrew]

ibid. *Jüdische Schule und Erziehung im Dritten Reich.* Frankfurt am Main, 1991, chapters 1-2.

Weisman, Debora. "Girls' Education in Jerusalem during the Period of British Rule." PhD diss. Hebrew University, 1994. [in Hebrew]

Yonai, Yosef. "The Schools in Haifa and Tel Aviv During the War." In *Citizens in War.* Edited by Mordechai Bar-On and Meir Chazan, Jerusalem and Tel Aviv, 2009.

Zimmermann, Moshe. "Basic Problems in the History of the Jews of Weimar." In *Weimar Jewry and the Crisis of Modernization, 1918-1933.* Edited by Oded Heilbruner, Jerusalem, 5754 [1994], 18-53. [in Hebrew]

Interviews with Yehuda Amichai and his Family Members in the Press, Radio and TV [alphabetically by the interviewer's name]

Abramson, Glenda. "Yehuda Amichai, A Kind of a Lay Prophet." *The Jewish Quarterly*, 35: 1 (129), 1988.

Ahi-No'omi, Amnon. "The Brawny Ones Refused to Leave the Classroom." *Yoman Hashavua*, December 11, 1983. [in Hebrew]

Amit, Dalia and Shmuel Huppert. Radio program on *Galgal Hamazalot* – a Literature and Culture Club. October 2, 1975. [in Hebrew]

Arad, Aryeh. "One from a City." Army Radio, September 5, 1989. [in Hebrew]

Baretzky, Nurit. "Private Property." *Maariv Sof Shavua magazine*, April 4, 1986. [in Hebrew]

Bar Yosef, Yosef. "Cold Lightning Does not Move Me." *Bamachane*, February 26, 1986. [in Hebrew]

Barzel, Aviva. Conversation with Yehuda Amichai. *Hadoar*, March 26, 1976, 325, 327. [in Hebrew]

Barzel, Bina. "Writing is a Necessity – Like Loving and Eating." *Yediot Acharonot*, June 1, 1973. [in Hebrew]

Bashan, Raphael. "Monologue of Yehuda Amichai - 'I Don't Remember When I Fled and from what God.'" *Yamim ve-Leilot Magazine, Maariv*, August 29, 1964. [in Hebrew]

Benning, Corinna. Broadcast on Radio Bavaria, May 4, 1998. Reproduced in *Zwischen Erinnern und Vergessen.* Author, Leo Christian. Würzburg, 2004, 247-257.

Beser, Yaakov. "Yehuda Amichai." In *Poets Talk about Themselves and their Writing*. Tel Aviv, 1971, 50-54. [in Hebrew]

Birman, Amnon. "Yehuda Amichai." *Kol Ha'ir*, September 29, 2000. [in Hebrew]

Carpel, Dalia. "Hoping for the Nobel." *Ha'ir*, November 3, 1989. [in Hebrew]

Chertok, Haim. "Yehuda Amichai." In *We Are All Close: Conversations with Israeli Writers*. New York: Fordham University Press, 1989, 49-61.

Cohen, Joseph. "Yehuda Amichai [essay and interview]." *Voices of Israel*. New York, 1990, 31-43.

Eliraz, Israel. "The Exception that Proves the Rule." *Yediot Acharonot*, February 17, 1961. [in Hebrew]

Evron, Edna. "National Poet? That's All I Need!" *Haaretz*, October 22, 1999. [in Hebrew]

Evron, Ram. "In the First Person," Channel 1, Israel television, [May-June?], 1998. [in Hebrew]

Eytan, Rachel. "Between Pen and Paper." *Haaretz*, January 1, 1965. [in Hebrew]

Fuchs, Esther. *Encounters with Israeli Authors*. Marblehead, MA: Micha Publications, 1982, 86-92.

Fuchs, Sarit. "Everything Is Still a Kind of Whirlwind." Interview with Emanuela Amichai, *Maariv-Sof Shavua*, January 26, 2001. [in Hebrew]

Furstenberg, Rochelle. "The Poet Revolutionary." *Jerusalem Report*, December 1, 1994.

Gonn-Gross, Tsippi (moderator). "With Our Love: Interview with Family Members." *Army Radio*, April 19, 2011. [in Hebrew]

Gutkind, Naomi. "The Poet, Criticism, and the Readership." *Hatzofeh*, November 20, 1981. [in Hebrew]

Halter, Aloma. "Poems, Prayers and Psalms." *Contact*, July 26, 1991, 11.

Hollander-Steingart, Rachel. "In My Heart Is a Museum." *The Jerusalem Post*, September 28, 1981.

Karpel, Dalia. "Hoping for the Nobel." *Ha'ir*, November 3, 1989. [in Hebrew].

Klein, Idit, Judith Rosenbaum, and Tanya Schlam. "The Joy of the Struggle: A Talk with Yehudah Amichai." *Urim v'Tumim*, 6: 2, Winter 1991, 26-28.

Krauze, Enrique. "Las vetas del pasado." *Vuelta* 165, August 1990. [in Spanish].

Joseph, Lawrence. "The Art of Poetry: Yehuda Amichai." *Paris Review* 44, Spring 1992, https://www.theparisreview.org/interviews/2095/yehuda-amichai-the-art-of-poetry-no-44-yehuda-amichai

Levit, Anat. "To Sing the Small Love Song." *Iton* 77, 72-73, January-February, 1986, 24-25. [in Hebrew]

Miro, Michael. "Writing is the Fruit of a Wonderful Laziness." *Pi Ha'aton*, April 1978, 6. [in Hebrew]

Montenegro, David. "Yehuda Amichai: An Interview." *American Poetry Review*, 16: 6, November-December 1987, 15-20.

Megged, Eyal. "Yehuda Amichai: Facing the End You Become Simpler." *Yediot Acharonot*, November 8, 1985. [in Hebrew]

Nagid, Haim. "I Think This Country Is a Paradise for Poets." *Maariv Literary Section,* May 15, 1977. [in Hebrew]

ibid. "Tchernichovsky Who?" *Yediot Acharonot Literary Section*, October 1, 1993. [in Hebrew]

Negev, Eilat "I'm a Happy Person." *7 Leilot magazine, Yediot Acharonot*, March 25, 1994. [in Hebrew]

ibid. "The Secular Prophet." *7 Leilot magazine, Yediot Acharonot*, April 3, 1998. [in Hebrew]

Nimrod, Noa. "A Hebrew Poet Abroad." *Jewish Chronicle*, August 21, 1959.

Nir, Liora (moderator). "A Propitious Time." Army Radio, October 7, 1974. [in Hebrew]

Nissim, Kobi. "They Always Threw Stones There." *Al Hamishmar-Hotam*, May 6, 1992. [in Hebrew]

Ohad, Michael. "Story Without Incident." *Dvar Hashavua*, January 31 , 1961. [in Hebrew]

Omer, Dan. "In This Burning Country Words Have to Be Shade." *Prosa* 25, September 1978. [in Hebrew]

Ormian, Dalit (host). "Daddy Wrote a Book on me." Episode of *Not by the Soul Alone* Series. *Voice of Israel*, June 10, 1973. [in Hebrew]

Punk, Liraz. "Even Poets Watch the World Cup." *Noar 97*, 1997, 90-98. [in Hebrew]

Yishai, Sarit. "Writing Poems Is like Chewing the Cud." *Haolam Haze*, March 28, 1983. [in Hebrew]

Yonatan, Natan (host). "Every poem." *Educational Television*, 1975. [in Hebrew]

Yuval, Shirli. "Words Absorb the Pain of My Life." *Olam Ha'isha* 119. [in Hebrew]

Zahavi, Alex. "Poetry as Consolation." *Davar-Masa*, May 7, 1976. [in Hebrew]

Zoritte, Ida. "Writers Tell about Their Works." *LaMerhav/Masa*, May 8, 1958. [in Hebrew]

Index

Note: Page numbers followed by "n" refer to notes.

About the Author

Dr. Ido Bassok is a poet, translator, and researcher in literature and history. He is a graduate of the Hebrew University of Jerusalem and the University of Grenoble, France, and has translated several French classics, including François Rabelai's *Gargantua and Pantagruel*, Georges Perec's *La vie mode d'emploi*, novels by Balzac and Claude Simon and philosophical works by Descartes, Rousseau and others. His historical and literary research focuses on Hebrew writers in pre-state Israel, including biographies in Hebrew of Shaul Tchernichovsky (Carmel, 2015) and Ya'akov Shabtai (Magnes, 2022). He has also written extensively on the world views and narratives of Jewish children and adolescents in interwar Poland.

www.ingramcontent.com/pod-product-compliance
Lightning Source LLC
Chambersburg PA
CBHW030624310726
48979CB00003B/870